CLASSIC CHEESE COOKERY

CLASSIC CHEESE COOKERY

PETER GRAHAM

GRUB STREET · LONDON

This new revised edition published by
Grub Street,
The Basement,
10 Chivalry Road,
London SW11 1HT

British Library Cataloguing in Publication Data

ISBN 1 904010 05 9

Typeset by Pearl Graphics, Hemel Hempstead
Printed and bound by Biddles Ltd, Guildford and King's Lynn

Contents

Acknowledgements

I should like to extend especial thanks to Elizabeth Carmichael, who kindly allowed me to consult her very wide-ranging and catholic collection of cookbooks, many of which cannot be found in libraries. I am grateful, too, to the food historians Philip and Mary Hyman, who provided much useful information about pre-twentieth-century cookbook writers and their recipes; to Tony Kitzinger, who gave invaluable help, to Randolph Hodgson, owner of that excellent cheese shop, Neal's Yard Dairy, in London, who brought me up to date on new developments in British cheese-making; to Dr Keith Walker, who helped me on various points of erudition; and to Richard Boston, who provided some savoury titbits of information.

I should also like to thank Elizabeth David, Eleanor Fishman, Professor Keith Roberts, Nigel White (formerly of the Milk Marketing Board), Dr Tag Gronberg, Professor Ginette Vincendeau, Ghislaine Bavoillot, Madeleine Terrasson, Roy Malkin, Paul Overy, Hugh Rance, Jonathan and Renée Fenby, Peter and Winifred Campbell, Mary Macleod, Dennis Walder, Judith B. Jones, Catherine Abbati, Claudia Roden, Jane Grigson and Mauro Terrosi.

The following chefs kindly gave me permission to reproduce their recipes (references to the recipes concerned will be found under their respective names in the index): Michel Bras, Jeanne Chabut, Guy Girard, Marie-Claude Gracia, Cosima Kretz, Jean Moreno, Carla and Bernard Phillips, Yvonne Puech and Louis-Bernard Puech.

Preface to the Third Edition

Although this is, strictly, a book about cheese cookery, not cheese, I do urge the reader always to go for the best-quality products available. One of the most crucial factors of cheese quality is the use of unpasteurized milk in its manufacture. Yet, in the last two or three years, misguided health authorities have tended increasingly to propagate the notion that raw-milk cheese is a potential health hazard *per se*. This is poppycock. It is plainly absurd to question the safety of traditional techniques and ingredients that have proved their worth for centuries. Any cheese, whether unpasteurized or not, may be unfit for human consumption *if not properly made or looked after*.

At about the time that the first edition of this book was published, a particularly virulent strain of the *Listeria monocytogenes* bacterium, which can under some circumstances cause listeriosis, an illness dangerous above all to pregnant women, was found in a consignment of Swiss Vacherin Mont d'Or cheese. In the ensuing panic, one of the world's greatest cheeses almost suffered the fate of the dodo. I am happy to report it is now thriving again.

And yet the food-safety fundamentalists – in the shape of some, but not all, British environmental health officers and European Union officials – are still pressing for a ban on cheeses made with unpasteurised milk.

Randolph Hodgson, a leading British cheese expert and founder member of the Specialist Cheesemakers' Association (SCA), says he is 'concerned that we are reaching a point where over-hygienic production will prevent us using some of the traditional cheesemaking methods which are crucial for making good cheese'. The SCA continues to campaign hard to prevent bureaucratic lunacy gaining the upper hand, while trying to keep the lines of communication open with the health authorities. Readers of this book can also do their bit, at a more basic level, simply by buying unpasteurized cheese whenever possible.

P.G.

Introduction

Imagine a world without cheese. A world where God or natural selection had organized things in such a way that milk – the primal food of every mammal, including man – inexorably went rotten (like fish or meat) when left for a time at room temperature, instead of coagulating, as it does, under the effect of natural bacteria and turning into a basic form of cheese. If milk did not have that magical property, generations of men and women would never have invented the hundreds of different kinds of cheese now in existence, and the world would definitely be a poorer place.

So we have much to be grateful for. Of course, we might still have ended up with only a dozen or so different cheeses. Instead we have anything from 700 to 2,000 varieties, depending on which authority and classification system one follows. The French alone have been responsible for inventing a large proportion of them, prompting the quip, variously attributed to Churchill and De Gaulle, that a nation that has 365 different cheeses must necessarily be ungovernable. Whether that is true or not, such a wide variety certainly denotes a very strong streak of individuality. Today's inventors of cheese are white-coated technicians in spotless laboratories who gear their talents to the findings of market researchers. The result, known as 'giving consumers what they want', is often insipid.

In the past the process was very different. Cheddar, Camembert, Parmesan, Gruyère and hundreds of less familiar varieties of cheese were devised down the centuries by anonymous farmers and dairymen and women working in often not very hygienic conditions. They were well served by serendipity, imagination and trust in their own taste buds. After much trial and error, they succeeded in perfecting their particular cheese, and handed down its secret for future generations.

These real cheese-makers were true alchemists. Look, for example, at the number of variables that go into the making of a cheese. They include: the type of pasture where the cows are put to graze, the time of year they are milked, the breed of cow, the type of coagulation induced, the way the curd is cut and pressed, the technique of salting, the shaping of the cheese, the length of curing, the place of curing, and the very specific temperatures required at each stage of manufacture. The end product, not surprisingly, assumes a multitude of guises, sizes, textures and flavours that is quite staggering given that most cheeses have but one ingredient: milk.

Tiny Pélardon goat cheeses, for instance, make hardly more than a mouthful, while huge cylinders of Cantal weigh up to 50 kilogrammes (a hundredweight) each. The surface of Pont-l'Evêque or Handkäse has deep folds and wrinkles, that of smoked Provolone is sensuously smooth. The rind of a proper farmhouse Saint-Nectaire is covered with yellow, grey and rust-coloured moulds reminiscent of lichen, while mass-produced Edam sports an aseptic wax covering. The crust of Stilton is as dry as sandstone, that of Boulette d'Avesnes as tacky as fresh paint.

The same multiformity continues within. Some cheeses have holes in them – hundreds of tiny ones, like Samsø, or scores of yawning cavities, like Emmental, or else the occasional solitary eye, like Gruyère. The exposed edge of Parmesan, which has to be split rather than cut, is as rugged as a cliff face. Slice into a really ripe Camembert, and its cut surface will bulge for a time like a full goatskin and eventually spill out over the plate. The crumbly white mass of Roquefort is riddled with blue-green *Penicillium roqueforti* mould, while Wensleydale, as Keith Waterhouse delightfully puts it in *Mondays, Thursdays*, 'has the colour and texture of a milkmaid's shoulder and when you bite into it you have a sensation of being tickled at the back of the throat by buttercups'.

The astonishing polymorphism of cheese is paralleled by its versatility of aroma and flavour. Here the epithets become more difficult to find, because cheese has rather few organoleptic points of comparison. While a wine can be described as flinty or carrying a hint of blackcurrant or raspberry, cheese tastes more like, well, cheese than anything else. True, there are several ways of objectively describing or suggesting the smell and flavour of a cheese – fresh, creamy, lactic, aromatic, nutty, sharp, pungent, strong-smelling and so on – but none of them circumscribes very precisely the actual experience of the taste buds and nose when one eats cheese.

To some people, the smellier cheeses recall, as that hallowed euphemism goes, 'certain parts of the human anatomy'. James Joyce spoke of 'the feety savour of green cheese'. Others are reminded of decomposition: I remember observing the reaction of two elderly American women tourists in a Paris café many years ago when they were served cheese sandwiches containing some really good Camembert (I could tell it was good because the smell carried to my table). One mouthful and the wretched sandwiches were abandoned with disgust: 'Aw, it tastes rotten!'

I have long been a cheese-lover, and in the course of living in and travelling round France for the last twenty years or so, as well as regularly visiting other major cheese-producing countries such as Britain, Italy and Switzerland, I have had plenty of opportunities to indulge that predilection. So it was not as a complete novice that I began researching this book. I expected the domain of cheese cookery to prove fascinating but somewhat limited. Surely the canon could not extend much beyond such familiar dishes as Welsh rabbit, cheese soufflé, fish in Mornay sauce, pasta and cheese, fondue, raclette, gratins like cauliflower cheese, quiche and cheesecake? How wrong I was: at the end of my labours, and after much ruthless whittling down, I still found myself with some

330 compulsive (to me) recipes. What I had not been prepared for was the sheer variety of cheese cookery – a variety that results from a combination of three factors: different cheeses, different accompanying ingredients and different cooking techniques.

There is much more involved in cheese cookery than merely using up a piece of old Cheddar. A glance at the checklist of different cheeses called for by the recipes in this book (pp. 13-22) will give some idea of the range of varieties that can be used. I, for one, had not been aware that cheeses like Maroilles or Reblochon took on a new and richer dimension when used in cooked dishes. Another surprise was the number of unexpected ingredients that combine successfully with cheese, from salt cod, smoked fish, mussels and prawns to snails, tripe, brains and cepe mushrooms. I did not expect Gorgonzola with honey and cream (p. 319), sweet/salt goat-cheese pie (p. 199), toasted cheese with gherkins, onions and vinegar (p. 92), or cheese, crab and apple gratin (p. 222) to be good – but they were.

Lastly, it was interesting to see how cooking techniques breed further variety, particularly when cheese is combined with that other primal food, eggs. For example, three very basic ingredients – cheese, eggs and cream (or milk) – can together create a host of subtly differing flavours depending on the way they are cooked (see Chapter Seven). Cheese in soup, not an altogether obvious combination, can produce some startlingly good results (see Chapter Two). The widespread use evolved by generations of peasant cooks of a cheap starchy envelope (pie, pancake, calzone, ravioli) enclosing a cheese-flavoured filling not only fulfils its original function (i.e. it ekes out the cheese), but also results in yet more textural and aromatic variations.

I could list other examples, but perhaps it is time to let you have a go yourself. I am sure you will find that, like cheese-making, cooking with cheese is an enjoyable form of alchemy – and one that offers few disappointments and great rewards.

CHAPTER ONE

Choosing and Using Cheese

CHECKLIST OF CHEESES

This checklist of cheeses is not intended to be encyclopaedic nor, indeed, objective. It is restricted to those mentioned in this book and aims merely to describe some of their characteristics and, wherever relevant, provide one or two hints on how to choose them. When the cheese is rare and/or very difficult to come by – but only in such cases – I have suggested possible alternatives. This in no way implies that the alternative is as good as, or even very similar to, the cheese it replaces. The aim is simply to suggest the most satisfactory substitute in the context of a recipe.

Appenzell (cow) A hard Swiss cheese with a distinctive and delicate tang, which results from its being marinated in white wine and spices during the curing process. Genuine Appenzell should show a bear rampant on its label. Possible alternatives: Beaufort, Gruyère.

Bagnes (cow) A semi-hard Swiss cheese mainly used in fondue and raclette. Mild yet full of character. Possible alternatives: Raclette.

Beaufort (cow) A hard French cheese. A subtly aromatic relative of Gruyère. Possible alternatives: Comté, Gruyère.

Bel Paese (cow) A semi-soft Italian cheese with a bland flavour.

Bleu d'Auvergne (cow) A semi-hard French blue cheese, which, like its cousin Bleu des Causses, can vary considerably in strength, texture and saltiness (so taste if possible before buying). The best Bleu d'Auvergne has a good tang, an almost buttery texture and is not too salty.

Bleu de Bresse (or Bresse Bleu) (cow) A semi-soft French blue cheese reminiscent of Gorgonzola.

Bleu de Gex (cow) A semi-hard French blue cheese. Aromatic with a touch of astringency. Possible alternatives: Stilton, Fourme d'Ambert.

Bleu de Sassenage (cow) A semi-hard French blue cheese similar to Bleu de Gex.

Blue Cheshire (cow) A semi-hard British blue cheese, coloured orange-red with annatto. Best when made with unpasteurized milk.

Blue Wensleydale (cow) A semi-hard British blue cheese similar to Stilton but smoother in texture and drier.

Boulette d'Avesnes (cow) A semi-soft French cheese containing tarragon. Its smell and flavour are fierce. Possible alternative: Maroilles.

Boulette de Romedenne (cow) A semi-soft Belgian cheese similar to Boulette d'Avesnes.

Brebis des Pyrénées (sheep) A semi-hard to hard French cheese. The term covers a range of cheeses that can vary considerably in strength and texture, from the mild and springy black-rinded Lou Palou, which may contain some cow's milk, to the harder and tangier Iraty and Laruns.

Bresse bleu See Bleu de Bresse.

Brie (cow) A soft French cheese that should have a pronounced, if sweet, smell when ripe. Brie de Melun is generally regarded as a finer cheese than Brie de Meaux.

Broccio (sheep) A fresh Corsican cheese, usually unsalted. Possible alternatives: ricotta romana, fresh ewe's-milk cheese, ricotta.

Brousse (sheep, goat) A fresh French cheese. The mainland version of Broccio, made with either ewe's or goat's milk.

Cabécou See Goat cheese.

Caerphilly (cow) A semi-hard British cheese with a tart, creamy taste and crumbly texture. Far superior when made with unpasteurized milk.

Camembert (cow) A soft French cheese, originally made in Normandy and now manufactured by dairies all over France. It varies enormously in quality. The words *Véritable Camembert de Normandie*, or VCN, on the box usually guarantee your getting the proper unpasteurized product with its insistent, sweet smell.

Cantal (cow) A semi-hard French cheese. It comes in three categories, *doux* (mild and creamy-tasting), *entre-deux* (medium-strong) and *vieux* (strong to pungent). The best categories for cooking are *doux* and *entre-deux*. *See also* Tomme fraîche de Cantal.

Cheddar (cow) A hard British cheese, now also made elsewhere in the world. It varies greatly. Rindless 'block' Cheddar is overbland, while unpasteurized Cheddar made on farms can mature to a rich and tangy cheese (the reason why much so-called 'farmhouse Cheddar' is disappointing is that it is manufactured industrially from pasteurized milk). Canadian, and occasionally American, Cheddar can be a very good strong cheese.

Cheshire (cow) A hard British cheese, sometimes coloured light orange-red with annatto, with a rich, subtle flavour. Unlike Cheddar, all Cheshire that calls itself 'farmhouse' is made from unpasteurized milk.

Chèvre See Goat cheese.

Comté (cow) A hard French cheese with a texture, a depth

of flavour and cooking qualities similar to those of its
cousin, Gruyère.

Cotherstone (cow) A semi-hard British cheese with a mild
lactic flavour and good melting properties.

Cottage cheese See Curd cheese.

Coulommiers (cow) A soft French cheese similar to Brie
but smaller.

Cream cheese See Curd cheese.

Crottin See Goat cheese

Curd cheese (cow) An unsalted fresh cheese (see recipe p.
370) that can vary in consistency from fairly liquid to
almost crumbly, depending on how thoroughly it has been
drained. The terminology of fresh cheeses is a vexed
question: curd cheese, lactic cheese, cottage cheese,
fromage blanc, fromage frais, quark (or quarg) and cream
cheese can be confusing terms because they are sometimes
used loosely or interchangeably. Certain writers, when
referring to cottage cheese, clearly have in mind something
that is identical with the curd cheese recipe in this book;
others are referring to the type of product usually marketed
as cottage cheese – a granular and rather tart fresh cheese
made from skimmed milk. Lactic cheese is just another
word for curd cheese (and is sometimes called lactic curd or
acid curd). Fromage blanc, fromage frais and quark are the
equivalent of fairly liquid curd cheese as far as taste and
cooking properties are concerned, though their fat content
and commercial manufacture may differ slightly. Cream
cheese, like its firmer French equivalent, Petit Suisse, is,
properly speaking, a fresh cheese with a very high fat
content (40-60 per cent), though so-called 'low-fat' cream
cheeses can be found on the market. Full-fat cream cheese
is not suitable in cooked dishes, as it tends to separate. For
all these reasons, whenever a recipe requires a fresh cheese
I have indicated curd cheese (sometimes specifying that it
should be fairly liquid or else well-drained). It can of course
be replaced by fromage blanc, fromage frais or quark if

you wish, and, in uncooked dishes, by cream cheese or even Petit Suisse mixed with a little milk (though to my mind the extra fat content of the last two cheeses adds nothing to the flavour). I would always avoid the grainy, acid commercial cottage cheese.

Danish blue See Mycella.

Derby (cow) A hard British cheese now made solely in block form. It is similar to Cheddar, but moister and has a more delicate flavour. Much Derby is rubbed with sage leaves and marketed as Sage Derby or Derby Sage.

Double Gloucester (cow) A hard British cheese occasionally made from the milk of Gloucester cows and mellow in flavour.

Dunlop (cow) A hard British cheese made in Scotland. Similar to Cheddar but slightly moister. Now made only by creameries.

Edam (cow) A semi-hard to very hard Dutch cheese. Often very salty, it is without much character when young, but matures into a very hard and flavourful cheese.

Emmental (cow) A hard Swiss cheese with large holes in its paste, often referred to erroneously as Gruyère. It has a subtle fruity flavour. Passable imitations of Emmental are made in France, Bavaria and Austria, but the original Swiss product has the edge.

Ewe's-milk cheese An unsalted or slightly salted curd cheese now made from ewe's milk in small quantities on some British farms. Very similar to Broccio and Brousse.

Feta (goat, sheep, cow) A semi-hard Greek cheese with a sharp, very salty flavour. It has a good deal of character when made, as it should be, from goat's or ewe's milk, or a mixture of the two. The Danish cow's-milk version is but a pale imitation. Feta made with goat's milk is now made on some British farms.

Fontina (cow) A semi-soft to semi-hard Italian cheese from the milk of Val d'Aosta cows. It has an elastic texture and a very delicate nutty flavour.

Fourme d'Ambert (cow) A semi-hard French blue cheese with a particularly subtle, slightly astringent flavour. The blueing occurs naturally. Possible alternative: Stilton.

Fromage blanc *See* Curd cheese.

Fromage frais *See* Curd cheese.

Goat cheese This term, like the French word *chèvre*, covers many types of cheese made from goat's milk. They range from the very fresh to the hard and pungently mature. The cheese that interests the cook is either fresh or medium-ripe. Fresh unsalted or slightly salted curd cheese is now being made from goat's milk in Britain, as are good imitations of French medium-ripe *chèvres* of the Crottin de Chavignol type. There are other Crottin-like goat cheeses produced in France, such as Cabécou, Chabichou, Pélardon, Picodon and Rogeret, some of which weigh as little as 30 g (1 oz).

Gorgonzola (cow) A semi-soft Italian blue cheese that takes its name from the little town of Gorgonzola near Milan. The best Gorgonzola – Mountain Gorgonzola – has a delicate, almost spicy flavour.

Gouda (cow) A semi-hard to very hard Dutch cheese, similar to Edam but less salty. Very mature Gouda, which has tiny holes in it, has a rich powerful flavour almost in the Parmesan league.

Grana *See* Parmesan.

Gruyère (cow) A hard Swiss cheese, one of the most widely used in cooking, usually in its grated form. The term Gruyère sometimes refers incorrectly to Emmental, which, whether Swiss-made or not, has large holes in its paste, whereas genuine Gruyère, which can only be Swiss, has just a few small holes. In flavour Gruyère is at once sweeter, more aromatic and tangier than Emmental.

Halumi (goat) A soft to semi-hard Cypriot cheese, which is very salty but quite mild.

Handkäse (cow) A soft German skimmed-milk cheese. It has a very distinctive and suggestive smell.

Kefalotiri (goat, sheep) A very hard Greek cheese made of goat's or ewe's milk (or a mixture of the two), and used for grating like Parmesan. It has a very salty, pungent flavour.

Labna (goat, cow) A fresh Middle Eastern cheese (see recipe p. 371) made from goat's- or cow's-milk yoghurt.

Laguiole (cow) A semi-hard French cheese made from the milk of Aubrac cows. Like Cantal, which it resembles closely, it can be eaten at various stages of maturity.

Lancashire (cow) A semi-hard British cheese with a whitish, crumbly paste. Its flavour changes considerably during ripening from mild and slightly acid to pungent. It is a good melting cheese. Best when made with unpasteurized milk.

Leicester (cow) A hard British cheese, dyed dark orange-red with annatto, with a close texture and nutty flavour that develops with age.

Manchego (sheep) A hard Spanish cheese with a rich, powerful but unaggressive flavour. Possible alternative: Brebis des Pyrénées.

Maroilles (cow) A semi-soft French cheese with a very strong and distinctive smell and a flavour that is only slightly less assertive.

Mascarpone (cow) A fresh Italian cheese (also known as Mascherpone), with a tart, sweet flavour and high cream content.

Mitzithra (sheep) A fresh Greek cheese made from ewe's milk and the whey left over from the manufacture of feta. Alternative: ricotta romana.

Mozzarella (buffalo, cow) A soft Italian spun-curd cheese with a fresh, slightly tart flavour and very good melting properties. It is only slightly salted. The genuine product, made from buffalo milk, has a more pronounced taste than the cow's-milk version, which is now manufactured all over the world.

Munster (cow) A soft French cheese whose flavour is surprisingly mild compared with its fierce smell.

Mycella (cow) A semi-hard Danish blue cheese. This creamy yellow cheese is the better-flavoured of the two Danish blues (the other is Danablu).

Oaxaca (cow) A soft Mexican spun-curd cheese with a mild flavour and excellent cooking properties. Possible alternative: mozzarella.

Parmesan (cow) A very hard Italian cheese made from partially skimmed milk. It is widely employed in cooking in its grated form. Strictly speaking, the term Parmesan should apply only to grana parmigiano-reggiano, but it is often used loosely outside Italy to refer to the wider family of grana cheeses, which includes grana padano, grana lombardo and grana lodigiano as well as grana parmigiano-reggiano. Each type of grana is made in carefully defined areas.

Pecorino (sheep) A semi-hard to very hard Italian cheese, widely used in cooking in its grated form. There are several types, including pecorino foggiano, pecorino romano, and pecorino siciliano, which contains pepper-corns in the paste. Pecorino is often used in the same way as Parmesan, though its flavour is sharper and usually much saltier. Possible alternative: Parmesan.

Pélardon *See* Goat cheese.

Petit Suisse *See* Curd cheese.

Picodon *See* Goat cheese.

Port-Salut (cow) A semi-soft French cheese with a softish texture and bland flavour.

Provolone (cow) A semi-soft to hard Italian spun-curd cheese which comes in several varieties and shapes. The two main types are *dolce* and *piccante*, which are, respectively, medium-strong and strong in flavour.

Quargel (cow) A soft Austrian cheese with a suggestive smell. Possible alternative: Handkäse.

Quark See Curd cheese.

Rabaçal (sheep, goat) A semi-hard Portuguese cheese made of ewe's or goat's milk, or both. Possible alternative: Brebis des Pyrénées.

Raclette (cow) A semi-hard French cheese recently devised specifically for use in the recipe raclette.

Reblochon (cow) A semi-soft French cheese with a very subtle, fruity flavour and a deceptively pervasive smell.

Ricotta (sheep, cow) An Italian cheese made from whey and much used in cooking. It is usually unsalted and sold as a fresh crumbly cheese, though in Italy it is sometimes salted and matured. Traditional ricotta – ricotta romana – is made from ewe's-milk whey left over from the making of pecorino romano.

Rigotte (cow, goat) A semi-hard French cheese made from cow's or goat's milk.

Rogeret See Goat cheese.

Roquefort (sheep) A semi-hard French blue cheese, made with ewe's milk from various parts of France but matured in the caves of Roquefort. It has a crumbly consistency. It has a very strong, salty flavour, and is often used almost as a condiment.

Saint-Nectaire (cow) A semi-soft French cheese with a pleasantly musty smell and nutty flavour.

Salers (cow) A semi-hard French cheese made from the milk of Salers cows. Like Cantal, which it resembles closely, it can be eaten at various stages of maturity.

Samsø (cow) A semi-hard Danish cheese with tiny holes in its paste. It has a sweet and nutty flavour. Possible alternative: Reblochon.

Sbrinz (cow) A very hard Swiss cheese with a strong aromatic flavour. It is widely used grated in cooking.

Stilton (cow) A semi-hard British blue cheese with a slightly creamy yet crumbly texture and a rich, complex flavour.

Tomme fraîche de Cantal (cow) A fresh French cheese with an elastic texture and a very mild, creamy flavour. It is immature Cantal that has been partly pressed but not salted. A good melting cheese. Possible alternatives: mozzarella, mozzarella and Caerphilly in equal quantities or Cotherstone.

Vacherin fribourgeois (cow) A semi-hard Swiss cheese mainly used in fondue. It has a delicate, slightly sharp flavour. Not to be confused with another Swiss cheese, Vacherin Mont d'Or. Alternative: Raclette.

Wensleydale (cow) A semi-hard British cheese with a flaky texture and almost honeyed after-taste. Now made only with pasteurized milk by creameries.

White Stilton (cow) A semi-hard British cheese with a crumbly texture and creamy flavour.

Yoghurt (cow, goat, sheep) Strictly speaking, yoghurt is a cultured milk, not a cheese (in cheeses proper, the whey is separated and drained from the coagulated milk). But a few recipes calling for yoghurt have been included here because it imparts a flavour similar to that of fresh cheeses such as quark or liquid curd cheese.

BUYING AND KEEPING CHEESE

All cheese except processed cheese is a living organism. This means it is constantly evolving (at a different rate depending on the type of cheese), either moving towards optimum ripeness or declining. A good store will sell cheese that is as near the peak of condition as possible. The golden rule of cheese buying should therefore be: with the exception of one or two types of cheese, avoid buying more than you need for two or three days' consumption.

In practice, of course, this may be difficult, as good cheese outlets do not lie thick on the ground throughout the country. But the number of specialized cheese shops and good cheese counters in department stores and supermarkets has increased spectacularly in Britain over the last few years. More and more care is now taken over the storing, presentation and selling of cheese. As a result, cheese buying has become much easier than it used to be.

However, there is still plenty of cheese in poor condition on sale, and it still gets sold to gullible customers. Some of those customers are people who believe that if a cheese is 'only' to be used for cooking it need not be of top quality. What a recipe for disaster! Just as a dish calling for wine can be spoilt by the employment of a 'cooking wine' (sharp, adulterated, or otherwise undrinkable) rather than a humble and palatable, or even very good, wine, so cheese cookery will be ruined by the use – or using up – of stale or second-rate cheese.

If you buy cheese from a shop that specializes in cheese or has a high cheese turnover, you are less likely to get stale specimens, fresh cheese that has gone off or sour, or hard, cracked and/or sweaty pieces of hard cheese. Look for shops that keep the exposed areas of their large cheeses covered with cheesecloth, plastic or cling-film when not being cut, give you samples of cheese to taste and let you sniff their Camembert and Brie. Most importantly, as Patrick Rance points out in his excellent handbook, *The Great British Cheese Book*, 'cheese buying cannot be hurried'.

When you have no alternative but to buy polythene-packed pre-sliced chunks of cheese from self-service shops and supermarkets, make sure they have not sojourned too long in the refrigerated unit (this is particularly liable to happen in the case of less well-known cheeses): over a long period, this can change the flavour of the cheese, whose surface may sprout unwelcome types of mould. When buying Camembert or Brie, be wary of specimens with large rust-brown patches on their rinds: this usually means they have reached the stage where they taste of little else but ammonia.

Cheese that was in excellent condition in the shop can deteriorate rapidly at home if it is not properly looked after. This is true even if you expect to consume it within a day or two, particularly in the often overheated modern home. Many people automatically put all their cheese in the refrigerator; others swear that no cheese should ever be refrigerated. But can there be any hard and fast rule when so many variables are involved? These include: the temperature at which the refrigerator has been set (usually too cold), the part of the refrigerator used, the temperature of the kitchen, and the type of cheese.

The main thing to keep in mind is that the ideal temperature for keeping a given cheese will be dictated by its type. All liquid or very soft fresh cheeses, and particularly unsalted ones, should not leave the refrigerator for longer than is necessary (curd cheese, ricotta and mozzarella fall into this category). They do best at a temperature of 4-6°C (34-43°F). Fresh goat cheeses are a case apart. If you want to keep them for several days, you can either wrap them in cling-film and refrigerate them (which may sharpen their flavour slightly, particularly if their salinity is low) or – better, to my mind – put them unwrapped on a plate under a cloche in a cool place such as a larder or cellar, where they will begin or continue to mature a little. They can even be left under a cloche at room temperature 20°C (68°F), in which case the ripening process will be speeded up and needs to be monitored carefully.

Similarly, blue cheeses and most soft and semi-soft cheeses (e.g. Camembert, Brie, Handkäse, Maroilles, Munster, Reblochon, Saint-Nectaire, to name but a few) will do much better in a cool or coolish place 10-15°C (50-59°F) than in the refrigerator – unless, by putting it at its lowest setting, you can obtain a temperature as high as 10°C (50°F). (By the way, remember that the 'warmest', or least cool, part of a refrigerator is at the top, under the ice-box, as cold air descends.) But they should be kept under a cloche or wrapped in cling-film. If they are whole cheeses and you want to keep them longer than two or three days, they will be happiest unwrapped in a tupper-ware box, which allows the cheese to breathe while preventing any moisture loss.

What if you have no cool place in or under the house and are therefore forced to choose between room temperature and a refrigerator that cannot be set at a higher temperature than, say, 6°C (43°F)? The soft and semi-soft cheeses mentioned above will just about survive twenty-four hours at that temperature. Blue cheese, on the other hand, whose living mould thrives at about 15°C (59°F) and does not like being chilled, will retain its flavour better at slightly too high a temperature (i.e. room temperature) than at one that is too low (below 10°C/50°F). If left at room temperature, it should be firmed up in the refrigerator for about half an hour before appearing on the cheeseboard.

All the harder cheeses (e.g. Cheddar and related British cheeses, Gruyère, Parmesan, Cantal) are best kept in not too cold a refrigerator with their cut surfaces tightly wrapped in cling-film. Special care has to be taken with Cantal after its removal from the refrigerator: it quickly goes soft and sweaty, and changes irreversibly in flavour, if allowed to remain at a temperature of over 22°C (72°F) for an hour or so. All the harder cheeses can be kept for up to a week in the refrigerator, but after that, however securely wrapped they may be, they deteriorate in flavour and pick up refrigerator odours.

There is one exception, however. Parmesan, like other very hard grating cheeses such as Pecorino, Sbrinz or old Gouda, will keep very well for long periods in the refrigerator when its exposed surface is well wrapped in cling-film. This is a boon for the cook. Powdery Parmesan sold in plastic packets is usually very low-grade stuff, and often contains a certain amount of pulverized Parmesan rind. Some good Italian shops sell ready-grated Parmesan of reasonable quality, but it tends to have lost much of its flavour through exposure to air. The best solution is to buy pieces of whole Parmesan and grate them as required by the dish you are cooking. In *An Omelette and a Glass of Wine*, Elizabeth David tells how Norman Douglas, when in France, used to carry such a chunk of Parmesan in his pocket whenever he went to a restaurant so as to be sure of getting his cheese freshly grated. It is not always easy to get hold of good Parmesan. Sometimes it has dried out in the shop, or else it is a second-rate grana passed off as grana parmigiano-reggiano (see Checklist of cheeses, pp. 13-22). If you can find a good supplier of Parmesan, it is worth, unless the shop is just round the corner, investing in a really large single piece of cheese weighing, say, up to 2 kg (4½ lb). If you carefully cover the Parmesan's exposed surface with cling-film, securing it to the edge of the rind with a few drawing-pins, and then wrap the whole thing in aluminium foil and leave it in the least cold part of the refrigerator, it will happily survive undimmed and unaltered in flavour for several months. Simply chip chunks off it as required. The advantage of this system is that it turns the Parmesan into yet another staple of your kitchen supplies like, for example, dried pasta and butter (with which it can be easily combined to make a delicious impromptu meal – see p. 151).

CHEESE AND WINE

That wine makes a good accompaniment to cheese is not something that any organizer of a wine and cheese party would dispute (by the way, several of the dishes in the chapter on Cold Entrées are suitable for such occasions). Many dinner party hosts believe in keeping the best bottle for the cheese course. But is cheese the ideal complement for a really good wine? Here, opinion is divided.

On one side, you have those who are convinced that it is, and who draw up long lists of specific wines matching specific cheeses (e.g. a Monthélie with Maroilles, or a Cooks Te Kauwhata Gewürztraminer with Gorgonzola). Such exercises, I must confess, strike me as otiose. In the middle stand those who, like myself, believe that while there may exist certain general guidelines the best judge in such matters is one's own palate and imagination. And then there are the purists who hold that no really good red wine should ever be drunk with cheese. They argue that either the cheese – especially a strong one – destroys the wine's subtler nuances, or else the tannin in the wine creates a bitter aftertaste in the mouth when combined with cheese.

The latter risk can be avoided by accompanying cheese with white wine, which contains very little tannin. The acidity of white wine cuts pleasantly through the high fat content of certain cheeses, such as those of the Gruyère family. Dry white wine is the traditional accompaniment to goat cheese in France, partly because the areas where the cheese is made often produce such wines. But it is equally good with a rustic red like a Marcillac or a Saint-Pourçain.

Many of the less aggressive cheeses are tailor-made for red wines not quite in the top league, making them seem smoother and richer than they really are (this is why wine-growers often serve cubes of cheese when you taste their wares). Parmesan and mature Gouda are both excellent with even a superior red wine, because their sweetness lessens the sensation of harshness that tannin leaves in the mouth. But the most successful accompaniment I have ever had for a big red wine was a medium-strong, close-grained Brebis des Pyrénées: not too pushingly aromatic, sweetish, but not as salty as Parmesan or Gouda, it both brought out and complemented the sophistication of the wine.

Blue cheese is a case apart. A light, not very sharp blue is happy with almost any wine. But the best foil for the bite of a really mature blue is a sweetish or sweet wine. Classic combinations are port *with* – not *in* – Stilton (see p. 315), and Sauternes or another good sweet white wine with Roquefort.

In his book *Guide du fromage*, Pierre Androuët asked several leading French writers to name their three favourite cheese and wine combinations. Four of them included Camembert. The wines they chose to go with it were, respectively, Savigny-les-Beaune, a young Côtes-du-Rhône, Beaujolais and Chambertin. This perplexed me when I read it, as I have always found there is something in the complex taste of a really good ripe Camembert which, when combined with wine, produces an unpleasantly soapy, almost bitter taste. For years, I imagined I was suffering from a blind spot or a wilful taste bud. So I was interested to read not so long ago about a wine and Camembert tasting held by the Association des Gastronomes Oenophiles. After a young Beaujolais, served slightly chilled, had been voted the best wine to go with the cheese, the organizer, André Vedel, pulled a rabbit out of his hat: a dry cider (which is made in the same part of Normandy as Camembert). It, too, was sampled with the cheese – and pronounced (rightly) a clear winner.

The question of which wine to serve with the cheese dishes in this book is something I have left readers to sort out for themselves, except for a few cases, where I have suggested a wine accompaniment that I have particularly enjoyed myself or that might not otherwise spring to mind.

CHEESE IN COOKING

Before using cheese in cooking, you will often be required to grate it. It is worth possessing a really sturdy conical or four-sided grater for this. When grating any cheese except a very hard one like Parmesan, your task will be made easier if you refrigerate it for an hour before use. If the cheese is only medium-hard, either by nature or because you have not had a chance to chill it, quite a lot of it will remain stuck to the grater, particularly if you use the finer holes. It is a nuisance to pick it out with a knife. A way to get round this is to rub a piece of stale bread two or three times up and down the grater so that the cheese is pushed through (a breadcrumb or two in the dish will not do any harm).

The behaviour of cheese during cooking is discussed under the headings of individual recipes. But as a general rule the things to avoid are: too fierce a heat (except when toasting), overcooking (which makes the cheese rubbery), and re-heating (which dries it out, except when the cheese has been blended with a sauce, in which case it should be re-heated *very* gently). The microwave is a boon for re-heating. Above all, do not allow cheese to reach anything like the point where it begins to burn. This will produce a bitter taste and result in the formation of acrolein, a highly poisonous substance (lethal dose = 1 teaspoon) that is produced in infinitesimal quantities when fats – including the fat in cheese – reach smoking point. Butter burns at a lower temperature than most oils, which is why good cookbooks always warn against heating butter beyond the light brown, *noisette* stage. The (fortunately) minute amount of acrolein produced when butter or cheese is burnt acts as an irritant and is therefore highly indigestible.

Many recipes for gratins tell you to dot the surface of the assembled gratin with diced butter, or to brush it with melted butter, before cooking. I do not see the point of this practice. If the gratin is put into a very hot oven, the coating of butter may reach smoking (burning) point. Butter is put on gratins for purely aesthetic reasons. If you want your dish to look glossier, melt your butter and brush it on *after* the gratin has finished cooking and just before serving – as Auguste Colombié suggests in his recipe for Moruc au gratin (p. 234).

Notes on ingredients commonly used in recipes

Herbs In recipes calling for herbs, I have always specified whether they should be fresh or dried. This is because herbs vary considerably in their ability to retain their original flavour after the drying process. Much depends, too, on how carefully and how recently they have been dried. The following herbs should, in my opinion, never be used in their dried state: parsley, chervil, chives, dill, basil and, above all, sage. Their flavour either vanishes during drying or turns into something different – and unpleasant. Tarragon, rosemary and mint are borderline cases: when you dry them yourself they retain something of their freshness, if only vestigially, for a month or two. After that, they begin to deteriorate (even mint tea, which is commonly made with dried mint, is far superior when the fresh herb is used). Winter and summer savory, thyme and wild thyme, on the other hand, dry well because of the large amount of essential oils contained in their leaves. They can therefore be used equally well either fresh or dried.

Garlic When chopping garlic for a raw or semi-cooked use, first peel and halve each clove lengthwise. If there is a nascent, green shoot down the middle, it should be prised out and discarded. Any green-tinted flesh at the tip of the clove should also be removed. The green parts are very bitter and sharp. It is usually more satisfactory to chop garlic finely than to put it through a garlic press or – dare I say it? – crush it with a pestle and mortar: these last two operations have the effect of squeezing out the garlic juice and produce a wet squidgy mass, which, if allowed to remain in contact with the air and thus oxidize, turns bitter and indigestible. In cooked uses, where a large amount of garlic is called for, the press can usefully be employed as long as the crushed garlic is immediately stirred into a liquid medium that will minimize oxidization.

Walnuts Walnuts, once shelled, go stale very quickly, which is why the pre-shelled walnuts available in shops often have a rancid after-taste. It is always well worth the bother of buying walnuts in their shells and cracking them as required. If possible, avoid those whose shells have been bleached pale buff and artificially dried.

Several recipes call for fresh or new walnuts, which become available in the autumn. The kernels are very sweet, but their moist skin is bitter and should be removed. If this is difficult, scald the nuts briefly in boiling water. The skin then peels off more easily.

Anchovies It is essential to use anchovies or anchovy paste of the finest quality in cheese dishes. The flavour of canned anchovies is sometimes affected by the corrosion of the metal by salt, so try to find ones that come in glass containers (e.g. Monégasque brand). Similarly, when buying anchovy paste, go for the very best quality, if possible the Italian brand Balena.

Quantities, weights and measures

Many cheese dishes can be served as either an entrée, a main course, or an accompaniment to the main course, so when a recipe says 'For 4', you have to decide at what point in the meal you are going to serve it and whether the quantities are right. The amount of, say, a cheese-topped vegetable gratin that your guests end up eating will vary considerably, depending on whether it is intended to be a main course or merely to accompany it.

Similarly, the exact proportions of ingredients indicated in the recipes should not be regarded as binding: everyone has his or her special penchant – a little more, or less, garlic, cream, cheese, sauce or whatever. The only recipes where the proportions should be respected are those involving emulsions, thickenings, pastry, yeast and certain very salty cheeses like Roquefort and feta.

When grated cheese is called for, I have given the amount by weight rather than by the number of tablespoonfuls required. This is because the quantity of cheese contained in a tablespoon varies depending on whether it has been grated finely or not. If you have no weighing machine to hand, you can convert weight into heaped tablespoonfuls by using the following rough calculation: 1 tbsp of coarsely grated cheese = 15 g (1/2 oz), while 1 tbsp finely grated cheese = 10 g (1/3 oz). As far as other ingredients are concerned, teaspoonfuls and tablespoonfuls should always be regarded as heaped except in the case of powdered or granular substances (salt, sugar, gelatine, flour and so on), when they are understood to be level spoonfuls.

By the way, please stick to *either* imperial *or* metric measurements. While the proportions remain the same within the two sets of measurements, the actual quantities may not necessarily correspond exactly.

Oven temperatures

Some modern ovens do not need to be pre-heated, though it never does any harm to be on the safe side and do so. *In all the recipes that follow, it is assumed that you will have pre-heated the oven to the indicated temperature before putting your dish into it.*

CHAPTER TWO

Soups

STRACCIATELLA   FOR 4-6

A speciality of Rome and the surrounding area, this very economical soup is visually unusual, with its tightly packed little flakes (*stracci*) of egg mixture suspended in a clear broth. The semolina *stracci* give the soup its sensuously soft texture; the Parmesan, its tang.

2 eggs	30 g (1 oz) freshly grated Parmesan
2 tbsp fine semolina	1 tsp parsley, very finely chopped
pinch freshly grated nutmeg	1.5 litres (50 fl oz) chicken stock

Put the eggs, semolina, nutmeg, cheese, parsley and 5 tablespoons of tepid stock into a mixing bowl and beat with a fork for 2-3 minutes. Bring the rest of the stock to simmering point. Lower the heat to moderate and pour in the egg mixture, whisking all the time. When the flakes appear, the soup is ready. Do not allow it to boil. Check seasoning and serve immediately, with extra grated Parmesan on the side if desired.

ZUPPA DI FINOCCHIETTI SELVATICI   FOR 4

Sardinian soup with wild fennel and fresh ewe's-milk cheese – a very basic yet flavourful staple dish eaten by the kind of poor Sardinian shepherds so vividly depicted in Vittorio de Seta's film *Banditi a Orgosolo*.

200 g (7 oz) tender wild fennel stems,   100 g (3¹/₂ oz) fresh ricotta romana
   peeled and coarsely chopped   *or* other fresh ewe's-milk cheese
150 g (5¹/₂ oz) bread, sliced   salt
3 tbsp virgin olive oil   50 g (2 oz) unsalted butter, melted

Boil the fennel in just over 1 litre (35 fl oz) of salted water until tender and reserve the liquid. Fry the bread in the oil until crisp, and place it in a deep oven dish. Strew it with the fennel, then with a layer of crumbled cheese. Pour in the fennel's cooking liquid – it should come up to, but not above, the level of the cheese. Add salt to taste and dribble melted butter over the top. Put into a fairly hot oven (190°C/375°F/Gas mark 5) until lightly browned.

Wild fennel grows all over Europe and can easily be identified with the help of a botanical handbook. If you cannot get hold of any, replace with an equal quantity of either garden fennel or Florentine fennel, combining the bulb part with as many of the feathery green leaves as have not been bruised during handling.

ZUPPA PAVESE   FOR 4
This soup features regularly on Italian restaurant menus. It is also used by some, apparently with some success, as a substitute for a prairie oyster.

150 g (5¹/₂ oz) good white bread,   4 very fresh eggs
   cut into 12 small slices   salt
100 g (3¹/₂ oz) unsalted butter   pinch freshly ground white pepper
1 litre (35 fl oz) chicken stock   100 g (3¹/₂ oz) freshly grated Parmesan

Fry the bread gently in butter on both sides until golden brown. Bring the stock to simmering point. Poach the eggs in it. When done, transfer each egg gingerly to a large hot soup plate (bowls will not do) and pour some stock over it. Season with salt and pepper. Sprinkle each slice of bread with finely grated cheese and arrange 3 slices round each egg. Serve the rest of the cheese on the side.

Toast can be used by the weight-conscious instead of fried bread, but in that case the baby (flavour) will be washed out with the bath water (calories).

VIENNESE CONSOMMÉ   FOR 4

3 eggs	1 litre (35 fl oz) beef stock
30 g (1 oz) flour	freshly ground pepper
3 tbsp milk	2 tbsp fresh chives, chopped
50 g (2 oz) freshly grated Gruyère	salt

Beat the eggs and flour together until well blended, then mix in the milk and finely grated cheese until a smooth batter is obtained. With the batter make two thin well-cooked 'omelettes', fold in half and leave to cool. Heat the stock. Cut the omelettes into thin slivers. When the stock is at simmering point, add a very little pepper and the chives, and check for salt. Put the omelette strips into hot soup plates or bowls, pour the stock over them, and serve.

The omelette slivers used in this recipe also make an attractive garnish for any clear soup of the minestrone type.

KÄSESUPPE MIT EIERN   FOR 4

Many British, Scandinavian, Dutch and German recipes for cheese soup call for flour as a thickening agent, and the end product often has a consistency uncomfortably reminiscent of glue. Here is a soup from Germany in which, as in many classic soups of French *haute cuisine*, eggs perform the same role as flour, but produce a far superior and more delicate result. The rich creaminess of the soup's flavour is tempered by the large amount of chives used.

250 ml (9 fl oz) milk	60 g (2 oz) freshly grated Emmental
5 eggs	750 ml (26 fl oz) chicken *or* beef stock
2 tbsp fresh chives, chopped	

Heat the milk until lukewarm. Break the eggs into a mixing bowl and beat them very thoroughly. Add the lukewarm milk, chives and cheese, and mix thoroughly. Bring the stock to the boil. Pour about 150 ml (5 fl oz) of it slowly into the egg and cheese mixture, whisking all the time. When everything is well blended, pour the mixture in one go into the stock, away from the heat, whisking energetically. The consistency of the soup should be such that it lightly coats the back of a spoon. If it is too liquid, cook for 1-2 minutes over a very low heat, stirring constantly. Do not allow the soup to reach anything near boiling point, or it will curdle. When it is ready, check seasoning and serve immediately in hot soup plates or bowls.

SORREL SOUP WITH BLUE CHEESE   FOR 4

This recipe is a real winner: the creamy, unastringent blue cheese acts as a perfect foil to the sharpness of the sorrel.

40 g (1½ oz) unsalted butter	2 tbsp double cream
50 g (2 oz) onion, finely chopped	200 g (7 oz) potato, peeled and diced
1 litre (35 fl oz) chicken stock	100 g (3½ oz) Gorgonzola *or*
100 g (3½ oz) sorrel, stemmed,	Bleu de Bresse, cut into small pieces
washed and shredded	1 tbsp fresh chives, finely chopped

Heat the butter in a large heavy saucepan and sweat the onion gently in it until soft. Add the potato and stock. Bring to the boil. When the potato is cooked, put the soup and sorrel (raw) into a blender, in several batches if necessary, and liquidize until smooth. Put the cream into the pan you have already used, add the cheese, and melt over a very low heat, stirring all the time. When the mixture is smooth, add the soup and chives, and reheat slowly, without boiling, until hot. Serve in hot soup plates or bowls.

I have borrowed the idea of using raw rather than cooked sorrel from Margaret Costa (via Jane Grigson's *Vegetable*

Book): this method retains the vividness of the vegetable's flavour and, to some extent, its colour.

SOUPE AU FROMAGE DU DOCTEUR   FOR 4

This idiosyncratic recipe comes (slightly adapted) from an excellent book called *Les Recettes des 'Belles Perdrix'*, published in 1930. The 'beautiful partridges' in question were the members of a women writers' dining club, La Belle Perdrix, which had been formed in mild protest at the fact that well-known gourmets' clubs such as Le Grand Perdreau, Le Club des Cent and Les Compagnons de Cocagne did not admit women to their ranks (though they were happy to enliven their banquets with a contingent of female guests). The book is a collection of recipes contributed by the club's members.

Whether the 'Docteur' refers to Dr Edouard de Pomiane (p. 241), who was on friendly terms with several members of La Belle Perdrix, or to some imaginary medic who might have prescribed this soup to an ailing patient remains a mystery. True, the soup's consistency does somewhat resemble that of invalid's pap. But its fairly assertive taste would be out of place in the sickroom.

70 g (2½ oz) chick peas	salt
1 large onion, peeled	freshly ground pepper
1 clove	150 g (5½ oz) white bread, sliced
70 g (2½ oz) haricot beans	70 g (2½ oz) freshly grated Parmesan
1 tsp meat glaze (*or* concentrated juice from a roast)	70 g (2½ oz) freshly grated Gruyère

Cook the chick peas in 1.5 litres (50 fl oz) of water with the onion, into which you have stuck a clove, for 2 hours. Add the beans and continue cooking for another hour. Check that the chick peas and beans are soft, then liquidize everything (after removing the clove). Dilute the meat glaze or juice from a roast in the mixture, and add salt and a little pepper to taste. Fill a deep oven dish with alternate layers of bread, grated Parmesan and grated

Gruyère, but, before sprinkling a final layer of Gruyère on top, pour the purée into the dish. Put into a fairly hot oven (190°C/375°F/Gas mark 5) for about 20 minutes or until golden brown. Serve in hot soup plates or bowls.

POLISH BEER SOUP WITH CURD CHEESE   FOR 4

A very old recipe. Just as the British once quaffed ale for breakfast, the Poles used to start the day by stoking up with this high-calorie soup, no doubt before confronting the rigours of their continental winter. Beer for breakfast gradually fell into disuse in both countries after the arrival of tea and coffee in Europe during the seventeenth century.

600 ml (21 fl oz) lightest possible beer	3 egg yolks
	40 g (1½ oz) sugar
300 ml (10 fl oz) crème fraîche *or* not very soured cream	150 g (5½ oz) very well drained curd cheese

Heat the beer in an enamel saucepan. When it reaches simmering point, add the cream and mix well. Beat the egg yolks with the sugar in a mixing bowl until pale yellow. Gently pour a little of the hot beer and cream into the egg mixture and stir until well blended, then pour everything back into the saucepan away from the heat, whisking all the time. Crumble the cheese into hot soup plates or bowls and pour the soup over it.

This rich soup cries out for something crunchy to go with it. In Poland croutons fried in butter would traditionally be served on the side. But in view of the cholesterol content of the soup plain toast might be a more sensible idea.

CHŁODNIK   FOR 4

Another Polish soup, this time iced, and ideal fare during a heat wave (Poland's summers can be as torrid as its winters are icy).

1 small raw beetroot
16 live freshwater crayfish
250 ml (9 fl oz) juice from jar of
   Polish dill-pickled sweet-sour
   cucumbers (diluted with water
   if necessary)
500 g (1 lb 2 oz) very liquid
   curd cheese

1/2 fresh cucumber, peeled
   and diced
8 radishes, finely sliced
1 tbsp fresh chives, finely chopped
1 tbsp fresh dill, finely chopped
4 hard-boiled eggs

Clean the beetroot, put into a small saucepan with enough water to cover it easily, cover and boil gently for 1 hour. Leave to cool in its liquid. Cook the crayfish in a court-bouillon for 10 minutes. When cool, shell them (do not throw away the heads and shells, as they can be used to make crayfish *fumet* or crayfish butter). Mix together thoroughly the pickled cucumber juice, curd cheese and 250 ml (9 fl oz) of the beetroot's cooking liquid. Add the crayfish tails, peeled and diced beetroot, along with the cucumber, radishes, chives and dill.

Check the seasoning (the pickled cucumber juice should provide enough salt), and put in the bottom of the refrigerator for 2-3 hours (if this amount of time is not available, you can cheat by putting a dozen ice cubes into the soup). Slice a hard-boiled egg into each previously chilled soup plate and ladle the soup over it, making sure that everyone gets their fair share of crayfish tails.

PERSIAN YOGHURT SOUP   FOR 4

An interesting soup from Claudia Roden's *A New Book of Middle Eastern Food*. It is 'given texture with chopped walnuts, and an unusual flavour from the herb fenugreek'.

30 g (1 oz) unsalted butter	2 tbsp fresh fenugreek, finely chopped
1 large onion, finely chopped	salt
1 tbsp plain flour	freshly ground pepper
40 g (1¹/₂ oz) walnuts, chopped	400 ml (14 fl oz) yoghurt

Melt the butter in a large pan. Fry the onion until pale golden. Add the flour and stir over a very low heat for a few minutes until well blended. Add the walnuts and fenugreek. Heat 600 ml (21 fl oz) of water to just below boiling point and remove from the heat. Pour one-third of the hot water into the pan in one go and beat vigorously. Add the rest of the water gradually, stirring constantly. Season to taste with salt and pepper, bring to the boil slowly and simmer covered for 15-20 minutes, until the soup thickens a little and has lost its floury taste.

Beat the yoghurt vigorously. Add a ladleful of the hot soup to it and beat well. Pour the mixture back into the soup gradually, stirring all the time. Leave over a low heat until it comes to just below boiling point, but do not allow the soup to boil, or it will curdle. Serve immediately.

If no fresh fenugreek is available, take precautions ahead of time: buy the unroasted seed from an Indian shop and sow it in a box like mustard and cress. Depending on its strength, you may need to use more than the quantity indicated above.

SOUPE AU FROMAGE   FOR 4

This recipe was given to me by the late Jeanne Chabut, who used to run a café-restaurant-hotel-grocery in the small Auvergne village where I live. It was a gruelling job, for in addition to cooking for customers and serving in the shop she had to milk the cows (she made and sold her own butter), feed the chickens and tend a large garden virtually single-handed (her husband Rémy drove the local bus).

Right up until her death Jeanne continued to thrive on hard work – in the best Auvergnat tradition. She was quite incapable of remaining idle, and spent all her waking hours gardening, making petit-point bedcovers for her children, bottling vegetables, making walnut wine and blackcurrant syrup, or fattening ducks and rabbits, which end up either in the deep-freeze (almost every household in the Auvergne now has one) or in the delicious pâtés she cans herself.

People came a long way to enjoy her cooking, and especially her cheese soup. Her husband used to go to the trouble of driving 100 km (62 miles) to the little medieval town of Salers to get the top-quality grade of Cantal (also called Salers). He kept the cheeses in his cellar, conscientiously turning them over and brushing their rinds every few days. What with sales of the cheese to customers and Jeanne's mammoth cheese soups, the Chabuts used to get through two of the 42-kg (93-lb) cheeses a week.

This cheese soup is a very simple dish; what counts is the quality of the ingredients.

50 g (2 oz) salt pork back fat *or* green bacon fat
1 onion, sliced
1 litre (35 fl oz) vegetable stock
freshly ground pepper

250 g (9 oz) rye bread, sliced
200 g (7 oz) young Cantal cheese (if possible from Salers)
1 tbsp double cream

Render the fat in a small frying pan and fry the onion until golden (do not allow to burn). Bring the stock to the boil, add the onion, its cooking fat and a little pepper. Simmer for 20 minutes. Put alternate layers of bread and very thinly sliced cheese into an ovenproof soup tureen, ending with a layer of cheese. Dribble the cream over the top and add the boiling-hot stock. Put into a moderate oven (180°C/350°F/Gas mark 4) for about 15 minutes, then serve in hot soup plates or bowls.

If you want to do as Jeanne Chabut and all self-respecting

Auvergnats do, i.e. *faire chabrot*, pour a little red wine into the soup when you have half finished it. It is supposed to be good for the health. It certainly did Jeanne no harm – but then it was the only time she ever drank anything alcoholic.

Very similar cheese soups exist in other mountain areas such as Savoie, Jura and Switzerland. The recipes are virtually identical, except that Gruyère or Comté is used instead of Cantal, and garlic sometimes replaces the onion.

POTAGE À LA JACOBINE   FOR 6

The basis of Soupe au fromage (see preceding recipe) goes back a very long way: in medieval times, cooks were already pouring hot broth over layers of bread and grated or sliced cheese. *Le Grand Cuisinier de toute cuisine*, an anonymous book published in 1540 which derived its recipes from a corpus of medieval cookery manuscripts, contains two soup recipes with cheese. One of them, Soupe à la Capilorde, calls for roast capon or partridge (boned), cinnamon and other '*menues épices*', and sliced hard-boiled egg yolks fried in lard or butter, as well as bread, cheese and stock. The other, Soupe Jacopine, is very similar, except that the birds may be partridges, spring chickens or pigeons (whether boned or not is left unspecified), and the whole thing is sprinkled with a mixture of cinnamon and sugar, both of them very common ingredients in medieval savoury dishes.

Just over a century after the publication of *Le Grand Cuisinier de toute cuisine*, Nicolas de Bonnefons brought out his three-part work, *Les Délices de la campagne*. Bonnefons, a former valet to the adolescent Louis XIV, was not only a cook, but also a gardener and seedsman (three years earlier he had brought out a book on gardening, *Le Jardinier françois*, which contains many interesting recipes for preserves). He was one of the first cooks to advocate that ingredients should taste of what they are, instead of being masked by an over-lavish use of seasonings and spices.

In his chapter on poultry, Bonnefons gives a recipe for Potage à la Jacobine, which is very similar apart from its garnishings (and spelling) to the one in *Le Grand Cuisinier de toute cuisine*. Here it is, adapted only slightly.

250 g (9 oz) white bread	40 g (1¹/₂ oz) unsalted butter
1.5 litres (50 fl oz) chicken stock	200 g (7 oz) freshly grated Gruyère *or*
1 whole boned breast (both halves)	mature Gouda
of a medium-sized chicken	6 slices lemon
salt	¹/₂ pomegranate
freshly ground pepper	

Slice the bread and bake in the oven until light brown. Place in the bottom of a deep oven dish. Bring the stock to the boil and pour enough of it over the bread just to cover. Leave for 10 minutes. Meanwhile season the chicken breasts with salt and pepper, and sauté them gently in butter on each side until cooked (i.e. springy to the touch) and very lightly browned. Sprinkle the cheese over the bread. Coarsely chop the chicken breasts and strew them over the cheese. Bring the rest of the stock back to the boil and pour into the dish. Place the dish in a moderate oven (180°C/350°F/Gas mark 4) for 15 minutes. Serve in hot soup plates garnished with lemon slices and a handful of pomegranate seeds.

SOUPE À L'AIL   FOR 4

The Auvergne is one of France's biggest garlic-producing areas, and the town of Billom, in the Puy-de-Dôme, famous for its university in medieval times, is now a major centre of garlic production (much of it is turned into powder and pills). There is so much garlic stored in its cellars and warehouses that you can smell it as you drive into town. Naturally, Billom's main culinary speciality is garlic soup.

200 g (7 oz) rye bread
6 cloves garlic
150 g (5¹/₂ oz) freshly grated young
  or medium-ripe Cantal (if too soft to
  grate, slice very thinly)

1 tbsp walnut oil
large pinch salt
freshly ground pepper

Cut the bread into thin slices and crisp it in the oven. Rub with the garlic. Put a layer of it into a hot soup tureen along with any remaining fragments of garlic. Sprinkle with a little grated cheese and a few drops of walnut oil. Add some salt and plenty of pepper. Repeat the operation until the bread is used up, and finish with a layer of cheese. Pour 1 litre (35 fl oz) of boiling water into the tureen and leave for 5 minutes until the cheese has completely melted. Serve in hot soup plates or bowls.

SOUPE À L'OIGNON GRATINÉE

One of the attractive features of many Paris café-restaurants is their democratic set of rules: even if the restaurant is quite pricey and full of smartly dressed people, at the bar you will often find a mêlée of office workers, students, winos and workmen in cement-bespattered overalls. Some such establishments serve one or two dishes on the *zinc*.

Until very recently the well-known Pied de Cochon restaurant in Les Halles (where the capital's main food market used to be located before it was moved out to the suburbs) kept up the tradition. You could wander in at any time of day or night and order one of its *plats du jour* at the bar – or else its great permanent speciality, *Soupe à l'oignon gratinée*, a bowl of aromatic tawny-coloured onion soup topped with a well-browned crust of grated cheese. The restaurant is still open 24 hours a day and still serves onion soup. But, as the meat porters and other market workers who used to throng the bar section had departed for the more dismal reaches of Rungis, the owners of the Pied de Cochon eventually ripped out the old decor, replaced it with modern kitsch – which they no doubt thought was in much better taste – and got rid of the *zinc* altogether.

Soupe à l'oignon gratinée – always abbreviated in Paris to just gratinée – was described by Alexandre Dumas as 'a soup beloved by hunters and venerated by drunkards' (for its sobering effect). But it is also the traditional dish of night owls, perfect for dealing with that little twinge of hunger that can nag you after a long show or late-night film.

Here are two versions of the soup, a classic one, and an extravagant curiosity described by that gastronome, wit, parodist, novelist and man-about-town Paul Reboux, in his delightful book *Plats nouveaux! 300 recettes inédites ou singulières*. The recipe was passed on to him by fellow gastronome Gaston Derys, who worked with Curnonsky (p. 242) on the short-lived magazine *La Table* and an *Anthologie de la gastronomie française*.

A Classic Gratinée   FOR 4

300 g (10½ oz) onions, very finely sliced
60 g (2 oz) unsalted butter
1 tsp flour
1 litre (35 fl oz) chicken stock
100 ml (4 fl oz) dry white wine
150 g (5½ oz) good white bread, sliced and toasted
200 g (7 oz) freshly grated Emmental freshly ground pepper

Sweat the onions gently in a heavy saucepan with the butter, stirring frequently with a wooden spoon. When they are translucent, sprinkle them with the flour, continue stirring and cook for a few more minutes until they begin to brown very slightly. Pour in the stock and wine, bring to the boil and simmer for 15 minutes.

In a deep oven dish (or four individual ovenproof soup bowls) put successive layers of toasted bread, cheese and onions. Add a little pepper, pour in the stock, and top with a thick layer of grated cheese. Put into a fairly hot oven (190°C/375°F/Gas mark 5) for 20 minutes or until the crust is well browned.

If using individual soup bowls, be careful not to fill them too full, as the soup will puff up slightly in the oven.

Some people prefer to liquidize the onion and stock, but the result is a less authentic, less chunky soup. In some versions of *gratinée*, just plain water or water in which haricot beans have been cooked is used instead of chicken stock.

GASTON DERYS' SOUPE À L'OIGNON ET AU CHAMPAGNE

A few years back [Gaston Derys told Paul Reboux] I used to dine from time to time with friends whose flat, though vast and comfortable, was located in a rather remote part of Paris.

The food was exquisite, the fellow guests pleasant, the women pretty. Time would go by so fast that it was one o'clock in the morning before we realized it. At that point – it was a tradition – the mistress of the house would herself concoct a tasty onion soup. We assisted her as best we could.

The lady's cook was of the not totally unjustified opinion that we tended to leave her kitchen in a shambles, and on one occasion took it into her head, alas, to leave us neither stock nor Gruyère with which to make our soup – a dish that had become a veritable institution and rite for us.

We therefore had no alternative but to replace the Gruyère with half a ripe Camembert that had been left over, and the stock with champagne.

Everyone was enthusiastic about the result, and we finally succeeded, after various improvements, in perfecting the following recipe, which we called *soupe à l'oignon Mado* as a tribute to the mistress of the house:

For 10 persons, take a frying pan and brown some onions in butter. Transfer them to a copper saucepan containing a litre of hot water, with a little salt, freshly ground pepper, a pinch of cayenne, a pinch of cinnamon and half a bay leaf. Add a bottle of dry champagne. Bring to a very gentle boil. Add half a ripe Camembert. Stir with a wooden spoon. Beat 6 egg yolks in a glass of old port and add the mixture to the soup. Then add a spoonful of armagnac. At all costs do not use any other spirit.

Toast some slices of bread and pour the soup over them.

I almost forgot: if they are in season, add 30 carefully peeled walnuts to the soup two minutes before serving.

This onion soup, taken at three or four o'clock in the morning, is an exhilarating tonic that forces one to take a blithely optimistic view of the world.

To be on the safe side, beat a little of the hot soup into the egg and port mixture before transferring it to the saucepan (which, of course, need not be made of copper). The champagne makes an otherwise cheap dish into a rather expensive one, but any good dry sparkling wine such as Clairette de Die, Blanquette de Limoux or Crémant de Loire will do equally well. The walnuts referred to are fresh ones; scald them in boiling water before peeling.

One suspects that the enviable feeling of exhilaration described by Derys had as much to do with the no doubt excellent wines that had been served into the small hours as with the virtues of this outlandish soup.

SOUPE GRATINÉE AU ROQUEFORT   FOR 4

A tasty variant of the preceding recipes.

300 g (10^1/$_2$ oz) onions, very finely sliced
60 g (2 oz) unsalted butter
1 tsp flour
pinch freshly grated nutmeg
200 g (7 oz) rye bread, sliced and toasted

70 g (2^1/$_2$ oz) Roquefort
freshly ground pepper
1 tbsp cognac
80 g (3 oz) freshly grated Gruyère

Sweat the onions gently in a heavy saucepan with the butter, stirring frequently with a wooden spoon. When they are translucent, sprinkle them with the flour, continue stirring and cook for a few more minutes until they begin to brown very slightly. Pour in 1 litre (35 fl oz) of water, add the nutmeg, bring to the boil and simmer for 15 minutes. In a deep oven dish (or four individual ovenproof soup bowls) put successive layers of toast, crumbled Roquefort and onions. Add a little pepper and the cognac, pour in the onions' cooking liquid, and top with the grated Gruyère. Put into a fairly hot oven (190°C/375°F/Gas mark 5) for 20 minutes or until the crust is well browned.

If using individual soup bowls, be careful not to fill them too full, as the soup will puff up slightly in the oven.

Roquefort is so salty that additional salt will probably be unnecessary.

GARBURE BÉARNAISE   FOR 8

I have met people from the Béarn, in the extreme south-west of France, whose eyes mist over with pride when they speak of their region's most celebrated dish, *garbure*. Their emotion is all the greater if they happen to be 'exiled' in Paris or some other city far from home: *garbure* then symbolizes the family hearth and culinary traditions they have left behind.

I say family hearth because *garbure* should properly be cooked in the fireplace, suspended from a *crémaillère* (pot-hook) over the embers. It is a sumptuous dish that, like an authentic Hungarian *gulyás* (goulash), really deserves to be – and often is – regarded more as a stew than a soup. It comes in several versions, the only common denominator of which is cabbage. That may not sound all that inspiring, but it is what goes in with the cabbage that really counts.

Garbure is one of the very few French rural dishes that edged its way into the kitchens of royalty in the eighteenth and nineteenth centuries. Menon's recipe, in his *Les Soupers de la cour* (1755), is interesting in that it does not include any potato, which was then still regarded as pig food, but does indicate parsnip, which has now virtually disappeared from French cuisine and is grown by the French, if at all, just 'for donkeys'. Antonin Carême devised an emasculated version of *garbure* he thought would appeal to the refined palates of his employers (Talleyrand, ambassadors, the English Prince Regent, the Rothschilds): it was called Potage garbure Crécy and consisted of carrots, breadcrumbs and grated Gruyère.

Genuine *garbure* is made of sterner stuff – as can be judged from the list of ingredients that follows.

1 ham bone (if possible)
3 cloves garlic
1 sprig thyme
1 small chilli
500 g (1 lb 2 oz) waxy potatoes, peeled and diced
1 small parsnip, peeled and diced
1 medium-sized Savoy cabbage, trimmed of its tougher ribs, washed and shredded
300 g (10^1/$_2$ oz) fresh haricot beans, shelled, *or* 150 g (5^1/$_2$ oz) dried haricot beans

200 g (7 oz) fresh broad beans, shelled, *or* 100 g (3^1/$_2$ oz) dried broad beans
1 wing or thigh *confit d'oie* (preserve of goose)
2 tbsp goose fat (from the jar *or* tin of *confit*)
200 g (7 oz) brown bread (wholemeal or rye)
100 g (3^1/$_2$ oz) Roquefort

Try to get hold of a ham bone, as it makes all the difference; ideally, it should be a *jambon de Bayonne* bone, but the bone of a cooked ham will do. If you are successful, put the bone in a large heavy saucepan along with the garlic, thyme and chilli, and boil in 2 litres (70 fl oz) of water. If you have no ham bone, use slightly salted water or meat stock.

When the bone has been cooking for 1 hour, add the potatoes and parsnip. After another 10 minutes, add the cabbage, fresh haricots and broad beans. Cook for 10 minutes, then add the goose and goose fat. Simmer for 20 minutes. Cut the bread into thin slices and place in the bottom of a large soup tureen along with the crumbled cheese. Remove the ham bone and sprig of thyme from the saucepan, and pour the soup over the bread and cheese. Leave for 5 minutes, then stir. Check seasoning and add salt if necessary (this will depend on the saltiness of the Roquefort and on whether or not you have used a ham bone). Serve in large hot soup bowls.

If dried haricot or broad beans are used, put them in with the ham bone; if you have no ham bone, boil them for 1 hour in water or stock before adding the potato and parsnip.

Most housewives in the Béarn use a different method of cooking *garbure*: they leave it to simmer away for two or three hours unsupervised so they can get on with other tasks. To my mind, the prolonged cooking of fresh vegetables, especially cabbage, destroys or denatures much of their flavour, which is why I have indicated a total cooking time of only 40 minutes.

Apart from cabbage, there is no strict canon for the ingredients that go into *garbure* (indeed, most versions do not call for Roquefort). Depending on the time of year, you can include, as replacements or additions, other seasonal vegetables like garden peas, carrots or turnips. In one delicious version roasted chestnuts are added to the soup at the last moment. Whatever goes into your *garbure*, it is best taken as a main course.

Alexis Soyer, the Frenchman who went to England in 1831 to seek his fortune and became a celebrated chef at the Reform Club, gives a soup recipe that is similar to the *garbure* above, except that he uses 'buttock of beef' instead of *confit*, and Cheddar instead of Roquefort. He gives the dish a suitably John-Bullish name: Potage à la Yeoman.

CHAPTER THREE

Cold Entrées

MARINATED GOAT CHEESES

One of the attractions of a summer's day in Haute Provence is not just the heat, or the sound of the cicadas, or the delicate grey of the undersides of the olive-tree leaves, but also the symphony of fragrant smells that fills the heavy air: whole hillsides and plateaux are covered with rosemary bushes, savory and thyme – not the rather insipid wild thyme found in Britain, but a woody plant with highly aromatic, grey-green leaves.

This experience can be remembered, anticipated or imagined when you taste these marinated cheeses.

6 semi-hard goat cheeses weighing about 70 g (2^1/$_2$ oz) each	1 bay leaf
	2 small dried chillies
3 cloves garlic, halved	10 black peppercorns, very
1 tiny sprig fresh rosemary	coarsely ground
1 sprig fresh *or* dried winter savory	about 500 ml (17 fl oz) virgin olive oil
1 sprig fresh *or* dried thyme	

Put the cheeses and flavourings into a jar or crock with enough olive oil to cover. The size of the container should be such that as little air as possible is left between the olive oil and the lid. Seal and put in a cool place for 3-4 weeks before consuming.

The cheeses should be semi-mature: neither mushy and bland, nor very hard and pungent. If they have been only lightly salted by the maker, sprinkle a little salt on them before marinating.

The quality of the olive oil employed is crucial to the success of the marinade. Use the smooth, very yellow virgin olive oil from Provence or the Nice area if possible. A particularly good brand is Alziari of Nice.

Other cheeses, made of cow's milk or of a mixture of cow's and goat's milk, and with the same consistency, may be similarly marinated – and often greatly improved in the process. Labna (p. 371), too, when well drained, can be rolled into walnut-size balls and given the same treatment.

KÖRÖZÖTT LIPTÓI (LIPTAUER) FOR 4-6

The Hungarians regard this cheese spread as an exclusively Hungarian creation (Liptói is the name of an ewe's-milk curd cheese from the former Hungarian county of Liptó, now in Czechoslovakia). But variations of this recipe are to be found all over the area once covered by the Austro-Hungarian Empire. Outside present-day Hungary, it is known – and marketed ready-made – as Liptauer. In Austria Liptauer is regarded as a rather peasanty dish, the sort of thing you order in a *Weinstube* and wash down with beer or new wine. It does not often find its way on to dinner tables.

Very similar dishes are also found both in Poland, where the mixture is unaccountably called *błoto* (which means 'mud'), and even in faraway Portugal, where a kind of fromage blanc is used and the texture is much more that of a dip.

225 g (8 oz) fresh ewe's-milk cheese	pinch salt
125 g (4¹/₂ oz) unsalted butter, softened	1 tsp paprika
	1 tsp capers, finely chopped
2 anchovies, finely chopped, *or* 2 tsp anchovy paste	¹/₂ tsp caraway seeds, coarsely crushed in a mortar
1 tbsp onion, finely chopped	1 tbsp fresh chives, chopped
1 tsp Dijon mustard	

Blend the cheese and butter together until fluffy. Incorporate all the other ingredients, cover and chill slightly for several hours (if possible overnight) to allow the flavours to intermingle. Take out and mix again. Check seasoning and add salt if necessary (this depends on the amount of salt in the anchovies). Serve with brown bread (wholemeal or rye).

If you blend the butter and cheese manually, make sure the butter is very soft, though not melting, otherwise it will not amalgamate properly.

This recipe is equally good when made with fresh goat cheese. You can also use ordinary curd cheese, in which case add a tablespoon of soured cream to sharpen the taste. In Austria an odoriferous local cheese called Quargel (rather similar to the German Handkäse) is sometimes included in the ingredients.

CERVELLE DE CANUT   FOR 4-6

This Lyonnais speciality, properly known as *claqueret*, owes its name to the city's once thriving silk industry (the words *cervelle de canut* mean 'silk-weaver's brains'). Whoever invented the name must, one supposes, have intended a visual, not a gustatory, analogy.

400 g (14 oz) not too liquid curd cheese	freshly ground pepper
small clove garlic, very finely chopped	1 tsp vinegar
1 tbsp fresh chives, finely chopped	3 tbsp dry white wine
salt	

Beat (*claquer*) the cheese with the garlic, chives, and salt and pepper to taste. Cover and leave for 24 hours in the refrigerator. Stir in the vinegar and wine, and serve with bread.

At a Lyon restaurant I was once served *cervelle de canut* that also contained some finely diced black radish – an excellent, though unorthodox, addition.

HERB CHEESE   FOR 4-6

Curd or cream cheese mashed together with the herbs of your choice. There are various commercial versions, the best-known of which is probably the French Boursin aux fines herbes.

The tradition of herb cheese, though, is a thoroughly English one, and goes back at least to Roman times. In the sixteenth century it was called 'spermyse' (etymology unknown), and varied so much in composition that Andrewe Boorde, in *A Compendyous Regyment or a Dyetary of Helth*, confessed he was unable to say exactly what its ingredients were:

> Spermyse is a chese the which is made with curdes and with the iuce of herbes: to tell the nature of it, I can not/consyderynge that euery mylke-wyfe maye put many iuces of herbes of sondry operacyon & vertue, one not agreynge with another. But and yf they dyd knowe what they dyd gomble [jumble] togyther without trewe compoundynge, and I knowynge the herbes, then I coulde tell the operacyon of spermyse cheese.

True to that spirit, I shall give here only a few suggestions and leave you, like the milk-wife, to experiment with others as the inspiration takes you.

400 g (14 oz) well-drained
  curd cheese
either 4 tbsp of any of the
  following herbs *or* combinations
  of herbs, finely chopped:
  chives
  chives and chervil

chives and tarragon
chives, chervil and tarragon
borage and chervil
or 3 tbsp fresh basil and 1 clove garlic,
  both finely chopped
salt
freshly ground pepper

Mix the cheese and herbs well, add salt and pepper to taste, cover and refrigerate for several hours or overnight. Serve with brown bread (wholemeal or rye).

CURD CHEESE AND BACON SPREAD   FOR 4

I owe this recipe to an old friend, Carla Phillips. She has always been an enthusiastic and inventive cook, never happier than when browsing through a recipe book or preparing a meal. For years she regaled family and friends with excellent food. Then one day, almost as a lark, she decided to go in for the *Sunday Times* Best Cook of Britain Competition – and won it. After that, she quite rightly decided, in 1986, to put her talents to a severer test by opening a restaurant, The Moorings, in Wells-Next-the-Sea (Norfolk). Her husband, Bernard, who is also a very good cook, threw up his teaching job so as to be able to help her in the kitchen (and collect cockles, pick samphire, and smoke grey mullet and trout for the restaurant).

8 slices streaky bacon, without rind	3 tbsp milk
350 g (12 oz) well-drained	2 tbsp horseradish, finely grated
curd cheese	freshly ground pepper

Fry or grill the bacon until thoroughly crisp, and drain well on paper towels. Blend the cheese with the milk. Crumble the bacon and add to the cheese mixture along with the horseradish and some pepper. Serve with brown bread (wholemeal or rye).

POTTED CHEESE

British potted cheese, like the French *fromage fort* (see following recipe), used to be an excuse for using up odds and ends of stale cheese. But versions of potted cheese using proper fresh cheese have appeared in recipe books ever since Hannah Glasse's *The Art of Cookery Made Plain and Easy* (1747). They vary considerably in their indications for the proportion of butter to cheese and in the amount of wine or sherry recommended. However, the great majority of the older recipes call for mace as a flavouring, while later versions tend to leave it out.

Has mace gone out of favour nowadays? If so, it is a pity. I have to admit to a special liking for its quite distinctive flavour, which is somehow subtler yet more insistent than that of nutmeg (mace is the dried aril – a husk-like cage – of the nutmeg). But maybe it especially appeals to me because powdered mace was the predominant aroma in the toy spice chest I used to play with when a small child.

This recipe comes from a book published in Edinburgh in 1804: *The New Practice of Cookery, Pastry, Baking, and Preserving*, 'being the country housewife's best friend, by Mrs Hudson and Mrs Donat, present and late housekeepers and cooks to Mrs Buchan-Hepburn of Smeaton, and published by her permission.'

600 g (1 lb 5 oz) Cheshire
100 g (3¹/₂ oz) unsalted butter
4 tbsp sweet sherry, Sauternes or
  other good sweet wine

3 g (¹/₁₀ oz) powdered mace
50g (2 oz) clarified butter (optional)

Blend or mash the cheese, unsalted butter, sherry or wine, and mace thoroughly. Press very firmly into a pot or pots. Cover with clarified butter and store in a cool place.

'This exceeds any cream cheese', remark Mrs Hudson and Mrs Donat. They had probably read Hannah Glasse, whose recipe for potted cheese concludes with the words 'a slice of this exceeds all the cream cheeses that can be made.' But their version differs substantially from Glasse's, which calls for a dry wine and twice as much mace.

The recipe can be made equally well with Cheddar or any other similar cheese. The clarified butter is unnecessary unless you intend to keep the potted cheese longer than a week.

FROMAGE FORT

Although listed in cheese books as a cheese, this French concoction is in fact a dish – a kind of mushy potted cheese. The term *fromage fort* falls short of the truth, for the kick it packs is quite definitely *fortissimo*.

French cuisine does not, on the whole, show a penchant for fiery, pungent flavours. But when the subject of strong or smelly cheese is broached the French display a mixture of awe and admiration. '*Ça dégage!*' they murmur, as they dig into a second helping of a ripe, runny Epoisses or a Gris de Lille, popularly known as Vieux Puant de Lille (Old Stinker of Lille) – the only cheese, by the way, that has ever been subject to a by-law: the city of Lille does not allow you to transport Gris de Lille in a taxi.

Gris de Lille has a bark that is worse than its bite. *Fromage fort* on the other hand, hits both palate and nose like a sledgehammer. There are several types of *fromage fort* made in various parts of France, some of them with picturesque names like Pétafine, Poustagnac, Fremgeye and Foudjou. In the Massif Central a few people still make one little-known version of *fromage fort* that goes by the harmless name of Fromagée (Auvergne) or Cofit (Rouergue). It consists simply of unsalted Tomme fraîche de Cantal and *eau de vie* mixed together in a crock, which is then left throughout the winter buried in hay in the barn or hayloft.

In his excellent and erudite book *Guide to Cheeses of France*, William Stobbs suggests that a competition should be held between *fromages forts* to find out which one is the real 'devil' of them all. To my mind, the winner would have to be Foudjou, from the lower Ardèche, which ideally is never emptied from the crock in which it is made, so that the 'culture' is passed on to the new mixture rather as in yoghurt-making. Not only does Foudjou get the top pungency rating from cheese experts, but it surely beats all records for cheese longevity: it has been claimed that the bottom of one crock containing Foudjou did not see the light of day for 15 years.

It is extremely rare to find *fromage fort* in French

restaurants. But there is a Paris café specializing in wine (La Tartine, 24 rue de Rivoli) that serves open sandwiches spread with an excellent *fromage fort*.

The version of *fromage fort* given here is based on a recipe that appeared in the third issue, devoted to Lyonnais cuisine, of *La France à table*, a magazine founded by Curnonsky (p. 242) in 1934. Each number dealt with a different region of France.

10 small goat cheeses (such as Pélardon, Rogeret or Picodon) that have been allowed to get very dry and hard	1 sprig fresh tarragon
	10 peppercorns
	3 allspice berries
	100 ml (4 fl oz) vieux marc de bourgogne
1 large leek, washed and sliced	
1 sprig fresh or dried thyme	

Grate or slice thinly the cheeses into a terrine or crock with a capacity of about 1.5 litres (53 fl oz). Boil the leek in 1 litre (35 fl oz) of water for 45 minutes. Strain the liquid, while still warm, over the cheese. Add the thyme, tarragon, peppercorns, allspice and *marc*. Cover tightly and leave for 1-2 weeks. Remove the herbs, stir well with a wooden spatula and serve with bread. Cover again after use. The *fromage fort* will keep for a month or two, getting more ferocious all the time.

MOZZARELLA WITH ANCHOVY   FOR 4

This simplest of dishes often forms part of the array of *antipasti* in good Italian restaurants. Cheese and anchovy, as will be seen from the many other recipes in which they feature, combine particularly well.

8 anchovy fillets	virgin olive oil
250 g (9 oz) mozzarella, cut into 8 slices	freshly ground pepper

Desalt the anchovies by soaking them briefly in tepid water and dabbing them dry with a paper towel. Place one anchovy on each slice of mozzarella, followed by a dribble of olive oil and some pepper.

YOGHURT WITH CUCUMBER   FOR 4
A cooling dish, found in Greece and all over the Middle East.

1 medium-sized cucumber, peeled and diced	3 cloves garlic, finely chopped
	1 tbsp fresh mint, finely chopped
salt	freshly ground pepper
250 ml (9 fl oz) yoghurt	

Sprinkle some salt over the cucumber and leave to drain for at least 30 minutes. Dab dry with paper towels and mix with the yoghurt. Add the garlic, mint and pepper, and leave in a cool place for 1-2 hours to infuse the flavours. Check seasoning before serving.

This can be eaten on its own with bread or, as in Greece, used to jazz up a hot dish like fried fish, aubergine or courgette.

CELERY WITH ROQUEFORT   FOR 4
An appetizer – quite literally.

110 g (4 oz) Roquefort	freshly ground pepper
80 g (3 oz) unsalted butter, softened	1 head celery
1 tbsp armagnac	

Mash the cheese, butter, armagnac and plenty of pepper together until smooth. Wash and dry the celery. Remove as much string as possible and trim off all but the palest leaves. Pack the cheese mixture into the groove of each stalk. Cut the stalks into 5-cm (2-in) lengths. Chill slightly before serving.

PARMESAN MOUSSE FOR 4

A popular Edwardian summer dish.

250 ml (9 fl oz) double cream	1 tsp made mustard
1¹/₂ tsp powdered gelatine	pinch cayenne
1 egg white	small pinch salt
125 g (4¹/₂ oz) freshly grated Parmesan	

Heat 1 tablespoon of the cream and 1 tablespoon of water gently in a very small pan, add the gelatine and stir until completely dissolved. Cool. Put the cream and gelatine mixture and the rest of the cream into a mixing bowl and whisk until firm. Whisk the egg white in another bowl with a tiny pinch of salt until very stiff, and fold delicately but thoroughly into the cream. Add the cheese (grated as finely as possible), mustard, cayenne and salt. Put a drop of vegetable oil on a piece of paper towel and lightly smear the inside of four dariole moulds or ramekins. Fill with the mixture and chill for at least 3 hours. Turn out by dipping the moulds very briefly in hot water. Serve with toast.

MOUSSE DE FROMAGE FRAIS DE CHÈVRE
AUX BLINIS DE SARRASIN FOR 6

A recipe given to me by Cosima Kretz and Jean Moreno (p. 251). It is an intelligent reinterpretation of the Russian classic, blinis with soured cream, and beautifully combines textures and tastes – warm, velvety and slightly sweet blinis with cold, sharp and slightly salty mousse.

The Mousse

400 g (14 oz) fresh goat cheese	3 tbsp armagnac
¹/₂ clove garlic, finely chopped	3 tsp powdered gelatine
375 ml (13 fl oz) double cream	salt
pinch cayenne	freshly ground pepper

Blend the cheese, garlic and cayenne. Heat the armagnac until lukewarm, put in the gelatine and stir until completely dissolved. Add to the cheese mixture and pass through a fine sieve. Whip the cream until firm and fold delicately but thoroughly into the mixture. Add salt and pepper to taste (the amount of salt will depend on how salty the cheese is). Put a drop of vegetable oil on a piece of paper towel and lightly smear the inside of six small dariole moulds or ramekins with a capacity of about 120 ml (4 fl oz) each. Fill with the cheese mixture and chill for at least 3 hours.

The Blinis

750 ml (26 fl oz) milk	good pinch salt
20 g ($^3/_4$ oz) fresh yeast	25 g (1 oz) caster sugar
250 g (9 oz) plain flour	1 tsp fine semolina
250 g (9 oz) buckwheat flour	2 egg whites
100 g (3$^1/_2$ oz) unsalted butter, melted	5 tbsp crème fraîche or soured cream
3 egg yolks	butter or oil for frying

Garnish

2 lettuce hearts	3 tomatoes

Heat the milk to a temperature of 35°C (95°F) and dissolve the yeast in it. Mix the plain and buckwheat flours together and sift into the milk, stirring until a smooth consistency is obtained. Leave to rise in a warm place for 25 minutes. Add the melted butter, egg yolks, salt, sugar and semolina to the batter and mix well. Whisk the egg whites with a small pinch of salt until very stiff and fold delicately but thoroughly into the mixture. Beat the crème fraîche a little to loosen it up, and stir into the batter.

Cook the blinis in the usual way (see method for pancakes, p. 175) in a non-stick frying pan with a little butter or oil; the quantities of batter given here should enable you to make 24 blinis measuring about 6 cm (2$^1/_2$ in) across. When little bubbles appear on the upper side, turn them over and cook for 1-2 minutes.

When each batch is done (the number of blinis in each batch will depend on the size of your pan), transfer to a shallow dish lined with paper towels in a cool oven (150°C/300°F/Gas mark 2).

Turn out the goat cheese mousses after dipping the moulds briefly in hot water, and place each in the middle of a large plate. Arrange around it 4 hot blinis alternating with 4 small lettuce leaves topped by a slice of tomato. Serve immediately.

CRÈME DE CAMEMBERT   FOR 6

For this and the following recipe – both typical of the Edwardian era and its love of novelty – it is essential to get hold of a top quality unpasteurized Camembert that is neither unripe (chalky) nor too ripe (runny).

1 ripe but firm Camembert	salt
dry white wine	freshly ground white pepper
100 g (3¹/₂ oz) unsalted butter, softened	freshly toasted breadcrumbs

Cut a thin layer of rind off the cheese. Place the cheese in a dish or very small enamel saucepan into which it fits snugly. Pour over enough white wine to immerse it, cover and leave in a cool place overnight. Discard the remaining wine, dab the cheese dry with paper towels and mash with the butter, adding a very little salt and some pepper, until an absolutely smooth paste is obtained.

Recipe books of the period tell you blithely at this point to give the Camembert its original shape. You will not find that easy using just your fingers unless you are very skilled at modelling. A better idea is to take a large piece of aluminium foil, fold it in half and line the bottom half of the Camembert box with it, allowing the sides to come up higher than the box. Dip a piece of paper towel in a very little oil and smear the inside of the improvised foil mould. Pack the cheese and butter mixture into the mould and press it down well. Refrigerate for 2 hours.

Take the mould out of the Camembert box and peel away the foil. Put the born-again Camembert on a serving plate and sprinkle the top and sides with a good coating of breadcrumbs, pressing them in with a knife so they adhere neatly. Chill for 1 hour before serving.

ICED CHEESE   FOR 4

This recipe comes from *The Dudley Book of Cookery and Household Recipes* (1909), collected and arranged by Georgiana Countess of Dudley.

60 g (2 oz) freshly grated strong Cheddar	pinch salt
	freshly ground pepper
1 egg yolk	1 tsp made mustard
good pinch cayenne ('as much as will cover a threepenny piece')	250 ml (9 fl oz) double cream
	small bunch parsley

'Mix the grated cheese with the yolk of 1 egg, then add the seasonings and lastly the cream. Mix all very smoothly and pour into a square mould. (A small mustard canister will answer the purpose.) Freeze in the usual manner for 3 hours, and when about to serve turn it out of the mould. It can be cut into neat small pieces and dished up in a circular form with small pieces of parsley to garnish it.'

MOCK CRAB   FOR 6

I have often pondered why traditional English cookery is so fond of mock this and mock that (heart masquerading as goose, for example, or onion and potato as sole, or walnuts and breadcrumbs as chicken cutlets). Does it, I wonder, have anything to do with the nineteenth-, as opposed to the seventeenth-, century Puritan ethic? If it is 'sinful' to enjoy goose, sole or chicken, making do with a poor substitute must have a salutary mortifying effect.

In France, where they have no such hang-ups, culinary deception usually takes the reverse form. The aim is to create a pleasant surprise (such dishes often carry the epithet *en surprise*). You imagine you are being fobbed off with something boring, but to your amazement there are unsuspected goodies within (see, for example, Escalopes savoyardes, p. 243).

Mock crab, also sometimes called crab cheese, is supposed, we are told, to recall the taste of the real crustacean. With a hefty effort of the imagination, one can just detect a distant kinship (and the colour is that of crab paste). However that may be, mock crab is excellent; it also makes a little cheese go a long way.

There is also a hot, toasted version of Mock crab (p. 94).

200 g (7 oz) freshly grated strong Cheddar	freshly ground pepper
200 g (7 oz) unsalted butter, softened	1 tsp made mustard
good pinch cayenne	1 tbsp tarragon vinegar
	1 tbsp anchovy paste

Blend the finely grated cheese and butter together until absolutely smooth. Then stir in the other ingredients. Serve with toast.

LITTLE CREAM CHEESES WITH ANCHOVY   FOR 6

This recipe, based on one in *Fifty Lunches* (1902) by Colonel Arthur Kenney Herbert ('Wyvern'), is really just a classier version of the preceding dish.

8 anchovy fillets	4 egg yolks
150 g (5¹/₂ oz) freshly grated Parmesan or Gruyère	200 ml (7 fl oz) double cream
1 tbsp made mustard	6 pre-cooked tartlet shells (made of short pastry with egg, p. 366)
1 tbsp wine vinegar	

Desalt the anchovies in tepid water and dab dry with paper towels. Blend them to a smooth paste with the finely grated cheese, mustard, vinegar and egg yolks. Whip the cream until stiff and fold into the mixture. Fill the pastry shells with the mixture. Serve cold.

COLD CHEESE CREAMS   FOR 4
A rich Edwardian cold savoury.

2 tsp powdered gelatine	pinch cayenne
300 ml (10 fl oz) milk	110 g (4 oz) freshly grated Parmesan
2 egg yolks	1 tsp unsweetened lime juice
salt	150 ml (5 fl oz) double cream
freshly ground pepper	4 sprigs chervil

Dissolve the gelatine in 2 teaspoons of hot water. Heat the milk gently until lukewarm. Beat the egg yolks thoroughly and whisk into the milk. Continue cooking over an extremely low heat, stirring all the time, until the mixture thickens very slightly. Away from the heat, add the dissolved gelatine, salt to taste, pepper and cayenne. Stir until smooth and leave to cool slightly. Add the finely grated cheese and the lime juice. Whip the cream until it almost doubles in volume. Fold into the mixture delicately but thoroughly. Pour into eight small dariole moulds or ramekins. Refrigerate. Unmould by dipping the moulds or ramekins briefly in hot water and turning out on to small plates. Decorate with sprigs of chervil and serve with green salad.

CANAPÉS
The range of possibilities here is enormous – after all, bread and any cheese is a form of canapé. But I suggest below some combinations that work particularly well. Also very good on canapés are Körözött liptói (p. 51), Herb cheese (p. 53), Curd cheese and bacon spread (p. 54), Potted cheese (p. 54) and Mock crab (p. 62).

For the greatest convenience – and particularly if the canapés have to be negotiated by guests who are standing up and clutching a drink in their other hand – the slices of bread should be trimmed of their crust, measure about 5 cm (2 in) square, and be cut thick enough to preclude their bending under their load and spilling it on to the floor. All quantities are for 20 fairly generously spread canapés.

Roquefort and Walnut

80 g (3 oz) Roquefort
80 g (3 oz) unsalted butter, softened
pinch cayenne

30 g (1 oz) walnuts, shelled
brown bread (wholemeal *or* rye),
    trimmed of crust

Blend the cheese, butter and cayenne to a smooth paste. Crush the walnuts in a mortar until they are about the size of peppercorns. Stir them into the cheese mixture. Spread on to the bread and chill slightly before serving.

Brie and Almond

80 g (3 oz) Brie without its rind
80 g (3 oz) unsalted butter, softened
small pinch cayenne
pinch salt

brown bread (wholemeal *or* rye),
    trimmed of crust
30 g (1 oz) flaked almonds, roasted

Blend the cheese, butter, cayenne and salt to a smooth paste. Spread on to the bread and sprinkle with almonds.

Curd Cheese, Watercress and Clementine

60 g (2 oz) watercress
100 g (3¹/₂ oz) curd cheese
salt
freshly ground pepper

good white bread, trimmed of crust
20 seedless clementine segments,
    peeled

Discard the tougher stalks of the watercress, wash thoroughly, plunge into plenty of boiling water for 30 seconds, drain in a colander, refresh under the cold tap and dry very thoroughly. Blend with the cheese (if you do not have a blender, chop as finely as possible and mix well with the cheese). Stir in salt and pepper to taste. Spread on the bread and press a clementine segment diagonally on to the middle of each canapé.

Peeling the clementine segments is a bother, but makes all the difference: their skin adds a quite unwelcome bitterness to the combination.

These canapés should not be made too long in advance, as the green tinge from the watercress tends to discolour after a time.

Fresh Goat Cheese and Prawn

1 small shallot, very finely chopped	60 g (2 oz) unsalted butter
1 tbsp fresh chervil, finely chopped	brown bread (wholemeal *or* rye),
100 g (3^1/$_2$ oz) fresh goat cheese	trimmed of crust
salt	20 cooked prawns, shelled
freshly ground white pepper	

Blend the shallot and chervil well with the cheese. Add salt to taste and a little pepper. Spread the mixture on the buttered bread and press a prawn diagonally on to the middle of each canapé.

SANDWICHES ANGLAIS   FOR 4

Nobody needs to be told how to make a straightforward English cheese sandwich. These Sandwiches anglais, however, which are really rolls more than sandwiches, are rather out of the ordinary. The basis of the recipe was published in the French cookery magazine *Luculla*, which appeared from 1911 to 1916, when it had to cease publication because of the wartime paper shortage.

4 hard-boiled egg yolks	pinch celery salt
100 ml (4 fl oz) double cream	pinch cayenne
60 g (2 oz) freshly grated Parmesan	4 large French rolls
1 tbsp Dijon mustard	

Blend the egg yolks, cream, cheese, mustard, salt and cayenne thoroughly. Chill slightly. Cut the rolls in half lengthwise and scoop out all the crumb. Fill one half with the mixture and press the other on top.

SMØRREBRØD

It is claimed that *nouvelle cuisine*'s emphasis on visual presentation was the result of Japanese influence – which may be partly true. But those neat little dollops of purée and bundles of *petits légumes* deployed around the edge of many a *nouvelle cuisine* confection surely have another model closer to home: Danish *smørrebrød*.

The decorativeness of these multi-ingredient open sandwiches makes them all the more appetizing. At least four times larger than canapés, and with the bread crust left on, they should be eaten with a knife and fork. Of the hundreds of combinations of *smørrebrød* that have been devised by Danish cooks, not a great many use cheese. But here are three original ones (quantities indicated are for 4; one piece of *smørrebrød* per person makes a light first course). I have halved the gigantic quantity of butter with which the Danes traditionally smother the bread base.

Parmesan, Cold Scrambled Egg, and Anchovy

6 eggs	4 slices brown bread
100 g (3^1/$_2$ oz) unsalted butter	(wholemeal *or* rye)
freshly ground pepper	16 anchovies
50 g (2 oz) freshly grated Parmesan	1 tbsp fresh chives, chopped

Beat the eggs thoroughly. Put half the butter into a thick saucepan and place in a bain-marie of boiling water. When the butter has melted, turn down the heat very low, pour in the eggs and scramble slowly, stirring and scraping all the time with a wooden spoon, until the eggs are cooked (they should have the consistency of thick cream and contain almost no lumps). Remove from the heat. Add plenty of pepper and stir in the finely grated cheese. Leave to cool. Desalt the anchovies in warm water and dab dry with paper towels. Butter the bread with the rest of the butter and spread the scrambled eggs evenly on it. Lay 4 anchovies in lattice formation on each piece and sprinkle with chives.

Blue Cheese and Cucumber

30 g (1 oz) Mycella *or*
  Bleu d'Auvergne
30 g (1 oz) curd cheese
pinch cayenne
salt
freshly ground pepper

about 1/3 large cucumber, unpeeled
75 g (2 1/2 oz) unsalted butter
4 slices brown bread
  (wholemeal *or* rye)
4 sprigs dill

Blend the two cheeses, the cayenne, a good pinch of salt and some pepper. Cut the piece of cucumber into two equal segments. Core each of them carefully and stuff firmly with the cheese mixture. Refrigerate for 2 hours, then cut into fairly thin slices. Arrange these, overlapping each other, in a fan formation on the buttered bread. Decorate each piece of *smørrebrød* with a sprig of dill.

Samsø and Onion

1 very large onion
200 g (7 oz) Samsø
75 g (2 1/2 oz) unsalted butter
4 slices brown bread
  (wholemeal or rye)

16 radishes
4 sprigs dill

Peel and halve the onion across its equator, then cut 2 slices about 6 mm (1/4 in) thick from the cut face of each half. Ease the outside ring off each of these slices. Cut the cheese into 4 slices the same thickness as the onion rings. Out of these slices cut 4 discs to fit into the onion rings. Place the cheese discs in the centre of the buttered bread slices, slip an onion ring over each one, place a radish rose on each corner of the slice, and decorate with a sprig of dill.

The remaining pieces of onions can be reserved for another dish, and the cheese trimmings for the hungry cook(s).

CROSTINI WITH PARMESAN
AND WHITE TRUFFLES   FOR 4

This is one of several Italian recipes that call for that superlative combination of flavours – cheese and white truffles.

60 g (2 oz) white truffles, preferably fresh	freshly ground white pepper
	1 tsp cognac *or* armagnac
60 g (2 oz) freshly grated Parmesan	1 tbsp single cream (*or* juice from
60 g (2 oz) unsalted butter, softened	truffle tin)
salt	good white bread, freshly toasted

Blend or mash together the truffles, finely grated cheese, butter, a little salt and pepper, brandy and cream (if the truffles are fresh; otherwise use the truffle juice in the tin). Leave for 1 hour so the flavours can intermingle. Spread on the toast.

CHEESE SAVOURY   FOR 4

This recipe and the one that follows come from a common-sense and rather interesting little book called *The Edinburgh Book of Plain Cookery Recipes* (1932), put together by the Edinburgh College of Domestic Science.

100 ml (4 fl oz) double cream	pinch salt
50 g (2 oz) freshly grated strong Cheddar	12 plain cheese biscuits (p. 352)
	cress
2 inner stalks celery, finely chopped	paprika
pinch cayenne	

Half-whip the cream. Stir in the finely grated cheese, celery, cayenne and salt. Pile neatly on to the biscuits. Decorate with a little cress and paprika.

KIPPER SAVOURY   FOR 4

60 g (2 oz) kipper, steamed, skinned
    and boned
60 g (2 oz) unsalted butter, softened
2 tbsp double cream
1 hard-boiled egg, finely chopped
pinch cayenne

small pinch salt
freshly ground pepper
12 thin rounds cooked beetroot
12 round plain cheese biscuits (p. 352)
1 tbsp fresh parsley, finely chopped

Blend or mash the fish, butter, cream, egg and seasonings together until fairly smooth. Cut 12 rounds of beetroot and lay one on each biscuit. Pile the mixture high on to the beetroot and sprinkle with a little parsley. Chill.

The presence of cheese in this recipe is restricted to the biscuit, but the nuance of flavour makes an admirable adjunct to the kipper.

SURPRISE BISCUITS   FOR 8

An amusing dish from *Savoury Cold Meals* (1927), by Mrs C. F. Leyel, foundress of the Society of Herbalists and the Culpeper House herb shops, and co-authoress, with Olga Hartley, of the seminal *Gentle Art of Cookery*.

6 large sprigs fresh parsley
10 anchovies
90 g (3 oz) unsalted butter, softened
16 plain cheese biscuits (p. 352)

100 ml (4 fl oz) double cream
30 g (1 oz) freshly grated Parmesan
4 hard-boiled egg yolks

Blanch the parsley sprigs, trimmed of their stalks, in boiling water for 1 minute. Refresh under the cold tap, squeeze dry in paper towels and chop very finely. Desalt the anchovies in warm water and dab dry with paper towels. Blend the parsley, butter and anchovies to a smooth paste. Spread on the cheese biscuits. Whip the cream until stiff and stir in the finely grated Parmesan. Put into a piping bag with a serrated nozzle and squeeze out a neat border round the edge of the biscuits. Sieve the egg yolks and sprinkle over the centre of each biscuit so the parsley and anchovy butter is masked. Serve slightly chilled.

CHAPTER FOUR
Deep-fried Dishes

Deep-fried food used to enjoy a much better reputation among gourmets than it does today. All over nineteenth-century Europe dainty deep-fried savouries – many of them containing cheese and bearing evocative names such as 'cheese *délices*', 'delights', '*délicieuses*' or '*aigrettes*' – were much appreciated for their crispness, which made an attractive contrast to the textural monotony of much of the typical diet at that time. As the Professor in Brillat-Savarin's *The Philosopher in the Kitchen* had remarked in 1825: 'Deep-fried foods are welcome at any banquet; they introduce an appetizing variety into the meal and are pleasant to the eye; they retain their original flavour, and can be eaten with the fingers, a quality which is always appreciated by the ladies.'

Nowadays the novelty has gone out of deep-fried foods, and crispness *qua* crispness is available from any good fish-and-chip shop. We are now more careful than we used to be about our fat intake, and accordingly tend to heed advice to steer clear of deep-fried food, fritters and the like.

Often, too, deep-fried food does not taste all that nice. Much of the trouble comes from faulty deep-frying techniques. Surely there can be nothing worse than a fritter that has soaked up almost the equivalent of its own weight in grease? I am possibly not alone in having been put off anything except the most expertly cooked fritters by my experiences at the school canteen. There used to be groans all round from us not very choosy young lunchers when Spam fritters were served: their leaden batter had absorbed both the veteran cooking oil and the unpalatable fat from the 'luncheon meat'.

The deep-frying possibilities of cheese, a rich ingredient with a high fat content, are limited – which explains the brevity of this chapter. There exist recipes for deep-fried cheese in batter, but, no doubt haunted by schoolboy memories, I could not bring myself to include any. But the deep-fried savouries given here, when correctly made, eaten in moderate quantities and accompanied or followed by a crisp green salad, can nonetheless make a pleasant entrée.

Basic deep-frying method

This method is valid, with minor variations, for all the recipes in this chapter except where otherwise indicated. The best kind of oil is one with a neutral taste and good frying properties, such as peanut, sunflower or safflower oil. Do *not* use rape-seed oil, which is thought to be carcinogenic at high temperatures. If you have an electric deep-fryer, pour in and heat the oil according to the manufacturer's instructions. Here is the procedure for deep-frying in an ordinary saucepan.

Pour enough oil into a large heavy saucepan to make a depth of at least 7.5 cm (3 in). Heat it to a temperature of about 170°C (325°F). A higher temperature will impart an unpleasantly burnt flavour to cheese or its egg-and-breadcrumb coating. Drop in, or lower in a frying basket, only small amounts at a time of whatever you are frying, so that the temperature of the oil does not drop appreciably. Make sure the pieces do not touch, otherwise they will stick together. Flip them over delicately with a fork, taking care not to pierce their protective shell: this will produce an evenly cooked surface. As soon as a golden-brown colour is obtained, remove the pieces with a slotted spoon and place on paper towels, turning them over on all their sides so that as much oil as possible drains off.

If, as is usually the case, you want to keep the pieces warm while you are frying another batch, transfer them to a shallow dish lined with several layers of paper towels in an oven preheated to 140°C/275°F/Gas mark 1. Serve (on a napkin if you want to do it in style) on a large warmed plate.

DEEP-FRIED CAMEMBERT

Ambrose Heath said, rightly, of deep-fried Camembert: 'This is an acquired taste, but you should set about acquiring it.' But you may already have been put off for life if you have been unfortunate enough to have tasted that monstrosity found on German and Danish menus, and newly fashionable in Britain: deep-fried Camembert with raspberry jam.

As a general rule, deep-fried food has a better texture and taste the smaller it is, hence the rather small pieces indicated here.

1 firm, medium-ripe Camembert	2 eggs, beaten
cayenne	slightly stale breadcrumbs
seasoned flour	oil for frying

Remove the corners and any hard bits of rind from the Camembert. Cut the cheese into 1-cm (½-in) cubes. Sprinkle with a very little cayenne. Dust the cubes on all sides with seasoned flour, shaking off any excess, then dip them, a few at a time, in beaten egg. Place them on a mound of breadcrumbs, sprinkle with more crumbs and turn on all sides so they are thoroughly coated. Repeat the egg and breadcrumb operation, then place the cubes on a platter and chill for 1 hour. Fry them in batches according to the basic deep-frying method (p. 72).

The point of the double egg-and-breadcrumb coating is to create a crisp shell that will prevent the melted cheese from oozing out into the oil.

DEEP-FRIED GRUYÈRE   FOR 4

250 g (9 oz) Gruyère	slightly stale breadcrumbs
seasoned flour	oil for frying
2 eggs, beaten	

Cut the cheese into 1-cm ($^{1}/_{2}$-in) cubes. Coat with flour, egg and breadcrumbs as described in the preceding recipe, chill for 1 hour and fry in batches according to the basic deep-frying method (p. 72).

Strong Cheddar can also be deep-fried in the same way.

DÉLICIEUSES   FOR 4

Also known as cheese meringues, délicieuses are indeed delicious if made correctly. The flavour of the cheese is diluted by the egg-white, so it is vital to use a variety with plenty of clout. Emmental or mild Cheddar, for example, will produce a disappointingly bland result.

oil for frying	250 g (9 oz) freshly grated Gruyère,
4 egg whites	strong Cheddar or Parmesan
small pinch salt	2 eggs, beaten
pinch cayenne	slightly stale breadcrumbs
seasoned flour	

Have your oil hot. Whisk the egg whites with the salt until very stiff. Mix with the finely grated cheese and cayenne, and form into little balls the size of large marbles. Coat with flour, egg and breadcrumbs as described in Deep-fried Camembert (p. 73), chill for 1 hour and fry in batches according to the basic deep-frying method (p. 72).

AIGRETTES   FOR 4

How this dish, which originated in France but only really came into its own in Edwardian Britain, got its name is something of a mystery. The original meaning of *aigrette* in French was 'heron' or 'egret'; it then came to mean, by extension, any tuft or plume. The connection between feathers and deep-fried pieces of cheese-flavoured choux paste is hard to see. Be that as it may, they make a nice, if rather substantial, savoury.

30 g (1 oz) unsalted butter	80 g (3 oz) freshly grated Parmesan,
100 g (3¹/₂ oz) sifted plain	Gruyère or strong Cheddar
flour	salt
2 eggs, beaten	freshly ground pepper
1 egg yolk	oil for frying

Put 250 ml (9 fl oz) of water and the butter into a saucepan, heat until the butter has melted, and bring to the boil. Away from the heat, add the flour and mix thoroughly with a wooden spoon. Put back on a gentle heat and cook, stirring all the time, until the mixture comes away from the sides of the pan. Allow to cool slightly. Blend in the eggs and then the egg yolk, followed by the finely grated cheese, a little salt and some pepper. Mix well, spread evenly on a lightly floured board or baking sheet, making a layer about 1 cm (¹/₂ in) thick, and chill for 1 hour. Cut into any small shapes you wish and fry in batches according to the basic deep-frying method (p. 72).

Aigrettes can also be deep-fried immediately after the addition of the eggs and cheese to the mixture. In this case, take teaspoonfuls of the mixture and push them with your finger into the hot oil.

PARMESAN RINGS   FOR 8

These tasty cheese quoits are to my mind the most satisfactory of all deep-fried cheese dishes. They are some trouble to make, but worth attempting for a large number of people. The recipes come from the *Larger Cookery Book of Extra Recipes*, by Mrs Agnes B. Marshall. This book, a stout, well-bound and authoritative volume, was the culinary bible of the British upper classes at the beginning of the 20th century.

Mrs Marshall was clearly a most enterprising woman. In addition to writing several cookery books and editing a magazine called *The Table*, she ran a highly reputed cookery school in London. It was there, Elizabeth David told me, that her own mother took some cooking lessons in 1905, shortly before her marriage. Mrs Marshall also had a shop next door to the school, which sold a range of products under her trademark (gelatine, 'coralline pepper', ice cream moulds, wines, soups and so on). She sent her squads of staff cooks all over the country to cook for special banquets, while she went on public lecture tours. In the course of each lecture she would give a cookery demonstration, called 'A Pretty Luncheon', which apparently never failed to enthral audiences. Newspaper reports speak of her 'skilled manipulation', 'dexterity', 'legerdemain' and 'conjuring', and describe her as a 'graceful, kindly lady', 'delightful to watch', who kept her listeners 'perfectly spellbound'. Mrs Agnes B. Marshall was clearly a woman of considerable charisma – and business sense, one imagines.

150 ml (5 fl oz) single cream	150 g (5½ oz) sifted plain flour
150 ml (5 fl oz) milk	4 eggs
large pinch salt	180 g (6½ oz) freshly grated Parmesan
pinch cayenne	1 egg, beaten
80 g (3 oz) unsalted butter	oil for frying

Put the cream, milk, salt, cayenne and butter into a saucepan, heat until the butter has melted and bring to the boil. Away from the heat, add the flour and mix thoroughly with a wooden spoon. Put back on a gentle heat and cook, stirring all the time, until the mixture comes away from the sides of the pan. Allow to cool slightly, then add the 4 eggs, one by one, followed by two-thirds of the finely grated cheese. Mix well and leave to cool

When the mixture has firmed up a little, put it into a forcing bag with a plain 1-cm (½-in) nozzle. Squeeze out the mixture and form small rings (this is much easier than might be supposed). Brush with beaten egg and fry in batches according to the basic deep-frying method (p. 72). Dust with the remaining Parmesan and serve immediately.

These rings are also nice cold, and, as Mrs Marshall remarks, 'can be used for ball suppers &c'.

FRIANDS SAVOYARDS FOR 6

To make authentic *friands savoyards* it is worth trying to get hold of Beaufort, or, even better, Beaufort *haute-montagne*, the produce of cows that graze at altitudes of almost 3,000 m (10,000 ft).

150 g (5¹/₂ oz) fresh or 15 g (¹/₂ oz) dried cepe mushrooms
25 g (1 oz) unsalted butter (if necessary)
400 ml (14 oz) béchamel sauce II (p. 357)
80 ml (3 fl oz) double cream
2 egg yolks

75 g (2¹/₂ oz) freshly grated Beaufort (*or* Gruyère)
75 g (2¹/₂ oz) ham, in one thickish slice
seasoned flour
2 whole eggs, beaten
slightly stale breadcrumbs
oil for frying

If you have fresh mushrooms, chop them finely and sauté in butter until lightly browned; if using dried ones, soak them in the milk to be used for the béchamel for at least 1 hour, then chop very finely. Make or re-heat the béchamel sauce (using the strained milk from the mushrooms, if they are dried ones). Away from the heat, stir in the cream and egg yolks, one by one, with a wooden spoon. Return to a low heat and cook briefly, stirring all the time, until the mixture thickens slightly. Remove from the heat and mix in the finely grated cheese, the ham, cut into tiny dice, and the mushrooms.

Spread the mixture evenly on a lightly floured board or baking sheet, making a layer about 1 cm (¹/₂ in) thick. Chill for a few hours. Cut into any small shapes you wish.

Coat with flour, egg and breadcrumbs as described under Deep-fried Camembert (p. 73), and fry in batches until golden brown according to the basic deep-frying method (p. 72). Do not overcook, otherwise the croquettes may burst. Drain on paper towels and serve immediately.

CROQUETTES À LA SEMOULE   FOR 6

This and the following recipe are for 'sandwiches' that are deep-fried in a frying pan rather than a saucepan or deep-fryer. This technique precludes the danger of the sandwiches falling apart in the oil.

450 ml (15 fl oz) milk	seasoned flour
large pinch salt	2 eggs, beaten
150 g (5¹/₂ oz) medium semolina	slightly stale breadcrumbs
200 g (7 oz) Gruyère *or*	oil for frying
strong Cheddar	

Put the milk and the same amount of water into a saucepan with the salt and bring to the boil. Pour in the semolina and cook gently for about 15 minutes, stirring frequently with a wooden spoon. The mixture should be quite thick. Turn it out on to a wet board or marble slab and, using a spatula dipped from time to time in hot water, spread it to make a layer about 6 mm (¹/₄ in) thick. Leave to cool. Cut into 5-cm (2-in) squares. Cut slices of cheese about 6 mm (¹/₄ in) thick into slightly smaller squares. Place the cheese slices on half the semolina squares and cover with the remaining squares. At this point you can, if you wish, press the edges of the sandwiches together to seal the cheese inside. Dust them on both sides with seasoned flour. Dip them in beaten egg and breadcrumbs, again on both sides.

Put enough oil into a frying pan to make a depth of about 1 cm (¹/₂ in) and heat until very hot but not smoking. Put in the croquettes and turn the heat down to medium. Fry in batches on both sides until golden brown.

As with other deep-fried dishes in which cheese, on its own, has to provide the dominant flavour, genuine Gruyère or strong Cheddar are mandatory. Mild cheeses such as Emmental will not do.

No doubt because they are thought to look prettier that way, these croquettes are supposed to be made in circular shapes. But this complicates matters considerably and results in a lot of unused scraps of semolina and cheese. This is why I have suggested squares rather than circles – after all, taste is not affected by geometry.

MOZZARELLA IN CARROZZA FOR 4

This evocatively named dish – the mozzarella is contained in 'a carriage' of bread – comes in two versions, one with anchovies and the other without. In my view the mild-tasting mozzarella on its own cannot stand up to the frying treatment, so I have given only the first version. If you want to try the other, just omit the anchovies.

8 anchovies
200 g (7 oz) mozzarella
8 slices good white bread,
  trimmed of crust

3 eggs, beaten
olive oil or lard for frying

Desalt the anchovies in warm water, drain and dab dry with a paper towel. Cut the mozzarella into slices 1 cm (1/2 in) thick and of slightly smaller dimensions than the bread. Place it on 4 slices of bread. Top with 2 anchovies per slice and cover with the remaining bread. Pour the well-beaten eggs into a large flat dish. Leave the sandwiches to soak in the eggs for about 30 minutes, turning them over once. Press the sides of the sandwiches together gently.

Put enough oil or lard into a large frying pan to make a depth of about 1 cm (1/2 in) and heat until hot but not smoking. Put in the sandwiches and turn the heat down to medium. Fry on both sides until golden brown. Drain on paper towels and serve immediately.

CHAPTER FIVE

Toasted Cheese

CHEESE ON TOAST

A slice of cheese placed on toast (buttered or not, as you like) and grilled until melted and golden brown is one of the most rudimentary of all cheese dishes, and quite distinct from the rabbits, Welsh or otherwise, which contain additional ingredients. The smell of cheese on toast is instantly appetizing and peculiarly evocative, which is probably why it haunted the dreams of Ben Gunn: 'Many's the long night I've dreamt of cheese – toasted mostly' (*Treasure Island*). The most frequently used cheese for cheese on toast is Cheddar, but Lancashire also has its devotees. For a creamy and slightly sharp taste similar to Lancashire's, however, I prefer toasted Caerphilly or Wensleydale. Toasted Leicester, too, is also held in great esteem. But here again, for mellowness and depth of flavour, I would not rate it as highly as genuine farmhouse Cheshire, Double Gloucester or, indeed, a really good Cheddar.

Cheese on toast does not necessarily have to be made with Cheddar-like cheese. Certain rich blue cheeses such as Stilton, Fourme d'Ambert and even Gorgonzola can be toasted. Other possibilities include young Cantal, medium-ripe Brebis des Pyrénées, Bagnes (the cheese used in raclette), young or medium-ripe Reblochon or Saint-Nectaire (these last two, like Bagnes, have a mild rind that has a delicious flavour when toasted and therefore should not be removed), and medium-ripe goat cheese.

Gruyère and its relatives are, on the whole, far from ideal for cheese on toast unless grated, very thinly sliced or already melted. A thick slab of such a cheese, when put under a grill, will have turned rubbery on top by the time it has been heated through. And if the cut surface has been exposed to air for any length of time and/or been left out of the refrigerator and allowed to sweat droplets of fat, it will not melt at all, but turn into the traditional sole of an old boot.

WELSH RABBIT AND ITS COUSINS

The expression 'Welsh rabbit' was a fanciful early eighteenth-century coinage to describe cheese on toast. It was probably an allusion to the tyrophilia (love of cheese) of the Welsh. There is much evidence that cheese was something of a national dish in Wales during Tudor times, to wit Shakespeare's conceit: 'I will rather trust a Fleming with my butter, Parson Hugh, the Welshman with my cheese, an Irishman with my aqua-vitae bottle or a thief to walk my ambling gelding than my wife with herself' (Ford in *The Merry Wives of Windsor*).

But the term Welsh rabbit was probably coined with derisive intent, for the epithet 'Welsh' commonly had a pejorative connotation in the eighteenth century (e.g. 'Welsh mile', 'Welsh comb', 'Welsh bait' and possibly 'to welsh'). A Welsh rabbit, then, would have been something like a poor man's rabbit, a second-best substitute. Not long after the coinage (and no later than 1785) someone – perhaps a disgruntled Welshman or an Englishman with an Oxford accent – was responsible for transmogrifying 'rabbit', a vulgar and confusing appellation, into the much more attractive and easily understood 'rarebit'. Cookbooks ever since have, understandably, tended to prefer the latter term.

Meanwhile, the folk etymologists, a breed whose ingenuity and imagination know no bounds, have been at work. One explanation of the expression Welsh rabbit, reported by Evan Jones in his *Book of Cheese*, is that Welsh wives, when they spied their menfolk returning from the hunt empty-handed, would quickly set cheese to melt before the fire as a substitute for game. The alternative form, Welsh rarebit, has been given an equally farfetched – and rather more *risqué* – explanation: it was usually served at the end of the meal with savouries, which, so the argument goes, were originally called 'rearbits', then 'rarebits', on early menus just as hors d'oeuvres were known as 'forebits'. According to the Oxford English Dictionary, by the way, there is no recorded use of either rearbit or forebit in any sense at all, culinary or otherwise. A pity.

The French have always prized the Welsh rabbit. To the best of my knowledge, the dish first appeared in a French cookbook in 1814, when Antoine Beauvilliers published a recipe for *wouelsche rabette* (*lapin gallois*) in his *L'Art du cuisinier*. But it really came into fashion when Anglomania was at its height around the turn of the 20th century. In *L'Art des mets*, published in 1959, the French gourmet Francis Amunatégui remembers the atmosphere, decades earlier, at the then very British restaurant, The Criterion, opposite the Gare Saint-Lazare in Paris. Anglophiles flocked there specially to order Welsh rabbit (by that time spelt correctly but usually abbreviated to *le welsh*) and wash it down with English ale in pewter mugs. The French waiters at The Criterion, he alleges, were specially trained to talk to customers with an English accent. (The Criterion may have served as a model for the café near the Gare Saint-Lazare in Joris-Karl Huysmans' *A Rebours* (1884), to which Des Esseintes repairs for refreshment just before embarking on a journey to London. He finds such a quintessentially English atmosphere there – tankards of ale, Stilton and a waiter who speaks to him incomprehensibly – that he sees no point in actually boarding a train and crossing the Channel, and goes home instead.)

When Amunatégui came to Britain on holiday, he made a pilgrimage to Wales in an attempt to hunt down the authentic Welsh rabbit:

My quest for *le welsh* was long and persistent. I saw

forbidding castles, rocky crags and blasted heaths; I partook of Scotch salmon, Cambridge sausages and Stilton cheese, but Welsh *welsh* was there none. Determined to keep my promise to myself, I finally found what I was seeking – in London. And not in a restaurant, if you please, but at the food counter of a department store. It is common knowledge that the food in England is not very good. You can imagine what it was like in a department store! The only resemblance between what I was served and a Welsh rabbit was its name. In other respects, it had more in common with rubber, horn and brick.

Welsh rabbit seems to encourage extravagant similes of this kind. Stella Irwin's *Stella's Cookbook*, published in Karachi during the heyday of the British Raj, has an introduction written by her husband, Lyn, which is titled 'Crimes of Karachi Cooks'. In it he writes:

> When Stella cooks Cheese Toast, it is golden brown and 'gooey', and tastes like a cherub in velvet pants. Even I can make a passable imitation, given a generous amount of ingredients to allow for wastage. Why is it, then, that Karachi cooks almost invariably produce something that looks and tastes like the fents [waste rags] from a textile mill and might just as well have been made by a verandah derzie [tailor]. Could it be that they pile on flour and then incinerate it?

Lyn Irwin clearly had a rather exaggerated opinion of his wife's cooking abilities: her recipe is simply Mornay sauce on toast.

There are countless versions of Welsh rabbit – from just plain cheese on toast to cheese that is melted with eggs and/or mustard and/or ale and/or wine, poured over toast and/or grilled. Then there are the 'rabbits' that are given other epithets (green, garlic, sage, horseradish, etc.) or nationalities (American, English, Irish, Scotch, etc.).

And last but not least comes the Continental contingent

of *croûtes*, *ramequins* (for a discussion of this word's multiple meanings, see p. 348) and *rôties*, the French and Swiss variations on the same theme.

Where authors have used the genteel 'rarebit', I have retained their spelling.

WELSH RAREBIT   FOR 4
A typically precise and meticulous recipe from Mrs Beeton's *Dictionary of Every Day Cookery* (1865).

good white bread	2 tsp made mustard
80 g (3 oz) unsalted butter	freshly ground pepper
250 g (9 oz) Cheshire or	
Double Gloucester	

'Cut the bread into slices about ½ in (1 cm) in thickness; pare off the crust, toast the bread slightly without hardening or burning it, and spread it with butter. Cut some slices, not quite so large as the bread, from a good rich fat cheese; lay them on the toasted bread in a cheese-toaster; be careful that the cheese does not burn, and let it be equally melted. Spread over the top a little made mustard and a seasoning of pepper, and serve very hot, with very hot plates. Note: Should the cheese be dry, a little butter mixed with it will be an improvement.'

The basic Welsh rabbit can be 'built on' in several ways. You can perch a poached egg on each portion, thus making a Golden buck or Buck rabbit. If you put a rasher of crisp-fried bacon between the toasted cheese and the poached egg, the dish becomes a Yorkshire rabbit.

WELSH RAREBIT WITH EGG   FOR 4
A recipe from *Savoury Breakfast, Dinner and Supper Dishes* (1904), by the famous Edwardian chef C. Herman Senn.

250 g (9 oz) freshly grated Cheshire	1 egg, beaten
30 g (1 oz) unsalted butter	salt
2 tbsp fresh breadcrumbs	freshly ground pepper
1 tsp made mustard	good white bread, toasted and buttered

Mix the finely grated cheese with the butter, breadcrumbs, mustard and egg. Beat well for a few minutes, season with salt and pepper to taste and spread on buttered toast. Put into a hot oven (220°C/425°F/Gas mark 7) until golden brown.

AMERICAN RABBIT   FOR 4

250 g (9 oz) Cheshire or American Cheddar, diced	2 tsp made mustard
pinch salt	90 ml (3 fl oz) light beer
freshly ground pepper	4 eggs, separated
pinch cayenne	good white or brown bread, toasted

Put the cheese, a little salt, plenty of pepper, the cayenne, mustard and beer in a heavy saucepan over a low heat and stir until the cheese melts and a smooth consistency is obtained. Beat the egg yolks and, away from the heat, stir them quickly into the mixture until thoroughly blended. Whisk the egg whites with a tiny pinch of salt until very stiff and fold delicately but thoroughly into the mixture. Return to a low heat and stir until the mixture thickens slightly. Pour the mixture over hot toast on very hot plates and serve immediately.

There are other versions of this recipe that call for either only egg whites or only egg yolks.

LADY SYSONBY'S TOASTED CHEESE   FOR 4

A very hot and spicy version of toasted cheese from *Lady Sysonby's Cook Book* (1935).

300 g (10¹/2 oz) Lancashire *or* Canadian Cheddar, diced	1/4 freshly grated nutmeg
small pinch salt	4 tsp made mustard
freshly ground white pepper	4 tbsp single cream
pinch ground ginger	340 ml (12 fl oz) mild draught beer
1¹/2 tbsp sugar	good white bread, rather thickly sliced and toasted

Put the cheese, salt, plenty of pepper, the mustard and cream in a heavy saucepan over a low heat and stir until the cheese melts and a smooth consistency is obtained. Keep warm.

Heat the beer, ginger, sugar and nutmeg in a saucepan until the sugar has dissolved and the mixture is very hot. Pour the hot melted cheese over rounds of toast on ovenproof plates, put under a fierce grill for 1-2 minutes until slightly brown on top, spoon the hot beer on to the plates (not on to the cheese) and serve. The beer will be soaked up by the toast.

SCOTCH RABBIT   FOR 4

This recipe, from *The Cook and Housewife's Manual* (1826) by Meg Dods (*nom de plume* of Scotswoman Christian Isobel Johnstone; other sources give her name as Christina Jane Johnstone), seems at first sight very similar to the last. But a very different taste is produced by the beer (stout) and the cheeses (Stilton, Gouda or Dunlop) she calls for. It is good to be able to report that Dunlop, which until recently was made only with pasteurised milk, can now be found in its genuine farmhouse form.

300 g (10¹/2 oz) Stilton, Gouda *or* Dunlop diced	freshly ground pepper
140 ml (5 fl oz) porter (stout)	good white bread, toasted and buttered
2 tsp made mustard	

Put the cheese, stout, mustard and plenty of very finely ground pepper into a fireproof or gratin dish. Place over a low heat and stir until the cheese melts and a smooth consistency is obtained. Put the dish under a fierce grill for a few minutes to brown. Serve with hot buttered toast on a separate plate.

Meg Dods concludes her recipe as follows:

> Observation: this is one of the best preparations of the kind that we are acquainted with. Some gourmands use red wine instead of porter, but the latter liquor is much better adapted to the flavour of cheese. Others use a proportion of soft putrid cheese, or the whole of it in that state. This is, of course, a matter of taste, and beyond the jurisdiction of any culinary dictator. To dip the toasts in hot porter makes another variety of this preparation.

The best kind of stout for this recipe is not Guinness, whose bitterness is accentuated by heat, but a sweet Scotch stout such as Mackeson's.

ENGLISH RABBIT   FOR 4

Pace Meg Dods (see preceding recipe), red wine, like stout, is also very good with toasted cheese, as in this recipe, which dates from the eighteenth century.

good white bread, rather thickly sliced and toasted	225 ml (8 fl oz) good red wine
2 tsp made mustard	300 g (10^1/$_2$ oz) Cheddar *or* Cheshire, thinly sliced

Put the toast in a large shallow gratin dish or baking tin. Smear with mustard. Pour the wine into the dish and leave for 5 minutes while the toast soaks it up. Cover the pieces of toast with the cheese and put under a moderate grill until it has completely melted and is golden brown on top.

GARLIC RABBIT   FOR 4

A dish my mother often used to make for supper, using the delicious wholemeal bread she baked herself. My grandmother (her mother-in-law) delighted in saying how much she detested garlic. So whenever she was present on such occasions, my mother deviously announced 'cheese on toast' (and included a little less garlic). Grandmother always came back for more.

300 g (10½ oz) freshly grated   3 cloves garlic, finely chopped
   Cheddar   freshly ground pepper
100 ml (4 fl oz) dry white wine   toasted wholemeal bread

Mash the cheese, wine, garlic and plenty of pepper to a paste. Spread thickly on pieces of toast. Put under a moderate grill until the cheese has completely melted and is golden brown on top.

When no white wine was to hand, my mother used milk instead.

RAMEQUIN   FOR 4

For the etymology and multiple meanings of *ramequin/* ramekin, see p. 348. Here, the word applies to a rich Swiss version of toasted cheese. The recipe comes from the fourth edition (1817) of the anonymous *La Cuisinière genevoise*, which first appeared in 1798.

225 g (8 oz) freshly grated Gruyère   pinch salt
2 eggs   freshly ground white pepper
110 g (4 oz) unsalted butter, softened good white bread, toasted
100 ml (4 fl oz) double cream

Blend or mash thoroughly the cheese, eggs, butter, cream, salt and pepper. Lay the pieces of toast on a baking tray. Spread the mixture over them and put under a moderate grill until golden brown on top.

CROUSTADES WITH CHEESE   FOR 4

A recipe redolent of Victorian high society from Mrs Agnes B. Marshall's *Larger Cookery Book of Extra Recipes* (p. 75) – and very useful if you have a lot of stale bread that needs using up. It is a bit of a bother but fun to make once in a while.

stale good white bread	pinch cayenne
oil for deep-frying	250 g (9 oz) Gruyère
6 tbsp double cream	400 ml (14 fl oz) Mornay sauce I (p. 358)

Cut the stale bread into 8 little blocks about 7.5 cm (3 in) square and 4 cm (1½ in) high. On the top, about 1 cm (½ in) from the edge, make a vertical incision all the way round the square down to 1 cm (½ in) from the bottom of the bread. Make no further incisions at this point. Deep-fry until a nice golden colour.

Mix the cream with the cayenne. Carve out the inner square of the fried bread pieces as follows: insert a knife horizontally into one side just above the base and swivel the blade to cut free the central cube of bread. Remove the cube and slice off its crisp outer surface for use as a lid. Put into each of these cavities a slice of cheese of the same dimensions as the lid and top with 2 teaspoons of cream. Cover with the bread lid.

Arrange the croustades in a shallow ovenproof serving dish. Make or re-heat the Mornay sauce. Put the croustades into a moderate oven (180°C/350°F/Gas mark 4) for about 20 minutes, remove, pour a little sauce over each of them and place under a fierce grill for a minute or two until golden brown. Serve immediately.

Mrs Marshall adds: 'This dish can be served as a savoury after the sweets, or for a second-course dish, and is very suitable for gentlemen when they return from hunting.' If not serving the croustades as a main course, halve the quantities per person.

CROQUE-MONSIEUR   FOR 4
No one quite knows how this toasted ham and cheese
sandwich, which first appeared on French menus around
the turn of the 20th century, got its name (*croquer* means
'to scrunch' or 'to munch', and gives us the word
croquette). An almost identical dish existed before then in
the Jura – and was called *ramequin*.

The breed of croque-monsieur widely available today in
French cafés is generally but a pale imitation of the
genuine dish.

120 g (4 oz) unsalted butter
8 thin slices good white bread
8 thin slices Gruyère *or* strong Cheddar } all of the same dimensions
4 thin slices ham

Butter the bread on one side only. Assemble the
sandwiches in the following order: slices of bread
(buttered side up), cheese, ham, cheese and bread
(buttered side down). Press the sandwiches down to make
them compact. Put them under a moderate grill until well
toasted on one side, turn over and brown on the other
side. The cheese should have completely melted and begun
to ooze out. Serve immediately.

You can also prepare croque-monsieur by gently frying the
sandwiches in butter on both sides until crisp, after
dipping them, if you like, on both sides in beaten egg. The
advantage of the toasted version is that it can be eaten
with the fingers and is an altogether lighter dish.

A croque-madame is a more recent invention: it is a
croque-monsieur with a fried egg on top.

RAMEQUIN DE FROMAGE   FOR 4
Yet another form of *ramequin* (p. 348). In its treatment of
the onion, which is only partially cooked, this dish
resembles the recipe given later for North Staffordshire
oatcakes with cheese (p. 183). It comes from one of the
most important of all French cookbooks, *Le Cuisinier*

françois by François Pierre de La Varenne. La Varenne worked as a cook for the Marquis d'Uxelles in the seventeenth century, and named a sauce of his invention, duxelles (p. 365), after his master.

75 g (2¹/₂ oz) unsalted butter	pinch salt
300 g (10¹/₂ oz) Gruyère, diced	freshly ground pepper
1 sweet onion, finely chopped	good white bread

Melt the butter in a thick saucepan over a gentle heat. Add the cheese, onion, salt and plenty of pepper. Stir until the cheese has completely melted. Spread the mixture on bread and put under a moderate grill for a few minutes until golden brown on top.

La Varenne did not specify what kind of cheese he had in mind. Any good melting cheese with plenty of character could be used instead of Gruyère.

SWISS CROÛTES   FOR 4

In Switzerland and the French Jura a *croûte* (which normally means just 'crust' in French) is the equivalent of Welsh rabbit.

4 large sweet onions	good white bread, quite thickly
80 g (3 oz) unsalted butter	sliced and toasted
large pinch salt	300 g (10¹/₂ oz) Gruyère, thinly sliced
freshly ground pepper	

Slice the onions as finely as possible (this is very important) and put into a large enamel saucepan. Pour a large quantity of boiling water over them, leave for 1 minute and drain well. Heat the butter in a large frying pan and gently sauté the onions, turning them over often, until slightly browned but not completely soft. Add salt and plenty of pepper, and stir well.

Place the pieces of toast on a lightly oiled baking tray or shallow gratin dish. Spread the hot onions over the toast, making the surface as even as possible. Arrange the slices of cheese on top and put under a moderate grill until the cheese has melted and turned golden brown. Serve immediately.

IRISH RAREBIT   FOR 4

This recipe looks weird at first sight, but turns out to be quite delicious. It comes from *Meatless Menus for Lunch, Dinner and Supper*, 'being a series of attractive menus arranged to give adequate nourishment', by Alfred Arm. The 'meatless' of the title is not just an old-fashioned term for vegetarian, but implies privation: the book was written at the time of the First World War meat shortage.

But why did Arm call his recipe *Irish* rarebit? Perhaps because the other nationalities had already been used up.

60 g (2 oz) unsalted butter	340 g (12 oz) Cheddar, diced
1¹/₂ large sweet onions, finely chopped	pinch cayenne
	1 tbsp fresh parsley, finely chopped
12 small gherkins, very finely chopped	1 tbsp fresh chives, finely chopped
	2 tsp fresh tarragon, finely chopped
120 ml (4 fl oz) best vinegar	good white bread, toasted

Heat the butter in a frying pan and gently sauté the onions, turning them over often, until translucent. Allow them to brown slightly. Add the gherkins and vinegar. Simmer uncovered until almost all the liquid has evaporated. Add the cheese and stir until completely melted. Mix in the cayenne and herbs. Spoon the mixture over toast and put under a fierce grill for a few minutes or until well browned on top.

HOT SANDWICHES   FOR 4

These sandwiches are an excellent way of using up surplus roast chicken (sorry, I don't like the associations of the word 'leftovers'). They are much more interesting than their name would suggest, containing as they do ham and an assortment of typically Edwardian condiments as well as chicken and cheese.

The recipe comes, slightly adapted, from a promotional booklet of recipes given away by Liebig in 1905, *Lemco Dishes for All Seasons* by Eva Tuite. Liebig at that time had to market its meat extract as Lemco (an acronym for Liebig's Extract of Meat Co.) because 'inferior meat extracts' were authorized in the British Empire to call themselves Liebig's Extract even though they had no relation with the genuine product (which, it will be remembered, had been devised by the eminent nineteenth-century German chemist Baron Justus von Liebig).

1/2 tsp meat extract or meat glaze	pinch cayenne
1 tbsp good curry powder	salt
225 g (8 oz) cooked chicken	freshly ground pepper
80 g (3 oz) ham	125 g (41/2 oz) unsalted butter
1 tsp chutney	16 very small slices good white bread
1 tsp capers	115 g (4 oz) freshly grated Cheddar
1 tsp lemon juice	8 small sprigs parsley

Dissolve the meat extract or meat glaze in 3 tablespoons of hot water, add the curry powder and mix to a smooth paste. Blend the chicken, ham, chutney and capers to the consistency of mincemeat, stir in the curry paste, add the lemon juice and cayenne, and mix well. Add salt and pepper to taste.

Reserve 40 g (1 1/2 oz) of the butter. Heat some of the remaining butter in a frying pan and gently sauté the slices of bread in batches on one side only, adding more butter as necessary. Spread the filling generously on half of these, fried side down, and top with the rest of the slices, fried side up. Mash the grated cheese with the 40 g (1 1/2 oz) of butter. Put little mounds of the cheese mixture on each sandwich and bake in a fairly hot oven (190°C/375°F/Gas mark 5) for about 15 minutes or until the cheese has completely melted and is brown on top. Garnish each sandwich with a sprig of parsley and serve immediately on hot individual plates.

SCOTCH WOODCOCK   FOR 4

A classic, very highly seasoned savoury of London's clubland, really better served with preprandial drinks than as a separate course of a meal.

4 large slices good white bread, trimmed of crust	2 tbsp anchovy paste
100 g (3¹/₂ oz) unsalted butter	freshly ground pepper
4 tbsp capers	60 g (2 oz) freshly grated Parmesan

Toast the bread and spread with butter while still hot. Chop the capers as finely as possible and mix with the anchovy paste and plenty of pepper, and spread on the toast. Sprinkle evenly with finely grated cheese and put under a fierce grill for a few minutes or until the cheese has browned. Using a sharp knife, cut the toast into fingers and hand round immediately on a hot serving plate.

MOCK CRAB TOASTS

Make mock crab as indicated on p. 62, but instead of serving it cold, grill and serve like Scotch woodcock (see preceding recipe).

REAL CRAB TOASTS   FOR 4

Real crab has a surprising affinity with cheese.

320 g (11 oz) crab meat, fresh if possible and including brown meat	2-3 tbsp dry white wine
60 g (2 oz) unsalted butter	salt
1 tsp made mustard	freshly ground pepper
pinch cayenne	8 slices good white or brown bread, toasted
1 tsp lemon juice	80 g (3 oz) freshly grated Gruyère
1 tbsp fresh parsley, finely chopped	or Cheddar

Blend the crab meat, butter, mustard, cayenne, lemon juice and parsley to a thick paste. Make it a little more liquid by mixing in some wine. Add salt and pepper to taste. Spread this mixture on the toast, sprinkle evenly with cheese and put under a fierce grill for a few minutes or until the cheese has melted and turned golden brown. Serve immediately.

FINNAN TOASTS   FOR 4

A succulent Scottish first course – as long as you use proper Finnan haddock, not the dyed and artificially flavoured version.

225 g (8 oz) cooked Finnan haddock, flaked
150 ml (5 fl oz) double cream
1 egg
freshly ground pepper

salt
115 g (4 oz) freshly grated Cheddar
1 tsp made mustard
8 large slices good white or brown bread, toasted

Put the haddock, cream, cheese, mustard, egg and pepper into a mixing bowl. Mix well and add some salt if necessary. Spread this mixture on the slices of toast and put under a moderate grill for about 10 minutes or until slightly brown on top.

CADOGAN CANAPÉS   FOR 4

Biting through warmed, but still raw, oysters is a great gastronomic and tactile experience, which is enhanced by spinach and Mornay sauce in this very stylish English savoury.

4 large slices good white bread 2.5 cm (1 in) thick
8 large leaves spinach
80 g (3 oz) unsalted butter
pinch freshly grated nutmeg

freshly ground pepper
8 oysters
400 ml (14 fl oz) Mornay sauce II (p. 358)

Scoop out a shallow oblong hollow in the top of each slice of bread. Toast on both sides. Trim the spinach leaves of their stalks and blanch, uncovered, in plenty of boiling salted water for 5 minutes, drain carefully so as not to tear the leaves, then dry thoroughly with paper towels. Melt the butter in a frying pan, add the nutmeg and plenty of pepper, put in the spinach leaves and delicately coat them with melted butter on both sides without cooking.

Open the oysters, reserving their liquid for the Mornay sauce. Wrap each oyster neatly in a spinach leaf and arrange two such parcels on each piece of toast. Dribble over any butter remaining in the pan. Make the Mornay sauce using the liquid from the oysters and allowing for its considerable degree of saltiness. Their liquid should amount to 100 ml (4 fl oz); if it does not, add water as necessary.

Put the toasts on lightly buttered small individual fireproof dishes, pour the sauce over them so they are completely masked, and bake in a hot oven (220°C/425°F/Gas mark 7) for 10 minutes or until the surface begins to brown. Serve immediately.

BOUQUETS EN SURPRISE   FOR 4

A romantic-sounding dish. But the French word *bouquet* means 'prawn', and was coined in the mid-nineteenth century on the analogy of *bouc* (billy goat) because of the prawn's 'whiskers'.

Surprising though it may seem, prawns combine very well with cheese, especially in this featherlight entrée.

24 prawns, live if possible	2 cloves garlic, finely chopped
juice of $1/2$ lemon	$1/2$ tsp Worcestershire sauce
150 g ($5^1/2$ oz) freshly grated	freshly ground pepper
Emmental *or* mild Cheddar	4 large slices good white or brown
2 eggs, separated	bread, toasted

If you are lucky enough to have live prawns, put them in a sauté pan over a high heat with 1-2 tablespoons of water and cook covered for about 5 minutes, shaking the pan occasionally. After that time, the prawns should be pinkish but not quite cooked. Drain off their cooking liquid and reserve. When the prawns have cooled a little, shell them.

If you have no live prawns, buy cooked ones from a reliable fishmonger rather than frozen ones, and shell. Marinate the shelled prawns in lemon juice for 30-60 minutes.

Mix thoroughly the cheese, egg yolks, garlic, Worcestershire sauce, 2 tablespoons of the prawns' cooking liquid and plenty of pepper. Put 6 prawns on each slice of toast. Whisk the egg whites with a tiny pinch of salt until stiff. Fold delicately but thoroughly into the cheese mixture. Put the pieces of toast on small individual fireproof dishes, pour the sauce over them so they are completely masked – hence *en surprise* – and place under a moderate grill until their surface puffs and browns. Serve immediately.

GREEN RABBIT   FOR 4

80 g (3 oz) watercress
175 g (6^1/$_2$ oz) freshly grated Cheddar
40 g (1^1/$_2$ oz) unsalted butter, softened

pinch salt
freshly ground pepper
4 large slices good white or brown bread, toasted
2 hard-boiled eggs, shelled and sliced

Wash the watercress and cut off its tougher stalks. Set aside 4 small sprigs. Blanch the rest, uncovered, in boiling salted water for 3 minutes, drain, refresh under the cold tap and dry well. Blend the cheese, butter, watercress, salt and a little pepper to a paste.

Put the pieces of toast on lightly buttered small individual fireproof dishes, cover with slices of hard-boiled egg, spread the cheese mixture over them and bake in a fairly hot oven (190°C/375°F/Gas mark 5) for 15 minutes or until the surface begins to brown. Garnish with sprigs of watercress, and then serve immediately.

This dish can also be made successfully by replacing Cheddar with the same amount of a blue cheese such as Gorgonzola, Bleu de Bresse, Bleu d'Auvergne, Fourme d'Ambert or Stilton.

SAGE RABBIT   FOR 4

This makes a nice change from ordinary Welsh rabbit or cheese on toast, but you *must* use fresh sage. What a world of difference there is between the sage flavour exploited by the Italians – in, say, *fegatini di pollo alla salvia* (sautéd chicken livers with fresh sage) – and that of certain English sage-and-onion stuffings. This is due to the fact that the mild, fresh herb is used in the first, and the musty, dusty, overpowering dried leaves in the second.

300 g (10½ oz) freshly grated
  Cheddar
1 clove garlic, finely chopped
120 ml (4 fl oz) mild beer

1 tbsp fresh sage, finely chopped
50 g (2 oz) unsalted butter, softened
good white or brown bread,
  toasted

Mash the cheese, garlic, beer, sage and butter thoroughly. Cover and leave in a cool place for 1 hour.

Spread the mixture on toast and put under a fierce grill until golden brown on top. Serve immediately.

HORSERADISH RABBIT   FOR 4

Like the preceding recipe, a refreshing variation on the basic cheese-on-toast theme. The dish will be incomparably improved if you use freshly grated horseradish, but this is not always possible and you may have to fall back on commercial grated horseradish. At all costs avoid a ready-made horseradish sauce of any description.

300 g (10½ oz) freshly grated
  Cheddar
4 tbsp freshly grated horseradish
2 tsp lemon juice

120 ml (4 fl oz) double cream
50 g (2 oz) unsalted butter, softened
good white or brown bread, toasted

Mash the cheese, horseradish, lemon juice, cream and butter thoroughly. Spread the mixture on toast and put under a fierce grill until golden brown on top.

The amount of horseradish indicated may seem excessive, but it should be remembered that heat destroys much of its pungency.

HERB CHEESE RABBIT
Gentle heat, as opposed to thorough cooking, can greatly enhance the flavour of some herbs, such as chervil, borage and basil. Spread toasted good white or brown bread with a thick layer of any of the mixtures suggested in the recipe for Herb cheese (p. 53) and bake in a moderate oven (180°C/350°F/Gas mark 4) for about 10 minutes or until just heated through, but not runny or browned.

CROÛTES AUX CROTTINS   FOR 4
In the 1970s, restaurants in France were swept by a sudden craze for toasted goat cheese, usually served with salad (a good idea) and often drowning in its dressing (a less good idea). Every aspiring exponent of *nouvelle cuisine* had to have the dish on his menu, usually dressed up as something like *Merveille caprine avec son escorte de feuilles du potager* (Caprine marvel with its escort of kitchen-garden leaves) or some such idiocy. I say 'his' menu advisedly, as most French women chefs astutely kept their distance from the more lunatic fringe of the *nouvelle cuisine* movement.

The toasted goat cheese craze then moved onto Britain. It remains a firm favourite for, whether trendy or not, it is an excellent straightforward dish when taken from time to time.

80 g (3 oz) unsalted butter	250 g (9 oz) medium-ripe Crottins,
4 large slices toast	Cabécous or any similar goat cheese
freshly ground pepper	

Butter the toast. Sprinkle with plenty of pepper. Cut the cheeses horizontally into slices about 6 mm (¼ in) thick and arrange on the slices of toast. Put under a moderate grill for about 5 minutes or until the surface of the cheese begins to brown.

I have indicated the amount of cheese by weight rather than by units, as such goat cheeses vary considerably in size. The cheese should be neither too fresh nor too hard – just dentable with the finger.

Goat cheese does not behave like other cheese when subjected to heat: it browns and goes soft, but does not run. So it is important not to wait desperately for it to spread over the toast: it won't. A slight browning is the sign that the cheese is ready to be served.

If you decide to serve this dish with salad – *mesclun* (p. 131) is an ideal foil – make sure it is lightly dressed and completely free of water droplets.

PETITS GRILLONS DE CHAVIGNOL
AUX BRINS DE SARRIETTE   FOR 4

A Provençal variation, with olive oil and winter savory, of the preceding dish. The recipe comes from *Les Fêtes de mon moulin* by Roger Vergé, whose splendid restaurant near Cannes, Le Moulin de Mougins, needs no introduction. His lavishly illustrated book – and I mean lavishly – contains some of the finest photographs of food I have seen, as well as many fascinating recipes, most, but by no means all, of which are much more sophisticated than this very simple snack.

The Crottin de Chavignol is the best-known of the Crottins. I am not quite sure what the *grillons* are doing in the name of the dish: *grillon* normally means 'cricket', the insect whose pleasant rasping is so characteristic of summer in Provence. Maybe it is 'chef-ese' for 'little grilled tit-bits'?

4 tbsp virgin olive oil

12 rounds 6 mm ($1/4$ in) thick from a French baguette loaf

250 g (9 oz) Crottins de Chavignol *or* Rigottes

2 large sprigs fresh winter savory

freshly ground pepper

Dribble a little olive oil over each round of bread and toast until golden brown. Cut the cheese horizontally into slices about 6 mm (¹/₄ in) thick and put one on each slice of toast. Sprinkle with a few drops of olive oil and plenty of pepper. Place a tiny sprig of winter savory on each piece of cheese. Put under a moderate grill for about 5 minutes or until the surface of the cheese begins to brown. Serve with a salad of rocket leaves.

CROQUE-BRIARD AU CUMIN   FOR 4
An original recipe given to me by Guy Girard (p. 261).

200 g (7 oz) ripe Brie	1 tsp paprika
120 g (4 oz) unsalted butter, softened	1 tsp caraway
8 large slices *pain brioché*, toasted	1 tbsp fresh chives, finely chopped

Trim the cheese of any hard or brown bits of rind, and mash thoroughly with 60 g (2 oz) of butter. Spread this mixture very thickly and evenly on 4 slices of toasted *pain brioché*, sprinkle with paprika and caraway, and top with another slice of toast. Butter the top with the rest of the butter, well softened, and sprinkle with a few chives. Place the sandwiches on a lightly oiled baking dish and bake in a fairly hot oven (190°C/375°F/Gas mark 5) for about 15 minutes.

Girard suggests serving these toasted sandwiches with a *mesclun* salad (p. 131) dressed with walnut oil and very good-quality vinegar.

The name *croque-briard* is an invention of Girard's, on the analogy of croque-monsieur. *Briard*, in lexicographers' jargon, means 'of, relating to, or characteristic of the Brie region'.

CRUMPETS AU ROQUEFORT   FOR 6

Elizabeth David's definitive and compelling discussion of muffins and crumpets in *English Bread and Yeast Cookery* – their history, recipes and meanings, including slang – does not embrace the kind of crumpet that Curnonsky (p. 242) had in mind when he called this recipe Crumpets au roquefort. The reason is simple: they are not crumpets at all. With an uncharacteristic imprecision, he uses the word to describe slices of a toasted cheese-filled Swiss-roll-like concoction. The presence of Cheddar and Worcestershire sauce in the dish no doubt explains why he felt tempted to use the English word 'crumpet'.

The recipe comes from *Lettres de Noblesse* (1935), a beautifully produced little book Curnonsky penned in praise of Roquefort for the company Roquefort Société. He writes:

> No doubt I am and shall remain one of those old French gourmets who prefer Roquefort *for what it is*, just as I prefer *foie gras* without salad. . . . [But] I do not object to Roquefort flirting with other products, as long as they, too, are of the finest quality.

Hence his recipe for these 'crumpets'.

150 ml (5¹/₂ fl oz) béchamel sauce I (p. 356)	2 tsp strong Dijon mustard
150 g (5¹/₂ oz) Roquefort, crumbled	freshly ground pepper
150 g (5¹/₂ oz) freshly grated Cheddar	1 tsp Worcestershire sauce (optional)
	pain de mie (white sandwich bread)

Make or re-heat the béchamel sauce, add the cheeses and heat in a double-boiler, stirring all the time, until a smooth consistency is obtained. Stir in the mustard, pepper and, if desired, Worcestershire sauce.

Cut the loaf of sandwich bread lengthwise into thin slices. Remove the crust. Spread the cheese mixture thinly on the slices (the number of slices will depend on the dimensions of the loaf).

Carefully roll up each slice like a Swiss roll, gently

pressing it so that everything stays in place. Place the rolls on a lightly oiled baking tray, with the flap end of the roll tucked underneath, and bake in a hot oven (220°C/425°F/Gas mark 7) for 15 minutes or until the bread is nicely toasted. Remove from the oven and leave for 1 minute. Using a very sharp knife, quickly cut the rolls crosswise into slices 1 cm (1/2 in) thick, arrange them overlapping each other on a very hot serving dish and serve immediately.

CHAPTER SIX

Melted Cheese

Fondue is the simplest of all cooked cheese dishes. In its best-known form, it is just cheese that has been melted – *fondu* – in a small amount of liquid. Yet, as with, say, cassoulet, there is sometimes acrimonious disagreement in France and French-speaking Switzerland over what it should, and especially should not, contain. Such gastronomic squabbles are pointless, and forget that, historically, one of the great virtues of cooking as a 'discipline' has been, paradoxically, its willingness to break the rules whenever given half a chance. So it is silly to claim, as some do, that a fondue containing eggs (as it does in some parts of France) is not a real fondue. Different yes, but hardly heretical, since there is no canon to be respected.

Where I would go along with the purists is in decrying the neologism 'fondue bourguignonne', the name given by a Swiss chef to a dish he invented in 1947: whether one likes his recipe or not (those chunks of steak that each guest cooks in boiling oil, then seasons with various sauces, are not to my taste), the word 'fondue' is inaccurate since nothing is melted. All it has in common with a cheese fondue is its *mise-en-scène* – a dish kept hot over a burner, a ritual pronging, a communal spirit.

FONDUE SUISSE   FOR 4-6

Swiss fondue (possibly the archetypal version of the dish since it would seem that the very term fondue is of Swiss origin) consists essentially of several cheeses melted with a little white wine and/or kirsch in a thick enamel or fireproof earthenware dish with a handle called a *caquelon*. The dish is placed on a burner and each guest dips pieces of bread into the mixture with a long fork, thus reverting to the medieval practice of eating out of a communal dish.

Whether or not it is atavism that makes the consumption of fondue in good company so pleasurable I do not know. But there are very few culinary preparations that are such effective icebreakers (this no doubt also accounts for the popularity of fondue bourguignonne as a dinner-party dish). In some bourgeois Swiss and French households where icebreaking is thought to be out of place fondue is served in individual dishes.

My first experience of a proper Swiss fondue was, not unsurprisingly, in Geneva. I had been told that one of the few restaurants still offering the genuine product was an old-fashioned establishment called Café Huissoud. As soon as I pushed open the door, I was hit by an especially pungent, insistent, heady odour. It seemed to be as integral a part of the place as the scuffed wooden tables, the clipped-on paper tablecloths, the newspapers on rollers and the sprinkling of solitary habitués at their appointed seats. Several diners had come specially for the fondue, which sat before them, imperceptibly bubbling in its *caquelon*. Those who had not yet reached the main course – fondue is quite definitely a *pièce de résistance* – were nibbling the dish that traditionally precedes it, *viande des grisons* (dried fillet of beef cut in paper-thin slices).

My fondue, when it came after a generous plate of *viande des grisons*, was immensely satisfying – apparently rich but quite uncloying. I have had a number of other fondues since, but none of them lived up to that first experience. The reason for this is partly gastronomic nostalgia, but not entirely: to achieve a proper fondue you must use the right ingredients. Here they are, in main-course quantities.

2 cloves garlic
2 tsp potato starch or arrowroot
250 ml (9 fl oz) very dry white wine
370 g (13 oz) Gruyère
180 g (6$^1/_2$ oz) Bagnes
5 tbsp kirsch

180 g (6$^1/_2$ oz) Vacherin fribourgeois
freshly ground pepper
plenty of uncrumbly good white *or* brown bread, cut into fairly large cubes

Crush the garlic and rub the fondue dish with it, leaving the fragments on the bottom. Dilute the potato starch or arrowroot in a little of the wine and set aside. Pour the rest of the wine into the dish. Cut all the cheese into very thin slices, keeping each variety in separate piles.

Put the Gruyère into the dish and place over a high heat until the first bubbles appear, then reduce the heat to very low and stir constantly but unhurriedly with a wooden spoon. When the cheese has melted, but not before, stir in the potato starch or arrowroot mixed with wine. When this is well blended, add the Bagnes. When it too has melted, add the kirsch and the Vacherin, and continue stirring until a smooth creamy consistency is obtained.

Add plenty of pepper, cover and carry immediately to the table, where the guests should be ready and, according to Swiss tradition, standing up when the lid is removed.

The white wine should be very dry and a little sharp, like the wines of the Geneva area. If you cannot find a Fendant or a Johannisberg, use a Muscadet or, better, a Gros Plant.

Don't despair if you cannot get hold of Bagnes or Vacherin fribourgeois – not to be confused with Vacherin Mont d'Or, that superb cheese which comes into season around Christmas (and whose manufacture was banned for a time by the Swiss authorities on the grounds that it could contain organisms that might be a health hazard). You can make a perfectly acceptable fondue by replacing them, or one of them, with an equivalent quantity of Emmental, Swiss if possible, or even one of those newfangled cheeses that go by the name of Fondue or Raclette. (By the way, anything that calls itself *fromage fondu* should be avoided at all costs; it has nothing to do with fondue, and is simply processed cheese.)

The Swiss insist that cheese for a fondue be cut into thin slices rather than grated, on the grounds that grating causes it to lose its taste (!). The real reason, of course, is that grating such a large amount of cheese takes much longer than slicing it.

Potato starch or arrowroot are the best thickeners, as they are virtually tasteless. Some purists make fondue without a thickener, but this flirts with the danger of the cheese and wine separating unappetizingly.

It is advisable to use real kirsch or Kirschwasser, and not kirsch fantaisie, which contains only 10 per cent kirsch. Alternatively, kirsch may be omitted altogether, in which case an equivalent quantity of extra white wine should be added.

As I have already suggested, it is a mistake to be uptight about the 'correctness' of ingredients that go into fondue. Even the Swiss sometimes ring the changes with different combinations of cheeses, with the addition of dried morels, with cider instead of wine, with shallots instead of garlic, or even with water instead of wine.

If you do not possess a special *caquelon* or fondue dish, use any heavy fireproof receptacle, with or without a handle, as long as it is at least 10 cm (4 in) deep and not too wide (the fondue should be fairly deep at the start of proceedings. You cannot, however, do without a burner, otherwise the fondue will congeal to an unprepossessing sludge.

Eating fondue requires some practice. Prong a piece of bread on your fork, swirl it round in the mixture to keep the latter well emulsified, lift it out and twirl it several times to wind up the strands of melted cheese (and to allow the morsel to cool slightly – failure to do this will give you a burnt tongue). Swiss tradition requires that anyone who loses his or her piece of bread in the fondue has to stand the other guests a bottle of wine – or pay some direr forfeit. When the *caquelon* is empty, there will be a thin layer of hardened, browned cheese stuck to the bottom. The Swiss compete to scrape up this delicious postlude, known variously as *la religieuse* (nun) or *la dentelle* (lace).

Fondue should be accompanied by the same white wine that was used in it. Some even push extravagance so far as to sip neat kirsch with it. The accepted wisdom, anyway, is that it is not a good idea to drink large quantities of *any* liquid, and especially cold liquid, while eating fondue. It apparently makes the cheese congeal in the stomach and causes indigestion. A cold fizzy drink can have disastrous consequences: some years ago an American at a French ski resort ate a large amount of fondue, gulped down two bottles of ice-cold cola – and died.

RACLETTE

A Swiss dish that is rarely encountered in its genuine version in either restaurants or private homes. The popularity of another Swiss dish, fondue (see preceding recipe) and of its bastard offspring fondue bourguignonne, led manufacturers of kitchen equipment to devise and market fondue sets. In the wake of their popularity, they scratched their heads to see if they could not also exploit that other Swiss speciality, raclette. That is how raclette sets were born. But the results they produce (cheese on toast without toast) are as different from a genuine raclette as chalk is from, well, cheese.

Here is how I was served raclette some years ago by a very Swiss couple living in Lausanne. Hours beforehand they had started a nice wood fire, so that when the time came to make the raclette there were plenty of red-hot embers and not too many flames. The husband cut a whole Bagnes cheese in half and carefully wiped the rind on both sides with a damp clean cloth. His wife put plates on the edge of the fireplace to get hot. He gripped the cheese with a special long-handled pair of tongs and held it horizontally in front of the embers, with the cut surface facing the heat, in exactly the same way that one used to toast bread or crumpets in the days when the toasting fork had not yet been superseded by the electric toaster.

Very soon the whole cut edge of the cheese, including the rind, blistered and bubbled, and the room filled with a mildly cheesy, nutty, smoky smell. Picking up the cheese and holding it with its toasted surface facing upwards at an angle of 45 degrees away from him, he executed a rather delicate downward movement with a broad-bladed knife that scraped (*racler* = to scrape) all the melted cheese off on to a tendered hot plate. As I was the guest, I was handed the first plate and told to eat up the raclette while it was still hot. The plate also contained gherkins, hot boiled potatoes and onion salad (see below). When I had finished, my plate was put back in the fireplace to warm up until it was again my turn to be served.

And so the meal proceeded, with everyone, including the master of ceremonies, successively tucking into their wrinkled dollops of cheese. We washed down the raclette with Fendant, one of those rather aggressive, strong white wines of the Valais region.

What made my experience so different from that now afforded by raclette sets was not just the lulling heat, heady wine and almost hieratic eating procedure (at once communal and separate), but the discreetly smoky taste of the cheese and its rind – the mild rind of a not too mature Bagnes turns aromatically crisp when toasted.

If you cannot get hold of Bagnes, one of the more widely marketed special raclette cheeses, such as Raclette, will make an acceptable substitute. You can also, if necessary, fall back on Italian fontina or its French equivalent, Fontal, but they are really too bland for this treatment. I have made unorthodox but perfectly tasty raclette with Saint-Nectaire and Reblochon, on both occasions with not very mature specimens. Their toasted rind, like that of Bagnes, is not only edible but also delicious.

Now for the problem of tongs. All is not lost if you do not possess the special Swiss cheese-grip. With a little ingenuity and the help of two pieces of plywood to prevent the surface of the cheese from being dented, you should find that a pair of ordinary coal tongs will serve your purpose. Another Swiss device is to place a very large flat stone or pile of bricks in front of the embers and perch the cheese on top on a trivet or upturned wire basket (were it put directly on the stone or bricks, conducted heat would soon melt the underside of the cheese and render the scraping operation messy).

Onion salad is the hallowed accompaniment to raclette in Switzerland. Pickled onions may be served instead, but to my mind, when combined with gherkins, they provide too sharp a note to the meal. Onion salad is surprisingly mild, since the onions are blanched. As it is little known outside Switzerland, I give the recipe here.

4 large sweet onions, very finely sliced	1 tbsp very dry, sharp wine (Fendant, Muscadet *or* Gros Plant)
4 tbsp oil	pinch salt
1 tsp best wine vinegar	freshly ground pepper
2 tsp strong Dijon mustard	

Pour plenty of boiling salted water over the onions and leave for a few minutes. Drain well. Make a salad dressing with the oil, vinegar, mustard, wine, salt and plenty of pepper. Mix in the onions while they are still hot. Leave to cool before serving.

SAVOURY TOSTED OR MELTED CHEESE

This recipe from the celebrated seventeenth-century English cookbook *The Closet of the Eminently Learned Sir Kenelme Digbie, Knight, Opened* is a kind of cheese fondue with added ingredients. Sir Kenelme lived in a less trammelled age than ours and, like his contemporaries, he saw nothing wrong in spelling the same word in two different ways on the same page. He had a similarly freewheeling attitude to ingredients, which are suggested as alternatives or possible additions rather than musts. A quick calculation shows that the total number of possible combinations of ingredients suggested by Sir Kenelme is a staggering ninety; were he alive today, we can be sure he would not know what to make of the fuss over what should or should not go into fondue.

> Cut pieces of quick, fat, rich, well-tasted cheese, (as the best of Brye, Cheshire, &c. or sharp thick Cream-Cheese) into a dish of thick beaten melted Butter, that hath served for Sparages [asparagus] or the like, or pease, or other boiled Sallet [vegetable], or ragout of meat, or gravy of Mutton: and, if you will, Chop some of the Asparages among it, or slices of Gambon of Bacon, or fresh-collops [fried bacon], or Onions, or Sibboulets [chives], or Anchovis, and set all this to melt upon a Chafing-dish of Coals, and stir all well together, to Incorporate them; and when all is of an equal consistence, strew some gross White-Pepper on it, and eat it with tosts or crusts of White-bread. You may scorch it at the top with a hot Fire-Shovel.

In the days before the grill was invented toasted cheese was obtained by holding a fire-shovel containing red-hot embers or a salamander (a special utensil developed for that purpose) over the dish.

STEWED CHEESE   FOR 4

This recipe is based on the one given in *The Cook's Dictionary* by Richard Dolby, who was head cook at the celebrated Thatched House Tavern in St James's Street in the nineteenth century. It is similar in spirit to Swiss fondue, except that the wine used is a sweet one.

225 g (8 oz) Cheshire	2 tsp made mustard (optional)
225 g (8 oz) Double Gloucester	freshly ground pepper
280 ml (10 fl oz) sweet white wine	
(Sainte-Croix-du Mont, Monbazillac)	

Cut the cheese into very thin slices and put in a heavy fireproof dish with the wine and 2 tablespoons of water. Place over a high heat. As soon as the liquid bubbles, turn down the heat to very low and stir constantly but unhurriedly with a wooden spoon. When the cheese has almost completely melted, add the mustard ('if approved') and continue stirring. When a smooth consistency is obtained, add plenty of pepper, carry to the table and serve on a burner. The melted cheese may then be spooned into guests' heated individual bowls and accompanied by toast, or, better to my mind, partaken of communally like a Swiss fondue (p. 105).

Dolby called for 'Lisbon wine', by which he almost certainly meant a sweet fortified white wine from Bucelas, just north of Lisbon, which was very popular in England at that time (today the only wine from Bucelas is dry). I have suggested a sweetish unfortified, white wine: even allowing for the evaporation of alcohol during heating, half a pint of 18°-19° wine does seem a little excessive.

GLOUCESTER CHEESE AND ALE   FOR 4

Elisabeth Ayrton says, in *The Cookery of England*, that this dish was sometimes served to travellers arriving at Gloucestershire or Oxfordshire inns when the meat and birds were finished. The combination of brown ale, mustard and cheese, which is also found in Scotch rabbit (p. 86), is a particularly satisfying one.

600 g (1 lb 5 oz) Double Gloucester, thinly sliced	1 tbsp made mustard
	freshly ground pepper
350 ml (12 fl oz) brown ale	brown bread, toasted

Cut the cheese into very thin slices and put into a heavy fireproof dish with 250 ml (9 fl oz) of the ale. Place over a high heat. As soon as the liquid bubbles, turn down the heat to very low and stir constantly with a wooden spoon. When the cheese has almost completely melted, add the mustard and continue stirring. When a smooth consistency is obtained, add plenty of pepper. Put plenty of hot toast on warmed plates. Heat the rest of the ale and dribble it over the toast, then swathe with the cheese mixture.

CHAPTER SEVEN

Cheese and Egg

EGGS STUFFED WITH ROQUEFORT   FOR 4-6

I have always found plain hard-boiled egg halves, with their forlorn half-moons of orange yolk (sickly yellow in battery eggs), somehow unfulfilled. They need something doing to them. The texture of dry egg white and crumbly yolk in the mouth is all right for picnics but less satisfactory on a dinner table. This is no doubt one of the reasons why cooks have always liked jazzing up hard-boiled eggs, if only with a squidge of mayonnaise. And if the yolk is taken out, mixed with something else that gives a complementary flavour and a smoother consistency, and put back again, then a whole new range of possibilities opens up. This and the following recipe are two such examples using cheese.

6 hard-boiled eggs, shelled
50 g (2 oz) Roquefort
2 tbsp double cream
pinch cayenne

pinch freshly grated nutmeg
freshly ground pepper
1 head radicchio

Halve the hard-boiled eggs lengthwise and remove the yolks. Mash these thoroughly with the cheese, cream, cayenne, nutmeg and plenty of pepper. Press this mixture into the hollows left by the yolks and pile up into a mound. Arrange the 12 egg halves on a serving plate and garnish with radicchio.

OEUFS GRANDSAY   FOR 8-12

This recipe comes from Edouard Nignon's *Eloges de la cuisine française* (1933). Nignon (1865-1935) is an intriguing figure. A working-class Breton, he started his career as a kitchen hand at the age of 10 and rose to become one of the most celebrated chefs of his day. He cooked for Tsar Nicholas II and Emperor Franz Josef, was chef at Claridge's in London, and eventually ran the famous restaurant Larue in Paris, where his customers – and friends – included Anatole France, Edmond Rostand, Sacha Guitry and Marcel Proust.

Something of that literary company must have rubbed off on to him, for when he retired to his native Nantes he wrote several books on gastronomy couched in sometimes hilariously flowery language interspersed with the occasional poem. Many of the recipes in *Eloges de la cuisine française* are redolent of another age, when the readers Nignon wrote for could afford to buy very expensive ingredients and employ regiments of cooks. Omelette Louis XV, for example, requires, 'for 12 gourmets', 18 pheasant's eggs and 24 boned and stuffed ortolan buntings (birds only fractionally larger than a sparrow). But Nignon also includes some excellent, more straightforward and extremely precise recipes that are well within the scope of even the single-handed modern cook. The following hors d'oeuvre, for example, is well worth going to the trouble of making if you have a large dinner party.

12 hard-boiled eggs, shelled	freshly ground pepper
60 g (2 oz) unsalted butter, softened	1 litre (35 fl oz) Mornay sauce V
60 g (2 oz) black truffle duxelles	(p. 359)
(p. 365)	24 small slices of bread for croûtons
40 g (1½ oz) ordinary duxelles	unsalted clarified butter for frying
(p. 365)	60 g (2 oz) freshly grated Parmesan
salt	

Halve the hard-boiled eggs lengthwise and remove the yolks. Blend or mash these thoroughly with the butter, the two duxelles, and salt and pepper to taste. Press this mixture into the hollows left by the yolks and pile up into a mound. Make or re-heat the Mornay sauce. Fry the croûtons in clarified butter until crisp and arrange in a circle on a fireproof dish. Place the stuffed eggs on the croûtons, pour the hot Mornay sauce over them, sprinkle with Parmesan and bake in a fairly hot oven (190°C/375°F/Gas mark 5) for about 15 minutes or until golden brown ('the colour of old gold' in Nignon's words).

Nignon suggests a 'garnish' that I think might usefully be omitted: 'Decorate the centre of the dish with two creamy lobsters à l'américaine.'

CAISSES À LA CASANOVA   FOR 4
A pretty dish, adapted from a recipe contributed by Lady Congreve to Dorothy Allhusen's A Medley of Recipes (1936).

250 g (9 oz) peas, shelled	20 g (³/₄ oz) freshly grated Parmesan
1 leaf mint, finely chopped	20 g (³/₄ oz) freshly grated Cheddar
3 hard-boiled eggs, shelled	salt
150 ml (5 fl oz) double cream	freshly ground pepper

Boil the peas uncovered in plenty of well-salted water for 5 minutes or until tender but not mushy. Pass them through a food mill, then press the resulting purée through a fine sieve until no fragments of skin remain. Stir in the mint. Mash the hard-boiled eggs with half the cream, about a third of the finely grated cheese, and salt and pepper to taste. Blend well. Put equal quantities of this mixture into four dariole moulds or ramekins. Make a second layer with the pea purée. Top with the rest of the cheese and cream mixed together. Put in a cool place for at least 2 hours before serving.

OEUFS EN COCOTTE AU PARMESAN
FOR 4

An easy, cheap and quickly made supper dish.

150 ml (5 fl oz) double cream
50 g (2 oz) freshly grated Parmesan
salt

freshly ground pepper
8 eggs

Put eight ramekins into a moderate oven (190°C/375°F/ Gas mark 5) to warm for 3 minutes. Warm the cream in a small saucepan, stir in the cheese, and add a little salt and plenty of pepper. Take the ramekins out of the oven, which should be kept on, and spoon equal amounts of the mixture into them. Delicately break an egg over the top and place the ramekins in a gratin dish that has been filled with enough hot water for them to be immersed two-thirds of the way up their sides. Bake for 7-10 minutes, depending on the size of the eggs. They are done when each yolk fades beneath a thin opaque white film. Serve at once with toast.

OEUFS ALASSIO
FOR 4

Another unusual recipe adapted from *Les Recettes des 'Belles Perdrix'* (p. 36).

4 egg yolks
40 g (1½ oz) freshly grated Gruyère
salt
freshly ground pepper

slightly stale good-quality white
bread, sliced
2 egg whites
butter and oil for frying

Mix the egg yolks with the finely grated cheese, a pinch of salt and plenty of pepper until a smooth paste is obtained. Cut 12 rounds about 6 cm (2½ in) in diameter out of the bread with a cutter or glass. Spread evenly with the mixture. Whisk the egg whites with a tiny pinch of salt until very stiff. Heat an equal quantity of butter and oil in a large frying pan until very hot (but not burning). Pile the egg whites on to each piece of bread and, using a spatula, carefully lower into the frying pan. Fry in batches until the bread is golden, transferring the pieces to a warm oven when they are done.

One would imagine from the method that the egg whites were supposed to remain raw. But although they stay fairly soft, they do cook slightly and acquire a distinctive savoury meringue taste.

FLORENTINE EGGS   FOR 4

750 g (1½ lb) spinach
300 ml (10 fl oz) Mornay sauce I
   (p. 358)
salt
freshly ground pepper
1 small clove garlic, very finely
   chopped

pinch freshly grated nutmeg
3 tbsp double cream
30 g (1 oz) unsalted butter
60 g (2 oz) freshly grated Parmesan
4 eggs

Wash the spinach thoroughly but do not dry. Put with no extra water in a large enamel or stainless steel saucepan, cover and cook over a low heat at first (to prevent sticking). Then, as the spinach gives off moisture, cook over an increasingly high heat. From time to time push the spinach down and turn it over so the leaves cook evenly. When almost all the liquid has evaporated, drain the spinach in a colander and press out as much moisture as possible. Make or re-heat the Mornay sauce.

Chop the spinach coarsely and transfer to a mixing bowl. Add salt to taste, plenty of pepper, the garlic, nutmeg and cream. Mix well and spread on the bottom of a medium-sized gratin dish, well-buttered and heated. Sprinkle the spinach with half the cheese and break the eggs gently over it. Cover with hot Mornay sauce and sprinkle with the rest of the cheese. Put in a fairly hot oven (200°C/400°F/Gas mark 6) for 5 minutes, then under a grill for 5 more minutes or until slightly browned.

EGG, LETTUCE AND CHEESE GRATIN FOR 4

This variation of the previous dish takes its cue from Elizabeth David's delicious recipe for a lettuce and egg gratin (without cheese) in *Summer Cooking*. Cooked, as opposed to raw, lettuce has an astringency that makes it, like spinach, an ideal accompaniment to cheese and egg.

500 g (1 lb 2 oz) lettuce (a good-sized specimen)
60 g (2 oz) unsalted butter
300 ml (10 fl oz) Mornay sauce I (p. 358)
3 tbsp cream

salt
freshly grated nutmeg
freshly ground pepper
6 hard-boiled eggs, shelled
30 g (1 oz) Parmesan

Wash the lettuce thoroughly and dry. Cut into thin strips and cook gently in the butter in a large frying or sauté pan. Turn the lettuce over from time to time so it cooks evenly. Make or reheat the Mornay sauce. When all the liquid from the lettuce has evaporated and the lettuce is soft, transfer to a gratin dish. Add the cream, salt to taste, nutmeg, pepper and Mornay sauce and stir well. Halve the hard-boiled eggs. Press the halves, yolk uppermost, into the lettuce mixture so they are completely covered. Sprinkle with cheese and bake in a fairly hot oven (200°C/400°F/ Gas mark 6) for 15 minutes or until slightly browned.

FONDUE WITH EGGS FOR 4-6

Fondue with eggs, which is found in various guises in the French Jura, Savoie, Limousin and Auvergne, as well as in Italy under the name of *fonduta* (which contains fontina, white truffles, and milk instead of white wine), has just as much right, *pace* the purists, to call itself fondue as the Swiss eggless version. Indeed, the concern of the French-speaking Swiss to keep eggs out of their hallowed recipe for fondue (p. 105), a concern that borders at times on the manic, seems to have little basis in historical fact. As I have already pointed out, the word fondue is of Swiss origin. When first recorded in French, in 1735, it meant 'scrambled eggs with cheese'. In 1796 the archly titled *Le Manuel de la friandise, ou les talents de ma cuisinière Isabeau mis en lumière* contained a recipe called Oeufs à la bonne Suisse, which is nothing other than a fondue with eggs. In 1825 Brillat-Savarin published a recipe for fondue 'as found among the papers of Monsieur Trollet, steward of Mondon, in the Canton of Berne' (Mondon is in the French-speaking part of the Canton). It is a straight recipe for scrambled eggs with cheese, and contains no wine. All this goes to show that whatever the French-speaking Swiss regard as fondue today, matters are not as simple as all that from a historical point of view.

Fondue with egg may not have quite the class of a properly made eggless Swiss fondue, but it is less rich, more digestible, more economical and more easily negotiated by the diner.

700 g (1¹/₂ lb) Gruyère *or* Emmental, *or* a combination of the two, thinly sliced	4 eggs, beaten
	large pinch freshly grated nutmeg
	freshly ground pepper
250 ml (9 fl oz) dry white wine	salt
2 cloves garlic, very finely chopped	

Put the cheese, wine and garlic into a heavy saucepan over a high heat. As soon as the first bubbles appear, turn down the heat to very low and stir constantly but unhurriedly with a wooden spoon until the cheese has completely melted. Away from the heat, pour in the beaten eggs and stir. Add the nutmeg, plenty of pepper and salt to taste. The mixture will be lumpy at this stage. Return to a low heat and continue stirring until the fondue becomes smooth and has the consistency of thick custard. Pour into very hot bowls and serve immediately with plenty of toast.

The bowls used should be thick and heavy, with maximum heat retaining properties.

If using Emmental alone, you may wish to give the dish some extra zap by increasing the quantities of garlic or adding a pinch of cayenne.

SCRAMBLED EGGS WITH CHEESE   FOR 4

It is hardly surprising that it is virtually impossible to get *proper* scrambled eggs in a restaurant: their preparation requires the undivided attention of the cook for at least 20 minutes, otherwise they will not have the correct creamy consistency that ensures that they retain their delicate and very characteristic taste.

The crumbly, fluffy mixture that goes by the name of scrambled eggs in British restaurants and cafés is a completely different animal, and sometimes quite edible too (except when, as is often the case, water has been added – and is clearly detectable – or when the eggs are of inferior quality and the colour of the dish unappetizing). I have included an English-style scrambled egg dish later on in this chapter. It calls itself not scrambled eggs, but Cheese muff (p. 121)!

150 g (5¹/₂ oz) unsalted butter	salt
4 slices good white bread, trimmed	freshly ground pepper
of crust	100 g (3¹/₂ oz) freshly grated
8 eggs	Parmesan

Heat 50 g (2 oz) of the butter in a frying pan. Cube the bread and fry gently on all sides until golden. Set aside. Rub the inside of a smallish, heavy saucepan with some butter and cut the rest up into dice. Bring some water in a larger saucepan to almost simmering point. Beat the eggs thoroughly in a mixing bowl with a little salt and plenty of pepper, and pour into the buttered saucepan. Place this in the hot water without its touching the bottom of the larger saucepan (with its arm resting on the side, it should float; if not, place a trivet or similar support in the water). Stir constantly with a wooden spoon over a very low heat (the water must never get anywhere near boiling point). As the mixture begins to warm up, add the diced butter gradually. Continue stirring for at least 15 minutes, running the wooden spoon over the bottom and sides of the pan to prevent more than a few lumps from forming.

Slowly re-heat the croûtons. When the eggs are done

(they should have turned into a thick custard-like mixture with only a few tiny lumps in it), add the finely grated cheese, give the mixture a stir or two, remove from the heat and continue stirring until the cheese has blended. Fold in the croûtons and serve immediately on warmed, but not hot, plates.

Properly made scrambled eggs like these, which would be almost cloyingly creamy if served on their own, are beautifully set off by the lurking, crisp fried bread. Don't tell your guests about the croûtons and observe their reactions as they crunch their first mouthful.

In Piedmont scrambled eggs with cheese often get a delicious last-minute addition: white truffles. Make the scrambled eggs as above, adding, along with the cheese, about a tablespoonful of truffles cut into paper-thin slivers. Decorate each portion with one or two extra slivers.

CHEESE MUFF   FOR 4

80 g (3 oz) unsalted butter
100 g (3½ oz) freshly grated
   strong Cheddar
1 tbsp fresh white breadcrumbs

8 eggs
large pinch salt
freshly ground pepper

Heat the butter in a large non-stick frying pan. Put in the cheese and stir until melted. Mix in the breadcrumbs. Pour in the eggs, well beaten, and add the salt and pepper. Cook over a low heat, stirring all the time, until the mixture thickens and, as one recipe book has it, 'can be pushed up into a soft muff-like form'.

CHEESE OMELETTE

A persistent mystique surrounds the cooking of omelettes. It is a question that can arouse strong feelings even in people who claim to be capable of cooking nothing else: they assert, variously, that no omelette is any good if it consists of more than 5 or 4 or even 3 eggs, if it does not contain at least a teaspoon of water/milk/cream to every egg, if it is not cooked in its own special pan, which is never washed but just wiped, and so on and so on.

I myself have always enjoyed omelettes of any size – even 12-egg monsters – cooked simply with a little butter in an all-purpose non-stick pan large or small enough to permit, depending on the number of eggs used, a normal omelette thickness and brief cooking time. Although the addition of a little milk, cream or butter to the egg mixture does no harm, an omelette does not really need any extra lubrication if it is prepared properly, i.e. with eggs that are lightly beaten just before use and cooked at a fairly brisk pace – neither so hurriedly that the butter burns nor so sedately that the omelette loses its soft, slightly runny inside.

As for the special, never-washed omelette pan, it has the advantage of preventing the omelette from sticking, but necessarily imparts a hint of rancidity. With the advent of non-stick pans, it has surely become obsolete.

Matters get somewhat more complicated when it comes to making cheese omelettes. Some of the cheese may be included in the egg mixture before cooking, but more usually all the cheese is added when the omelette is almost done. The problem in the latter instance is that if the cheese is to melt properly the eggs have to be so hot they run a serious risk of getting overcooked. Hence the need either to add only a small final filling or, when (as is usually the case) the filling is more substantial, to melt the cheese beforehand.

Cheese omelette I   FOR 4

8 eggs

40 g (1½ oz) freshly grated
   Parmesan

30 g (1 oz) unsalted butter

pinch salt

freshly ground pepper

40 g (1½ oz) freshly grated Gruyère

Break the eggs into a bowl and stir briefly but vigorously with a fork, making sure that all the yolks are broken and mixed in with the rest. Add the Parmesan and beat for 20 seconds. Melt the butter over a high heat in a large non-stick frying pan, making sure it coats the whole surface and part of the sides. When it has completely melted and begins to foam, pour in the egg mixture and reduce the heat to low. As the edges of the omelette cook, lift them at various points and, tilting the pan, allow the uncooked egg on the surface of the omelette to run over the edge and come into contact with the hot pan. Sprinkle with salt and plenty of pepper. When there remains only a thin layer of runny egg on top, sprinkle the omelette with the finely grated Gruyère (which must be at room temperature) and immediately fold over; the heat of the omelette is sufficient to melt the cheese. Transfer to a warm, but not hot, serving dish.

Cheese Omelette II   FOR 4

2 tbsp double cream	30 g (1 oz) unsalted butter
80 g (3 oz) freshly grated Gruyère	pinch salt
8 eggs	freshly ground pepper

Put the cream and the cheese into a small thick saucepan and heat gently until the latter has melted, stirring all the time. Set aside and keep warm. Break the eggs into a bowl and beat for 30 seconds. Melt the butter over a high heat in a large non-stick frying pan, making sure it coats the whole surface and part of the sides. When it has completely melted and begins to foam, pour in the eggs and reduce the heat to low. As the edges of the omelette cook, lift them at various points and, tilting the pan, allow the uncooked egg on the surface of the omelette to run over the edge and come into contact with the hot pan. Sprinkle with salt and plenty of pepper. When there remains only a thin layer of runny egg, dribble the melted cheese evenly over the omelette, fold and transfer to a warm, but not hot, serving dish.

BRIE OMELETTE   FOR 4

2 tbsp double cream	30 g (1 oz) unsalted butter
80 g (3 oz) ripe Brie, trimmed	pinch salt
of its rind	freshly ground pepper
8 eggs	

Proceed as in Cheese omelette II (above), using Brie, instead of Gruyère, cut up and gently melted in cream.

BROCCIO OMELETTE   FOR 4

The presence of mint in this Corsican classic betrays the island's fundamentally Italian cultural roots (mint is used extensively in Italian cooking). In mainland France any mention of English cooking will immediately spark considerable mirth about that 'abomination', mint sauce. But I have met a few French gourmets who, after a visit to England, were honest enough to admit they had changed their minds about mint sauce (they must have been fortunate enough to get a properly made one).

To make a really authentic Broccio omelette, you will need the wild mint, pennyroyal (*Mentha pulegium*), though the cultivated kind will do.

125 g (4^1/$_2$ oz) Broccio	30 g (1 oz) unsalted butter
8 leaves fresh pennyroyal (or 4 leaves	pinch salt
fresh garden mint), finely chopped	freshly ground pepper
8 eggs	

Mix the cheese with the mint and refrigerate for 2 hours. Proceed as in Cheese omelette I (p. 122), using Broccio instead of Parmesan, and omitting the Gruyère.

FOURME D'AMBERT OMELETTE   FOR 4

I first tasted this simple, subtle omelette not in Ambert, in the Auvergne, where the blue Fourme d'Ambert is made, but at Jacques Mélac's jolly wineshop-cum-bistro in Paris (42 rue Léon-Frot). Mélac, like the vast majority of Paris café owners, hails from the Auvergne, and this is reflected in the choice of dishes that feature on his tiny menu. More unusually, he stocks a number of obscure Auvergne wines (Marcillac, Corent, Châteaugay) in addition to the better-known Saint-Pourçain. The received wisdom that wines make a poor marriage with eggs is a gross exaggeration: any of the rustic wines just mentioned goes very well with this omelette.

2 tbsp double cream	30g (1 oz) unsalted butter
80 g (3 oz) Fourme d'Ambert	pinch salt
8 eggs	freshly ground pepper

Proceed as in Cheese omelette II (p 123), using Fourme d'Ambert, instead of Gruyère, mashed and gently melted in cream.

MAROILLES OMELETTE   FOR 4

This is a dish that very rarely finds its way on to restaurant menus because of Maroilles' spectacular smelliness (p. 203). But the chef François Benoist, of the restaurant Chez Les Anges in Paris, who grew up in the north of France where the cheese is made, used to rustle up this dish for himself (a whiff of his youth?) even if he did not make it for his elegant customers.

2 tbsp double cream	30 g (1 oz) unsalted butter
60 g (2 oz) Maroilles	pinch salt
8 eggs	freshly ground pepper

Proceed as in Cheese omelette II (p. 123), using Maroilles, instead of Gruyère, cut up and melted gently in cream.

PARMESAN OMELETTE   FOR 4

8 eggs
30 g (1 oz) unsalted butter
small pinch salt

freshly ground pepper
80 g (3 oz) freshly grated Parmesan

This is the same as Cheese omelette I (p. 122), except that a further 40 g (1½ oz) of Parmesan, instead of Gruyère, is added before the omelette is folded.

ROQUEFORT OMELETTE   FOR 4

2 tbsp double cream
60 g (2 oz) Roquefort
8 eggs

30 g (1 oz) unsalted butter
freshly ground pepper

Proceed as in Cheese omelette II (p. 123), omitting the salt and using Roquefort, instead of Gruyère, mashed and gently melted in cream.

PARMESAN AND SPINACH OMELETTE   FOR 4

There are several versions of this Italian *frittata* (omelette), with the proportion of spinach to cheese and egg varying enormously (it is sometimes like an almost solid *sformato*). The recipe given here results in something that is recognizably an omelette.

300 g (10½ oz) spinach
50 g (2 oz) fresh white breadcrumbs
1 clove garlic, finely chopped
1 tsp fresh marjoram, finely chopped
tiny pinch freshly ground allspice

pinch salt
freshly ground pepper
60 g (2 oz) freshly grated Parmesan
8 eggs
30 g (1 oz) unsalted butter

Wash the spinach thoroughly but do not dry. Put with no extra water in a large enamel or stainless steel saucepan, cover and cook over a low heat at first (to prevent sticking). Then, as the spinach gives off moisture, cook over an increasingly high heat. From time to time, push the spinach down and turn it over so the leaves cook evenly. When almost all the liquid has evaporated, drain the spinach in a colander and press out as much moisture as possible. Chop coarsely.

Soak the breadcrumbs in a little water (or milk) and squeeze dry. In a mixing bowl, put the spinach, breadcrumbs, garlic, marjoram, allspice, salt, plenty of pepper, cheese and eggs. Mix thoroughly. Heat the butter in a large non-stick frying pan until completely melted and foaming, pour in the mixture, turn down the heat and cook gently, without lifting up the edges, until only a thin layer of uncooked egg is visible on the surface. Fold in half and transfer immediately to a warm, but not hot, serving plate.

OMELETTE SAVOYARDE   FOR 4

In mountain areas with rigorous climates, omelettes, like soups, tend to be filling, energy-packed affairs that the local inhabitants hungrily dispatch as a first course. For the more sedentary, this omelette from Savoie (like the following one from Auvergne) makes an ample main course for a light lunch or supper.

60 g (2 oz) unsalted butter	2 tbsp cream
125 g (4¹/₂ oz) *jambon de Savoie*	small pinch salt
or lean smoked bacon, trimmed	freshly ground pepper
of its rind, thinly sliced	100 g (3¹/₂ oz) freshly grated Beaufort
8 eggs	*or* Gruyère

Butter an oven dish with half the butter. Cut the ham or bacon into narrow strips and put into a mixing bowl with the eggs, cream, salt, pepper and half the cheese, finely grated. Beat together for about 30 seconds. Heat the rest of the butter in a large non-stick frying pan until completely melted and beginning to foam, pour in the mixture and turn down the heat. Cook for 1-2 minutes without touching the omelette so that it firms up just enough underneath for you to be able to fold it. At this point it should still be very runny. Transfer the folded omelette to the buttered oven dish, sprinkle with the rest of the cheese, and put in to a hot oven (220°C/425°F/Gas mark 7) for 5 minutes or until the cheese has a nice crust.

Cooking this omelette may require a little practice: as the omelette spends a short spell, folded, in the oven, it is not easy to tell exactly when it is done (it should remain moist in the middle).

There are no hard and fast rules about what goes into an Omelette savoyarde, though it is most often made as in the above recipe. If you happen not to have any ham, you can follow the version given by Austin de Croze in his *Les Plats régionaux de France*: his ham-less omelette is cooked entirely on top of the stove, with some pre-fried potatoes and a little chopped chervil and tarragon folded in at the last moment.

OMELETTE BRAYAUDE   FOR 4

This omelette is named after the *brayauds* (peasants in ancient costume) who on 11 June each year march through the streets of Riom in the Auvergne in honour of the town's patron saint, Saint Amable. The omelette, which is cooked right through instead of being kept moist in the centre, is more like a thick galette than a classic omelette.

50 g (2 oz) lard	1 clove garlic, finely chopped
175 g (6 oz) potatoes, peeled and diced	8 eggs, lightly beaten
	freshly ground pepper
salt	100 g (3¹/₂ oz) young Cantal, cut in very thin slivers
100 g (3¹/₂ oz) *jambon d'Auvergne* (*or* similar raw ham), sliced	100 ml (4 fl oz) double cream

Heat the lard in a large non-stick frying pan. Dry the diced potatoes and cook them in the lard over a high heat for a few minutes, then reduce the heat as low as possible, sprinkle with a little salt and cover. Cut the ham into thin strips. When the potatoes are very nearly cooked, turn up the heat a little, stir in the ham and garlic, and pour the eggs over the whole thing. Sprinkle with a little more salt and some pepper.

When the omelette has browned on one side, turn it over on to a warm serving dish, then slide it back into the pan so it cooks on the other side for 3-4 minutes. Lay the slivers of cheese very flat on the omelette while it cooks on the other side, so they come into contact with its warm surface and begin to melt. Heat the cream to almost boiling point, pour over the omelette and serve immediately.

OMELETTE SOUFFLÉE AU FROMAGE   FOR 2

An ethereal concoction that for some inexplicable reason regularly engenders a feeling of well-being among guests. It makes an ideal, insubstantial first course. Because the egg whites swell, 2 small omelettes of the size indicated below are more easily negotiated by the cook than one big one when catering for four people.

40 g (1¹/₂ oz) freshly grated
    Parmesan
4 eggs, separated
salt

40 g (1¹/₂ oz) unsalted butter,
    softened
freshly ground pepper

Stir the very finely grated cheese and half the butter, in little dice, into the egg yolks until well blended. Whisk the egg whites with a pinch of salt until stiff and fold delicately but thoroughly into the yolks. Heat the rest of the butter in a medium-sized nonstick frying pan until it begins to foam and pour in the mixture, making an even surface with a spatula. Cook over a medium heat, shaking from time to time. When the omelette's underside has browned a little, fold it over and serve immediately.

COLD CHEESE OMELETTE WITH TOMATO   FOR 4

Cold omelette may strike you as repulsive: cold sticky egg yolk, congealed butter and general insipidity. But such unpleasantness can be circumvented by using olive oil instead of butter, cooking the omelette a little bit longer, and giving it a filling with plenty of personality.

Is it the coldness that puts you off? The question of cold food in general is a very interesting one. Do our taste buds perceive it differently from hot food? Harold McGee, in his immensely learned yet very readable handbook *On Food and Cooking*, says that although our sensitivity to taste is affected by the temperature of food, no definite pattern has yet been found. Experimental work has simply shown that maximum taste sensitivity occurs at between 22°C and 41°C (72°F and 105°F). This would explain why cold dishes, as every scullion knows, need to be salted more liberally than hot ones.

But I wonder whether matters are not more complicated than that. Smell plays an important role in taste, and the smell of cold food is very different and, to my mind, often more complex and subtle than that of the same food hot. This is certainly true of wine. Compare the full nose of, say, a red wine drunk at the correct temperature – between 12°C and 18°C (48°F and 64°F) depending on the type of wine – and the unsubtle, debilitated smell of the same wine mulled. Cold omelettes are surely a case in point. Like cold (pink) roast beef and cold Charter pie (if you have never tasted this superb dish, hurry and make it – the recipe is in Jane Grigson's *Good Things*), a cold omelette does not have much in common with its hot version. The egginess has greater impact, the filling more individuality. If you are not convinced, please at least try the following recipe.

8 eggs	salt
40 g (1¹/₂ oz) freshly grated	freshly ground pepper
Parmesan	200 ml (7 fl oz) tomato sauce (p. 364)
2 tbsp virgin olive oil	

Proceed as in Cheese omelette I (p. 122), using olive oil

instead of butter, cooking the omelette until the eggs are completely set and replacing the Gruyère with tomato sauce, which should be spread evenly over half the surface. Fold the other half of the omelette over the tomato mixture and leave to cool. When cool, cover snugly with aluminium foil and balance a small terrine or similar not too heavy, oval object on top. Leave overnight in a cool place. To serve, cut into slices crosswise and arrange on a serving dish with, if you like, a garnish of *mesclun* salad (radicchio, rocket, chervil, young dandelion).

CHEESE SOUFFLÉ

Soufflés, like omelettes, can cause nervous tension. With omelettes, as I have already suggested, any tension there may be is usually between the cook and the cooked-for: each prospective consumer of the omelette has his or her own very clear idea about how it should be cooked, how runny it should be and so on. Problems with soufflés, on the other hand, arise between the cook and the cooked: there can be much nail-biting between the moment when the soufflé is put into the oven and when it is taken out. Will the soufflé perform as it should, in other words will it rise properly in the oven and stay up long enough to be presentable by the time it gets to the table? This is a problem that has exercised the mind of many a cook; and it has led to the devising of 'foolproof' variations on the soufflé technique.

Soufflés are in fact rather easy to make as long as the basic procedure is scrupulously followed – and as long as you have a fairly modern, easily controlled oven and don't live in a large mansion with miles of draughty corridors between kitchen and dining room.

The soufflé is a relatively recent dish. Although a recipe for what was in effect a kind of soufflé appeared in Vincent La Chapelle's *Le Cuisinier moderne* in 1735, the term was not used until 1829, when the advent of new ovens using an air draught system rather than hot coals made possible the constant cooking heat needed for soufflés. Although many of the earliest soufflés, particularly those of Carême, who pioneered the dish as we know it, were sweet, cheese soon became an important, and sometimes the main, ingredient. It is perfectly suited to the soufflé technique, which enhances not only the flavour but also the aroma of whatever goes into it.

There are two basic forms a soufflé can take: you can cook it informally in a large mould and portion it out at table, thus risking the ire of your less well-behaved and greedier guests, who will *always* convince themselves that they have been short-changed, complaining that they did not get enough of the soufflé's deliciously browned crust, or enough of its succulent creamy centre or enough *tout court*. This hazard can be circumvented by cooking individual small soufflés, which have the added advantage of offering a higher ratio of crust to centre, but which also tend to dry out rather easily. It is up to the host to weigh up all these pros and cons before deciding on logistics.

As will be seen from the range of recipes given here, the soufflé is a very versatile dish. Not only can it accommodate a wide range of ingredients or combinations of ingredients, but even its texture, at first sight unvarying, can be given subtle nuances depending on what goes into – or rather is left out of – it. Eggs (usually both yolks and whites) are of course a recurring ingredient. But in many recipes flour is completely dispensed with, or replaced by potato, semolina, cornflour or even bread (in which case the soufflé turns into something almost indistinguishable from a cheese pudding – see p. 146). Milk is left out in other versions.

Even the basic cheese soufflé varies considerably. This is why I have given two basic formulae here. Cheese soufflé I is very fluffy and light, and has a muted cheese flavour; Cheese soufflé II tastes much more strongly of cheese and has a rich, almost tacky texture. The types of cheese indicated are only suggestions; you can make a soufflé with virtually any cheese.

Cheese Soufflé I   FOR 4

50 g (1³/₄ oz) unsalted butter
40 g (1¹/₂ oz) plain flour
310 ml (11 fl oz) milk
3 egg yolks
60 g (2 oz) of any of the following
  cheeses, freshly grated *or* finely
  crumbled: Cheddar, Cheshire,
  Wensleydale, Gruyère, Parmesan,
  Gruyère and Parmesan in equal

quantities, Roquefort,
Bleu d'Auvergne, Fourme d'Ambert,
Stilton, medium-ripe goat cheese,
Maroilles (for precautions, see
recipe for Goyère p. 203)
freshly grated nutmeg
salt
freshly ground pepper
5 egg whites

Butter generously the whole of the inside of a 1.4-litre (50-fl oz) soufflé mould – it should be about 14 cm (5¹/₂ in) across and 9 cm (3¹/₂ in) deep. Sprinkle with a little flour, tilting, turning and tapping the mould so the flour tumbles round and covers the whole buttered surface with a thin film. Turn the mould upside down and tap out any excess flour.

Melt the butter gently in a heavy saucepan. Heat the milk in another pan. Blend the flour with the butter and cook slowly, stirring all the time, for 2-3 minutes without browning. When the milk almost reaches boiling point, pour it over the butter and flour mixture, away from the heat, and whisk until absolutely smooth. Return the pan to the heat, bring to the boil and cook gently for about 1 minute, stirring. Remove from the heat, allow to cool slightly and beat in the egg yolks one by one. Stir in the grated cheese and add nutmeg, salt (very little if using Roquefort) and plenty of pepper to taste (the mixture should be highly seasoned at this point, as it will be diluted by the egg whites). Whisk the egg whites with a small pinch of salt until very stiff.

Take a large spoonful of whipped egg whites and quickly stir into the cheese mixture to slacken it, then fold in the rest delicately but thoroughly. Turn the mixture into the mould, filling it about three-quarters full, and bake immediately in a fairly hot oven (200°C/400°F/Gas mark 6) for 25-30 minutes. *Do not open the oven door for at least 20 minutes.* The soufflé should have browned nicely and risen well above the sides of the mould.

You have two options at this point. If your guests are ready and close to hand – if, for example, you are eating in the kitchen – serve immediately: the soufflé will have a creamy centre, which, as Elizabeth David observes, 'supplies [it] with, as it were, its own sauce'. But if you want, or need, to be on the safe side, cook the soufflé for a further 3-4 minutes to make it less liable to immediate collapse.

The 'musts' for the success of the soufflé are as follows: the egg whites must be whisked until very stiff – therefore there must be no speck of egg yolk or grease in the bowl; the whisking should be done with a balloon whisk or, just as well but with less effort, by a hand-operated whisk with interlocking paddles (an electric beater at a slow speed can be used, but should be of the type you can move around the bowl in order to reach the whole of the egg-white mass); the whites must be folded in quickly and the soufflé baked immediately; all temptations to open the oven door before the indicated time must be resisted (this is less of a problem now that ovens with windows have become the rule); and, last but not least, guests must be ready, with forks poised.

The buttered soufflé mould can, if desired, be sprinkled with grated cheese instead of flour before the mixture is poured into it. Equally you can, if you wish, score the surface of the mixture deeply with a spatula, forming either a circle about 3 cm (1 in) from the edge or a hot-cross-bun-like pattern: this will make the cooked soufflé look more attractive.

If you decide to make four individual soufflés, you will need four small soufflé moulds or large ramekins with a capacity of about 350 ml (12 fl oz) each. Pour an equal amount of the soufflé mixture into each mould, again filling them only about three quarters full. Bake in a fairly hot oven (200°C/400°F/Gas mark 6) for 12-16 minutes. *Do not open the oven door for at least 10 minutes.*

If made with Gruyère alone or with Cheddar, Cheshire

or Wensleydale, this soufflé will have a very mild cheese flavour. A fairly tangy goat cheese or any of the blue cheeses suggested, especially Roquefort, make a refreshingly piquant change from the classic cheese soufflé.

Cheese Soufflé II   FOR 4

50 g (1³/₄ oz) unsalted butter
40 g (1¹/₂ oz) plain flour
250 ml (9 fl oz) milk
4 eggs, separated
170 g (6 oz) of any of the following
  cheeses, freshly grated *or* mashed:
  Cheddar, Cheshire, Wensleydale,

Gruyère, Gruyère and Parmesan in
equal quantities, fresh goat cheese,
fresh ewe's-milk cheese
freshly grated nutmeg
salt
freshly ground pepper

Proceed exactly as for Cheese soufflé I, whether making one big soufflé or four small ones, but turn the heat of the oven up to very hot (240°C/475°F/Gas mark 9) for the last quarter of the cooking time.

Don't be disappointed if the soufflé does not puff up quite as toweringly as in the preceding version. It will make up for its lower profile with a more assertive flavour. It is, of course, possible to make a cheese soufflé using different, intermediate proportions of egg whites, egg yolks and cheese to the ones indicated in the two versions described above. Its texture will vary accordingly.

If you are using fresh goat or ewe's-milk cheese, a tablespoon of finely chopped fresh chives can be rewardingly added to the mixture.

SEMOLINA CHEESE SOUFFLÉ   FOR 4-6

As the soufflé technique has the effect of heightening the flavours of its various ingredients, this recipe is not for those who have been put off semolina for life by the nauseating pap served at school meals. I am fortunate in that the predominant memory of semolina bequeathed to me by my childhood is of a fragrant, cinnamon-dusted cold pudding called semolina halva (nothing to do with the sticky almond sweetmeat called halva) made by Greek friends of the family. To me, then, the discreet additional flavour of semolina in this soufflé makes a pleasant change from the classic version, even though its texture is far less pneumatic.

50 g (1³/4 oz) unsalted butter	4 eggs, separated
600 ml (21 fl oz) milk	salt
120 g (4 oz) fine semolina	freshly ground pepper
170 g (6 oz) freshly grated Cheddar, Gruyère or Gruyère and Parmesan in equal quantities	pinch freshly grated nutmeg

Take a large soufflé mould or four small individual soufflé moulds of the dimensions indicated in Cheese soufflé I (p. 133); butter generously and sprinkle with flour as explained in that recipe. Bring the milk to the boil in a heavy saucepan and pour in the semolina. Cook over a gentle heat, stirring all the time, for about 5 minutes, by which time the mixture will have thickened. Add the butter and cheese, and stir until a smooth consistency is obtained. Remove from the heat and allow to cool slightly, then stir in the egg yolks, one by one, until well blended. Season well with salt, pepper and the nutmeg.

Whisk the egg whites with a tiny pinch of salt until very stiff. Take a large spoonful of whipped egg whites and quickly stir into the cheese mixture to slacken it, then fold in the rest delicately but thoroughly. Turn the mixture into the mould(s) and bake immediately in a fairly hot oven (200°C/400°F/Gas mark 6) for about 40 minutes or until the soufflé has risen slightly and is golden brown on top. *Do not open the oven for at least 30 minutes.* Serve immediately.

IMITATION SOUFFLÉ FOR 4

This recipe comes from *Eating without Fears* (1925) by G. F. Scotson-Clark – and is actually rather tastier than it sounds. I cannot resist quoting Scotson-Clark's preamble to the recipe:

> Have you ever tried to make a soufflé ? A real soufflé is a sort of *ignis fatuus* or will o' the wisp. It is like the brilliant genius who dies in his 'teens. It is the tragedy of the kitchen. Many a soufflé has come from the oven with all the promise of perfection, only to wilt and sag before it reached the dining table. A puff of cold air, a false step on the part of its honoured bearer, apparently even a whisper, is enough to turn its proud rounded apex into a mean and uninteresting hollow, like a dried-up dew pond. By chance the partner in my sorrows evolved the following, and I can recommend it as being very like a soufflé. And it has the great advantage of behaving itself and standing up under all the cares of this world.

4 tbsp cornflour
1¹/₂ tbsp baking powder
pinch salt
250 ml (9 fl oz) milk
4 eggs

60 g (2 oz) unsalted butter
120 g (4 oz) freshly grated strong
  Cheddar
pinch paprika

Put the cornflour, baking powder and salt into a bowl and mix thoroughly. Add enough milk to cream the mixture. Beat the eggs vigorously in a mixing bowl until they froth, add the rest of the milk and beat again. Stir in the cornflour mixture and beat again. Take a pie dish with a capacity of about 1 litre (35 fl oz) and butter it with a little less than half the butter. Strew the bottom of the dish with the rest of the butter, cut into tiny dice, and the grated cheese. Re-beat the egg mixture and pour gently into the pie dish, sprinkle with a little paprika and bake in a moderate oven (180°C/350°F/Gas mark 4) for 20-25 minutes or until it is nicely risen and golden brown all over. 'Then eat it', Scotson-Clark concludes.

You can use any pie dish, oval or round, and even quite a flat one, for this dish. Soufflés always used to be cooked in rather shallow oval dishes until the straight-sided soufflé mould was introduced.

CHEESE SOUFFLÉ WITHOUT FLOUR   FOR 4

After a soufflé that replaces flour with cornflour and baking powder, here is one that contains no flour at all. It comes from the mid-nineteenth-century *My Receipt Book: A Treasury of Six Hundred Receipts in Cooking and Preserving &c., &c.,* 'compiled entirely from private resources and personal experience' by 'A Lady'.

250 ml (9 fl oz) double cream	4 eggs, separated
60 g (2 oz) unsalted butter	salt
110 g (4 oz) freshly grated Cheddar	freshly ground pepper

Put the cream and butter into a saucepan over a low heat. Beat until thoroughly blended and leave to cool. Stir in the cheese and egg yolks. Add salt and pepper to taste. Butter a pie dish with a capacity of about 1 litre (35 fl oz). Whisk the egg whites with a small pinch of salt until very stiff. Take a large spoonful of whipped egg whites and stir quickly into the cheese mixture to slacken it, then fold in the rest delicately but thoroughly. Turn the mixture into the buttered pie dish and bake immediately in a hot oven (220°C/425°F/Gas mark 7) for about 20 minutes or until well puffed up and golden brown. *Do not open the oven door for at least 15 minutes*. Serve immediately.

FAVORITES À LA PARMESAN   FOR 4

Another form of soufflé without flour, subtly different from the preceding recipe. It forms part of the collection of recipes published under the title *The Cookery Book of*

Lady Clark of Tillypronie, and was given to Lady Clark by Lady Playfair in 1887 – complete with its Anglo-French epithet '*à la* Parmesan'.

60 g (2 oz) freshly grated Parmesan	1 egg white
2 tbsp double cream	pinch cayenne pepper
4 tbsp milk	salt
4 egg yolks	

Put the finely grated cheese, cream, milk, egg yolks and egg white into a mixing bowl and beat vigorously until thoroughly blended. Add cayenne pepper and salt to taste. Pour into four small ramekins and bake in a hot oven (220°C/425°F/Gas mark 7) for about 12 minutes or until puffed up and slightly cracked on top. Serve immediately.

HOT CHEESE CREAMS   FOR 4

This recipe not only does without flour but also dispenses with egg yolks. The result is more like a savoury meringue than a soufflé.

5 egg whites	2 tbsp double cream
salt	120 ml (4 fl oz) tomato sauce (p. 364)
30 g (1 oz) freshly grated Parmesan	2 tbsp fresh parsley, finely chopped

Whisk the egg whites with a pinch of salt until very stiff. Add the cheese, cream and some more salt, and stir thoroughly. Spoon the mixture into eight small ramekins. Place these on a trivet or wire rack in a sauté pan, pour in enough boiling water to come two-thirds of the way up the sides of the ramekins. Cover and cook over a low heat for about 15 minutes. The water should simmer almost imperceptibly. Heat the tomato sauce. Remove the cheese creams from the pan, sprinkle with parsley and serve immediately with tomato sauce.

CHEESE ROULADE   FOR 4

This is a rather spectacular, up-market cross between a classic soufflé and a stuffed cheese omelette. It has certain advantages over both preparations: the soufflé mixture and its accompanying flavours are not fused as in a soufflé, but arranged in discrete layers that produce a different effect on the palate; and the texture is incomparably lighter than that of a cheese omelette.

90 g (3¹/₂ oz) unsalted butter	Parmesan in equal quantities, fresh
250 ml (8 fl oz) milk	goat cheese, fresh ewe's-milk cheese
40 g (1¹/₂ oz) plain flour	freshly grated nutmeg
4 eggs, separated	salt
170 g (6 oz) of any of the following	freshly ground pepper
cheeses, freshly grated or mashed:	150-200 g (5¹/₂-7 oz) filling
Cheddar, Gruyère, Gruyère and	(see suggestions below)

Line a shallow baking tin measuring about 35 x 25 cm (14 x 10 in) with greaseproof paper. Butter the exposed side of the paper generously. Melt 50 g (1³/₄ oz) of butter gently in a heavy saucepan. Heat the milk in another pan. Blend the flour with the butter and cook slowly, stirring all the time, for 2-3 minutes without browning. When the milk almost reaches boiling point, pour it over the butter and flour mixture, away from the heat, and whisk until absolutely smooth. Return the pan to the heat, bring to the boil and cook gently for about 1 minute, stirring.

Remove from the heat, allow to cool slightly, and beat in the egg yolks one by one. Stir in the grated cheese and add nutmeg, salt and plenty of pepper to taste (the mixture should be highly seasoned at this point, as it will be diluted by the egg whites). Whisk the egg whites with a small pinch of salt until very stiff. Take a large spoonful of whipped egg whites and quickly stir into the cheese mixture to slacken it, then fold in the rest delicately but thoroughly.

Pour the soufflé mixture into the tin and spread evenly all over the surface with a palette knife. It should be about 6 mm (¹/₄ in) deep. Place immediately in a moderate oven (180°C/350°F/Gas mark 4) and bake for 15 minutes or until firm. Remove from the oven and leave for 1-2 minutes to cool, then invert the baking tin on to a buttered sheet of greaseproof paper of larger dimensions. Remove the tin, then peel the greaseproof paper off the soufflé. When the soufflé has completely cooled, with a sharp knife trim a 6-mm (1/4-in) strip off the two shorter edges of the soufflé and discard (or eat).

Spread the filling evenly over the surface of the soufflé, leaving a 1-cm (1/2-in) margin free on all edges. With extreme care, prise up one of the longer edges with a piece of greaseproof paper and roll up the soufflé as tightly as possible without breaking it. Lay it delicately, with its flap underneath, on a shallow oval or oblong ovenproof dish. Melt 40 g (1½ oz) of butter and brush the roll all over with it. Bake the roll in a moderate oven (170°C/325°F/Gas mark 3) for 15-20 minutes and serve immediately.

Here are some suggested fillings for the roll. For a soufflé mixture containing:

Cheddar, or Gruyère or half Gruyère and half Parmesan:
150 g (5½ oz) duxelles (p. 365), made with cepes if possible

Fresh goat cheese:
200 g (7 oz) basil and garlic herb cheese (p. 53)

Fresh ewe's-milk cheese:
200 ml (7 fl oz) tomato sauce (p. 364)

Other fillings are possible, of course, using for example some of the ingredients that go into the soufflés that follow – or anything else that takes your fancy, as long as it is not out of key with the cheese.

SMOKED TROUT SOUFFLÉ   FOR 4

This soufflé produces an extraordinarily subtle smoky aroma if you can get hold of properly smoked trout or salmon trout.

50 g (1³/₄ oz) unsalted butter
40 g (1¹/₂ oz) plain flour
310 ml (11 fl oz) milk
3 egg yolks
60 g (2 oz) freshly grated Cheddar *or* Gruyère

freshly grated nutmeg
salt
freshly ground pepper
200 g (7 oz) smoked trout *or* smoked salmon trout
5 egg whites

Make a soufflé mixture as indicated in Cheese soufflé I (p. 133), using Gruyère or Cheddar. Check the saltiness of the smoked fish before adding salt. Flake the fish finely. Incorporate it into the soufflé mixture before folding in the egg whites. Bake in a fairly hot oven (200°C/400°F/Gas mark 6) for a little longer than a normal cheese soufflé, about 35-40 minutes. *Do not open the oven door for at least 25 minutes.* Serve immediately.

The same method can be used to make a Finnan haddock soufflé. Simply replace the smoked trout with the same quantity of good quality poached and flaked haddock (use the milk in which it was poached to make the soufflé mixture).

Equally, you can make a crab soufflé by replacing the trout with an equivalent quantity of crab meat. A can of top-quality crab will do, but because of the soufflé's aroma-enhancing qualities it is more than ever worth going to the trouble of procuring fresh crab (and using both its white and its brown meat).

SPINACH SOUFFLÉ   FOR 4
Yet another successful spinach and cheese marriage.

500 g (1 lb 2 oz) fresh spinach
50 g (1³/₄ oz) unsalted butter
40 g (1¹/₂ oz) plain flour
250 ml (9 fl oz) milk
4 eggs, separated
170 g (6 oz) freshly grated Gruyère

and Parmesan in equal quantities,
or fresh goat cheese or fresh ewe's
  milk cheese
freshly grated nutmeg
salt
freshly ground pepper

Wash and cook the spinach as described on p. 126. Chop finely.

Make a soufflé mixture as indicated in Cheese soufflé II (p. 135), using the cheese(s) listed above. Incorporate the drained spinach into the soufflé mixture before folding in the egg whites. Bake in a fairly hot oven (200°C/400°F/Gas mark 6) for a little longer than a normal cheese soufflé, about 35-40 minutes. *Do not open the oven door for at least 25 minutes*. Serve immediately.

OEUFS À LA CANTALIENNE   FOR 4
An uncharacteristically featherlight dish from the Auvergne.

4 eggs, separated
salt
pinch freshly grated nutmeg
pinch freshly ground pepper

20 g (³/₄ oz) unsalted butter
2 tbsp double cream
100 g (3¹/₂ oz) Cantal

Make sure the eggs are very fresh and brought to room temperature. Separate the egg yolks from the whites carefully so as not to break the yolks, which should be set aside in their half shells. Whisk the egg whites with a small pinch of salt until very stiff. Gently fold in the nutmeg, pepper and some more salt, and transfer to a buttered soufflé dish. Make little hollows on the surface of the beaten egg whites with the back of a spoon, and carefully place an egg yolk in each of them. Dribble the cream over the whole thing and strew with grated Cantal (if the Cantal is too soft to grate, cut into very thin slices and lay on top). Bake in a fairly hot oven (190°C/375°F/Gas mark 5) for 20 minutes or until puffed up and golden brown. Serve immediately.

JERUSALEM ARTICHOKE SOUFFLÉ   FOR 4

The unusual feature of this soufflé is that it contains neither flour nor milk. The Jerusalem artichokes (see p. 294), once puréed and rid of their knobbly, rather earthy appearance, reveal an ethereal subtlety of flavour.

40 g (1½ oz) unsalted butter	4 eggs, separated
450 g (1 lb) Jerusalem artichokes	salt
pinch freshly grated nutmeg	4 extra egg whites
freshly ground pepper	
90 g (3 oz) freshly grated Gruyère	
or Cheddar	

Butter a 1.4-litre (50-fl oz) soufflé mould (for dimensions see p. 133). Wash, peel and halve the artichokes. Plunge into plenty of boiling salted water and cook until just tender (they can equally well be steamed). Blend to a purée and put in a thick-bottomed saucepan with the butter, nutmeg and plenty of pepper. Heat gently, stirring all the time until the butter has melted. Add the cheese and continue stirring until a smooth mixture is obtained. Away from the heat, add 4 egg yolks one by one. Add salt to taste. Whisk 8 egg whites with a pinch of salt until very stiff. Take a large spoonful of the whites, stir quickly into the soufflé mixture to slacken it, then fold in the rest delicately but thoroughly.

Turn the mixture into the soufflé mould and bake immediately in a hot oven (220°C/425°F/Gas mark 7) for about 35 minutes. *Do not open the oven door for at least 25 minutes.* Alternatively, you can put equal quantities of the mixture into four small buttered and floured soufflé moulds and bake for 15-18 minutes. Serve immediately.

HARENG SAUR SOUFFLÉ   FOR 4

This soufflé – it has rather more the texture of a pudding
– contains potato but no flour or milk. It makes a nice
substantial luncheon dish.

1 kg (2¹/₄ lb) floury potatoes
4 fillets *hareng saur*
2 tbsp fresh dill, finely chopped
3 eggs, separated
80 g (3 oz) freshly grated Gruyère *or*
  Cheddar

freshly ground pepper
salt
250 ml (9 fl oz) double cream

Butter a 1.4-litre (50-fl oz) soufflé mould (for dimensions,
see p. 133). Wash the potatoes but do not peel. Cook
uncovered in plenty of boiling *unsalted* water until tender.
Cut up the fish as finely as possible. Peel the potatoes
while still hot and mash thoroughly with the fish. Add the
dill, egg yolks, cheese and plenty of pepper, and beat
vigorously for at least 2 minutes (you can use a blender for
this series of operations if you like). Check seasoning: it
may need a little salt. Whisk the egg whites with a tiny
pinch of salt until very stiff.

Take a large spoonful of the whites and stir quickly into
the potato mixture to slacken it, then fold in the rest
delicately but thoroughly. Turn the mixture into the
soufflé mould and bake immediately in a hot oven (220°C/
400°F/Gas mark 7) for about 35-45 minutes or until
slightly risen and brown on top. *Do not open the oven
door for at least 30 minutes*. Heat the cream to almost
boiling point. Unmould the soufflé, place on a deepish hot
serving dish, and pour the cream over it.

As with other soufflés, you can also make four small
individual soufflés. If you decide to do that, bake for
about 20 minutes; do not unmould the soufflés, stick a
sprig of dill in the top of each one and serve with the hot
cream on the side.

CHEESE PUDDING   FOR 4

'The leaden syllables Cheese Pudding' (Jane Grigson) denote a concoction that, when badly made, deserves to feature in the chamber of horrors of British cooking. It is the archetypal 'slapped together', lazy man's dish.

One such lazy man is Wilson Midgley, author of *Cookery for Men Only, or I.Y.G.T.T.L.A.F.* [if you go to the larder and find] (1948), who deems the cheese pudding far superior to the cheese soufflé. Before explaining, in a perfunctory twenty-seven words, how to rustle up a cheese pudding, Midgley dismisses the merits of the cheese soufflé as follows:

> Do not heed feminine warnings about this. They are couched in terms of steamed soufflés which have been blown up with white of egg, and, under the least provocation or no provocation at all, flop, and in any case must be eaten at once, almost before you get them out of the oven. But most men are not interested in eating air.

Curious how obsessed male British cookery writers seem to be (cf. G. F. Scotson-Clark, p. 137) with the contingent detumescence of the genuine soufflé . . .

Midgley's recipe for cheese pudding relies on the classic ingredients for the dish, but naturally does not require the egg whites to be separated and whisked until stiff. The whisking process, however, greatly improves the end result, as in the recipe below. It comes from *In the Kitchen* (1875) by Elizabeth S. Miller, who 'respectfully' dedicates her book to the cooking class of the Young Ladies' Saturday Morning Club of Boston, Massachusetts. For some reason, she calls her recipe 'Ramakins, or *Ramaquin à la Ude*, Cook to Louis XVI' – yet another connotation of the elusive word ramekin (p. 348); but its ingredients and method are those of a classic cheese pudding.

50 g (2 oz) fresh white breadcrumbs
6 tbsp milk
60 g (2 oz) unsalted butter, softened
$1/3$ tsp mustard
$1/3$ tsp salt

small pinch cayenne
110 g (4 oz) freshly grated strong
  Cheddar
2 eggs, separated

Put the breadcrumbs into the milk and cook for a few minutes, stirring from time to time. Remove from the heat and allow to cool a little. Stir in the butter, mustard, salt, cayenne, cheese and egg yolks, beaten. Whisk the egg whites with a tiny pinch of salt until very stiff. Fold delicately but thoroughly into the mixture. Pour into a lightly buttered pie-dish and bake immediately in a moderate oven (180°C/350°F/Gas mark 4) for about 40 minutes or until risen and golden brown. Serve immediately. 'A delightful dish for tea', remarks the author.

CHEESE BATTER PUDDING   FOR 4

A thrifty recipe from the *Edinburgh Book of Plain Cookery Recipes* (1932).

225 g (8 oz) sifted plain flour
pinch salt
2 eggs

570 ml (20 fl oz) milk
80 g (3 oz) freshly grated Cheddar
25 g (1 oz) lard

'Measure the flour and salt into a basin, make a well in the centre, and drop in the eggs. Add a little milk and draw in the flour gradually, adding enough milk by degrees to make a smooth thick batter. Beat thoroughly till covered with air bubbles. Stir in the cheese and the remainder of the milk. Cover, and leave to soak for 1 hour if possible. Pour into a greased pie-dish or Yorkshire pudding tin, and bake in a hot oven (220°C/425°F/Gas mark 7) for 30-40 minutes till well risen and brown. Serve in the same dish, or cut in pieces and serve on a hot ashet.'

'Ashet', a legacy, like many other Scottish culinary terms,

of the Auld Alliance, means 'a serving dish' and comes from the French *assiette*.

As with Yorkshire pudding, it is best to pre-heat the pie dish or baking tin before pouring in the mixture.

As it stands, this dish is probably better eaten as an accompaniment to, say, roast meat than on its own. If you want to make a light main course of it, add some crumbled crisp-fried bacon or well-sautéd caramelized onions to the batter before baking.

CHAPTER EIGHT

Pasta, Gnocchi and Polenta

Pasta, gnocchi and polenta are examples of the Italians' genius for turning cheaply obtainable starch into a palatable food. In the search for an accompaniment capable of making that food enjoyable as well as palatable, cheese has naturally played an important role: it can provide both lubrication and crispness, but its major contribution is, of course, flavour. The freshly grated Parmesan that the Italians automatically sprinkle on many of their pasta, gnocchi and polenta dishes performs the function almost of a condiment. This chapter, therefore, does not attempt to cover the whole range of dishes where grated Parmesan is used; it restricts itself to those where various cheeses (chiefly Parmesan, ricotta and mozzarella) play a predominant role.

As any Italian will tell you, it is preferable, whenever possible, to use fresh pasta (whether bought or home-made). Both its texture and its flavour are superior to the dried product. More and more shops are selling a variety of types of fresh pasta. And simple pasta-making machines (of the 'wringer' type) are now widely available and within the reach of most pockets. If you are likely to be making pasta regularly, it is worth investing in one of the more sophisticated machines that take in flour and eggs at one end and magically extrude the finished product at the other; they save so much time that they soon pay for themselves. It is also possible to roll out your dough with the help of nothing but a rolling pin, but getting an even thickness requires quite a knack.

BASIC PASTA DOUGH
TO MAKE ABOUT 500 G (1 LB 2 OZ) OF DOUGH

310 g (11 oz) sifted plain flour   3 eggs, beaten
pinch salt

Put almost all the flour on a flat working surface, add the salt and make a well in the middle. Pour the beaten eggs into the well and, using the fingertips, gradually blend with the flour. Work into a ball, scraping up any dough that adheres to the working surface and flouring the surface and your hands as necessary with the rest of the flour. Use your palms and wrists to knead the dough vigorously, stretching it out occasionally, for at least 10 minutes. The dough at this point should be soft, elastic and dry on the surface. If it is sticky, work in a little more flour. Form into a ball, flour lightly and leave for about 20 minutes before rolling out.

If you do not have a hand-operated pasta-making machine, use a rolling pin to make a large circle (or several circles) of dough about 2 mm ($1/12$ in) thick. Make sure the whole area is of exactly equal thickness. Cut as required.

If the number of eggs in proportion to the flour varies in some recipes, proceed in exactly the same way, adding a little water if necessary.

For the more straightforward types of pasta – spaghetti, tagliatelle, lasagne and their relatives – the dried, factory-made product gives perfectly acceptable results as long as you make sure it contains at least 5 eggs per kilogramme ($2^{1}/4$ lb).

The boiling of pasta is simple enough if one or two basic rules are observed. Use large quantities of already boiling, well-salted water – at least 1 litre (35 fl oz) of water per

100 g (3½ oz) of pasta, with about 8 g (¼ oz) of salt per litre added to the water when it boils. The addition of a few drops of oil, as suggested by some authorities, is quite unnecessary.

After putting in the pasta, stir to ensure that it does not stick together, cover, bring back to the boil, take off the lid, stir again and cook vigorously for as long as is necessary to produce an *al dente* texture (this means that the pasta is not yet mushy and offers resistance 'to the tooth'; it must be chewy but without a hint of brittleness).

Fresh pasta takes upwards of only three or four minutes to cook, depending on its thickness. With dried pasta, the suggested cooking time will usually be found on the packet. When it is cooked (the only way to find out is to fish out a piece and bite it to test the texture), put it immediately in a warmed colander just long enough for most, but not all, the cooking water to drain off (the residue helps to keep the pasta moist and hot). If for any reason the pasta has to wait in its cooking water, be it only for a few seconds, add a glassful of cold water to it to stop the cooking process.

Once drained, pasta cools at an alarmingly quick rate, so have both your serving bowl and the plates nice and hot – and your guests ready and waiting. It is better in my view to mix the pasta with its sauce or accompanying ingredients in a very hot serving bowl. If guests have to do their own mixing on their plates, there is a far greater heat loss.

FETTUCCINI AL BURRO   FOR 4

It would be hard to think of a more basic cheese dish. But it is a great standby if you are in a hurry or have not had time to shop (as long as there is some dried fettuccine in your store cupboard and you have taken the precaution, as suggested on p. 25, of stashing away a large hunk of Parmesan in your refrigerator).

400 g (14 oz) fresh fettuccine *or*
  tagliatelle
75 g (2½ oz) unsalted butter

freshly ground pepper
100 g (3½ oz) Parmesan, freshly
  grated

Cook the pasta as indicated on p. 150. While it is cooking, soften the butter in the heated serving dish. Add plenty of pepper. Drain the pasta, turn out into the dish, add the finely grated cheese, mix well and serve immediately. More cheese may be served on the side if desired.

TAGLIATELLE CON PESTO   FOR 4

Of all the dishes calling for that invention of the gods, pesto sauce, this is possibly the one that best sets it off: the low-key pasta offers no competition to or distraction from the symphonic combination of basil, garlic, cheese and pine-nuts.

The recipe here is for tagliatelle, but any type of pasta may be used. In Genoa, the spiritual home of pesto, they prefer trenette (a kind of square-edged spaghetti).

400 g (14 oz) fresh tagliatelle   125 g (4½ oz) pesto sauce (p. 362)

Cook the pasta as indicated on p. 150. While it is cooking, put the pesto sauce in the warmed serving bowl. Drain the pasta and turn out into the bowl, mix well and serve immediately.

TORSETTI AL MASCARPONE E NOCI   FOR 4

Torsetti (also called fusilli, and, in Britain, 'twists') are short screw-shaped pieces of pasta. Thay have the useful ability to attract and retain, by capillary action, liquid sauces like the one described here, which consists mainly of the Italian cream cheese, mascarpone (or mascherpone). Since torsetti cannot, as far as I know, be made with domestic pasta-making machines and are not often found fresh in the shops, you may have to fall back on the dried version – or else use fresh pasta of a different type (in which case the sauce will tend to form a pool in the bottom of the serving bowl).

400 g (14 oz) fresh or dried torsetti	40 g (1¹/₂ oz) walnut pieces, chopped
300 g (10¹/₂ oz) mascarpone	salt
1 clove garlic, finely chopped	freshly ground pepper

Cook the pasta as indicated on p. 150. While it is cooking, put the mascarpone into a small heavy saucepan over a low heat, add the garlic, walnuts, salt to taste and plenty of pepper, and stir until hot and liquid (the mascarpone must not boil). Transfer to a warmed serving bowl, pour the drained pasta over it, mix well and serve immediately. Freshly grated Parmesan may be served on the side if desired.

SPAGHETTI WITH CHICKEN LIVERS AND LEMON   FOR 5

Gremolata, a mixture of finely chopped parsley, garlic and lemon peel, is an essential element of an authentic Milanese *osso buco* (it is sprinkled over it at the last moment). The same wonderfully refreshing, piquant combination of garlic and lemon peel predominates in this highly original recipe, which Elizabeth David hunted down in the Tuscan countryside with her customary flair. It originally appeared in the sixth issue of *Petits Propos Culinaires*, a fascinating series of booklets containing 'essays and notes on food, cookery and cookery books', published by Prospect Books, and was reprinted in *An Omelette and a Glass of Wine*.

Here is how Elizabeth David discovered the dish:

It was given to me some years ago by Giovanna, the young Tuscan girl who cooked it in a country restaurant, now alas vanished, in a remote part of the Chianti district of Tuscany. Far from any town or village, lost among the trees on a gentle hill overlooking a man-made reservoir, the restaurant didn't even have a name. We called it the Lake Place.

There was no telephone. If we wanted to make sure
of a table we would drive up the previous day to
order our meal, but sometimes we would take a
chance, arriving at midday and hoping that Giovanna
would have some of her freshly-made pasta for us.
We were never disappointed. Giovanna was the most
original and gifted pasta cook, and it was on the day
when we had turned up without warning that she
first gave us this delicious dish.

100 g (3¹/₂ oz) chicken livers
  (3 large livers)
150 ml (5 fl oz) olive oil
4-5 cloves garlic
salt
100 g (3¹/₂ oz) lean raw ham
  (*or* coppa)
zest of 1 lemon, coarsely grated
  (without any of the bitter white pith)

freshly ground pepper
1 whole egg
4 egg yolks
200 g (7 oz) freshly grated Parmesan
  or pecorino
large pinch freshly grated nutmeg
500 g (1 lb 2 oz) fresh spaghetti

Cut the cleaned chicken livers into small pieces. Heat the
olive oil in a sauté pan. Crush the garlic with some salt on
a board. Cut the ham into fine strips. Put the chicken livers
into the hot oil, add the ham, garlic, salt, lemon peel and
pepper. The cooking of all these ingredients should take
scarcely 3 minutes. The chicken livers will be spoiled and
tasteless if they are overcooked.

In a mixing bowl, beat the whole egg and the 4 yolks.
Add the finely grated cheese and the nutmeg. Cook the
spaghetti as indicated on p. 150, drain and turn out into a
heated serving bowl. Quickly pour the egg and cheese
mixture into the sauté pan containing the hot olive oil,
chicken livers, garlic and ham. Mix all together very
thoroughly, away from the heat. Now mix the sauce with
the pasta, turning it over and over as if you were mixing a
salad. The eggs cook in the heat from the pasta and hot
oil.

LASAGNA VERDI OÙ FOURN   FOR 6

The title of this recipe for baked green lasagne is written not in one of those weird Italian dialects like Sardinian or Friulian, but in Niçois. The cuisine of Nice, not surprisingly because of its history and proximity to the Italian border, has much in common with that of Italy. But even when using thoroughly Italian ingredients such as pasta, it often adds an individual touch.

This sumptuous dish, which comes from Jacques Médecin's *Cuisine Niçoise*, differs from the classic Bolognese version in that it calls for minced pork as well as raw ham and is enriched with generous amounts of cream and Parmesan. Most definitely a main course.

400 g (14 oz) fresh green lasagne	400 ml (14 fl oz) beef stock
200 g (7 oz) raw ham	200 g (7 oz) very ripe tomatoes,
2 medium-sized onions	peeled, seeded and coarsely
2 small carrots	chopped
2 stalks celery	200 g (7 oz) chicken livers
80 g (3 oz) unsalted butter	pinch freshly grated nutmeg
2 tbsp virgin olive oil	salt
160 g (5 1/2 oz) minced beef	freshly ground pepper
100 g (3 1/2 oz) minced lean pork	200 ml (7 fl oz) double cream
4 tbsp white wine	200 g (7 oz) freshly grated Parmesan

Cook the lasagne for about 3 minutes or until half-cooked (its cooking will be completed in the oven) as indicated on p. 150. To be on the safe side, do this in batches, stirring often and standing poised with a fork to separate the pieces if they try to stick together. Drain and set aside in a bowl of cold water.

Chop the ham, onions, carrots and celery as finely as possible. Melt 50 g (2 oz) of butter gently in a sauté pan. As soon as it stops foaming, add the chopped ingredients and cook for about 10 minutes over a medium heat, stirring often. When the mixture begins to take colour, transfer to a large heavy saucepan. Heat the olive oil in the sauté pan and brown the minced beef and pork, stirring well with a wooden spoon so that no lumps form. Add the white wine, turn up the heat and cook, still stirring, until all the liquid has evaporated. Transfer the meat to the saucepan. Add the beef stock and tomatoes. Bring to the boil, then turn down the heat, cover and leave to simmer for 1 hour, stirring occasionally.

Meanwhile, melt 30 g (1 oz) of butter in the sauté pan and brown the chicken livers gently for a few minutes. Cut them into very small dice and add, along with the nutmeg, salt and pepper, to the sauce in the saucepan after it has been cooking for about 50 minutes. Butter a large gratin dish. Put in a layer of lasagne (about 1 cm/1/2 in deep) and cover with some of the sauce, cream and Parmesan (the exact amount will depend on how many layers of lasagne will fit into the dish). Repeat the operation until all the lasagne is used up, and finish with a layer of sauce and cream. Sprinkle plenty of Parmesan on top.

Bake in a moderate oven (180°C/350°F/Gas mark 4) for between 15 and 30 minutes, depending on the temperature of the sauce when added to the lasagne. Turn up the heat about 5 minutes before serving. When golden brown on top, carry to the table, cut into slices in the dish and serve with a spoon or fish slice.

CANNELLONI CON LA RICOTTA   FOR 4

Home-made cannelloni are much easier to deal with than bought dried cannelloni, whose perfect cigar-like tubes are very tiresome to stuff. If you have to rely on dried pasta for this recipe, it is a better idea to use lasagne pieces, even if they are not quite the proper shape.

1 small onion, finely chopped
1 small carrot, finely chopped
1 stick celery, finely chopped
3 tbsp olive oil
400 g (14 oz) tomato pulp
salt
freshly ground pepper
12 cannelloni squares measuring
  about 12 x 12 cm (5 x 5 in), made
  from a 400-g (14-oz) sheet of
  fresh dough

200 g (7 oz) mozzarella
110 g (4 oz) ham
200 g (7 oz) ricotta, sieved
2 eggs, beaten
pinch freshly grated nutmeg
3 tbsp fresh basil, finely chopped
80 g (3 oz) freshly grated Parmesan

Fry the onion, carrot and celery gently in the oil for a few minutes, stir in the tomato pulp, some salt and plenty of pepper, and simmer, stirring from time to time, for about 20 minutes. If necessary, add 1-2 tablespoons of water during the simmering process. Cook the pasta squares as indicated on p. 150, in batches, for about 3 minutes or until half-cooked, making sure they do not stick together in the water. Drain and lay out to dry on a large cloth or paper towels.

Chop the mozzarella and ham finely, and mix thoroughly with the sieved ricotta, eggs, nutmeg, and a little salt and pepper. Spread this mixture equally over the pasta squares, roll them up in Swiss-roll fashion and place them side by side in a buttered ovenproof dish. Stir the basil into the tomato sauce and pour it over the cannelloni. Sprinkle with Parmesan and bake in a moderate oven (180°C/350°F/Gas mark 4) for about 25 minutes or until golden brown.

MACARONIS AU GRATIN   FOR 4

Macaronis au gratin, a Lyonnais speciality that is also eaten all over France, is the French version of that British wartime staple, macaroni cheese (see following recipe). I remember some years ago making a pilgrimage to Léa Bidaut's restaurant, La Voûte, in the old part of Lyon, in order to taste the cooking of that celebrated *mère lyonnaise*. Despite her fame, her bistro still had a nice, no-nonsense family atmosphere: the wireless was blaring out a football commentary (the 'local' team, Saint-Etienne, was playing a crucial match) and, in between bouts of cooking, Léa would wander into the dining room and comment on the state of play to her waitresses.

Having read that Léa made a delicious *Macaronis au gratin*, I was all the more eager to sample it because of the appalling connotations that macaroni cheese can have for anyone who has experienced British school meals. It came to the table, sizzling hot in a little individual gratin dish, as a separate course in the middle of a substantial meal. I waited expectantly for it to cool a little, and tasted it. What a disappointment! Although rich and creamy and delicious in its way – and naturally an enormous improvement on school macaroni cheese – it struck me as lacking in character. In fact, it had simply been cast in the wrong role: instead of being served on its own, it should have accompanied, say, a *boeuf bourguignon* or a veal stew or some other pillar of *cuisine bourgeoise*. The rest of the meal, by the way, was superb.

The following recipe is for an unassertive macaroni cheese with only a hint of cheese, similar to the one I tasted at La Voûte; it should accompany a meat dish that does not have a creamy sauce.

400 ml (14 fl oz) Mornay sauce I
  (p. 358)
400 g (14 oz) macaroni

80 g (3 oz) unsalted butter
1 clove garlic, finely chopped

Make or re-heat the Mornay sauce. Cook the pasta as indicated on p. 150. Butter a large pre-heated gratin dish. Put the cooked and drained macaroni into it, stir in the rest of the butter, the garlic and the Mornay sauce. Put in a fairly hot oven (200°C/400°F/Gas mark 6) for 15 minutes or until slightly browned.

MACARONI CHEESE   FOR 4

This is a substantial, satisfying dish that bears as little relation to wartime or school-canteen macaroni cheese as foie gras does to liver paste. It is based on the recipe for Maccaroni à la Reine given by Eliza Acton in the first edition of her influential *Modern Cookery for Private Families* (1845).

400 g (14 oz) macaroni	freshly ground white pepper
450 ml (16 fl oz) double cream	large pinch freshly ground mace
300 g (10¹/₂ oz) Cheddar, thinly sliced	(*or* freshly grated nutmeg)
50 g (2 oz) unsalted butter	pinch cayenne
pinch salt	

Cook the pasta as indicated on p. 150. Put the cream in a heavy saucepan and melt the cheese in it over a low heat, stirring all the time. Mix in the butter and seasonings. Put the cooked and drained macaroni into a gratin dish and pour the sauce over it, stirring well until all pockets of air have escaped. Put in a fairly hot oven (200°C/400°F/Gas mark 6) for 15 minutes or until slightly browned.

A nice green salad should come hard on the heels of this very rich dish (viz. the proportions of cheese and cream to pasta). Eliza Acton suggests a variation on this 'very excellent and delicate mode of dressing maccaroni': half the quantity of Stilton 'free from the blue mould', instead of Cheddar, 'would have a good effect in the present receipt'.

MACARONADE   FOR 4

Succulent *Daube à la provençale* or *à la niçoise*, the beef stew that simmers away gently for anything up to six hours, produces a large amount of deep-flavoured juice. This can be mopped up with potatoes – or else used in this *macaronade*, served on the side. Alternatively you can set aside the excess juice from the *daube* for another day, when the *macaronade* can be served on its own as an entrée or light main course.

400 g (14 oz) penne, large macaroni *or* rigatoni	freshly ground pepper
150 g (5¹/₂ oz) freshly grated Parmesan *or* Gruyère	600-900 ml (21-32 fl oz) *jus* (cooking liquid) from a *daube* or similar beef stew

Cook the pasta as indicated on p. 150 until just before the *al dente* stage is reached, and drain. Put a layer of it in a deep gratin dish and sprinkle with cheese and some pepper. Repeat the operation until all the macaroni, but not all the cheese, is used up. Pour in enough hot *daube* juice just to cover the macaroni, sprinkle with the remaining cheese (there should be a generous handful), and put the dish into a hot oven (220°C/425°F/Gas mark 7) for about 10 minutes or until the liquid begins to bubble.

TIMBALE MILANAISE   FOR 6-8

Pasta dishes reached France earlier than they did Britain, but they only really caught on in the eighteenth century, when they began to appear regularly in the cookbooks of Menon, Marin and *Le Cuisinier gascon*. The eighteenth century was also the period when the ragout was in vogue in both France and Britain (this was no banal meat stew, but a rich combination of sometimes exotic ingredients). The two were brought together by the author of *Le Cuisinier gascon* in his recipe for a *pâté de macaronis à l'italienne*, a kind of raised pie containing pasta (in fact, broad ribbons of pasta; macaroni was synonymous with pasta at the time), chopped ham, truffles, mushrooms, beef marrow, butter, cinnamon, Parmesan, beef juice and *coulis*. There was nothing particularly Italian about the dish, the epithet *à l'italienne* (and later *milanaise*) simply serving to indicate the presence of pasta.

In the nineteenth century the more usual term for this kind of pie, because of its shape, was timbale, which also means 'kettledrum' or 'tympanum' in French (curiously, timbale and tympanum are etymologically quite distinct words). Mrs Beeton, introducing her recipe for Timbale milanaise in her *Dictionary of Every Day Cookery*, describes it as an elegant dish [which] belongs to "high-class cooking"'.

When French *grande cuisine* was at its height towards the end of the nineteenth century, Timbale milanaise was a spectacular creation, lavishly decorated with pastry shapes. The version given here is a much less complicated affair, which omits the pastry and the decoration (in other words, it is a kind of mould). It is based on an extraordinarily detailed recipe, covering three and a half large pages, in the form of a report on a cookery lesson by Auguste Colombié, published by the French cookery magazine *Le Pot au feu* in 1900. As Elizabeth David tells us in *French Provincial Cooking*, Colombié was 'one of the great teaching cooks of the latter part of the nineteenth century' and, 'to the great indignation of his professional colleagues ("Giving away professional secrets – we shall be out of work", they said), founded the first cookery school in Paris for *les dames et demoiselles du monde*'.

Some of the ingredients in Timbale milanaise are rather expensive and/or hard to come by. But it makes a spectacular effect at a dinner party, and, as Colombié remarks, 'it is time-consuming but not difficult to make, and almost everything can be prepared the previous day.'

125 g (4¹/₂ oz) sheep's sweetbreads
175 g (6 oz) unsalted butter
60 g (2 oz) cultivated mushrooms
60 g (2 oz) black truffles
3 tbsp white wine
150 ml (5 fl oz) Madeira
125 g (4¹/₂ oz) cockscombs
125 g (4¹/₂ oz) *rognons de coq*
about 250 ml (9 fl oz) *jus* (cooking liquid from a *daube or* similar stew)
1 wing and ¹/₂ breast (i.e. one side) of a chicken, cooked

¹/₄ bay leaf
1 small onion
2 cloves
about 200 g (7 oz) fresh spaghettoni (thick spaghetti)
15 g (¹/₂ oz) plain flour
2 tbsp tomato purée
pinch freshly grated nutmeg
freshly ground pepper
salt
60 g (2 oz) freshly grated Gruyère
60 g (2 oz) freshly grated Parmesan

The Filling

This can be prepared in advance. Soak the sweetbreads in cold water for several hours. Drain, dab dry with a paper towel and cut into dice of about 1 cm (½ in). Heat 50 g (2 oz) of butter in a small frying pan until foaming, and sauté the sweetbreads over a fairly high flame (but without browning the butter) for 4-5 minutes. Drain off any excess butter and set the sweetbreads aside in a mixing bowl.

Wipe the mushrooms clean without peeling them; if you need to dip them in water to remove any sand, do so briefly and only just before cooking them. Chop finely the mushrooms (caps and stalks) and the truffle(s). Put them in a heavy saucepan with the white wine, 3 tablespoons of Madeira, the cockscombs, the *rognons de coq* (along with their jelly if they are canned) and enough of the *jus* to immerse everything. Cover and bring very slowly to the boil. At the first bubble, remove from the heat and leave the ingredients to cool in the liquid.

Skin and bone the chicken pieces and cut into 6-mm (¼-in) dice (this operation is better not carried out in advance).

The Pasta

Put the bay leaf and onion, studded with the cloves, in 2 litres (70 fl oz) of well-salted water. Bring to the boil. After 15 minutes, add the pasta. As soon as the water comes back to the boil, put the saucepan over the lowest heat possible so that it scarcely simmers. Leave the pasta to poach for about 15 minutes (twice as long if dried pasta is used). Drain and lay out on a towel to cool.

Take a mould with a capacity of about 2 litres (70 fl oz), if possible with slightly rounded corners at the bottom. Butter the inside very generously with 50 g (2 oz) of butter. Cover the bottom of the mould with flat coils of pasta; push them close together so there is no gap. Now line the sides of the mould with pasta: take a piece of pasta and lay it round the edge, making it adhere to the butter and overlap on itself; continue with the other pieces, one after the other, so they form a neat spiral up the whole of the inside of the mould. Cut the remaining pasta into 2-cm (1-in) lengths.

The Sauce

Melt 30 g (1 oz) of butter in a heavy saucepan. When it foams, add the flour, turn down the heat to low and cook gently for 2-3 minutes, stirring all the time to keep the mixture smooth. The flour should turn golden but not brown. Add the liquid in which the ingredients of the filling have cooked, the remaining *jus* and the tomato purée. Mix well and bring slowly to the boil. Add the remaining Madeira, the nutmeg and pepper. Move the saucepan partly away from the heat so that the liquid bubbles very gently on only one side. Leave for about 20 minutes, removing from time to time the skin that forms on the side that is not bubbling.

Transfer the sauce to a larger saucepan, add salt if necessary (this will depend on the amount of salt in the *jus* and the jelly from the cans) and mix in the filling (but not the cut-up pasta). Bring almost to the boil, then, away from the heat, add the cheese, the cut-up pasta and the rest of the butter cut into little pieces. Stir until the butter has melted and a smooth mixture is obtained. Turn into the mould, filling it right to the top. Cover with a disc of buttered aluminium foil and place in a fairly hot oven (200°C/400°F/Gas mark 6) for 30 minutes. Leave to settle for 2-3 minutes after removing from the oven, then turn the timbale out on to a warm dish and serve immediately.

You are unlikely to be able to get hold of cockscombs and *rognons de coq* in the required quantities unless you have a very friendly butcher. Canned cockscombs are available, but hard to obtain, in France. In any case, you can make up any shortfall in these two ingredients by increasing the amount of sweetbreads accordingly. If sheep's sweetbreads are unavailable, calf's will do instead.

RAVIOLI CON LA RICOTTA   FOR 6

To people who have never visited Italy ravioli may call to mind mass-produced envelopes of pasta containing preservative-zapped mini-portions of some dubious, dry, vaguely meat-flavoured filling, the whole swathed in a second-rate tomato sauce. Needless to say, such ravioli bear little relation to the home-made thing.

In Italy ravioli and its numerous cousins (tortelli, tortellini, marubini, pansotti, offelle, agnolotti, a(g)nolini, cappelletti) as often as not contain meatless fillings, usually with one or more types of cheese delicately combined with a variety of apposite ingredients. The simplest and most classical of these dishes is Ravioli con la ricotta.

If you are likely to be making ravioli-type pasta frequently, the acquisition of a special metal tray (or trays) divided into serrated ravioli-shaped compartments will prove an undoubted boon. Such trays are available from good kitchen equipment suppliers.

100 g (3¹/₂ oz) freshly grated
  Parmesan
300 g (10¹/₂ oz) ricotta, sieved
2 eggs
salt
freshly ground pepper
a sheet of fresh pasta made with
  400 g (14 oz) flour and 3 eggs
  (p. 150)

1 egg, beaten with a few drops
  of water
90 g (3 oz) unsalted butter
5 leaves fresh sage, chopped

For the filling, put 50 g (2 oz) of Parmesan, the ricotta, 2 eggs, salt and pepper into a mixing bowl and blend well. Lay the sheet of pasta on a lightly floured surface. Place little dollops of filling (1 well-heaped teaspoon each) in a straight line about 5 cm (2 in) apart and about 5 cm (2 in) from the edge of the pasta sheet. Brush the outer uncovered strip of pasta with beaten egg and fold over the fillings, pressing down between each lump. Using a pastry wheel, cut the half-formed ravioli free from the rest of the sheet of pasta, then complete the operation by cutting crosswise between each lump. Press down all the cut edges to make sure they adhere well.

If using a ravioli tray, cut the sheet of pasta in half. Flour one sheet lightly and place, floured side down, on the tray, pressing it down into each compartment. Spoon the filling into the compartments. Place the other sheet of pasta on the tray; run a rolling pin over the top and – hey presto! – the ravioli are made (little teeth on the tray sever them from each other).

As you make the ravioli, transfer them to a lightly floured tea-towel; do not allow them to touch each other. Boil in plenty of salted water until *al dente* (10-15 minutes); test to make sure that the serrated edge of the ravioli, where there is a double thickness, is cooked. Remove with a slotted spoon and transfer to a colander. When drained, lay the ravioli in a very hot deep serving dish. Heat the butter to the point when it is just beginning to change colour, stir in the sage, and pour immediately over the ravioli. Sprinkle with the remaining Parmesan and serve immediately.

TORTELLI DI ZUCCA   FOR 6

A recipe from the region of Modena, in Emilia Romagna. The use of macaroons in a savoury dish provides an unusual medieval touch. Tortelli are a form of ravioli that may be square, crescent shaped or triangular.

1 kg (2¹/₄ lb) pumpkin
150 g (5¹/₂ oz) freshly grated
  Parmesan
50 g (2 oz) toasted breadcrumbs
50 g (2 oz) very dry macaroons
  (*amaretti*), crushed
1 egg
pinch freshly grated nutmeg

pinch salt
freshly ground pepper
a sheet of fresh pasta made with
  400 g (14 oz) flour and 3 eggs
  (p. 150)
1 egg, beaten with a few drops of
  water
90 g (3 oz) unsalted butter

Slice the pumpkin, remove the seeds and cottony fibre (but not the skin) and bake in a hot oven until soft. Peel, cut into dice, put into a mixing bowl and mash thoroughly. Add the cheese, breadcrumbs, macaroons, egg, nutmeg, salt and pepper, and mix well. Using this mixture and the sheet of pasta, make, cook and drain the tortelli according to the same procedure as for the ravioli in the preceding recipe. Lay the tortelli in a very hot deep serving dish. Pour melted butter over them, and serve immediately.

In Emilia Romagna this dish is sometimes accompanied by a *ragù* (the true Bolognese sauce of spaghetti bolognese), but in my view it does very well on its own.

TORTELLI CON BIETOLE   FOR 6
This dish can take two forms: one includes chopped ham and/or chicken in the filling, and the other (given here) is a meatless, Lenten version.

900 g (2 lb) Swiss chard tops, washed and trimmed of their ribs
300 g (10¹/₂ oz) ricotta, sieved
60 g (2 oz) freshly grated Parmesan
2 eggs
salt
freshly ground pepper
pinch freshly grated nutmeg

a sheet of fresh pasta made with 400 g (14 oz) flour and 3 eggs (p. 150)
1 egg, beaten with a few drops of water
90 g (3 oz) unsalted butter
5 leaves fresh sage, chopped

Boil the Swiss chard tops in a very little salted water until tender, drain, chop finely and press out as much moisture as possible. Put into a mixing bowl with the ricotta, Parmesan, 2 eggs, salt, pepper and nutmeg. Mix thoroughly. Using this mixture and the sheet of pasta, make, cook and drain the tortelli according to the same procedure as for the ravioli on p. 165. Lay the tortelli in a very hot deep serving dish. Heat the butter to the point when it is just beginning to change colour, stir in the sage, pour over the tortelli and serve immediately.

If Swiss chard is unavailable, spinach may be used instead. The tortelli will taste distinctly different, but equally good.

MARUBINI   FOR 6

A rich dish from the Cremona region in Lombardy. Strictly speaking marubini are a round kind of ravioli. But, not wishing to embark on another description of how to make filled pasta, I suggest you follow the basic procedure for ravioli already described and make square marubini. As I have already remarked, taste is not affected by shape.

110 g (4 oz) freshly grated Parmesan	2 eggs
200 g (7 oz) toasted breadcrumbs	pinch salt
pinch freshly grated nutmeg	freshly ground pepper
a sheet of fresh pasta made with	1 egg, beaten with a few drops
400 g (14 oz) flour and 3 eggs	of water
(p. 150)	90 g (3 oz) unsalted butter
75 g (2¹/₂ oz) beef marrow	

In a mixing bowl put the Parmesan, breadcrumbs, melted beef marrow, 2 eggs, salt, pepper and nutmeg. Mix thoroughly. Using this mixture and the sheet of pasta, make, cook and drain the marubini according to the same procedure as for the ravioli described on p. 165. Lay the marubini in a very hot deep serving dish. Pour melted butter over the marubini. Serve immediately, with more Parmesan on the side.

HUNGARIAN NOODLES WITH DILL   FOR 4

Pasta found its way from Italy to Hungary, as well as to France and Britain, at a very early date. It is believed to have been brought there by Beatrice, the Italian bride of Matthias Corvinus, King of Hungary and Bohemia, in the fifteenth century. But soon pasta dishes were given a distinctive non-Italian flavour by local ingredients, such as those used in this recipe (lard, soured cream, dill).

Hungarian noodles are normally made with fewer eggs

than the Italian original, but fresh tagliatelle will serve perfectly well. If making the pasta dough yourself, use a proportion of 1 egg to 400 g (14 oz) of flour.

30 g (1 oz) lard	freshly ground pepper
200 g (7 oz) ewe's-milk curd cheese *or* ricotta	400 g (14 oz) fresh flat noodles *or* tagliatelle
4 tbsp soured cream	3 tbsp fresh dill, finely chopped
salt	

Put the lard, cheese, soured cream, salt to taste and pepper into a serving bowl. Warm in a slow oven until the lard has melted. Stir well and leave in the oven until the noodles are ready. Cook and drain the noodles as indicated for pasta on p. 150. Turn out into the serving bowl, add the dill, mix thoroughly and serve immediately.

SAVOURY PIEROGI WITH CHEESE   FOR 4

These are a Polish version of ravioli made with a dough that contains buckwheat flour but no eggs. Like their Italian counterparts, *pierogi* can be filled with almost anything: cabbage and mushrooms, sauerkraut and mushrooms, minced beef, kasha, bilberries or curd cheese. For a sweet version of *pierogi* with cheese, see p. 343.

175 g (6 oz) buckwheat flour	1 egg, beaten with a few drops of water
225 g (8 oz) plain wheat flour	
salt	50 g (2 oz) unsalted butter
250 g (9 oz) well-drained curd cheese	250 g (9 oz) soured cream
1 egg yolk	

Put the sifted buckwheat flour into a mixing bowl and add, by degrees, about 150 ml (5 fl oz) of boiling water, kneading all the time. Add the wheat flour and a pinch of salt, and continue to knead until a smooth dough is obtained. Roll out or put through a pasta-making machine: the sheet of dough should be slightly thicker than that of Italian pasta.

Beat the cheese with the egg yolk and a pinch of salt. Using this mixture and the sheet of dough, make, cook and drain the *pierogi* according to the same procedure as for ravioli (p. 165). Lay them in a very hot deep serving dish and pour melted butter over them. Serve with soured cream on the side.

GNOCCHI ALLA PIEMONTESE   FOR 4

Broadly speaking, gnocchi can be made with flour and potato, flour and milk, semolina or even maize flour. This very simple recipe from Piedmont combines potato gnocchi with the local cheese, fontina. Precisely because of its simplicity, it is worth hunting down some really tasty potatoes, which can make a useful contribution to the final result. Making gnocchi, like pasta, is very labour-intensive, and if you are thinking of making them regularly it is worth investing in a gnocchi-making machine.

1 kg ($2^1/4$ lb) best potatoes	1 egg yolk
salt	about 300 g ($10^1/2$ oz) plain flour
freshly grated nutmeg	200 g (7 oz) fontina

Boil the potatoes in their skins. Peel and mash them in a mixing bowl. Add salt to taste, nutmeg, the egg yolk and, little by little, the flour, first mixing it in with a fork, then kneading the mixture with the fingers until a soft but unsticky dough is obtained. Add a little extra water if necessary to make it hold together. Roll the dough, piece by piece, into several long sausage-like lengths about 2.5 cm (1 in) thick. Cut these crosswise into sections about 3.5 cm ($1^1/2$ in) thick, and bend each piece slightly round your finger into the shape of a comma. Lay the gnocchi on a lightly floured tea towel as you make them, being careful not to let them touch each other, and leave them to dry for about 30 minutes.

Bring plenty of salted water to the boil in a broad saucepan and drop in the gnocchi in batches. Keep the water on a gentle boil. The gnocchi are done 3-4 minutes after they float to the surface. Take them out with a slotted spoon, drain and arrange in a gratin dish, making alternate layers of gnocchi and slivers of fontina as the batches are cooked. Finish with a layer of cheese, and put into a fairly hot oven (190°C/375°F/Gas mark 5) for about 15 minutes or until golden brown.

These gnocchi are nice served with tomato sauce (p. 364) on the side.

CROZETS   FOR 6

National borders tend to run along natural frontiers such as rivers and mountain ranges. But common cultural and culinary features are often found on both sides of the divide, either because of a common heritage or because of shifting political borders. Northern France's Mimolette cheese, which is very similar to Gouda, shows the influence of Flemish occupation. Vacherin and Gruyère-type cheeses are found on both sides of the Franco-Swiss border. So it is no surprise to find, in the upper Dauphiné just over the French border from Val d'Aosta (home of the preceding recipe), another kind of potato gnocchi dish with cheese, *crozets*. There is a major difference, however: *crozets* call for a local blue cheese, Bleu de Sassenage.

600 g (1 lb 5 oz) potatoes	about 400 g (14 oz) plain flour
4 eggs	125 g (4½ oz) Bleu de Sassenage,
2 tsp walnut oil	crumbled
salt	125 g (4½ oz) freshly grated
freshly ground pepper	Gruyère

Boil the potatoes in their skins. Peel and mash them in a mixing bowl. Add the eggs, oil, salt, pepper and flour, mixing well until a soft but unsticky dough is obtained. Add a little extra water if necessary to make it hold together. Roll the dough, piece by piece, into long sausage-like lengths about 2.5 cm (1 in) thick. Cut these crosswise into sections about 3.5 cm (1½ in) thick, and bend each piece slightly round your finger into the shape of a comma. Lay the gnocchi on a lightly floured tea towel as you make them, being careful not to let them touch each other, and leave them to dry for about 30 minutes.

Bring plenty of salted water to the boil in a broad saucepan and drop in the *crozets* in batches. Keep the water on a gentle boil. The *crozets* are done 3-4 minutes after they float to the surface. Take them out with a slotted spoon, drain and arrange in a gratin dish, making alternate layers of *crozets*, blue cheese and Gruyère as the batches are cooked. Finish with a layer of Gruyère and put in a fairly hot oven (190°C/375°F/Gas mark 5) for about 15 minutes or until golden brown.

If you cannot obtain Bleu de Sassenage, you can make do with Bleu de Gex from the Jura or, indeed, any other mild creamy blue cheese.

GNOCCHI À LA FRANÇAISE   FOR 4

The first mention of gnocchi in France was in *Le Cuisinier gascon*, where they appear as *nioc*. But they did not catch on until the second half of the nineteenth century, when they were described variously, by chefs and cookbook writers, as *nioki*, *niokys*, *niocchi*, *nioccki*, *gnoki*, *gnoquis*, *gniocchi* and *gnocci*. Such quaint spellings must, one imagines, have resulted from French chefs hearing the words in Italian kitchens or restaurants and trying, desperately, to find a phonetic equivalent; nineteenth-century France was also introduced to some British dishes camouflaged as *misies paës* (mince pies), *plumbuting* and *wouelsche rabette* (p. 82).

The French have another dish, called *noques*, which is also often eaten in a gratin with a cheese sauce, and which, if the *Dictionnaire de l'Académie des Gastronomes* is to be believed, is not yet another misspelling of gnocchi but derives from the German word for dumpling, *Knödeln* – not to be confused with *Nudeln* (noodles). It is from *Knödeln* that the quenelle-like *knepfs* or *knèfles* of Alsace are derived (they are thought to have originated in Jewish cooking). Farther east, and all the way to Moscow, there are countless other similar concoctions, many of them very stodgy, which are served with cheese, curds or soured cream, and the full range of which this book cannot begin to embrace.

Although potato gnocchi (see the two preceding recipes) are sometimes eaten by the French, they tend to prefer the flour-milk-and-egg version given here.

300 ml (10 fl oz) milk	large pinch salt
200 ml (7 fl oz) double cream	pinch cayenne
150 g (5¹/₂ oz) flour	pinch freshly grated nutmeg
3 eggs	350 ml (12 fl oz) Mornay sauce I
3 egg yolks	(p. 358)

Put the milk and cream in a saucepan with the salt, cayenne, nutmeg and pepper. Bring to the boil, remove from the heat and pour in the flour in one go, stirring immediately and vigorously to prevent lumps from forming. Put the pan back on a moderate heat and cook, stirring all the time, until the mixture begins to leave the sides of the pan. Again remove from the heat, then blend the eggs and egg yolks one after the other. Make or re-heat the Mornay sauce.

Bring plenty of salted water to the boil in a broad saucepan. Put the dough into a forcing bag with a plain round nozzle about 1 cm (¹/₂ in) in diameter. Squeeze out knobs of dough about 2 cm (1 in) long into the water, cutting them off with a knife. Dip the knife in the water from time to time so the dough does not stick to it. Simmer the gnocchi for about 4 minutes or until they begin to swell. Take them out with a slotted spoon, drain and arrange in a warm gratin dish. Smother in hot Mornay sauce and put under a medium grill until slightly browned.

POLENTA ALLA FRUMENTINO   FOR 4
A cheap and filling peasant dish from northern Italy that relies on that well-tried combination, anchovies and mozzarella.

250 g (9 oz) maize flour	175 g (6 oz) mozzarella
80 g (3 oz) anchovies	freshly ground pepper
115 g (4 oz) unsalted butter	

Bring 1 litre (35 fl oz) of salted water to the boil and pour in the maize flour. Stir until smooth, then cook over a low heat, stirring constantly, for about 20 minutes or until the mixture is quite thick and begins to come away from the sides of the pan. Turn it out on to a moistened marble slab or large board. Using a spatula dipped frequently in hot water, spread it out evenly to a thickness of about 1 cm (1/2 in). Leave to cool.

Desalt the anchovies in warm water, dab dry with paper towels and chop coarsely. Butter a gratin dish and melt the rest of the butter. Cut the polenta into smallish squares and put one layer of them, overlapping each other, on the bottom of the gratin dish. Strew with anchovies and thin slices of mozzarella, pour over some melted butter and add plenty of pepper. Repeat the operation until all the polenta is used up, finishing with mozzarella and butter. Put into a fairly hot oven (190°C/375°F/Gas mark 5) for about 15 minutes or until golden brown.

POLENTA ALLA PIEMONTESE   FOR 4
This method of treating polenta, which is similar to the last but uses different and richer ingredients, is called *pasticciata* (pie) in Piedmont, but it is in fact a gratin.

250 g (9 oz) maize flour	80 g (3 oz) freshly grated Parmesan
80 g (3 oz) unsalted butter	15 g (1/2 oz) white truffle, cut into
250 g (9 oz) fontina	paper-thin slivers

Make the polenta as described in the preceding recipe.

When cool, cut into smallish squares and put one layer of them, overlapping each other, on the bottom of a buttered gratin dish. Cover with thin slices of fontina, some grated Parmesan and butter cut into small pieces. Repeat the operation until all the polenta is used up, finishing with a layer of fontina and pieces of butter. Put into a fairly hot oven (190°C/375°F/Gas mark 5) for about 20 minutes or until golden brown. Strew the top with shavings of truffle and serve.

CHAPTER NINE

Pancakes

The principle involved here – of a rather tasteless starchy envelope enclosing a tasty filling – is the same as for ravioli, pasties, turnovers and their relatives. But stuffed pancakes have an important advantage: they are much more quickly and more easily prepared. It does not matter if they leak, since they were never supposed not to, and they can easily be kept warm or cooked in advance and stuffed at the last moment.

A few basic rules should be observed when making pancakes.

1. Leave the batter to stand in a cool place for at least 2 hours before use.

2. Use a thick pan, if possible a special crêpe pan, so the heat is distributed evenly. Barely grease it, by wiping, for example, with a piece of paper towel dipped in oil or clarified butter (unclarified butter burns very easily).

3. Have the pan nice and hot before pouring in the first ladleful (or half-ladleful) of batter. Tip the pan so the batter is distributed evenly, then turn down the heat to medium while cooking.

4. When little holes appear on the surface of the pancake, turn it over with a palette knife or fish slice, or by pulling one side of it up towards you with your fingers and flipping it over. Cook only for about 30 seconds on the other side. Pancake-tossing should be left to the experts, and even then there may be problems: Paul Levy

tells, in his amusing *Out to Lunch*, how the very expert cook and cookbook writer Julia Child tried, 'in an act of sheer hubris' on television, to toss a gigantic potato crêpe, which remain lodged in the studio rafters.

QUARKPFANNKUCHEN   FOR 4
Delicious, if bland, German curd-cheese pancakes.

130 g (4¹/₂ oz) fairly liquid curd cheese	pinch salt
90-120 ml (3-4 fl oz) milk	freshly ground pepper
120 g (4 oz) sifted plain flour	4 eggs, beaten
	oil or clarified butter for frying

Beat the cheese and milk together until a smooth and rather liquid consistency is obtained (the amount of milk will depend on how liquid the cheese is; if making the cheese yourself, you can ensure that it remains fairly liquid). Pour the mixture, along with the flour, salt, pepper and eggs, into a blender and blend for 1 minute. Pour into a bowl, cover and leave in a cool place for 2 hours. Cook the pancakes in the usual way.

A good accompaniment to roast meat.

A very similar dish, called *sanciaux au fromage*, is made in central France in the Berry, the Nivernais and the Bourbonnais.

PANNEQUETS AU FROMAGE   FOR 4
Pannequet is one of several English culinary terms that chefs, who were often illiterate, phonetically transcribed into the French language in the eighteenth century (see also p. 171). No prizes, in this context, for guessing what the English original was.

140 ml (5 fl oz) milk
3 eggs
$1/2$ tsp salt
150 g ($5^1/2$ oz) sifted plain flour
2 tbsp oil

oil or clarified butter for frying
400 ml (14 fl oz) Mornay sauce V
(p. 359)
80 g (3 oz) freshly grated Gruyère

Put the milk, an equal amount of water, the eggs, salt, flour and oil into a blender and blend for 1 minute. Pour into a bowl, cover and leave in a cool place for 2 hours. Cook 8 pancakes in the usual way.

Make or re-heat the Mornay sauce. Spoon some of it on to each pancake and roll up. Arrange the pancakes in one layer in a large buttered gratin dish, sprinkle with grated cheese, and bake in a hot oven (220°C/425°F/Gas mark 7) for 15 minutes or until the surface has begun to turn golden brown.

BARLEY PANCAKES WITH CHEESE   FOR 4

A felicitous invention of Elizabeth David's, from her encyclopaedic *English Bread and Yeast Cookery*.

420 ml (15 fl oz) milk
85 g (3 oz) strong plain flour
85 g (3 oz) barley flour
15 g ($1/2$ oz) yeast
4 eggs

oil or clarified butter for frying
225 g (8 oz) Cheddar
freshly ground pepper
pinch freshly grated nutmeg
40 g ($1^1/2$ oz) unsalted butter

Warm 280 ml (10 fl oz) of the milk. Put the two flours together in a bowl, add the salt and mix well. Cream the yeast with a little of the warmed milk, add it to the flour, then mix to a batter with the rest of the warmed milk. Cover the bowl and leave to rise for one hour or a little longer, until the batter is spongy and bubbly.

Beat in the eggs and then the rest of the milk, which does not have to be warmed. Again cover the bowl and leave the batter to rise for the second time, for another hour, or longer if necessary.

Cook the pancakes in the usual way. The quantities

given will make a dozen or more very thin 18-cm (7-in) pancakes.

Cut the cheese into sticks about 2 cm (1 in) wide. Put 2 of these portions of cheese on each pancake, seasoning with pepper and nutmeg. Arrange the pancakes one on top of the other in a shallow round gratin dish. Pour over them a little melted butter.

Put in the centre of a moderately heated oven (180°C/350°F/Gas mark 4) for about 15 minutes, or until the cheese begins to melt and the pancakes are well heated through.

'Barley flour has a very particular flavour, earthy and rather primitive', says Elizabeth David. 'I like it very much, but it's not to everyone's taste.' I, for one, share her liking for it.

She also says that the cheese used for the filling does not have to be Cheddar. Other English cheeses, such as Double Gloucester, Lancashire or Wensleydale, do very well. So does a soft melting cheese such as Port Salut or Bel Paese. She adds that as she invented these cheese-filled barley pancakes herself, 'there is no sacred tradition involved'.

PANCAKES STUFFED WITH CHEESE AND HAM   FOR 4
This recipe from the Bernese Alps is a superior version of *crêpes au jambon*, that classic of French everyday cooking that has now, in its frozen form, become God's gift to working mothers, canteen managers and lazy restaurateurs.

140 ml (5 fl oz) milk	oil or clarified butter for frying
3 eggs	400 ml (14 fl oz) Mornay sauce I
1/2 tsp salt	(p. 358) made with only
150 g (51/2 oz) sifted plain flour	250 ml (9 fl oz) milk
2 tbsp oil	5 tbsp dry white wine
80 g (3 oz) unsalted butter	pinch cayenne
8 very thin slices raw smoked Swiss	120 g (4 oz) Gruyère, diced
ham, or similar raw ham	80 g (3 oz) freshly grated Gruyère

Put the milk, an equal amount of water, the eggs, salt, flour and oil into a blender and blend for 1 minute. Pour into a bowl, cover and leave to stand in a cool place for 2 hours.

Melt some unsalted butter in a large pan and cook the slices of ham gently for 1-2 minutes each on one side only, adding more butter as necessary. Cook 8 pancakes in the usual way in oil or clarified butter. Make or re-heat the Mornay sauce. Pour the wine into it, add the cayenne and stir over a low heat for 2-3 minutes. On each pancake, put a slice of ham, a little Mornay sauce and some diced cheese. Roll up the pancakes, lay in a buttered shallow gratin dish, cover with the rest of the sauce and sprinkle with grated cheese. Bake in a fairly hot oven (200°C/400°F/Gas mark 6) for 20 minutes or until the surface begins to turn golden brown.

ENTRÉE SUZETTE   FOR 4

Another unusual recipe from *Les Recettes des 'Belles Perdrix'* (p. 36).

140 ml (5 fl oz) milk	7 thin slices ham
3 eggs	7 thin slices *langue écarlate* (cured
1/2 tsp salt	tongue)
150 g (5 1/2 oz) sifted plain flour	200 g (7 oz) Gruyère, very thinly
2 tbsp oil	sliced
oil or clarified butter for frying	

Put the milk, an equal amount of water, the eggs, salt, flour and oil into a blender and blend for 1 minute. Pour into a bowl, cover and leave to stand in a cool place for 2 hours. Cook 8 pancakes in the usual way.

Place 1 pancake in a buttered round gratin dish only slightly larger than the pancakes, followed by a slice of ham, a slice of tongue and some slivers of cheese. Make a pile of pancakes in the dish by repeating the operation 7 times, finishing with a pancake and a topping of cheese. Put into a moderate oven (180°C/350°F/Gas mark 4) for

25-30 minutes or until the cheese has begun to ooze out and the topping is golden brown. Serve by cutting into segments like a cake.

FRIED CHEESECAKES   FOR 4

These 'cheesecakes' from rural New England are in fact very light savoury pancakes. The lemon-rind and cheese combination is a novel one.

60 g (2 oz) sifted plain flour	freshly ground pepper
1 tsp lemon zest (without any bitter white pith), finely grated	200 ml (7 fl oz) soured cream
175 g (6 oz) freshly grated Cheddar	4 egg yolks, beaten
large pinch salt	oil or clarified butter for frying

Put the flour, lemon zest, cheese, salt and pepper into a mixing bowl. Blend, then add the soured cream and egg yolks. Beat until thoroughly mixed. Cover and leave to stand in a cool place for 2 hours. Cook the pancakes in the usual way.

In New England these 'cheesecakes' often accompany grilled bacon or ham.

CRESPÉOU AÏ MUSCLÉ   FOR 4

These are Niçois pancakes stuffed with cheese and mussels, from Jacques Médecin's *Cuisine Niçoise*. The Niçois word *crespéou*, the Italian *crespolini*, the French *crêpes* and the old English 'crisps' or 'cresps' all mean 'pancakes'. They derive from the Latin adjective *crispus*, which means 'wrinkled', 'crinkled' or 'curled' ('crisp' is still used in this sense in English to describe curly hair). But to most British minds, of course, a crisp nowadays denotes a sliver of deep-fried potato (often, alas, denatured with onion and/or cheese and/or vinegar flavouring, monosodium glutamate, E260, E262, E330, etc., etc.).

120 g (4 oz) sifted plain flour
30 g (1 oz) cornflour
2 whole eggs
5 tbsp milk
1 onion, sliced
1 clove garlic, finely chopped
2 tbsp fresh parsley, coarsely chopped
1 litre (scant 2 pints) mussels
1/4 tsp salt

1/4 tsp baking powder
3 tbsp virgin olive oil
oil *or* clarified butter for frying
30 g (1 oz) unsalted butter
1 egg yolk
120 g (4 fl oz) double cream
freshly ground white pepper
100 g (3 1/2 oz) freshly grated
Parmesan

Put 100 g (3 1/2 oz) of flour, the cornflour, salt, baking powder, 2 tablespoons of olive oil and 2 eggs into a bowl and mix thoroughly. Gradually add the milk diluted with 5 tablespoons of water until a smooth batter is obtained. Cover and leave to stand in a cool place for 2 hours.

Bring 250 ml (9 fl oz) of water to the boil in a large saucepan with the onion, garlic and parsley. Add the scrubbed and bearded mussels, cover and cook over a high heat for 3 minutes, shaking frequently. Remove mussels with a perforated spoon, discarding any that have refused to open. Cover and simmer the liquid for 20 minutes. You should have about 250 ml (9 fl oz) of liquid after this reduction (the mussels give off some liquid): if the quantity is less, make it up with water; if more, reduce uncovered. Keep the liquid hot. Shell the mussels and set aside in a bowl.

Cook the pancakes in the usual way and keep warm. Heat the butter in a small thick-bottomed saucepan, stir in the rest of the flour and cook over a slow heat for 2-3 minutes without browning. Strain the mussels' hot cooking liquid into the pan, whisk well and leave over a very low heat. Put the egg yolk, cream, plenty of pepper and three-quarters of the cheese into a bowl and mix well. Add gradually to the sauce, away from the heat, beating well until smooth. Stir in the mussels gently. Check seasoning.

Put 2 tablespoons of filling on to each pancake, roll up and arrange in an oiled gratin dish large enough to take all the pancakes in a single layer. Cover with the remaining sauce, sprinkle with the rest of the cheese and bake in a hot oven (220°C/425°F/Gas mark 7) for 10-15 minutes or until the surface begins to turn brown.

QUESADILLAS   FOR 4

There are countless versions of these Mexican snacks, which consist simply of a folded-over tortilla with a filling. Very often the filling contains cheese. A particular favourite is Oaxaca, rich spun-curd cheese with good melting properties.

250 g (9 oz) Oaxaca, young provolone *or* mozzarella

2 tbsp fresh *epazote or* fresh coriander leaves, finely chopped

2 (poblano) chillies, peeled and cut into strips

8 frozen uncooked tortillas, defrosted

oil for frying

Place equal portions of the cheese, *epazote* and chillies on one half of each tortilla, not too near the edge. Fold over and press down the edges of the dough. Cook for about 2 minutes on each side in hot oil at least 1 cm (1/2 in) deep. Drain on paper towels and serve immediately.

ATAÏF WITH CHEESE   FOR 4

A recipe from Claudia Roden's *A New Book of Middle Eastern Food*, surely the definitive work on the subject. Normally *ataïf* (pancakes) are served sweet. However, she says, 'a more uncommon but most excellent way of preparing them is to stuff them with cheese.'

15 g (1/2 oz) yeast

225 g (8 oz) plain flour

1 tsp salt

oil for frying

250 g (9 oz) halumi *or* mozzarella

Dissolve the yeast in 120 ml (4 fl oz) of lukewarm water. Allow it to stand in a warm place for 10 minutes or until it begins to bubble. Sift the flour into a large bowl. Add the salt and the yeast mixture and work it into the flour.

Add about 300 ml (10 fl oz) of lukewarm water gradually, stirring constantly until the batter is smooth. Cover and leave to stand in a warm place for about 1 hour. The soft, almost liquid batter will rise and become bubbly and a little elastic.

Cook the pancakes in the usual way in a little oil. The batter will remain in a small, round, fattish shape. (Do not try to spread it out too much.) When the pancake loses its whiteness, becomes bubbly and comes away from the pan easily, lift it out with a palette knife (*ataïf* for stuffing are cooked on one side only.)

Put a small slice of cheese on one side of each pancake, fold over and seal by pressing down. Deep-fry in hot oil until golden and drain well on paper towels. Serve hot or cold, preferably hot.

Claudia Roden gives two other fillings for the pancakes:

250 g (9 oz) freshly grated Wensleydale, Gouda, Edam *or* Canadian Cheddar, mixed with 1 egg and black pepper to taste; *or* 250 g (9 oz) crumbled feta seasoned with white pepper and mixed with a few finely chopped chives.

I prefer to fry these pancakes in plenty of oil in a frying pan rather than deep-fry them.

NORTH STAFFORDSHIRE OATCAKES
WITH CHEESE AND ONIONS   FOR 4

To me, the smell of toasted oatmeal brings back memories of the scrumptious oatmeal-coated grilled herrings that my mother often used to cook for us during the lean post-war years. But I am not alone in finding the smell of toasted oatmeal particularly evocative. Philip Oakes's autobiography, *From Middle England*, contains a vivid passage in which he describes how, as a boy in the Potteries, he would stand outside the oatcake shop for an hour at a time watching the man inside making 'a tender, tottering pile' of oatcakes, while 'the mouthwatering smell of toasted oatmeal seeped under the shop door'.

North Staffordshire oatcakes (nothing like the much harder, crumbly Scottish variety) are one of the very few regional English specialities that have held their own against the food industry's attempts to make everything taste the same. A pity, then, as Eleanor Fishman remarks in her interesting booklet on the subject, *The Staffordshire Oatcake Recipe Book*, that such oatcakes are still little known outside North Staffordshire and Derbyshire, and that the number of oatcake shops there has diminished since Philip Oakes's childhood.

Fortunately, oatcakes are easy to make oneself. They go particularly well with cheese, as in this recipe, based on one in Fishman's book. In it, the onions make a vital contribution, in rather the same way that they do in some kebabs: subjected briefly to the heat of the grill, they only half-cook, and are at once crunchy, sharp and caramelly.

115 g (4 oz) fine oatmeal	1/2 tsp sugar
115 g (4 oz) plain flour	oil *or* clarified butter for frying
1/2 tsp salt	200 g (7 oz) freshly grated Cheshire
225 ml (8 fl oz) milk	salt
7 g (1/4 oz) fresh yeast	freshly ground pepper

Sift the oatmeal and flour into a warm basin. Add the salt and stir well. Mix the milk with an equal amount of water and heat until lukewarm. Dissolve the yeast in a little of the liquid and add the sugar. Set aside in a warm place for a few minutes to rise. Pour the yeast mixture and the liquid into the flour and mix well. Cover and leave in a warm place for about 1 hour.

Make 8 small or 4 large oatcakes. Cook them on both sides like pancakes on a well-greased bakestone (if you are lucky enough to have one) or in a heavy frying pan. Put the oatcakes under the grill to toast slightly on one side. Spread grated cheese on the untoasted side and sprinkle with chopped onion, a little salt and plenty of pepper. Put under not too fierce a grill until the cheese has thoroughly melted and the onions are just beginning to brown. Serve immediately as they are, or folded over.

CHAPTER TEN

Pies and Tarts

CALZONI

Calzoni are a kind of turnover much appreciated in the Naples area. They are made with the same dough as that of another Neapolitan speciality – which has made its way in the world – the pizza.

15 g (1/2 oz) fresh yeast
375 g (13 oz) sifted plain flour
1 tsp salt
4 tbsp virgin olive oil
150 g (51/2 oz) mozzarella,
  cut into slivers

120 g (4 oz) good salami, thinly sliced
  and coarsely chopped
1 clove garlic, finely chopped
1 egg, beaten

Dissolve the yeast in a little warm water. Put the flour into a mixing bowl, make a well in the centre, and add the yeast, salt and 1 tablespoon of oil. Blend well, adding more warm water as necessary, until you have a smooth, stiff dough. Work the dough with the palm of your hand until it is fairly soft and elastic. Form into a ball and place in a floured bowl. Cover with a cloth and leave in a warm place, not in direct heat, and away from draughts, for 3 hours.

Divide the dough into four equal parts. On a lightly floured surface, roll out into rounds 6 mm (1/4 in) thick. Mix together the cheese, salami, garlic and 2 tablespoons of olive oil. Place equal amounts of this mixture on half of each round of dough 1 cm (1/2 in) from the edges. Moisten the edges with beaten egg mixed with a little water and fold the dough over the filling. Press the edges down well and crimp with a fork. Brush the whole surface of the calzoni with the remaining oil, place on a lightly oiled baking sheet, and bake in a hot oven (220°C/425°F/Gas mark 7) for about 20 minutes or until golden brown.

Calzoni are sometimes deep-fried, which makes for a much less digestible dish and carries the risk of spillage. They can also be made in larger sizes: the above ingredients, for example, will make two large ones instead of four small ones.

Italian raw ham (*prosciutto*) can partly or entirely replace the salami in the filling. You can experiment with any number of fillings, varying the type of cheese you put with the salami, or not using salami at all and combining several cheeses.

ENGLISH CHEESE PASTIES   FOR 4

C. Anne Wilson tells us, in her erudite *Food and Drink in Britain*, that pasties, sometimes baked, sometimes deep-fried in lard, have been a favourite dish in England since medieval times, when the nobler tables were often laden with such luxuries as venison or porpoise pasties. In subsequent centuries the pastry of the pasty (sometimes also called patty) might be flavoured with saffron and its filling include beef marrow, dried fruit and spices, a lineage that resulted in mince pies.

Nowadays English pasties are made of more mundane stuff. They usually contain just cheese and some seasonings, though in Cornwall they add a few potatoes as well. They are tasty as long as a generous amount of good quality cheese with plenty of personality is used.

250 g (9 oz) chilled short pastry (p. 366)

200 g (7 oz) strong Cheddar, Cheshire *or* Double Gloucester, cut into slivers

60 g (2 oz) unsalted butter, cut into very small dice

pinch cayenne

freshly ground pepper

1 egg, beaten

Divide the pastry into four equal parts. On a lightly floured surface, roll out into rounds 3 mm (1/8 in) thick. Mix the cheese and butter together with the cayenne and plenty of pepper (you will probably not need to add any salt unless the cheese is very lightly salted). Place equal amounts of this filling on half of each round of pastry 1 cm (1/2 in) from the edges. Moisten the edges with beaten egg, and fold the dough over the filling. Press the edges down well and crimp with a fork. Brush the whole surface of the pasties with beaten egg. Place on a lightly oiled baking sheet, and bake in a fairly hot oven (200°C/400°F/ Gas mark 6) for 30-40 minutes, or until nicely browned.

RISSOLES DE SAINT-FLOUR   FOR 4

French *rissoles* have nothing to do with British rissoles and all that they evoke. They are pastry turnovers identical with *chaussons*. The French word comes from the Latin *russeolus* (reddish-brown), no doubt because *rissoles* brown in the oven. The English 'rissole' was sometimes spelled 'rishew' in Elizabethan times and, according to one theory, derives from the Norman French *réchauffées* (re-heated meats).

These *rissoles* are a speciality of that most forbidding of Auvergnat towns, Saint-Flour.

400 g (14 oz) chilled flaky pastry (p. 367)	pinch salt
	pinch freshly grated nutmeg
170 g (6 oz) well-drained curd cheese	freshly ground pepper
110 g (4 oz) young Cantal, cut into slivers	1 tbsp fresh chives, finely chopped
	1 tbsp fresh chervil, finely chopped
3 egg yolks	1 egg, beaten

Divide the pastry into four equal parts. On a lightly floured surface, roll out into rounds about 15 cm (6 in) in diameter and 4 mm (1/6 in) thick. Into a mixing bowl, put the curd cheese, Cantal, egg yolks, salt, nutmeg, plenty of pepper, chives and chervil. Mix thoroughly until a smooth paste is obtained. Place equal amounts of this filling on half of each round of pastry 1 cm (¹/₂ in) from the edges. Moisten the edges with beaten egg and fold the dough over the filling. Press the edges down well and crimp with a fork. Brush the whole surface of the *rissoles* with the rest of the beaten egg. Place on a lightly oiled baking sheet, and bake in a fairly hot oven (190°C/375°F/Gas mark 5) for about 45 minutes.

You can also make these *rissoles* with short pastry and deep-fry them. They are correspondingly heavier. Some authorities swear that genuine Saint-Flour *rissoles*, the ones traditionally sold on market days in that town, were always made that way. Possibly. But then deep-frying is a cooking technique much better suited to the market square than baking.

In another version a little diced ham is added to the cheese filling.

CHAUSSONS À LA FOURME D'AMBERT   FOR 4
These are turnovers with a simple filling of blue cheese and cream, as in Fourme d'Ambert omelette (p. 124).

400 g (14 oz) chilled short pastry
(p. 366)
200 g (7 oz) Fourme d'Ambert,
crumbled
5 tbsp double cream
30 g (1 oz) unsalted butter, softened

2 eggs
1 tbsp fresh chives, finely chopped
1 tbsp fresh parsley, finely chopped
freshly ground pepper
salt

Divide the pastry into four equal parts. On a lightly floured surface, roll out into rounds about 15 cm (6 in) in diameter and 4 mm (¹/₆ in) thick. Into a mixing bowl, put the cheese, cream, butter, 1 egg, chives, parsley and plenty of pepper. Mix thoroughly until a smooth paste is obtained. Add a little salt if necessary. Place equal amounts of this filling on half of each round of pastry 1 cm (¹/₂ in) from the edges. Moisten the edges with beaten egg, and fold the dough over the filling. Press the edges down well and crimp with a fork. Brush the whole surface of the *chaussons* with the rest of the beaten egg. Place on a lightly oiled baking sheet, and bake in a fairly hot oven (190°C/375°F/Gas mark 5) for about 45 minutes.

FIB PASTRIES WITH CHEESE FOR 4

These little triangular envelopes of filo pastry enclosing melted cheese could justifiably be called 'melting moments' were that niche not already occupied by a kind of English teacake. Bible-paper-thin filo pastry is as difficult to make as it is evanescent on the palate. Fortunately, good-quality ready-made filo is now widely available.

This recipe comes from Claudia Roden's *A New Book of Middle Eastern Food*.

140 g (5 oz) feta	freshly ground white pepper
110 g (4 oz) curd cheese	250 g (9 oz) ready-made filo pastry
2 tbsp fresh mint, finely chopped	60 g (2 oz) unsalted butter, melted
2 tbsp fresh chives, finely chopped	

Mash the cheeses, herbs and pepper to a paste and leave for 1 hour. Take the required amount of standard-sized filo pastry out of the packet, which should be resealed hermetically and put back in the refrigerator to prevent the remaining sheets from drying out. Cut the sheets lengthwise into four rectangular strips about 8 cm (3 in) wide and place them under a damp tea towel.

Take one strip at a time and brush on one side with melted butter. Put a teaspoon of the filling at one end of the strip, about 2.5 cm (1 in) from the short edge. Fold one corner down over the filling, like a dog-ear, making a triangle. Then fold the triangle containing the filling over on to the next bit of the strip. Continue in this fashion, folding horizontally and diagonally in turn, until the whole strip is folded and you end up with a triangular package. Tuck the loose end neatly into the fold. Filo pastry is so unbelievably thin that even after such a long series of folds the package does not increase enormously in size. Repeat with the other strips of dough.

Place the pastries on lightly oiled baking sheets, brush them with melted butter and bake in a cool oven (150°C/300°F/Gas mark 2) for 30-45 minutes, or until crisp and golden. Serve immediately on hot plates.

PROFITEROLES MARTHE PAGER FOR 6

We usually associate profiteroles with hot chocolate and ice cream. But their savoury version, which consists simply of stuffed *ramequins* (p. 348) can be equally satisfying, as in these cheese profiteroles with a sorrel-flavoured filling.

150 g (5½ oz) unsalted butter	40 g (1½ oz) freshly grated Parmesan
salt	100 g (3½ oz) sorrel, trimmed of its
175 g (6 oz) sifted plain flour	stalks
6 eggs	4 hard-boiled egg yolks
freshly ground pepper	2 tbsp fresh chives, very finely chopped
40 g (1½ oz) freshly grated Gruyère	250 ml (9 fl oz) double cream

Put 90 g (3 oz) of butter, a large pinch of salt and 340 ml (12 fl oz) of water in a heavy saucepan and heat slowly. Make sure the butter has completely dissolved by the time the water comes to the boil. When it boils, remove from the heat, pour in the flour in one go and beat vigorously with a wooden spoon. Return to the heat and continue beating until the mixture comes away from the sides of the pan. Remove the pan from the heat and stir in the eggs one after the other (make sure each one has been thoroughly blended before putting in the next one). Add plenty of pepper and the cheeses, and stir well.

Using a tablespoon or a forcing bag with a plain large nozzle, place neat mounds of the mixture about 5 cm (2 in) in diameter on 2 oiled baking sheets, leaving plenty of space between each profiterole (they swell considerably during cooking). Bake both sheets at the same time in a hot oven (220°C/425°F/Gas mark 7) for about 20 minutes, or until the profiteroles have swollen in size and browned slightly. Reduce the heat to fairly hot (190°C/ 375°F/Gas mark 5) for another 15-20 minutes, or until the profiteroles are firm and crisp to the touch. Transfer to a rack, make a slit in the side of each of them and leave for a further 5 minutes or so in the oven, with the heat off and the door ajar. Test a profiterole by looking into the slit. The centre should be hollow. If there is a lump of semi-cooked, soft pastry in the centre, scoop it out with a teaspoon after slicing the top off the profiterole. Proceed in the same way with the rest if necessary. Leave to cool.

Wash and shred the sorrel. Heat the rest of the butter and a little salt in a large non-stick frying pan and gently sauté the sorrel, turning it over frequently with a wooden spoon, until it has acquired an almost purée-like consistency. Transfer the cooled contents of the pan to a mixing bowl, add the hard-boiled yolks, chives and plenty of pepper, and mix well. Whip the cream until stiff and fold into the mixture. Add more salt to taste. Slice the tops off the profiteroles (if you have not already done so), fill with this mixture and replace the tops. Chill very slightly or leave in a cool place for 1 hour. Serve with a green salad.

The sorrel in this recipe can be replaced by an equivalent quantity of spinach, trimmed of its stalks.

FEUILLETÉS AU FROMAGE DE CHÈVRE ET AU COULIS DE TOMATES AU BASILIC FOR 4

A summery recipe given to me by Cosima Kretz and Jean Moreno (p. 251).

500 g (1 lb 2 oz) tomatoes, peeled and seeded
1 large sweet onion
2 cloves garlic
pinch salt
pinch freshly ground pepper

18 fresh basil leaves
250 g (9 oz) flaky pastry (p. 367)
2 medium-ripe goat cheeses of about 60 g (2 oz) each (Crottins *or* Cabécous)
2 egg yolks, beaten

Blend the tomatoes, onion, garlic, salt, pepper and 10 basil leaves. Pour the mixture into a heavy saucepan and cook over a low heat until reduced to the consistency of a thickish purée-like sauce, or *coulis*. Keep hot.

On a lightly floured surface, roll out the pastry about 2 mm (1/12 in) thick. Cut eight rounds about 8 cm (3 in) in diameter. Put a quarter of a goat cheese on half of each round. Moisten the edges of the pastry with egg yolk. Fold over and crimp with a fork so the *feuilleté* is well sealed. Brush the whole surface with egg yolk. Place on a lightly oiled baking sheet and bake in a moderate oven (180°C/350°F/Gas mark 4) for 15-20 minutes or until the surface begins to brown.

Put the *feuilletés* on hot individual plates (two per plate), spoon the hot tomato *coulis* around, but not on top of, them, decorate with a basil leaf and serve immediately.

If you prefer a more assertive basil taste, instead of blending the basil leaves with the tomatoes at the start of operations, stir the finely chopped basil leaves into the hot *coulis* just before assembling the *feuilletés* on the plates.

FEUILLETÉS AU ROQUEFORT   FOR 4

This dish, which became a favourite on *nouvelle cuisine* menus, often suffers from being overdry and oversalty. This is because chefs, worried about the waistlines of their weight-conscious Yuppie customers, tend to stint on the proportion of cream to Roquefort. Roquefort is so packed with taste and salt that it needs a bland foil like cream in order to give of its best. So don't baulk at the quantity of cream indicated here.

5 tbsp good sweet white wine (Sauternes, Monbazillac) *or* fortified wine (Muscat)
350 ml (12 fl oz) double cream
250 g (9 oz) puff pastry (p. 368)

1 egg, beaten
170 g (6 oz) Roquefort, crumbled
pinch freshly grated nutmeg
freshly ground white pepper

Put the wine into a heavy saucepan over a high heat and boil for 1 minute. Add the cream, bring to the boil, turn down the heat and simmer uncovered, stirring from time to time, until the liquid has reduced by a third. Cover and keep warm.

On a lightly floured surface, roll out the pastry to a rectangle 16 x 32 cm (6 x 12 in) and about 5 mm (just under 1/4 in) thick. With a sharp knife, cut it into four rectangles 8 x 16 cm (3 x 6 in). Place these, floured side up, on a lightly oiled baking sheet and brush their tops with a little beaten egg (do not allow any egg to dribble down the cut edges). Bake them in a hot oven (220°C/425°F/Gas mark 7) for about 15 minutes, or until well puffed up.

While the pastry is cooking, add the cheese, nutmeg and pepper (but no salt: that is amply provided by the Roquefort) to the reduced hot cream and stir over a gentle heat until a smooth consistency is obtained. When the *feuilletés* are ready, remove them from the oven and, as quickly as possible, slice each of them delicately in half horizontally. Put the four bottom halves on hot individual plates, spoon most of the hot sauce over them, cover with the other half of pastry, pour remaining sauce over the top and serve immediately.

A good accompaniment to this dish is some more of the sweet wine used in it. If that sounds outlandish, remember how well port goes with Stilton.

SPANAKOPITTA   FOR 4

Greek spinach pie – another dish calling for featherlight filo pastry.

1 kg (2 1/4 lb) spinach	225 g (8 oz) feta, crumbled
200 g (7 oz) unsalted butter	1 tbsp fresh dill *or* aniseed leaves,
pinch freshly grated nutmeg	finely chopped
salt	freshly ground pepper
1 large sweet onion, finely sliced	5 eggs, beaten
225 g (8 oz) well-drained curd cheese	225 g (8 oz) ready-made filo pastry

Wash the spinach and cut off any tough stems. Shake off excess moisture, chop coarsely and cook gently in 40 g (1½ oz) of butter in a large sauté pan with nutmeg and a little salt, pressing down and turning over with a wooden spoon until tender. If there is a lot of liquid, tilt it to one side of the pan, pushing the spinach up towards the other side, and reduce the liquid to 1-2 tablespoons over a high heat.

Put 30 g (1 oz) of butter in a small heavy frying pan and sweat the onion, covered and over a very low heat, until translucent but not browned. Into a large mixing bowl, put the two cheeses, the spinach and its remaining liquid, onion, dill or aniseed, plenty of pepper and the eggs. Mix thoroughly and add salt if necessary (feta can be very salty).

Melt the remaining butter. Butter a gratin dish or baking tray, preferably rectangular and slightly smaller than the dimensions of the filo pastry sheets. Into it put 4 sheets, each brushed on one side with butter, one on top of the other, allowing them to overlap the sides. Spread the filling evenly over the pastry and top with the rest of the sheets, each brushed with butter. Fold the overlapping sheets back over the top, brush with butter, make two to three small slashes in the surface with a sharp knife and sprinkle with a very little water (to prevent the pastry from curling up and burning). Bake in a fairly hot oven (190°C/375°F/Gas mark 5) for about 45 minutes or until the surface is golden brown.

Spanakopitta can also be made with puff pastry if you cannot get hold of filo pastry.

TIROPITTA
Greek cheese pie. Make it exactly like Spanakopitta (see preceding recipe), replacing the spinach with an additional 150 g (5½ oz) of well-drained curd cheese and 75 g (2½ oz) of freshly grated kefalotiri or Parmesan.

KALLITSOUNAKIA   FOR 4
Unusual little cheese pies from Crete that are filled with mitzithra, the Greek equivalent of ricotta.

300 g (10¹/₂ oz) mitzithra
2 tbsp fresh chives, finely chopped
freshly ground pepper
salt
300 g (10¹/₂ oz) chilled short pastry
  (p. 366), with chilled orange juice

replacing chilled water (in an equal
quantity) as the moistening agent
1 egg yolk, beaten
2 tbsp sesame seeds

Mix the cheese, chives, plenty of pepper and salt to taste. On a lightly floured surface, roll out the pastry 3 mm (¹/₈ in) thick and cut rounds of about 10 cm (4 in) in diameter. Spoon equal amounts of cheese on to the middle of each round, moisten the edges with water and bring them together over the filling. Seal well, crimping with a fork. Brush the pies with egg yolk and sprinkle with sesame seeds. Place on a lightly oiled baking sheet and bake in a fairly hot oven (200°C/400°F/Gas mark 6) for 20-25 minutes or until golden brown.

KREATOPITTA   FOR 4-6
Another Cretan pie, which contains lamb, cheese and spearmint. During the Second World War British officers helped the Cretans to resist the German occupation. Would it be frivolous to suggest, I wonder, that their feelings of camaraderie might have been heightened by a common predilection – shared, as far as I know, with no other Europeans – for the mint and lamb combination?

However that may be, this recipe is an original way of using up the remains of a leg of lamb.

60 g (2 oz) unsalted butter
1 onion, finely chopped
350 g (12 oz) lean raw lamb or
   250 g (9 oz) lean cooked lamb, cut
   into small cubes
200 g (7 oz) feta, crumbled
4 tbsp double cream
2 tbsp fresh chives, finely chopped

2 tsp fresh spearmint or 1 tbsp fresh
   mint, finely chopped
salt
freshly ground pepper
400 g (14 oz) chilled short pastry
   (p. 366)
1 egg yolk, beaten
2 tbsp sesame seeds

Heat the butter in a frying pan and put in the onion and the raw meat pieces. Sauté over a medium heat until the meat is well cooked and the onion translucent and slightly browned. If using already cooked meat, add the cubes to the onion when it is nearly cooked. Transfer the meat and onion to a mixing bowl. Add the cheese, cream, chives, spearmint or mint, a little salt and plenty of pepper. Mix well.

Divide the pastry into two pieces, one very slightly larger than the other. On a lightly floured surface, roll out the larger piece to a circle about 6 mm (1/4 in) thick and place on a lightly oiled baking sheet. Spoon the lamb and cheese filling neatly and compactly on to the centre of the pastry, leaving a 4-cm (11/2-in) margin free on the edge. Roll out the other piece of dough to the same thickness and place it over the filling; it should be large enough to cover it completely. Fold the edge of the bottom round of pastry back over the edge of the top round, fold again so the border rests against the enclosed filling, and seal well by crimping with the thumb and fingers. Brush the surface with egg yolk, cut one or two slits in it with a sharp knife and sprinkle with sesame seeds. Bake in a fairly hot oven (190°C/375°F/Gas mark 5) for 45-60 minutes or until the pastry begins to turn golden brown. This pie is best served hot, but also makes a nice cold dish.

LABNA PIES   FOR 4
These pies get the best out of labna.

90 g (3 oz) pine-nuts   1 tbsp virgin olive oil
300 g (10¹/₂ oz) fairly dry labna   400 g (14 oz) chilled short pastry
  (p. 371)   (p. 366)
1 tbsp fresh mint, finely chopped

Put the pine-nuts on a baking tray and bake in a moderate
oven until the colour of roasted peanuts. Mix them well
with the labna, mint and olive oil. On a lightly floured
surface, roll out the pastry 3 mm (¹/₈ in) thick and cut eight
rounds about 12 cm (5 in) in diameter. Spoon equal
amounts of the cheese mixture on to the middle of each
round, moisten the edges with water and bring them
together over the filling. Seal well, crimping with a fork.
Place the pies on a lightly oiled baking sheet and bake in a
fairly hot oven (200°C/400°F/Gas mark 6) for 20-25
minutes or until golden brown. Serve hot or cold.

TOURTE DE POMMES DE TERRE   FOR 4-6
A potato pie from the Auvergne. Potato in pastry sounds
a bit like stodge in stodge. Surprisingly, it is not – as long
as you give the pie plenty of seasoning and use the best-
quality waxy potatoes available.

400 g (14 oz) waxy potatoes   2 tbsp fresh parsley, finely chopped
250 g (9 oz) fairly liquid curd cheese 400 g (14 oz) chilled short pastry
large pinch salt   (p. 366)
freshly ground pepper   1 egg yolk beaten
3 cloves garlic, finely chopped

Wash, peel and steam the potatoes (if they are new
potatoes of a thin-skinned variety, they need not be
peeled). Cut them into fairly thick slices and put into a
mixing bowl with the cheese, garlic, parsley, salt and
plenty of pepper. Mix well, but without breaking up the
potatoes.

Divide the pastry into two pieces, one slightly larger than the other. On a lightly floured surface, roll out the larger piece to a circle about 6 mm (1/4 in) thick and place on a lightly oiled baking sheet. Put the filling neatly and compactly on to the centre of the pastry, leaving a 4-cm (1½-in) margin free on the edge. Roll out the other piece of dough to the same thickness and place it over the filling; it should be large enough to cover it completely. Fold the edge of the bottom round of pastry back over the edge of the top round, fold again so the border rests against the enclosed filling and seal well by crimping with the thumb and fingers. Brush the surface with egg yolk, and cut one or two slits in it with a sharp knife. Bake in a fairly hot oven (190°/375°F/Gas mark 5) for 45-60 minutes or until the pastry begins to turn golden brown.

Tourte de pommes de terre is best served hot, but also makes a nice cold picnic dish (the potatoes will have absorbed all the liquid).

A farmer's wife near where I live in the Auvergne has devised a tasty variation of this pie. Whenever she or someone in her family comes across just one or two cepes in the woods, she adds them to the potatoes. If served on their own, the mushrooms would reduce to a measly teaspoonful per person. Cepes have plenty of flavour (see p. 279) so even a small specimen gives this pie an extra dimension. Just chop the mushroom fairly finely and sauté in butter until it begins to turn brown, then mix with the ingredients of the filling.

PETITS PÂTÉS AU FROMAGE DE
CHÈVRE À LA SANCERROISE FOR 4

These are pies, not pâtés (for a discussion of the word pâté, see following recipe), with a succulent centre of melted goat cheese.

350 g (12¹/₂ oz) chilled short pastry (p. 366)

4 medium-ripe goat cheeses of about 60 g (2 oz) each (Crottins *or* Cabécous)

40 g (1¹/₂ oz) unsalted butter, melted
freshly ground pepper

4 small sprigs – flowering sprigs if possible – of wild *or* garden thyme

1 egg yolk, beaten

On a lightly floured surface, roll out the pastry. Cut four rounds 12-15 cm (5-6 in) in diameter (depending on the size of the cheeses) and four rounds 5-7 cm (2-3 in) in diameter. Place 1 cheese on each larger round, brush with melted butter, sprinkle with plenty of pepper and stick a sprig of wild thyme flowers in the top. Brush the edges of the small round with egg yolk. Draw the pastry of the larger round up the sides of the cheese to form a cylindrical casing, top with the smaller round, moistened side down, and press the edges securely together, crimping with the fork. Place on a lightly oiled baking sheet, brush all over with egg yolk and bake in a hot oven (220°C/425°F/Gas mark 7) for 20-25 minutes or until the pastry has begun to turn golden brown.

The natural partner for these pies is, of course, a white Sancerre.

PÂTÉ DE FROMAGE DE CHÈVRE FOR 4-6

Pâté is a confusing term; it is related to such words as pastry, pasty, patty, pasta and paste – indeed, in current English usage it usually denotes something like a paste, i.e. a smooth mixture of finely minced liver and/or other meat. But things are not quite as simple as they seem. In French pâté originally signified 'something enclosed in pastry'. And although by the early nineteenth century its sense was occasionally extended to include meat paste or foie gras *without* a pastry crust, the word continued until quite recently in France to be used mostly in the sense of a 'pie' – and a pie in general, irrespective of its contents. In Britain, until the Edwardian period and afterwards, potted meat was the expression normally used to describe what would now be called pâté.

To confuse matters further, this Savoyard *pâté de fromage de chèvre*, from Austin de Croze's *Les Plats régionaux de France*, is neither a pie nor what we would now call a pâté, but a tart – and a very strange sweet-salt one at that. Potatoes, spinach and Swiss chard are occasionally included in sweet dishes in France, but this combination of very sweet pastry with a very savoury filling is as far as I know unparalleled.

300 g (10¹/₂ oz) chilled sweet short pastry (p. 368)
400 ml (14 fl oz) béchamel sauce I (p. 356)
3 egg yolks
freshly ground pepper

1 slice ham, chopped
4 small fresh goat cheeses of about 60 g (2 oz) each, crumbled
30 g (1 oz) freshly grated Parmesan (optional)
1 tbsp sugar

On a lightly floured surface, roll out the pastry 3 mm (¹/₈ in) thick. Use it to line a 25-28-cm (10-11-in) flan tin, with a removable bottom if possible, and bake blind in a fairly hot oven (200°C/400°F/Gas mark 6) for 15 minutes.

Make or re-heat the béchamel sauce, remove from the heat and allow to cool a little. Stir in the egg yolks, plenty of pepper, the ham, the goat cheeses and, if you like, the Parmesan. Mix well and pour into the pastry shell, sprinkle with sugar and bake in a fairly hot oven (190°C/375°F/Gas mark 5) for 25-30 minutes or until the tart has puffed and browned. Remove from the oven, leave to firm up for 5 minutes, then transfer to a hot dish and serve immediately.

The combination of Parmesan and sugar is *very* odd. The Parmesan can be omitted if you like or replaced by the same amount of a less pungent cheese, such as Gruyère or very mature Gouda.

TOURTE D'HERBES
FOR 4

The recipe for this tart comes from *Le Ménagier de Paris* (written in 1392 or 1393, and first published only in 1846). One of the very earliest French manuscripts to contain recipes, it was written anonymously by an elderly member of the Parisian legal profession for his 15-year-old bride in the hope that when she remarried after his death his memory would not be disgraced by her ignorance.

The author, whose personality comes across with extraordinary vividness, touches on various topics – gardening, cleaning, disinfesting, going to market, the selection and treatment of servants, horses, hawking – in addition to cooking and the devising of menus. The book is an invaluable source for practical details of everyday life in a prosperous middle-class household towards the end of the fourteenth century.

I cannot resist quoting the text of the original recipe, which is written in marvellously rough-hewn medieval French:

Pour faire une tourte. Prenez .iiii. pongnees de bectes, .ii. pongnees de percil, une pongné de cherfeuil, ung brain de fanoul et deux pongnees d'espinoches, et les esliziez, et lavez en eaue froide, puis hachiez bien menu. Puis broyez de deux paires de frommage; c'est assavoir du mol et du moyen; et puis mectez des oeufz avec ce – moyeul et aubun – et les broyez parmy le frommage. Puis mectez les herbes dedens le mortier et broyez tout ensemble, et aussi mectez y de la pouldre fine; ou en lieu de ce ayez premierement ou mortier .ii. cloches de gingembre et sur ce broyez vos frommages, oeufz et herbes. Et puis gectez du vieil frommage de presse ou autre gratuisié dessus celles herbes, et portez au four, et puis faictes faire une tarte et la mengiez chaude.

I have interpreted this as follows:

300 g (10½ oz) chilled short pastry (p. 366)

110 g (4 oz) well-drained curd cheese

110 g (4 oz) medium-ripe goat cheese, crumbled

170 g (6 oz) Swiss chard tops

85 g (3 oz) spinach

40 g (1½ oz) fresh chervil, chopped

85 g (3 oz) fresh parsley, chopped

1 tbsp fresh fennel, chopped

1 pinch each, powdered ginger, cinnamon, crushed clove and crushed cardamom seeds

large pinch sugar

3 eggs, separated

salt

85 g (3 oz) freshly grated Gruyère

On a lightly floured surface, roll out the pastry 3 mm (⅛ in) thick. Use it to line a 25-28-cm (10-11-in) flan tin, with a removable base if possible, and bake blind in a fairly hot oven (200°C/400°F/Gas mark 6) for 15 minutes.

Trim the Swiss chard tops of all white stalk and the spinach of its tougher stems. Wash thoroughly and blanch together uncovered in plenty of boiling salted water for 5 minutes. Drain well, squeeze out as much moisture as possible and chop. Put into a mixing bowl with the chervil, parsley, fennel, spices, sugar and egg yolks. Mix thoroughly and add salt to taste. Whisk the egg whites with a tiny pinch of salt until stiff, and fold them in delicately but thoroughly. Turn the mixture into the pastry-lined tin and spread evenly. Sprinkle with grated cheese. Bake in a fairly hot oven (190°C/375°F/Gas mark 5) for 30-40 minutes or until the surface begins to brown. Remove from the oven, leave to firm up for 5 minutes, then transfer to a hot dish and serve immediately.

This tart is equally good cold.

Bartolomeo Platina, writing about half a century later than the author of *Le Ménagier de Paris*, has a very similar recipe, called Tarte bourbonoise. It is made with Swiss chard tops, parsley, marjoram flowers and leaves, curd cheese, eggs and saffron.

GOYÈRE   FOR 4-6

Goyère, a word of obscure origin that looks like a hybrid between Gruyère and *gougère*, is a redoubtable Maroilles tart from northern France. After cooking it for the first time, I was irresistibly reminded of the words used by my classics master at school to explain to his sniggering pupils that the perfect tense in ancient Greek indicated 'a past act with the effects remaining'. Maroilles is already one of the smelliest cheeses in the world. When heated in the filling of *goyère*, its smell is magnified many times and spreads to every nook and cranny of the house. What is more, it lingers on – and on. Not a good time for a chance visitor to drop in. Take the precaution, then, of making *goyère* during clement weather, so that once it has been cooked and eaten every window can be flung open and the mephitis banished.

Yet the tart tastes delicious. This is only apparently a paradox. For it is a curious fact about the human taste mechanism that, unless we suffer from a total aversion to smelly cheese, we can be repelled by the smell (alone) of a cheese, but enjoy it once it is in the mouth – at which point we are in fact both tasting *and* smelling it via the air passage at the back of the mouth. Why this should be so has not yet, as far as I know, been satisfactorily explained by the experts on the psychology and physiology of taste.

300 g (10^1/$_2$ oz) chilled short pastry (p. 366)	3 eggs, separated
250 g (9 oz) Maroilles	50 g (2 oz) unsalted butter, softened
170 g (6 oz) curd cheese	freshly ground pepper
	salt

On a lightly floured surface, roll out the pastry 3 mm (^{1}/$_8$ in) thick. Use it to line a 25-28-cm (10-11-in) flan tin, with a removable base if possible, and bake blind in a fairly hot oven (200°C/400°F/Gas mark 6) for 15 minutes.

Blend or mash the Maroilles, including its rind if it is not too dry, with the curd cheese, egg yolks and butter until smooth. Add plenty of pepper and a little salt to taste. Whisk the egg whites with a tiny pinch of salt until stiff and fold in delicately but thoroughly. Turn the mixture into the pastry-lined tin and bake in a hot oven (220°C/425°F/Gas mark 7) for about 30 minutes or until the mixture has puffed up and its surface has begun to turn golden brown. If it seems to be browning too soon, protect by laying a sheet of aluminium foil on top. Remove from the oven, leave to firm up for 5 minutes, then transfer to a hot dish and serve immediately.

Goyère is sometimes made with a bread dough, like the *flamiche* of the following recipe.

FLAMICHE DE DINANT   FOR 4-6

Flamiche (sometimes spelled *flamique*) is a Flemish word meaning cake or tart. *Flamiche* is found not only in Belgium and the part of northern France once occupied by the medieval principality of Flanders, but also in Burgundy, where, presumably, it was introduced when the influence of Flemish culture was at its height there in the fifteenth century.

Flamiche varies considerably in nature from place to place. In one version, monstrous quantities of cheese and butter are folded into pastry before baking in rather the same way that butter is folded into puff pastry. Other *flamiches* are straightforward cheeseless tarts or pies, often with a leek filling. In northern France *flamiche* is sometimes indistinguishable from *Goyère* (see preceding recipe).

The version given here, which has a bread-dough crust, is from Dinant in Belgium, where an annual *flamiche*-eating contest is organized. The winner, who usually manages to put away about 2 kilogrammes (4¹/₂ lb) of the stuff at a sitting, is crowned *Roi de la flamiche*, 'according to the 1,000-year-old rites of Belgian Gaul'.

The cheese that is called for in this recipe, the odoriferous Boulette de Romedenne, is difficult to find outside Belgium, but you can always fall back on Maroilles or, if you are feeling daring, its even more pungent cousin Boulette d'Avesnes. So when making *flamiche*, take the same precautions as for *goyère*.

7 g (¹/₄ oz) fresh yeast
150 g (5¹/₂ oz) sifted plain flour
1 tsp salt
2 tsp oil
120 g (4 oz) unsalted butter,
   softened

280 g (10 oz) Boulette de Romedenne
   or Maroilles *or* 200 g (7 oz)
   Boulette d'Avesnes
4 eggs
freshly ground pepper
salt

Dissolve the yeast in a little warm water. Put the flour into a mixing bowl, make a well in the centre, and add the yeast, salt and oil. Blend well, adding more warm water as necessary, until you have a smooth, stiff dough. You will probably need about 120 ml (4 fl oz) of water in all. Work the dough with the palm of your hand until it is fairly soft and elastic. Form into a ball and place in a floured bowl. Cover with a cloth and leave in a warm place, not in direct heat, and away from draughts, for 3 hours.

Blend the butter, cheese and eggs until a smooth consistency is obtained. Sprinkle with plenty of pepper. Add a little salt if necessary. Put the dough in a ball in the middle of a lightly oiled 25-28-cm (10-11-in) flan tin, with a removable base if possible, and press it out to cover the whole base. Cover with cling-film and leave in a warm place for about 30 minutes to rise again, then work it up the sides of the tin. The dough should cover the tin very thinly.

Turn the filling into the dough-lined tin and bake, first in a hot oven (220°C/425°F/Gas mark 7) for 15 minutes, then cover the filling with aluminium foil and bake in a fairly hot oven (190°C/375°F/Gas mark 5) for about another 20 minutes or until the filling has set. Remove the foil for the last 5 minutes of baking. Remove the tart from the oven, leave to firm up for 5 minutes, then transfer to a hot dish. Serve immediately.

QUICHE LORRAINE   FOR 4-6

I would not presume to add anything to Elizabeth David's
witty and authoritative discussion of the quiche lorraine in
the *Tatler* of September, 1985 (except that, perhaps
intentionally, she did not mention in her remarks on the
Küchen, a bread-dough version of the quiche made in
some parts of Alsace, that *Küchen* is in fact the word from
which quiche derives). She quite rightly points out that the
quiche lorraine usually served in London wine bars and
indeed most restaurants in France is not authentic because
it contains cheese (e.g. Gruyère, Cheddar), whereas the
genuine version has a filling that consists solely of cream,
eggs and a little streaky bacon.

So what is quiche lorraine doing here, in a book of
cheese recipes? Elizabeth David goes on to say that in
Lorraine itself quiches sometimes also contain 'plain,
fresh, skimmed-milk curd cheese'. A Lorraine-born friend
of mine makes a tidy quiche according to a family recipe
that includes the latter ingredient. The result is perfectly
balanced: the cream provides the richness, the smoked
bacon the aroma, the curd cheese a wonderful fluffiness
and wobbliness, and the eggs just enough binding to hold
the whole thing together. Here is her recipe.

300 g (10¹/₂ oz) chilled short pastry (p. 366)	6 tbsp double cream
90 g (3 oz) good smoked streaky bacon, sliced not too thinly	4 eggs, beaten
200 g (7 oz) well-drained curd cheese	freshly ground pepper
	salt

On a lightly floured surface, roll out the pastry 3 mm
(¹/₈ in) thick. Use it to line a 25-28-cm (10-11-in) flan tin,
with a removable base if possible, and bake blind in a
fairly hot oven (200°C/400°F/Gas mark 6) for 15 minutes.

Cut the bacon into thin strips and sauté gently in a
lightly oiled frying pan until crisp but not hard. Put the
curd cheese, cream and eggs into a mixing bowl. Add the
bacon, any fat it has rendered and plenty of pepper. Blend
thoroughly. Add salt to taste (check the saltiness of the

bacon). Turn the mixture into the pastry-lined tin, making sure that the bacon is evenly distributed. The filling should not completely fill the pastry shell, as it will puff up during cooking. Bake in a fairly hot oven (200°C/400°F/Gas mark 6) for about 30 minutes or until the filling has puffed up and begun to brown. If it seems to be browning too soon, protect with aluminium foil. Remove from the oven, leave to firm up for 5 minutes, then transfer to a hot dish and serve immediately.

As Elizabeth David points out, the original quiche lorraine was often made with bread dough like *flamiche* (see preceding recipe). If you want to try it that way, follow the procedure for Tarte aveyronnaise (see following recipe), using a not very deep tart tin and filling it with the above mixture instead of the Roquefort-flavoured one.

The Hungarians make a delicious quiche-like curd tart with dill. Follow the procedure in the above recipe, replacing the cream with soured cream and the bacon with 4 tablespoons of finely chopped fresh dill and a large pinch of salt.

TARTE AVEYRONNAISE   FOR 4-6

Like Feuilletés au roquefort (p. 192), this recipe exploits the glorious combination of Roquefort and cream. It was invented by Elizabeth David, who subtitles it 'Roquefort quiche' on the grounds that it calls for a bread dough instead of short pastry (see my remarks on the quiche under the preceding recipe). The recipe comes from her *English Bread and Yeast Cookery.*

7 g (1/4 oz) fresh yeast	6 tbsp double cream
140 (5 oz) strong plain flour, preferably unbleached	100-115 g (3 1/2-4 oz) Roquefort
	4 tbsp milk
1 tsp salt	pinch freshly grated nutmeg
3 eggs	freshly ground pepper

Cream the yeast with 2 tablespoons of tepid water. Warm

the flour in a bowl, add the salt, 1 egg and the creamed yeast. Mix all the ingredients into a light dough. Add 3 tablespoons of cream and with your hand beat the dough into a soft batter. Dry this by sprinkling it with a little flour, form it into a bun and cover the bowl with a plate or cloth. Leave in a warm place for about 2 hours, until the dough has doubled in volume and is light and spongy. Break it down, sprinkle again with flour and reshape into a bun.

Mash the cheese to a paste. Add 3 tablespoons of cream. Stir rather gently until the two are blended. Beat 2 eggs and the milk – the blender can be used for this operation but *not* for mixing the cheese and cream – and combine the two mixtures. Add the nutmeg and plenty of pepper (but no salt, because of the saltiness of Roquefort). Gentle stirring with a fork or spoon is necessary now, and there is no cause for worry if there are a few recalcitrant lumps of cheese in the filling. They will smooth themselves out during the cooking. On the other hand, over-vigorous whisking can curdle the cream and the cheese, a minor disaster that does not affect the flavour but results in rather a flat filling when the quiche is cooked.

Butter and flour a 25-cm (10-in) not too deep tart tin, with a removable base if possible (or else two 15-cm (6-in) tins of the same kind). Work the dough into a ball, put this into the centre of the tin. Sprinkling the dough with flour from time to time, press it out gently with your knuckles until it covers the base of the tin. Leave it, covered with a sheet of greaseproof paper and in a warm place, for about 25 minutes, until it has again become very pliable and is sufficiently risen to be gently pressed out again to line the sides of the tin.

Spoon the filling into the dough-lined tin, and put this quickly on to a baking sheet on the centre shelf of a hot oven (220°C/425°F/Gas mark 7). Bake for 15 minutes before reducing the oven heat to 190°C/375°F/Gas mark 5, covering the filling with buttered paper and cooking the quiche for another 10 minutes.

Elizabeth David adds:

There is a good case for the use of two small tins for this quiche, rather than one large one. It is a question of synchronization. In small tins the yeast pastry and the fillings are ready at precisely the same moment, whereas in one big tin the filling tends to cook more quickly than the dough. To a certain extent this depends upon your oven. It is in any case a wise precaution to use the buttered greaseproof paper covering as directed.

Roquefort varies a good deal in quality. If it is very strong use a little less, and make up the difference with extra cream or milk.

CHEESE TART   FOR 4-6

There are countless versions of plain cheese tart and they can taste very different from one another. It is not so much the recipe as the cheese that makes the difference. So here is an all-purpose formula that can be used for whichever cheese or cheeses you happen to feel like using or have to hand.

300 g (10$^{1}/_{2}$ oz) chilled short pastry (p. 366)	4 eggs, beaten
200 g (7 oz) freshly grated cheese (see suggestions below)	large pinch freshly grated nutmeg
200 ml (7 fl oz) double cream	freshly ground white pepper
	salt
	pinch cayenne (optional)

On a lightly floured surface, roll out the pastry 3 mm (1/8 in) thick. Use it to line a 25-28-cm (10-11-in) flan tin, with a removable base if possible, and bake blind in a fairly hot oven (200°C/400°F/Gas mark 6) for 12 minutes.

Put the cheese, cream, eggs, nutmeg, plenty of pepper, salt to taste (depending on the cheese used) and cayenne, if desired, into a mixing bowl and blend thoroughly. Turn the mixture into the pastry-lined flan tin and bake in a fairly hot oven (190°C/375°F/Gas mark 5) for 30-45 minutes, or until the mixture has set and its surface begun to brown. If it seems to be browning too soon, protect by laying a sheet of aluminium foil on top. (The time needed to cook this tart will depend partly on the type of cheese used.) Remove from the oven, leave to firm up for 5 minutes, then transfer to a hot dish and serve immediately.

Here is a by no means exhaustive list of possible cheeses or cheese combinations to use in the above tart.

200 g (7 oz) of any of the following:
   Gruyère, Emmental, Cheddar, Cheshire, Double Gloucester, Appenzell, fontina, young Cantal or
100 g (3¹/₂ oz) each of:
   Parmesan or pecorino or Sbrinz or mature Gouda and Gruyère or Emmental or mozzarella or ricotta or Gorgonzola; Cheddar and Wensleydale; well-drained curd cheese and Brie or Camembert; Tomme fraîche de Cantal and medium-ripe Cantal or Fourme d'Ambert.

To add an authentic touch to the tart if it contains Italian cheese(s), use dry white wine instead of water when making the short pastry, as is sometimes done in Italy. You can even risk tautology and use, as the Swiss do, cheese pastry (p. 369) for the cheese tart.

TARTE AUX CARDONS   FOR 4-6

This is a useful dish to make if you do not have enough cardoons to make Chardoons à la fromage (p. 296). It also brings into play a classic combination of the Lyonnais and Bresse area, cardoons with beef marrow.

300 g (10¹/₂ oz) chilled short pastry
   (p. 366)
450 g (1 lb) cardoons, trimmed of
   their leaves
200 ml (7 fl oz) Mornay sauce V
   (p. 359)

freshly ground pepper
pinch freshly grated nutmeg
salt
80 g (3 oz) beef marrow
80 g (3 oz) freshly grated Gruyère

On a lightly floured surface, roll out the pastry 3 mm (1/8 in) thick. Use it to line a 25-28-cm (10-11-in) flan tin, with a removable base if possible, and bake blind in a fairly hot oven (200°C/400°C/Gas mark 6) for 20 minutes.

Wash the cardoons, cut into sections and blanch in boiling acidulated and salted water for about 30 minutes or until tender but not mushy. Drain and remove all string and hard skin. Cut into very small pieces and put into a mixing bowl. Make or reheat the Mornay sauce and add to the cardoons along with plenty of pepper and the nutmeg. Mix well and add salt to taste. Cut the beef marrow into thin slices and poach in very little salted water at barely a simmer. As soon as the slices become translucent, remove them carefully with a perforated spoon and drain.

Spoon half the cardoon mixture into the pastry-lined flan tin. Even out the surface and arrange the marrow slices on top, sprinkle with plenty of pepper and cover with the rest of the cardoon mixture. Strew the surface of the tart with finely grated cheese and bake in a hot oven (220°C/425°F/Gas mark 7) for about 20 minutes or until the surface of the tart begins to brown. Remove from the oven, leave to firm up for 5 minutes, then transfer to a hot dish and serve.

PIZZA AI QUATTRO FORMAGGI   FOR 6-8

The Neapolitan pizza started life humbly as an archetypal working-class dish that could be either savoury or sweet. It was a useful way of using up surplus bits of bread dough and a handy vehicle for cheap flavourful seasonings (anchovies, black olives, tomatoes, cheese, fresh fruit) that would make plenty of starch go a long way. Its low cost price was the main reason, no doubt, why the pizza's potential was soon spotted by restaurateurs. It was quickly and successfully exported, in its savoury version, from Naples to the rest of Italy, then to pizzerias and freezers all over the world.

The pizza one is likely to get in a pizzeria can, as we all

know, be anything from tasty to mundane to unchewable, depending on the scrupulousness and skill of its cook(s). But a home-cooked pizza – and I don't mean a re-heated frozen version – is a startlingly delicious dish. I grant that it does not have the authentic slightly smoky aroma of a pizza baked in a wood-fired oven; but it more than makes up for that by the lavishness of its topping – as in this recipe from Florence for a pizza with four types of cheese.

The whole point of this dish is that the cheeses occupy different areas on the surface of the pizza, but do not mingle. This means that you have to make either several individual pizzas (which is tedious) or one large one. The siting of the various cheeses on the surface of one large circular pizza is highly problematic if each guest is to get a fair share of each cheese. This is why I suggest you make a large rectangular pizza and cut it crosswise.

15 g (½ oz) fresh yeast	110 g (4 oz) freshly grated Gruyère
375 g (13 oz) sifted plain flour	110 g (4 oz) freshly grated pecorino
1 tsp salt	110 g (4 oz) Gorgonzola, crumbled
3 tbsp virgin olive oil	110 g (4 oz) mozzarella, thinly sliced
2 cloves garlic, finely chopped	freshly ground pepper

Dissolve the yeast in a little warm water. Put the flour into a mixing bowl, make a well in the centre and add the yeast, salt and 1 tablespoon of oil. Blend well, adding more warm water as necessary, until you have a smooth, stiff dough. Work the dough with the palm of your hand until it is fairly soft and elastic. Form into a ball and place in a floured bowl. Cover with a cloth and leave in a warm place, not in direct heat, and away from draughts, for 3 hours.

Put the dough in a ball in the centre of a well-oiled shallow rectangular baking tray measuring about 25 x 35 cm (10 x 14 in), and press it out into a thin layer that covers the whole tray. Cover with cling film and leave in a warm place for 15 minutes. Brush with plenty of olive oil and strew with garlic. Cover the dough lengthwise with four parallel bands of each cheese (grated, crumbled or sliced as the case may be) in such a way that its surface is completely covered. Sprinkle with plenty of freshly ground pepper.

Bake in a hot oven (220°C/425°F/Gas mark 7) for 15 minutes, then turn down the heat to fairly hot (190°C/375°F/Gas mark 5) for another 10-15 minutes. Make sure that the underneath is brown and the cheese completely melted and bubbling. Remove from the oven and cut into crosswise slices, so that each portion contains a strip of each cheese.

If you do not have a shallow baking tray of the right dimensions, you can equally well cook this pizza on a baking sheet. Simply turn up the dough slightly at the edges to make a rim and leave a narrow strip of uncovered dough all round the edge when adding the cheese topping.

CHEESE TARTLETS   MAKES 8 TARTLETS

Like their much larger relation the Cheese tart (p. 209), these decorative concoctions can contain virtually any cheese or combination of cheeses. Hot, they make a nice, light first course, with a little salad to relieve their nakedness on the plate, and cold, they can serve as picnic or buffet fare.

300 g (10½ oz) chilled short pastry (p. 366)	2 eggs, separated
140 ml (5 fl oz) double cream	pinch freshly grated nutmeg
80 g (3 oz) freshly grated Gruyère	freshly ground white pepper
80 g (3 oz) freshly grated Parmesan	pinch cayenne (optional)
	salt

On a lightly floured surface, roll out the pastry 3 mm (⅛ in) thick. Cut eight 10-cm (4-in) rounds. Fit each round into a lightly oiled 7-cm (3-in) tartlet tin, crimping the surplus pastry on the edge to form a border. Bake blind in a fairly hot oven (200°C/400°F/Gas mark 6) for 10 minutes.

Heat the cream in a medium-sized saucepan, add the

finely grated cheeses and stir over a gentle heat until smooth. Away from the heat, stir in 2 egg yolks, the nutmeg, plenty of pepper and, if desired, the cayenne. Add a little salt if necessary. Whisk the egg whites with a tiny pinch of salt until stiff. Fold in delicately but thoroughly. Put the mixture into the pastry shells and bake in a fairly hot oven (190°C/375°F/Gas mark 5) for about 15 minutes or until puffed up and golden brown on top. Remove from the oven, leave for a minute or two to firm up, then transfer to hot plates and serve immediately.

The classic partnership of Gruyère and Parmesan indicated above can be replaced by any of the cheeses or cheese combinations suggested in the recipe for Cheese tart (p. 209).

TALEMOUSE BIEN DÉLICATE   MAKES 8 TARTLETS

The talemouse or talmouse is a kind of cheese tartlet with turned-up sides that appears regularly in cookbooks from the Middle Ages on. The fourteenth-century manuscript *Le Viandier*, by Guillaume Tirel, known as Taillevent, has a telegraphic recipe for it. But we learn more about what it was supposed to look like in the version given in 1654 by Nicolas de Bonnefons in his *Les Délices de la campagne* (p. 41), on which the recipe below is based.

The talemouse had reached Britain by 1600 at the latest and later became a well-established part of the cookery canon. *The Cookery Book of Lady Clark of Tillypronie* (pp. 138-9) contains no less than four recipes for 'talmouses'. One of them is contributed by a Mrs Pellet, who, like de Bonnefons, insists on the shape of the tartlet; 'Turn up the sides so as to make each [tartlet] the shape of a three-cornered hat.' In the Bordeaux area an identically shaped cheese tartlet is made that is called *corniotte* or *chapeau de curé* (priest's hat). Historically, the talemouse has another clerical connection: under the Ancien Régime the inhabitants of Sarcelles, then a village near Paris, traditionally offered the tarts to the Archbishop of Paris.

Yet the origins of the word talemouse are shrouded in mystery. It may come from the Old French *talemelier* (baker). But the word also means 'a slap in the face' and may equally well derive from *taler* (to beat) and *mouse* (muzzle). Another medieval word for the tartlet was *casse-museaux* (muzzle-breaker). Wondering what possible connection there could be between a three-cornered hat and a slap in the face, I turned to that marvellous fund of erudite and quaint information, the Larousse *Dictionnaire du XIX siècle* (published in the nineteenth century, and not to be confused with later editions of Larousse encyclopaedias). Under talmouse it says that the word does indeed mean *casse-museaux* because '*le nez s'y enfonce bien avant quand on la mange.*'

The entry goes on, in opinionated Johnsonian fashion, to describe the talmouse as a '*pâtisserie indigeste qui ne pourrait plaire qu'à des estomacs grossiers*'. But it none the less gives a recipe for it (indicating, by the way, that the dollop of filling to be put into each tartlet should be 'as large as a lady-apple' – a reminder that there was a time, alas long past, when lady-apples were so common that they could be used as a culinary standard of comparison).

350 g (12¹/₂ oz) chilled short pastry (p. 366)	40 g (1¹/₂ oz) plain flour
	1 whole egg
80 g (3 oz) unsalted butter, softened	2 egg yolks
110 g (4 oz) well-drained curd cheese	freshly ground white pepper
110 g (4 oz) freshly grated Gruyère	salt

On a lightly floured surface, roll out the pastry 3 mm (¹/₈ in) thick. Cut eight 15-cm (6-in) rounds. Fit each round into a lightly oiled 7-cm (3-in) tartlet tin, allowing the surplus pastry to overlap the edge. Prick the bottom and sides of the shell.

Blend the butter, cheeses, flour, egg, 1 egg yolk and plenty of pepper. Add salt to taste. Spoon the mixture into the pastry-lined tartlet shells. Moisten the edges of the pastry, and turn up the sides to make a shape like that of a three-cornered hat. Press the pastry together, but not all the way to the top, so there is an opening that allows the filling to puff and brown a little. Beat the remaining egg yolk and brush the talemouses with it. Bake in a moderate oven (180°C/350°F/Gas mark 4) for about 40 minutes or until golden brown. Remove the tartlets from the oven, leave to firm up for a minute or two, then transfer to hot plates and serve immediately.

CHAPTER ELEVEN

Cheese and Fish

GRATIN DE MOULES CORALIE   FOR 4

Mussels and onions – two complementary sweetnesses –
are often paired together. In this interesting recipe, a kind
of gratinéed risotto that comes from *Les Recettes des
'Belles Perdrix'* (p. 36), Gruyère provides a third, but not
pleonastic, sweetness.

1 litre (scant 2 pints) mussels
120 ml (4 fl oz) dry white wine
100 g (3¹/₂ oz) unsalted butter
1 onion, finely chopped
100 g (3¹/₂ oz) rice
200-300 ml (7-10 fl oz) veal *or*
  chicken stock

1 tbsp double cream
120 g (4 oz) freshly grated
  Gruyère
freshly ground pepper
salt

Scrub and beard the mussels. Discard any that do not
close up tight during handling or that have broken shells
(this, as the *Caterer & Hotelkeeper* once put it with
characteristic bluntness, means that 'the creatures inside
are dead and might make customers ill if eaten').

Put the mussels and the wine in a large sauté pan over a
high heat and cover. Shake the pan gently for a few
minutes. When the mussels have opened a little, strain off
the liquid and reserve. Shell the mussels, discarding any
that have not opened at all.

Heat 60 g (2 oz) of butter in the sauté pan and gently
sweat the onion until translucent but not browned. Add

the rice and stir for 1-2 minutes so all the grains are well coated with butter. Pour in the mussels' cooking liquid and a little hot stock, stir and leave to cook slowly. As the rice absorbs the liquid, add more hot stock and stir. By the time the rice is done (it should remain slightly firm), there should be no more liquid, just a tablespoon or two of creamy sauce.

Add the shelled mussels, the rest of the butter, the cream, half the cheese and plenty of pepper. Mix well but gently, so as not to damage the mussels. Add a little salt if necessary. Turn the mixture into a gratin dish, top with the rest of the cheese and bake in a fairly hot oven (190°C/375°F/Gas mark 5) for about 20 minutes or until the surface turns golden brown.

GRATIN DE PALOURDES   FOR 4

This rich Breton recipe gets the best out of carpet-shells (*palourdes*), which seem to me to have the finest flavour of the clam family. It also works well with any other small shellfish – cockles, clams, venus shells and indeed razor-shells (if you can catch them).

48 carpet-shells	350 ml (12 fl oz) double cream
400 ml (14 fl oz) dry white wine	150 g (5^1/$_2$ oz) freshly grated
50 g (2 oz) unsalted butter	Gruyère
150 g (5^1/$_2$ oz) onions, finely	freshly ground pepper
chopped	salt
3 cloves garlic, finely chopped	2 tbsp fresh parsley, finely chopped

Scrub the carpet-shells. Put them and 120 ml (4 fl oz) of the wine in a large sauté pan over a high heat and cover. Shake the pan gently for a few minutes. When the carpet-shells have opened, strain off the liquid and reserve. Shell the carpet-shells, discarding any that have not opened at all.

Heat the butter in the sauté pan and gently sweat the onions and garlic for a few minutes. Add the rest of the wine and the carpet-shells' cooking liquid, and simmer uncovered until an almost syrupy consistency is obtained. Add the cream and continue to cook gently, stirring from time to time, until the sauce thickens a little (it should coat the back of a spoon). Away from the heat, stir in the cheese and add plenty of pepper, a little salt to taste and the parsley.

Put the carpet-shells, in equal amounts, in four small, not too deep fireproof dishes. Pour the sauce over them and place them under a fierce grill until the surface turns golden brown. Serve immediately.

The more usual way of doing this gratin is to put the carpet-shells and dollops of sauce into empty half-shells, then brown them under the grill. The trouble with this method is that the shells do not sit upright and the sauce spills messily over the dish – which is why I have opted for a visually less exciting but culinarily more satisfactory procedure.

If you possess a set of those special earthenware snail dishes with cavities that look like solitaire boards, put a carpet-shell into each cavity, top with sauce and brown under the grill. The advantage of such dishes is that they have extraordinary heat-retaining properties – so you can take your time over eating the carpet-shells.

In a variation of this recipe, the cream and Gruyère are replaced by 400 ml (14 fl oz) of Mornay sauce II (p. 358) made with the carpet-shells' cooking liquid.

PRAWN GRATIN   FOR 4
On 26 January 1660 Samuel Pepys enjoyed:

> a very fine dinner – viz a dish of marrow-bones, a leg of mutton, a loin of veal, a dish of fowl, three pullets, and two dozen of larks all in a dish; a great tart, a neat's tongue, a dish of anchovy, a dish of prawns and cheese.

Pepys does not say how the prawns and cheese had been

cooked or whether he had any appetite left at that point in the meal. But they probably made a tasty morsel; for, surprising though it may seem until one has sampled them together, the two ingredients combine well, as in the following treatment based on a Polish recipe.

140 g (5 oz) good white bread, trimmed of crust	1 tbsp flour
120 ml (4 fl oz) milk	250 g (9 oz) curd cheese
700 g (1½ lb) prawns, live if possible	140 g (5 oz) freshly grated Gruyère
120 ml (4 fl oz) dry white wine	freshly ground pepper
120 g (4 oz) unsalted butter	pinch freshly grated nutmeg
	salt

Put the bread to soak in the milk. Put the prawns and wine in a large sauté pan over a high heat and cook covered for about 5 minutes, shaking the pan from time to time. The prawns should be pinkish but not quite cooked. Drain off their cooking liquid and reserve. When the prawns have cooled a little, shell them. (If you cannot get live prawns, buy cooked ones – if possible, fresh, not frozen – from a reliable fishmonger, shell them and marinate for 1 hour in lemon juice.)

Pulverize the shells in a blender and put them in a small saucepan with the butter. Heat gently, stirring, until the mixture begins to bubble. Pour through the finest strainer or muslin into the sauté pan. Add the flour, mixing well, then the bread, any milk that has not been absorbed by it, the prawns, their cooking liquid, the curd cheese, half the Gruyère, plenty of pepper and the nutmeg. Mix well and add salt to taste. Place the pan over a gentle heat and stir until the mixture thickens a little. Turn it into a gratin dish, sprinkle with the rest of the Gruyère and bake in a hot oven (220°C/425°F/Gas mark 7) for about 15 minutes or until the surface turns golden brown.

Depending on the dryness of the curd cheese and the amount of liquid given off by the prawns, this dish may remain fairly liquid. It is best served with plenty of rice or boiled potatoes.

You can, of course, replace the prawns with shrimps. The flavour will be subtly different and just as good, though the shelling will take much longer.

PRAWNS WITH FETA   FOR 4

A powerfully flavoured Greek version of prawns and cheese.

900 g (2 lb) prawns, live if possible
120 ml (4 fl oz) dry white wine
4 tbsp virgin olive oil
2 onions, finely sliced
3 cloves garlic, finely chopped
500 g (1 lb 2 oz) tomatoes, peeled,
  seeded and coarsely chopped

2 tbsp fresh parsley, finely chopped
pinch salt
freshly ground pepper
175 g (6 oz) feta, crumbled

Put the prawns and wine in a large sauté pan over a high heat and cook covered for about 5 minutes, shaking the pan from time to time. The prawns should be pinkish but not quite cooked. Remove them with a perforated spoon. When they have cooled a little, shell them. (If you cannot get live prawns, buy cooked ones – if possible, fresh, not frozen – from a reliable fishmonger, shell them and marinate for 1 hour in lemon juice.)

To the prawns' cooking liquid, add the olive oil, onions and garlic. Cook over a medium heat, stirring, until most of the liquid has evaporated. Add the tomatoes and the parsley. Simmer covered for 10 minutes, then uncovered for a further 20-30 minutes or until you have a not too liquid sauce.

Add a very little salt if necessary (remembering that the feta used in the topping is very salty), plenty of pepper and the shelled prawns. Mix well and put the mixture in four small individual soufflé dishes or large ramekins, sprinkle with feta and bake in a hot oven (220°C/425°F/Gas mark 7) for about 15 minutes or until the cheese has completely melted and begun to brown on top.

KRABBGRATIN   FOR 4

An unusual, successful Scandinavian combination of flavours: spicy-sweet crab flesh, nutty-sweet cheese and clean-sweet apple.

400 ml (14 fl oz) Mornay sauce I
  (p. 358)
340 g (12 oz) cooked crab meat, fresh
  if possible
4 eggs
1 small clove garlic, very finely
  chopped

pinch cayenne
freshly ground white pepper
1 crisp-flavoured apple
salt
80 g (3 oz) freshly grated Gruyère

Make or re-heat the Mornay sauce in a fairly large saucepan. Stir in the crab meat, eggs, garlic, cayenne and pepper. Peel and core the apple and grate it into the mixture. Mix thoroughly and add salt to taste. Pour the mixture into individual soufflé dishes or large ramekins, sprinkle with cheese and bake in a moderate oven (180°C/350°F/Gas mark 4) for 25-30 minutes or until the surface turns golden brown and a sharp-pointed knife, when inserted, comes out clean.

If using canned crab meat, use the juice in the can to make Mornay sauce II instead of I. It is worth going for the finest-quality canned crab: its flavour is incomparably superior to that of the cheaper brands.

CROQUETTES BLANKENBERGEOISES   FOR 4

In this recipe from Belgium, the prawn and cheese combination can be served to your guests *en surprise*, as the prawns are not visible.

300 g (10^1/$_2$ oz) prawns, live if
   possible
400 ml (14 fl oz) béchamel sauce II
   (p. 357)
120 g (4 oz) freshly grated Gruyère
2 egg yolks
freshly ground pepper

pinch freshly grated nutmeg
pinch salt
plain flour
2 eggs, beaten
slightly stale breadcrumbs
oil for deep-frying

Put the prawns into a sauté pan with a few tablespoons of water and cook over a high heat for about 5 minutes. They should be pinkish but not completely cooked. Remove the prawns with a perforated spoon. Boil down the cooking liquid to 1-2 tablespoons and reserve. Shell the prawns.

Make or re-heat the béchamel sauce. Away from the heat, stir in the finely grated cheese, the egg yolks, plenty of pepper, the nutmeg, the prawns' cooking liquid, a little salt to taste and the prawns. Leave to cool. Spread the mixture evenly on a lightly floured board or baking sheet, making a layer about 2 cm (1 in) thick. Chill for a few hours.

Cut the mixture into small pieces. Coat with flour, egg and breadcrumbs as described under Deep-fried Camembert (p. 73) and fry in batches until golden brown according to the basic deep-frying method (p. 72). Do not overcook, otherwise the croquettes may burst. Drain on paper towels and serve immediately.

WHITING WITH CURD CHEESE   FOR 4

A potent recipe that jazzes up the rather dull flavour of whiting.

700 g (1^1/$_2$ lb) whiting fillets
juice of 1 lemon
large pinch salt
freshly ground pepper
250 g (9 oz) curd cheese

4 cloves garlic, finely chopped
3 tbsp fresh parsley, finely chopped
80 g (3 oz) stale breadcrumbs
50 g (2 oz) freshly grated Parmesan

Put the whiting fillets into a shallow dish with the lemon

juice and plenty of salt and pepper. Leave to marinate for 1-2 hours in a cool place, turning the fillets over at least once.

Place the fillets, folded over on themselves, in a buttered gratin dish into which they fit neatly. Put the curd cheese, garlic, parsley, breadcrumbs and juice from the marinade into a bowl and mix well. Check for salt. Spread this mixture evenly over and around the fillets, as well as in the fold. Sprinkle the Parmesan over the top and bake in a moderate oven (180°C/350°F/Gas mark 4) for 30-40 minutes or until lightly browned on top.

FISH GRATIN WITH MORNAY SAUCE   FOR 4

This very basic dish works with almost any nice fresh-looking fillet that catches your eye at the fishmongers' (or, for that matter, with frozen fish), though the use of a very delicately or subtly flavoured fish such as red mullet, monkfish or salmon carries, in my view, a risk of overkill.

800 g (1³/₄ lb) fish fillets
500 ml (18 fl oz) hot Mornay sauce II (p. 358)

1 small clove garlic, finely chopped
60 g (2 oz) duxelles (p. 365) (optional)

Poach the fish in a mild court-bouillon (without vinegar) or steam it in aluminium foil until it is *almost* but not quite cooked. Keep 100 ml (3¹/₂ fl oz) of the court-bouillon or cooking juices (supplementing the latter if necessary with fish stock) for the Mornay sauce. Make the Mornay sauce.

Butter a gratin dish and strew it with garlic. If you want an additional mushroomy flavour, stir the duxelles into the hot Mornay sauce. Arrange one layer of fillets on the bottom of the gratin dish. Pour some sauce over them, add another layer of fish, making the surface as flat as possible, and add the rest of the sauce. Bake in a hot oven (220°C/425°F/Gas mark 7) for 10 minutes or until the surface begins to turn golden brown.

RAIE AU PARMESAN   FOR 4

In France skate is almost invariably served swimming in *beurre noir*, a treatment that at its best is boring, and to my mind, repulsively rich, but at its worst – as when the butter overheats and burns, producing minute quantities of a poison called acrolein (p. 29) – highly indigestible.

But the French have another, now largely forgotten, way of cooking skate, which dates from at least as far back as the eighteenth century: *Raie au fromage* or *au parmesan*. The piquant touch that capers traditionally give the skate in the *beurre noir* recipe is here provided by pickling onions.

This recipe has been adapted from François Marin's *Les Dons de Comus ou les délices de la table*. Marin was one of the most important of eighteenth-century French cookbook writers and a leading figure in the movement of the period known as *nouvelle cuisine* (many of whose precepts have been adopted by exponents of 'modern' *nouvelle cuisine*).

Like the earlier Vincent La Chapelle, Marin reacted against the heavy use of spices to which chefs commonly resorted at the time in order to mask the true flavour of often second-rate produce. And, in what is to my knowledge the first ever discussion in print of cheese cookery, he stressed the need to use high-quality cheeses in prime condition.

16 small pickling onions, peeled	1.2kg (2 lb 10 oz) skate *or* ray
500 ml (17 fl oz) milk	(thornback if possible) skinned and
large pinch salt	cut into 4 pieces
freshly ground pepper	90 g (3 oz) unsalted butter
1/2 lemon, thinly sliced	175 g (6 oz) freshly grated Parmesan
2 tbsp fresh parsley, finely chopped	2 egg yolks
2 tbsp fresh chives, finely chopped	1 tbsp Dijon mustard
1/2 tsp fresh *or* dried thyme	100 g (3 1/2 oz) stale breadcrumbs
50 g (2 oz) *beurre manié* (p. 364)	fried croûtons (optional)

Blanch the pickling onions for 20 minutes in boiling salted water and drain. Put them in a large sauté pan with the milk, salt, pepper, lemon, parsley, chives and thyme. Bring to simmering point and beat in the *beurre manié*. Put in the skate and poach gently for 15 minutes, turning the pieces over once. Remove the skate. Continue to simmer the cooking liquid until the consistency of single cream is obtained. Remove the onions and strain the sauce into a saucepan.

Using 30 g (1 oz) of the butter, butter a gratin dish large enough to hold the skate pieces in one layer. Sprinkle the bottom of the dish with half the cheese. Place the skate in the dish with the onions arranged in rows between each piece. Heat the sauce to almost simmering point, then, away from the heat, beat in the rest of the butter, cut into little pieces. When it has melted, add the egg yolks and mustard, and whisk, if necessary over a low heat, until the sauce thickens a little.

Pour the sauce over skate and onions. Mix the rest of the cheese with the breadcrumbs, sprinkle over the dish and bake in a hot oven (220°C/425°F/Gas mark 7) for 10 minutes or until the surface begins to turn brown. Serve with fried croûtons if desired.

SOLE À LA FLORENTINE   FOR 4

Sole has a pleasant, firm texture and an excellent, versatile flavour; what is more, it has few bones and is easily filleted. No wonder, then, that around 1900 it became the darling of *haute cuisine* chefs, who dressed it up in a multitude of often meretricious guises. It was not infrequently accompanied by lobster and truffles, and given evocative names like 'Otéro', 'Walewska', 'Victoria' and 'Prince Albert'. A 1929 fish cookbook in my possession lists no less than 160 ways of cooking – or rather accompanying – sole. But not all *haute cuisine* recipes for the fish are extravagant or overcomplicated, to wit this classic, Sole à la florentine.

8 sole fillets

salt

120 ml (4 fl oz) fish *fumet*, made
from the bones and trimmings

3 tbsp dry white wine

600 g (1 lb 5 oz) spinach

50 g (2 oz) unsalted butter

pinch freshly grated nutmeg

400 ml (14 fl oz) Mornay sauce II
(p. 358)

30 g (1 oz) freshly grated Parmesan

freshly ground pepper

Put the sole fillets, seasoned with salt, into a lightly buttered, heated large gratin dish. Bring the *fumet* and wine to the boil in a saucepan and pour over the fish. Transfer the baking dish to a moderate oven (180°C/350°F/Gas mark 4) and poach for about 10 minutes. The fillets should be only just cooked, tender but still springy when prodded. Remove the fillets carefully from the liquid and keep warm (but not hot). Pour the cooking liquid into a small saucepan and reduce until you have about 100 ml (3½ fl oz) left. Set aside for the Mornay sauce.

Trim the spinach of its tougher stalks, wash thoroughly, and put in plenty of boiling salted water. Cook uncovered for about 5 minutes, drain, chop coarsely and squeeze out as much liquid as possible. Melt the butter in a large frying pan. Add the spinach and nutmeg and cook gently, stirring and tossing all the time, until all the liquid has evaporated. Lay the spinach on the bottom of the gratin dish and keep warm.

Make the Mornay sauce, using the sole's reduced cooking liquid. Lay the sole fillets on the spinach and sprinkle with pepper. Pour the Mornay sauce over them as evenly as possible, sprinkle with finely grated Parmesan and bake in a very hot oven (230°C/450°F/Gas mark 8) for 5 minutes or until the surface begins to turn golden brown.

PAUPIETTES DE TRUITE AU LAGUIOLE
ET AUX OIGNONS NOUVEAUX   FOR 4

The cards were stacked against Michel Bras when he took over his parents' hotel-restaurant, Lou Mazuc, in Laguiole (pronounced 'lie-yol') in 1979. Winters in Laguiole, a town of just over 1,250 inhabitants on the windswept plateau of the Aubrac, 1,000 m (3,280 ft) above sea level, are so rigorous that the hotel-restaurant had to close down from mid-October to April. And there was little local demand for the kind of sophisticated cuisine that Bras was creating, even though it was rooted in local culinary tradition. Despite all these handicaps, Bras turned Lou Mazuc into a place of culinary pilgrimage. He then moved his hotel-restaurant to an ultra-modern building he had built on a hill overlooking Laguiole. Now called simply Michel Bras, it has moved high into the French culinary firmament, and now boasts three Michelin stars and a 19/20 rating in the Gault-Millau Guide. Anyone wishing to eat, let alone stay, there during July or August now has to book months ahead.

But fame has not gone to Bras' head, and his cooking style remains brilliantly simple, as can be judged from the following recipe (which uses the local cheese, Laguiole, a relative of Cantal).

60 g (2 oz) young Laguiole, diced	4 large spinach leaves, trimmed of
160 g (5^1/$_2$ oz) unsalted butter	their stalks
1 small egg	8 trout fillets (i.e. from 4 trout)
4 shallots, finely chopped	salt
30 g (1 oz) raw ham, chopped	freshly ground pepper
30 g (1 oz) white bread, soaked	200 ml (7 fl oz) dry white wine
in water	12 very small spring onions

Blend the cheese with 3 tablespoons of water until smooth. Add 40 g (1^1/$_2$ oz) of butter, the egg, half the shallots, the ham and the bread (squeezed dry), blend until smooth and set aside in a cool place for 30 minutes.

Wash the spinach leaves thoroughly, and put in plenty of boiling salted water. Cook uncovered for 5 minutes. Drain and lay out the spinach leaves flat on tea towels.

Spread them equally with the cheese mixture. Place 2 trout fillets in the middle of each leaf, season with salt and pepper, and wrap up to make a neat paupiette. Put the paupiettes in a baking dish into which they fit neatly, add 4-5 tablespoons of dry white wine, cover tightly with aluminium foil and bake in a fairly hot oven (200°C/400°F/Gas mark 6) for 15-25 minutes.

Trim the spring onions and remove and discard their green tops. Cook in boiling salted water until tender. Drain and set aside. In a small heavy saucepan, bring the remaining wine to the boil, add the rest of the shallots and reduce until you obtain a jam-like consistency. Add the rest of the butter, 4 tablespoons of water and the spring onions, finely sliced. Bring to the boil and cook, stirring frequently, until the mixture homogenizes to a sauce. Put the paupiettes on to hot plates, pour the sauce around them and serve immediately.

BRACIOLE DI PESCE SPADA   FOR 4

Swordfish are plentiful around Sicily and the Sicilians have many ways of cooking them. This recipe, quite apart from producing a delicious result, must be one of the rare cases in cheese cookery where the technique used to melt the cheese is a charcoal grill.

7 tbsp virgin olive oil	50 g (2 oz) breadcrumbs
1 onion, finely sliced	120 g (4 oz) mature provolone,
120 g (4 oz) swordfish flesh, coarsely	grated *or* diced
chopped, and 4 large very thin	2 eggs
slices swordfish	salt
2 tbsp fresh parsley, chopped	freshly ground pepper

Heat 6 tablespoons of olive oil in a frying pan and gently sauté the onion until it is translucent but not browned. Add the chopped swordfish flesh and parsley, and continue to cook for 12 minutes. Stir in the breadcrumbs. Put the mixture into a blender along with the cheese and eggs. Blend, and add salt and pepper to taste.

Beat the swordfish slices, but not too hard, with the side of a meat cleaver. Season with salt and pepper. Spread the filling evenly over the slices, leaving a small margin uncovered near the edges. Roll the slices up like a scroll and secure at two or three points with toothpicks or cocktail sausage sticks. Brush with olive oil and grill, turning over once, for 10-15 minutes, if possible over a fire of charcoal or, even better, vine stumps. Whether grilling from above or below, keep the heat moderate.

Like grilled tunny fish, swordfish done in this way requires only one accompaniment: a squeeze of lemon juice. This recipe, by the way, can be made equally well with tunny fish.

If possible, try to get hold of mature provolone, which has a sharp taste and is hard enough to be grated; failing that, any cheese with plenty of tang, like mature Canadian Cheddar, will do.

POUPETOUN   FOR 4

An oddly un-Provençal dish from Provence. I have used the Provençal word *poupetoun* because the French spelling *poupeton* also refers to a kind of meat roll or *ballottine* (in that sense, it is the dimunitive of *poupée*). Originally a way of using up the remains of a bouillabaisse, *poupetoun* can also be made from the remains of any fish dish – or indeed with fresh fish bought specially for the purpose.

90 g (3 oz) good white bread,
   trimmed of crust
150 ml (5 fl oz) milk
4 eggs, separated
60 g (2 oz) freshly grated Parmesan
600 g (1 lb 5 oz) cooked fish
   (see note below)

120 ml (4 fl oz) double cream
1 clove garlic, finely chopped
   (if necessary)
Salt
freshly ground pepper

Soak the bread in the milk. Bone the fish meticulously and blend with the cream, soaked bread, egg yolks, cheese and, if using fish that has *not* been left from a bouillabaisse or similarly garlicky dish, garlic. Add salt and plenty of pepper to taste. Whisk the egg whites with a small pinch of salt until stiff and gently fold into the mixture. Butter a soufflé mould. Turn the mixture out into the mould (which it should not fill completely).

Cook in a bain-marie in a fairly hot oven (190°C/375°F/Gas mark 5) for about 30 minutes or until cooked (a pointed knife, when inserted, should come out clean). Allow to settle for 5 minutes, then unmould on to a hot serving dish.

This dish may be accompanied either by tomato sauce (p. 364), or, in more peasant fashion, by tomatoes fried in olive oil.

If buying fish specially for the *poupetoun*, just steam it, or cook it in a well-spiced court-bouillon and allow to cool before use. As the fish ends up by being boned and blended, the dish provides a good opportunity to use one of those species that are tasty but difficult to negotiate because of their forest of bones, e.g. large fresh sardines (pilchards) or conger eel.

GENERAL GRUDGER   FOR 4-6

An Anglo-Indian curiosity from E. H. Parry's *Cookery and Other Recipes* (Allahabad, 1910), a book heavily redolent of the British Raj, with its advertisements in the front for 'improved "Cawnpore Tent Club" pith helmets', Madame E. Thick's drill skirts, and Charles & Co., chemists whose 'dispensary is entirely under European control'.

The publishers interleaved the book with blank ruled pages for notes and recipes. My kitchen-soiled, battered (possibly in both senses) copy enables one to chart the itinerary of an anonymous family (diplomats? soldiers?) as they moved around the British Empire: on the interleaved pages, written in at least three different anonymous hands (grandmother? mother? daughter?) there are Australian, Malaysian, Indian, Singhalese and South African recipes.

One such manuscript recipe is for General Grudger. I must confess that I have no idea how the dish came to acquire its curious name.

The 'other recipes' of the book's title include cocktails (e.g. 'P. & O.'), 'How to keep cheese from drying in India', 'How to clean ivory knife handles' and other apposite household hints.

30 g (1 oz) sultanas	110 g (4 oz) freshly grated Cheddar
3 tbsp milk	20 prawns, cooked and shelled
1 kg (2 lb 3 oz) potatoes	3 hard-boiled eggs, shelled and sliced
salt	4 tbsp breadcrumbs
freshly ground pepper	2 tsp good curry powder
60 g (2 oz) unsalted butter	2 tbsp fresh parsley, finely chopped
3 tbsp mango chutney	

Put the sultanas to soak in the milk. Wash and cook the potatoes in plenty of boiling salted water until tender. Peel and mash, adding salt and pepper to taste. Butter a pie dish with half the butter. Put a thin layer of mashed potato on the bottom of the dish and follow this with layers of chutney, cheese, potato, prawns, hard-boiled egg, cheese and potato, in that order. Fry the breadcrumbs gently in the remaining butter. When crisp, mix with the curry powder, sultanas and parsley. Make a small well in the centre of the layered pie dish and fill with the mixture. Bake in a fairly hot oven (190°C/375°F/Gas mark 5) for 20 minutes.

DAHI WALI MACCHI FOR 4

Fresh haddock baked in a yoghurt sauce – an aromatic recipe from *Madhur Jaffrey's Indian Cookery*, and one that she describes as one of her favourite dishes.

175 g (6 oz) onions
1 kg (2 lb 3 oz) fresh haddock fillets
   about 2.5 cm (1 in) thick
425 ml (15 fl oz) yoghurt
2 tbsp lemon juice
1 tsp sugar
1½ tsp salt
¼ tsp coarsely ground pepper
2 tsp freshly ground cumin

2 tbsp freshly ground coriander seeds
¼ tsp garam masala
¾ tsp cayenne
1 tsp fresh ginger, peeled and
   finely grated
3 tbsp oil
40 g (1½ oz) cold unsalted butter,
   diced

Cut the onions into 3-mm (⅛-in) thick slices and line a large shallow baking dish with them. The dish should be large enough to hold the fish in a single layer. Cut the fish fillets crosswise into 8-cm (3-in) long segments and lay them over the onions.

Put the yoghurt into a bowl. Beat it lightly. Add the lemon juice, sugar, salt, pepper, cumin, coriander, garam masala, cayenne and ginger. Mix well. Add the oil and mix again. Pour this sauce over the fish, making sure that some of it goes under the pieces as well. Cover (with aluminium foil if necessary) and bake in the upper third of the oven for 30 minutes or until the fish is only just done.

Carefully pour out all the liquid from the baking dish into a small saucepan. Keep the fish warm. The sauce will look thin and separated. Bring it to the boil. Boil rapidly until about 350 ml (12 fl oz) of sauce remains. Take the saucepan off the heat. Put in the pieces of butter and beat them in with a whisk. As soon as the butter has melted, pour the sauce over the fish and serve.

Jaffrey adds that, although not traditionally eaten that way, the dish is also very good cold, with a green salad on the side.

MORUE AU GRATIN   FOR 4

Like Timbale milanaise (p. 160), this clever combination of salt cod and cheese comes, slightly adapted, from the magazine *Le Pot au feu* (issue of 13 March 1900). This recipe, too, was demonstrated at a lecture by Auguste Colombié.

> Ladies [he began], the *morue au gratin* we are going to make today is an excellent dish, which looks very pretty and is easy to prepare. It is one of the best ways to make salt cod attractive to people who eat it more out of resignation than for pleasure.

The resignation arose no doubt from the frequency of consumption: in the days before refrigerated lorries carried fresh fish the length and breadth of the land, salt fish loomed much larger in the everyday diet than it does now.

500 g (1 lb 2 oz) salt cod	salt
1 tsp lemon juice	freshly grated nutmeg
80-120 ml (3-4 fl oz) milk	freshly ground pepper
400 ml (14 fl oz) Mornay sauce II	pinch sugar
(p. 358), made with 1^1/$_2$ times	140 g (5 oz) unsalted butter
the quantity of cheese indicated	1 egg yolk
500 g (1 lb 2 oz) yellow waxy	1 whole egg
potatoes (Jaune de Hollande if	3 tbsp double cream
possible)	50 g (2 oz) freshly grated Parmesan

Soak the salt cold for at least 24 hours (some authorities recommend 48 hours or even more; I have found that a day is enough if plenty of water is used, if it is changed several times, and if, as Colombié suggests, the cod is placed on an upturned wire basket or similar object that prevents it from sitting on the bottom of the receptacle, where the water is saturated with salt). Scrape off any scales but leave the skin (which adds flavour).

Place the cod in a saucepan with 2 litres (70 fl oz) of water, the lemon juice and 4 tablespoons of milk. Set uncovered over a very low heat. As it heats up, move the cod gently around so the hot liquid envelops it well. As soon as the water just begins to simmer, cover and put over the lowest setting of an electric plaque or on a heat diffuser (if you have a kitchen range as Colombié did, place the pan on a cool part of the surface). Leave for 20 minutes, then set aside, still in its water. Set aside 100 ml (3½ fl oz) of the liquid for the Mornay sauce.

Scrub and peel the potatoes. Boil in plenty of boiling salted water for 20-30 minutes or until cooked. While they are cooking, make the Mornay sauce and keep warm. Drain the potatoes and leave them in the saucepan for 1-2 minutes to dry out. Mash them quickly in a very hot mixing bowl, add a little salt, the nutmeg, a little pepper, the sugar and 80 g (3 oz) of butter, chilled and diced. Beat vigorously with a wooden spoon for 5-6 minutes. Add the egg, egg yolk and cream, and mix well. If the mixture is too firm to be put through a forcing bag, add a very little milk, taking care not to make it too liquid. Keep warm.

Butter a shallow gratin or baking dish with 30 g (1 oz) of butter. (With a manic precision that was a reaction against the usual vagueness of recipe directions in his day, Colombié specifies that it should be 'about 34 cm (13½ in) in diameter'!) Put the mashed potatoes into a forcing bag with a cannelated nozzle and squeeze out into a fluted design around the edge of the dish. If you do not have a forcing bag, use a spoon to mould the potato into a series of neat mounds.

Remove the salt cod from its cooking liquid, and flake, but not too finely. Check its degree of saltiness. If almost all the salt has been removed during soaking, add a little. Put a layer of sauce on the bottom of the dish, then a layer of cod; repeat the operation, finishing with sauce. Sprinkle the sauce with the finely grated cheese. Brush the mashed potato with milk and bake in a very hot oven (230°C/450°F/Gas mark 8) for 10 minutes or until the potato has begun to brown. Remove from the oven, brush the surface of the sauce with melted butter to glaze it, and serve immediately.

CHAPTER TWELVE

Cheese and Meat

POULET BOURBONNAIS FOR 4

An uncomplicated peasant dish that has nothing to do with the noble House of Bourbon (whose adjective is *bourbonien*). It comes from the Bourbonnais region, which lies between the Berry and the Auvergne in central France.

50 g (2 oz) unsalted butter	120 ml (4 fl oz) dry white wine
1 small onion, sliced	400 ml (14 fl oz) Mornay sauce IV
1 small, good-quality chicken	enriched with 2 egg yolks as in
(about 1.2 kg/2³/₄ lb), trussed	Mornay sauce V (p. 359)
large pinch salt	100 g (3¹/₂ oz) freshly grated Gruyère
freshly ground pepper	

Heat the butter in a heavy oval casserole and cook the onion gently until it just begins to turn brown. Sprinkle the chicken, inside and outside, with salt and plenty of pepper. Put it on its side in the casserole, cover and cook over a low heat for 45-60 minutes, turning it over once.

When the chicken is just cooked (you should be able to prise a leg away from the body easily, but the thigh socket should still be slightly pink), take it out and place on a board. There will normally be a certain amount of juice in the casserole. If there seems to be a lot of fat, tilt the casserole and remove as much as possible with a bulb baster or spoon. Pour in the wine (and about the same quantity of water if there is very little chicken juice) and, over a high heat, deglaze the bottom of the casserole with a wooden spoon. Reduce the liquid until there is about 100 ml (3½ fl oz) left. Put this liquid through a fine strainer, check its seasoning (it should be quite salty) and set aside for use in the Mornay sauce.

Cut the chicken into four pieces (two breast pieces and two legs), arrange neatly in one layer in a large buttered gratin dish and keep warm. Make the Mornay sauce. Pour it over the chicken, sprinkle with cheese, and bake in a fairly hot oven (190°C/375°F/Gas mark 5) for 15-20 minutes, or until the surface begins to turn golden brown. For this, as for the following recipes, it is essential to procure a good-quality farm chicken, not a gelatinous broiler that will fall apart in the casserole. Also to be avoided are certain maize-fed specimens that ooze staggering amounts of yellow fat during cooking.

If you want to be really authentic, use white Saint-Pourçain, a homely wine from the Bourbonnais, for the deglazing, and serve the same appellation at table (either a chilled white or a cool red).

POULARDE GRATINÉE DE L'AUBERGE   FOR 4

A luscious recipe served by the brothers Pierre and Jean-Paul Haeberlin at their Auberge de l'Ill, in Alsace, probably the most unassuming of France's Michelin three-star restaurants. It comes from their handsome book, *Les Recettes de l'Auberge de l'Ill*.

1 good-quality chicken of about 1.5 kg (3½ lb), trussed	500 ml (17 fl oz) Mornay sauce V (p. 359)
30 g (1 oz) unsalted butter	120 g (4 oz) foie gras truffé
large pinch salt	100 g (3½ oz) freshly grated Gruyère
freshly ground pepper	

Rub the chicken with the butter, the salt and plenty of pepper. Roast in a fairly hot oven (200°C/400°F/Gas mark 6) for about 1 hour or until done. Make or re-heat the Mornay sauce. Remove the chicken from the oven and cut into four pieces (two breast pieces and two legs). Remove as much bone as is possible while leaving the four pieces whole.

Cut the foie gras into four slices. Place on the bottom of a buttered gratin dish. Lay the chicken pieces on them, cover with Mornay sauce, sprinkle with grated cheese and put into a very hot oven (230°C/450°F/Gas mark 8) for about 10 minutes or until golden brown.

The Haeberlin brothers suggest the chicken be served with Wasserstriwela (an Alsatian kind of noodle) and a lamb's lettuce salad on the side.

BEIRA ALTA CHICKEN   FOR 6

A recipe from Portugal's most mountainous area, Beira Alta, which lies in the centre-east of the country.

1 good-quality chicken of about 2 kg (4^1/$_2$ lb), trussed	200 g (7 oz) well-drained curd cheese
2 thin slices *presunto or* Bayonne ham	120 g (4 oz) unsalted butter
	salt
	freshly ground pepper

Make an incision in the skin of the chicken at one end of one side of the breast, prise it away from the flesh and insert a slice of ham. Do the same on the other side. Mash the curd cheese with 60 g (2 oz) of butter, some salt and plenty of pepper. Stuff the chicken's inner cavity with this mixture and sew up the opening. Melt the rest of the butter and brush the chicken with it. Sprinkle with a little salt and place in a baking dish. Roast unhurriedly, so as not to burn the butter, in a moderate oven (180°C/350°F/Gas mark 4) for about 90 minutes, basting from time to time.

This dish is very good with new potatoes, which should be roasted and basted in the same dish as the chicken.

CHICKEN MARINATED IN YOGHURT AND SPICES   FOR 6
This is one of my favourite Indian dishes. The apparently plethoric combination of different flavours and aromas combines into a symphonic whole.

1 good-quality chicken of about 1.5 kg (3^1/$_2$ lb)	10 cloves garlic
2 red peppers, seeded	250 ml (9 fl oz) yoghurt
3 green chillies, seeded	large pinch salt
2 tbsp roasted coriander seeds	30 g (1 oz) clarified butter
seeds of 4 cardamom pods	200 g (7 oz) onions, finely chopped
2 tbsp ground almonds	4 cloves, pounded
large pinch cinnamon	1 tbsp fresh mint, chopped
2 tbsp freshly grated ginger	pinch ground saffron
large pinch freshly grated nutmeg	1 tsp freshly ground pepper
	140 g (5 oz) spring onions, finely sliced

Cut the chicken into 8 pieces, skin and prick all over with a fork. Blend the peppers, chillies, coriander and garlic with the yoghurt and salt. Put the chicken pieces into a bowl. Cover thoroughly with the marinade and press down to make as compact and airless a mass as possible. Cover and leave in the refrigerator or a cool place overnight or for at least 12 hours.

Heat the clarified butter in a casserole until very hot. Put in the chicken pieces, with any bits of marinade adhering to them, and cook briskly for a few minutes, turning them over from time to time until slightly browned. Remove from heat. Take out the chicken pieces. Line the bottom of the casserole with a bed of chopped onions. Add to the remaining marinade the cardamom seeds, ground almonds, cinnamon, ginger, nutmeg, cloves, mint, saffron and pepper, and mix very thoroughly. Roll the chicken pieces in this mixture and lay them delicately on the bed of onions in the casserole with all the remaining marinade. Strew the top with spring onions.

Transfer to a moderate oven (180°C/350°F/Gas mark 4) for about 75 minutes, shaking the casserole vigorously from time to time. Resist any temptation to raise the lid, leaving that pleasure for when you bring the dish to the table. Serve with boiled rice.

VEAU À LA VIKING   FOR 4

Veal with cheese is one of those combinations that is so *right* that it is found in many European cuisines – French, Polish, German, Swiss and, of course, Italian.

This recipe comes from *Les Recettes des 'Belles Perdrix'* (p. 36), and is named after one of the restaurants where the women belonging to the Belles Perdrix dining club used to meet, the Restaurant des Vikings in Paris.

4 large, thin veal escalopes weighing 125 g (4¹/₂ oz) each, as nearly as possible of equal dimensions	salt
	freshly ground pepper
3 tbsp olive oil	150 g (5¹/₂ oz) freshly grated Gruyère
juice of 1 lemon	150 g (5¹/₂ oz) freshly grated Parmesan
2 tsp armagnac	
40 g (1¹/₂ oz) unsalted butter	

Cut all gristle and transparent skin off the edge of the escalopes and trim if necessary to make them almost exactly the same size. Place each under a piece of cling-film and beat briefly but not too hard. After this treatment they should be no more than 6 mm (¹/₄ in) thick. Put them in a dish and pour the olive oil, lemon juice and armagnac over them, making sure the liquid reaches into every cranny. Cover and set aside in a cool place for several hours.

Heat the butter gently in a small casserole. Lay 1 escalope on the bottom, sprinkle with a little salt and plenty of pepper, and cover neatly with a third of each cheese. Repeat the operation, pressing down each layer of cheese with the following escalope, and finishing with an escalope. Pour the marinade over the escalopes. Cover and cook very slowly for 45-60 minutes.

When done, remove to a hot serving plate. Using a wooden spoon, quickly deglaze the bottom of the casserole with enough water to make about 100 ml (3¹/₂ fl oz) of liquid (the amount will depend on how much cooking juice remains). Reduce by half over a high heat. Slice the mound of escalopes crosswise and arrange so they overlap each other, dribble the juice over them and serve immediately.

SCALOPPINE DI VITELLO ALLA MODENESE   FOR 4

As I have already pointed out, the marriage of veal and cheese is a common event, but it often develops – especially in Italy – into a *ménage à trois*, with ham, either raw or cooked, adding a piquancy to the relationship, as in these delicate little veal slices from the Modena region.

8 small thin veal escalopes of about 60 g (2 oz) each	breadcrumbs
juice of ¹/₂ lemon	80 g (3 oz) unsalted butter
salt	4 thin slices prosciutto *or* similar raw ham
freshly ground pepper	250 g (9 oz) mozzarella, thinly sliced
1 egg, beaten	

Sprinkle the escalopes with lemon juice, salt and pepper. Dip in a little beaten egg, then in breadcrumbs. Heat the butter in a very large frying pan and fry the escalopes gently for 7-8 minutes on each side, in two batches if necessary. Transfer to a shallow gratin or baking dish. Place half-slices of ham, then slices of cheese, on each escalope. Put in to a hot oven (220°C/425°F/Gas mark 7) for 10 minutes or until the cheese has melted and begun to brown.

ESCALOPES AU POTIRON   FOR 4

Veal escalopes with pumpkin and cheese? It sounds an odd combination, but works admirably well. As we have seen in other dishes, 'sweet' cheeses like Gruyère or Parmesan are never happier than when accompanied by a complementary sweetness in this case, pumpkin.

The recipe comes from *Radio-Cuisine* by Dr Edouard de Pomiane. De Pomiane was the most engaging of France's prewar gastronomic luminaries: he was full of *joie de vivre*, totally devoid of pretension or self-importance, greedy, sociable, gastronomically curious and scientifically on the ball. In his writing he could switch effortlessly from serious books on diet and cooking techniques, such as *Bien Manger pour Bien Vivre* or *Conserves Familiales et Microbie Alimentaire*, to tongue-in-cheek works like *Vingt*

Plats Qui Donnent la Goutte (published by the manufacturers of a patent medicine for gout, Pipérazine-Midy, the book describes twenty dishes likely to encourage gout in those who do *not* take the medicine).

While his Angevin friend and colleague Maurice Edmond Sailland assumed the Polish-sounding *nom de plume* of Curnonsky (in fact from the Latin *cur non?* – 'why not?' – at the suggestion of the humorist Alphonse Allais), the aristocratic-sounding Edouard de Pomiane was in fact called Edouard Pozerski and was of Polish stock. This latter fact may explain his interest in the cuisines of countries other than France.

In a popular series of radio programmes called 'Chroniques Gastronomiques Radiodiffusées' De Pomiane regaled listeners with hundreds of interesting recipes, reminiscences and breezy chit-chat. But radio reception was not always perfect. Fed up with having to reply to requests for written versions of the recipes he had given over the air, he published them, in two volumes, as *Radio-Cuisine* (1936).

In his chapter on the pumpkin he bemoaned the fact that the street songs of Parisian oyster vendors and chickweed sellers (the chickweed was for cage-birds) had been drowned by traffic noise, and that most shop fronts had been modernized. But he was glad to note that cheese merchants, with their sign 'Beurre, oeufs, fromages', were respecting tradition by placing a huge, partly cut pumpkin on a stool by their shop entrance as if to say to passers-by: 'Make pumpkin soup; you'll need to buy milk for that.' De Pomiane was writing – or rather speaking – in 1936. Needless to say, the pumpkins in front of cheese shops have long since vanished.

500 g (1 lb 2 oz) pumpkin
12 g (¹/₂ oz) flour
5 tbsp double cream
100 g (3¹/₂ oz) freshly grated
  Gruyère
pinch freshly grated nutmeg

freshly ground pepper
salt
5 veal escalopes of 125 g (4¹/₂ oz)
  each
60 g (2 oz) unsalted butter
4 slices ham

Slice the pumpkin, remove the seeds and cottony fibre (but not the skin) and bake in a hot oven until soft. Peel, cut into small pieces and put into a saucepan with a little water. Cover and place over a high heat. As soon as the liquid begins to bubble, turn the heat down to low and cook for about 15 minutes or until the pumpkin has turned to a mush and there is almost no liquid remaining. Keep the pan on a very low heat.

In a small mixing bowl, blend the flour and the cream. Pour into the pumpkin purée, stir and cook over a medium heat for 30 seconds. Add half the cheese, the nutmeg, plenty of pepper and salt to taste. Mix well and set aside.

Cut all gristle and transparent skin off the edge of the escalopes. Heat the butter in a frying pan over a medium heat and brown the escalopes on both sides, then cook them gently for 10 minutes. Warm a large gratin dish and arrange the escalopes in it side by side. On each of them lay a slice of ham. Pour over the pumpkin sauce, sprinkle with the rest of the cheese and put in a fairly hot oven (190°C/375°F/Gas mark 5) for 20 minutes or until the surface begins to turn golden brown.

De Pomiane suggests that a 'good, very sweet Sauternes' should be drunk with this dish.

ESCALOPES SAVOYARDES   FOR 4
One of the most congenial restaurants in the Paris of the Sixties was a cheap little place in the Rue Cochin run by an amiable Savoyard – and fanatical rugby fan – whose name has since slipped my memory. Invariably wearing a vest, he beavered away on his own, in a tiny overheated kitchen by the restaurant entrance. The long, narrow dining-room stretched back and down under ancient vaults. People went to his restaurant to eat *à la bonne franquette*, an expression that is used only in connection with eating and hospitality, and which literally means 'simply and without ceremony' but implies bonhomie and unpretentiousness as well.

The Savoyard's set menu invariably started with a series of copious, ultra-fresh *hors-d'oeuvre variés* and continued with some old favourite – or reinterpretation – of *cuisine bourgeoise*. Magnum bottles of good *vin ordinaire* stood on each table, and the two pert waitresses (his daughters) followed the informal Italian practice of charging you according to the level the wine in your bottle had sunk to by the end of the meal.

One of the best dishes produced by the Savoyard in his little kitchen was of his own invention. It appeared on the menu simply as Escalope savoyarde. He could equally well have called it Gratin dauphinois en surprise. It certainly surprised me and my friends the first time we were served it.

600 g (1¹/₄ lb) good waxy potatoes, peeled
500 ml (17 fl oz) milk
150 ml (5 fl oz) double cream
pinch freshly grated nutmeg
4 thin escalopes of about 125 g (4¹/₂ oz) each
40 g (1¹/₂ oz) unsalted butter

2 cloves garlic, finely chopped
4 small pieces of smoked bacon cut from the lean end of the rasher, trimmed of rind
salt
freshly ground pepper
200 g (7 oz) freshly grated Gruyère

Slice the potatoes very thinly. Do not rinse, as the starch in their juice will help prevent the milk and cream from curdling. Bring the milk to simmering point in a large saucepan, add the potatoes and poach gently for about 10 minutes (the potatoes should be about half-cooked). Strain the milk into another pan, add the cream and nutmeg to it and mix.

Cut all gristle and transparent skin off the edge of the escalopes. Fold in half and score lightly on the outside of the fold so they stay closed. Heat the butter in a frying pan and cook the folded escalopes gently for about 5 minutes on each side. They should be very slightly browned.

Butter a gratin dish generously and strew the garlic over the bottom. Slip a piece of bacon into the fold of each escalope and lay the escalopes in the dish. Arrange about a third of the potatoes in a layer around them, with the slices overlapping each other. Sprinkle salt, pepper and about a quarter of the cheese over them. Repeat the layering operation twice more, but, before adding the final generous topping of cheese, pour the milk and cream over the potatoes and escalopes. By the time the topping has been added, the gratin dish should be no more than three-quarters full, otherwise it may boil over in the oven. The escalopes must be undetectable. Bake in a fairly hot oven (190°C/375°F/Gas mark 5) for 25-30 minutes.

POLPETTE DI VITELLO   FOR 4

As Elizabeth David wrote in 1954, 'the only English translation of *polpette* would be rissoles, or meat balls, both of which have acquired a sinister connotation since the days of the meat shortage.' Since then, fast-food hamburgers, kingburgers and the rest have added their own unsavoury presence to the rogues' gallery of minced meat concoctions. This is a pity, because a properly made hamburger or meat ball can be excellent, particularly when made from really tasty cuts of beef that are too tough to be cooked like steaks yet lose much of their character when made tender by stewing or braising.

When veal, by definition tender, is minced, the purpose is usually to combine it intimately with another ingredient – for instance cheese, as in these *polpette di vitello*. Although they come from Sicily, analogous *polpette* were once (and possibly still are) made elsewhere in Italy. There is a similar recipe in Bartolomeo Platina's influential *De Honesta Voluptate* (1474), one of the earliest printed books to devote considerable space to recipes: the mixture, instead of being fried, is fashioned into egg shapes, wrapped in pig's caul and spit-roasted.

80 g (3 oz) good white bread

2-3 tbsp milk

600 g (1¹/₄ lb) lean minced veal

1 clove garlic, finely chopped

1 tbsp parsley, finely chopped

4 eggs

80 g (3 oz) freshly grated Parmesan

large pinch salt

freshly ground pepper

pinch freshly grated nutmeg

breadcrumbs

olive oil for frying

Soak the bread in milk or water for a few minutes, then squeeze it dry. Put the bread, veal, garlic, parsley, 2 eggs, cheese, salt, plenty of pepper and nutmeg into a mixing bowl and mix thoroughly. Beat the remaining eggs. Flouring your hands lightly from time to time, form the mixture into neat little scone-shaped *polpette* (this quantity of minced veal should make about 16). Coat them in beaten egg, roll in breadcrumbs and fry gently in olive oil until firm and crisp.

The *polpette* can also be fried without the addition of an egg and breadcrumb coating. They are normally eaten hot, but are also good cold (in which case they are better without egg and breadcrumbs) with a green salad.

SALTIMBOCCA   FOR 4

Saltimbocca, which literally means 'jump in the mouth', is a classic combination of veal and ham that features quite often on the menus of Italian restaurants, both in Italy and elsewhere. Sometimes it includes cheese as well, sometimes not. Sometimes the little veal escalopes are rolled up and secured with a toothpick, sometimes not. Whichever way it is made (here, of course, it includes cheese), it is an attractive and light meat dish.

12 small thin veal escalopes of
  about 50 g (2 oz) each
salt
freshly ground pepper
2 tbsp good cooking oil
80 g (3 oz) unsalted butter
100 ml (3½ fl oz) dry white wine

6 thin slices prosciutto *or* similar
  raw ham
200 g (7 oz) mozzarella, thinly sliced
250 ml (9 fl oz) tomato sauce (p. 364)
1 tbsp fresh sage, finely chopped
1 tbsp fresh parsley, finely chopped
50 g (2 oz) freshly grated Parmesan

Cut all pieces of gristle and transparent skin off the edge of the escalopes, cover with cling-film and beat, but not too hard, to make them as thin as possible. Season on both sides with salt and pepper. Heat the oil and butter in a large frying pan. Put in the escalopes, in batches, and brown them for 1 minute on each side. Transfer to a hot buttered baking dish large enough to take them in one layer.

Using a wooden spoon, deglaze the frying pan with white wine, reduce the liquid by half and pour over the escalopes. On each of them lay a half-slice of raw ham and a slice of mozzarella. Heat the tomato sauce, add the sage and parsley, and stir over a very low heat for 1-2 minutes. Pour over the escalopes, sprinkle with Parmesan and put into a fairly hot oven (200°C/400°F/Gas mark 6) for 15 minutes or until golden brown.

If you have no fresh sage – and it *must* be fresh – use the same amount of fresh or dried wild marjoram (oregano) instead.

The dish can be given a warmer inflection by the use of 3 tablespoons each of Marsala and water to deglaze the pan instead of white wine.

PAIN PERDU AU FROMAGE   FOR 4

Another unusual recipe from Paul Reboux's *Plats nouveaux!* (p. 44). Normally *pain perdu* is a sweet dish in which stale bread is ingeniously turned into a tasty pudding rather like bread-and-butter pudding. In Reboux's reinterpretation it becomes a sumptuous, savoury main course that still has the merit of being very economical.

250 g (9 oz) stale bread (white *or* wholemeal), rather thickly sliced
300 ml (10 fl oz) milk
60 g (2 oz) unsalted butter
4 whole eggs, beaten
120 ml (4 fl oz) béchamel sauce II (p. 357)
175 g (6 oz) freshly grated Gruyère
100 g (3½ oz) ham, finely chopped
200 ml (7 fl oz) double cream
4 egg yolks
100 ml (3½ fl oz) meat juice *or* 1 tbsp meat glaze dissolved in 6 tbsp boiling water
1 tbsp fresh tarragon, finely chopped
1 tbsp fresh parsley, finely chopped
1 tbsp fresh chives, finely chopped

Soak the bread slices on both sides in the milk for 1 hour. Heat the butter in a non-stick frying pan. Dip the bread slices in beaten egg and fry them gently on both sides until the egg has coagulated. Mix the béchamel with 120 g (4 oz) of cheese and spread it on the bread. Sprinkle with chopped ham and the rest of the cheese. Put in a fairly hot oven (200°C/400°F/Gas mark 6) for about 15 minutes or until the cheese topping melts and begins to turn golden brown.

While the *pain perdu* is in the oven, beat the cream and egg yolks together thoroughly in a small saucepan. Heat the meat juice, or meat glaze and water, to boiling point in another pan and pour it slowly into the cream and egg-yolk mixture, whisking all the time. Put over a gentle heat, add the herbs, and stir until the sauce has thickened slightly and is nice and hot (on no account must it be allowed to get anywhere near boiling point). Pour into a hot sauceboat and serve with the *pain perdu*.

GRATIN D'ENDIVES AU JAMBON   FOR 4

An enduring favourite in French households at all levels of society. Why? As Jane Grigson says in her *Vegetable Book*, 'the combination of the watery, faintly bitter chicory, with the mild smokiness of good ham and the rich flavour of the Mornay sauce, makes an irresistible dish.'

8 firm thick chicory heads

50 g (2 oz) unsalted butter

1 tsp lemon juice

pinch sugar

salt

freshly ground pepper

8 thin slices ham

400 ml (14 fl oz) Mornay sauce I

  (p. 358)

30 g (1 oz) freshly grated Parmesan

Trim and wipe clean the chicory heads. Melt the butter in a casserole large enough to take the chicory in a single layer. Put in the chicory, sprinkle with lemon juice, sugar, a little salt, plenty of pepper and 1-2 tablespoons of water. Cover and cook very gently until the chicory is tender. The time needed for this will vary. Check that the vegetables do not stick, adding a little water if necessary.

Transfer the vegetables and cooking liquid to a gratin dish large enough to take the 8 chicory heads neatly in one layer. Wrap each head in a slice of ham and arrange in the dish. Smother in Mornay sauce, sprinkle with cheese and put in a fairly hot oven (200°C/400°F/Gas mark 6) for 15-20 minutes or until the surface begins to turn golden brown.

PORK STUFFED WITH CHEESE   FOR 8

This dish, which achieves an interesting interpenetration of flavours, is a variation on Porc Sylvie in *Mastering the Art of French Cooking*, by Simone Beck, Louise Bertholle and Julia Child.

2 kg (4^1/$_2$ lb) loin of pork, untrussed

  and without rind

2 tsp salt

1 tsp freshly ground pepper

250 ml (9 fl oz) dry white wine

100 ml (3^1/$_2$ fl oz) olive oil

5 cloves garlic, crushed

1 tsp fresh or dried thyme

1 tbsp fresh sage, finely chopped

2 tbsp fresh parsley, finely chopped

^{1}/$_2$ bay leaf, broken into several pieces

6 juniper berries, crushed

250 g (9 oz) Gruyère, very thinly sliced

30 g (1 oz) unsalted butter

1 tbsp oil

Place the joint on its end on a board, so it stands up like a stumpy pillar. Make three or four vertical, parallel cuts about 3 cm (1 in) apart, from the top to within 1 cm (1/2 in) of the bottom. The meat will look ragged at this point, but you will tie it into shape later. Place it as it is, lengthwise, in a dish into which it fits neatly. Rub with the salt and pepper. Mix together the wine, olive oil, garlic, thyme, sage, parsley, bay leaf and juniper berries, and pour over the pork. Make sure the liquid penetrates the slits in the meat. Roll the meat over and over so it is completely coated. Cover and set aside in the refrigerator or a cool place for at least 12 hours.

Scrape off the marinade ingredients. Insert slices of cheese neatly into the slits so they are completely filled. Close the meat to re-form the roast and tie up with string to hold it in shape. Strain the marinade and keep the liquid.

Heat the butter and oil in a casserole over a fairly high heat, put in the pork and brown it briefly on all sides, basting from time to time. Add the marinade liquid and reduce quickly to about half its volume. Test the liquid for salt, adding a little more if necessary. Cover the casserole and place in a moderate oven (170°C/325°F/Gas mark 3) for 2-2 1/2 hours. Baste several times during cooking with the juices in the casserole.

Remove the meat and allow to firm up for 15 minutes before carving. Cut it crosswise so that each slice has lardings of cheese. Remove any excess fat from the juices in the casserole, strain into a hot sauceboat and serve with the meat.

FILET DE PORC AU ROQUEFORT
ET AUX AMANDES   FOR 4

The film-maker Alain Resnais once described in an interview how he had wandered into a cinema with a friend not knowing anything about the film advertised outside, but attracted by the promise of good acting from Tony Curtis and Burt Lancaster. The film turned out to be the classic *Sweet Smell of Success*. He was sure, he said, that he derived greater enjoyment from seeing the film blind, so to speak, than he would have if he had read the rave reviews it got and gone specially to see it.

The same is true, surely, of eating out. It is always a great pleasure, of course, to read praise of a restaurant by a food writer or guide book and to go along and confirm for oneself the accuracy of the judgement passed. But isn't it much more satisfying to hap upon a restaurant, to scrutinize the menu posted outside, to tingle with anticipation as one realizes that here is a chef with ideas, originality and even daring, to go in and sample the food, and to find the food lives up to one's expectations?

This all too rare experience happened to me some time ago when I was passing through the little village of Sournia in the wilds of the Fenouillèdes, in the Roussillon area of south-west France. Although it had only one food store and no hotel, Sournia did boast the Auberge de Sournia. This excellent restaurant (at the time of my visit it was in no food guide) was run by Cosima Kretz, an amiable young woman from Bavaria, whose imaginative chef, Jean Moreno, learned his trade at several well-known restaurants, including the excellent La Tamarissière in Agde.

One of the dishes I tasted that day was this interesting pork tenderloin with Roquefort (the recipe for which was later given to me by Kretz and Moreno). The use of ground almonds as a thickening agent for sauces was common in earlier centuries. Here, the smooth flavour of almonds and cream provides a perfect riposte to the aggressiveness of Roquefort.

800 g (1³/₄ lb) tenderloin of pork, trimmed of all fat
80 g (3 oz) unsalted butter
500 ml (17 fl oz) double cream

125 g (4¹/₂ oz) Roquefort, crumbled
freshly ground white pepper
4 tbsp ground almonds

Cut the pork into little slices about 1 cm (¹/₂ in) thick. Heat the butter in a large frying pan until it is just about to change colour and cook the pork slices gently for about 5 minutes on each side. Remove and keep warm.

Put the cream, cheese and some pepper into the pan,

turn up the heat and reduce for a few minutes, stirring all the time, until a smooth and sauce-like consistency is obtained. Blend in the ground almonds. Pour the sauce over the pork and serve immediately. A good accompaniment is boiled rice or fresh pasta.

As is usual when a fair amount of Roquefort is called for, there is no need to add any salt.

RAAN MASALEDAR   FOR 6

A leg of lamb in a spicy yoghurt sauce – an aromatic dish from *Madhur Jaffrey's Indian Cookery*.

a leg of lamb of about 2.5 kg (5^1/$_2$ lb)	4 2-cm (1-in) cubes of ginger, peeled
50 g (2 oz) blanched almonds	and coarsely chopped
225 g (8 oz) onions, coarsely chopped	4 fresh hot green chillies, coarsely
8 cloves garlic	chopped
2 tbsp ground cumin seeds	600 ml (21 fl oz) yoghurt
4 tsp ground coriander seeds	^{1}/$_2$ tsp cloves
^{1}/$_2$ tsp cayenne	16 cardamom pods
freshly ground pepper	5-cm (2-in) stick of cinnamon
3^1/$_2$ tsp salt	10 black peppercorns
^{1}/$_2$ tsp garam masala	4 tbsp sultanas
6 tbsp oil	15 g (^{1}/$_2$ oz) slivered almonds

Get your butcher to remove the H bone so as to make a deep pocket to hold a stuffing, to cut the protruding leg bone as close to the end of the meat as possible so it fits into the baking dish, and to remove all fat and skin from the outside of the leg. Alternatively, do all these operations yourself.

Put the leg in a baking dish. Blend to a paste the whole almonds, onions, garlic, ginger, green chillies and 3 tablespoons of yoghurt. Put the remaining yoghurt into a mixing bowl and beat lightly with a fork or whisk until smooth and creamy. Add the blended paste, the cumin, coriander, cayenne, pepper, salt and garam masala. Mix. Push plenty of the mixture into all the openings in the lamb. With a sharp paring knife make deep slashes all over the meat and push in as much spice paste as possible with your fingers. Spread the remaining paste over and around the meat, cover with cling-film and refrigerate for 24 hours.

Let the meat come to room temperature and remove the cling-film. Heat the oil in a small frying pan, put in the cloves, cardamom, cinnamon and peppercorns. When the cloves swell – this takes just a few seconds – pour the hot oil and spices over the lamb. Cover the baking dish tightly either with its own lid or with aluminium foil and bake for 90 minutes. Uncover and bake for a further 45 minutes, basting three or four times with the sauce. Scatter the sultanas and slivered almonds over the top of the leg and bake for another 5-6 minutes. Remove from the oven and allow to firm up in a warm place for 15 minutes.

Put the lamb on a warm serving plate. Remove all the fat from the top of the sauce with a spoon or bulb baster; fish out the whole spices with a slotted spoon and discard. Pour the sauce around the leg and serve.

PIÈCE DE BOEUF AU BLEU D'AUVERGNE   FOR 4

It would seem that the only cheese that combines successfully with beef is blue cheese (*pace* Messrs McDonald's *et al.*). Why this should be is a mystery; perhaps it has something to do with the tang of really tasty, well-hung beef, which needs a piquancy to set it off.

This rump steak with Bleu d'Auvergne is a popular dish on the menu of the Hôtel Beauséjour. It was devised by Louis-Bernard (Loulou) Puech, the son of the owners, who, after a spell working with a couple of leading French chefs (Claude Peyrot of Le Vivarois in Paris, and Lucien Vanel of Vanel in Toulouse), returned to his home village to take over the kitchens of his parents' hotel-restaurant. Steering a middle course between traditional Auvergnat cooking and imaginative 'modern' cuisine, he has succeeded in turning it into one of the very best restaurants in the Cantal. He won a Michelin star in 1966.

4 tbsp double cream

120 g (4 oz) Bleu d'Auvergne

4 thick pieces of rump steak totalling
  1 kg (2¹/₄ lb)

30 g (1 oz) unsalted butter

1 tbsp oil

small pinch salt

freshly ground pepper

100 ml (3¹/₂ fl oz) dry white wine

Mash the cream and cheese together in a small bowl until a fairly smooth consistency is obtained. Trim the meat of *all* fat and gristle and bring to room temperature. Heat the butter and oil over a high heat in a very large frying pan until the foam begins to subside, put in the steaks, reduce heat to medium and cook for 4-5 minutes on each side. When tiny drops of red liquid begin to ooze out of the meat, remove to a hot dish, season with a little salt and plenty of pepper, and keep warm.

Deglaze with the wine over a high heat, scraping the bottom of the pan with a wooden spoon. When the liquid has reduced to 1-2 tablespoons, add the cream and cheese mixture, turn down the heat and, shaking the pan all the time, beat the mixture with a whisk until it has turned into a smooth sauce and is on the point of boiling. Put the steaks on hot individual plates, spoon the sauce over them and serve immediately.

It is worth trying to get the very best-quality Bleu d'Auvergne for this dish. Taste a bit to check its saltiness before adding any salt to the steaks.

Blue cheese, especially when given added pungency by the warming process, can spell death to a subtle wine. A rustic red wine with a pronounced *goût du terroir*, such as Marcillac from the Rouergue, would make a perfect partner for this dish. It should be served cool, but not chilled.

STEAK AU ROQUEFORT   FOR 4
A recipe given to me by Guy Girard (p. 261). Although it looks at first sight similar to the preceding one, the 'sheepy' taste of Roquefort, the toasted nuts and the shallot produce an altogether different result.

120 g (4 oz) Roquefort	4 thick pieces of rump steak totalling
80 g (3 oz) unsalted butter	1 kg (2¼ lb)
2 tsp parsley, very finely chopped	2 tbsp good cooking oil
2 tsp chives, very finely chopped	2 shallots, very finely chopped
1 tbsp pine-nuts	100 ml (3½ fl oz) dry white wine
1 tbsp hazelnuts, crushed to the	2 tbsp double cream
size of peppercorns	freshly ground pepper
1 tbsp slivered almonds	

Mash the cheese and 50 g (2 oz) of butter together in a small bowl with the parsley and chives until a fairly smooth consistency is obtained. Put the nuts into a shallow tin or tart mould and bake in a moderate oven (180°C/350°F/Gas mark 4) until they have turned the colour of roasted peanuts.

Trim the meat of *all* fat and gristle and bring to room temperature. Heat the rest of the butter and the oil over a high heat in a very large frying pan until the foam begins to subside, put in the steaks, reduce heat to medium and cook for 4-5 minutes on each side. When tiny drops of red liquid begin to ooze out of the meat, remove to a hot dish and keep warm. Pour off the fat.

Put the shallots and wine into the pan and cook over a high heat, scraping the bottom with a wooden spoon. When the liquid has reduced to 1-2 tablespoons, add the cream and plenty of pepper, turn down the heat and cook for 3-4 minutes. Add the cheese and butter mixture a little at a time, turn up the heat and, shaking the pan all the time, beat the mixture until it has turned into a smooth sauce and is on the point of boiling. Put the steaks on hot individual plates, spoon the sauce over them, sprinkle with roasted nuts and serve immediately.

GRAS-DOUBLE À LA NANCÉIENNE FOR 4

Two cities have given their names to the classic French tripe recipes *tripes à la mode de Caen* and *gras-double à la lyonnaise*. This tripe dish from Nancy, in Lorraine, is less well known – but none the less excellent. *Gras-double* is the paunch of beef – or blanket tripe – and is not fatty as its name might suggest (*double* is an old word for paunch). It is milder and 'meatier' than other parts of the animal's stomach, and a good thing to start with if one is trying tripe for the first time.

1 kg (2¼ lb) pre-cooked (but not bleached) blanket tripe	1 bay leaf
50 g (2 oz) unsalted butter	1 tsp fresh *or* dried thyme
1 tbsp flour	2 tbsp fresh parsley, chopped
large pinch salt	200 ml (7 fl oz) dry white wine
freshly ground pepper	120 g (4 oz) freshly grated Gruyère
2 shallots, chopped	3 egg yolks
2 cloves garlic, chopped	juice of 1 lemon

Cut the tripe into small strips about 6 mm (¼ in) thick. Heat the butter in a casserole, put in the tripe, sprinkle with flour, salt and plenty of pepper, and cook over a medium heat, tossing and stirring all the time, until slightly browned. Add the shallots, garlic, bay leaf, thyme, parsley, white wine and enough water just to cover the tripe. Bring to the boil, cover, lower heat and simmer for about 1 hour.

Remove any excess fat with a spoon or bulb baster and fish out the bay leaf. Stir in the cheese, cover and leave for 5 minutes over a low heat. Beat the egg yolks and lemon juice together in a bowl until thoroughly blended. Still beating, ladle a little of the tripe's cooking liquid into the bowl. Remove the casserole from the heat, pour the contents of the bowl into it and stir. The sauce should thicken very slightly. Serve immediately with, for instance, boiled potatoes or rice.

If the sauce does not thicken slightly in the final stage,

return the casserole to a low heat for 1-2 minutes, stirring all the time. It must on no account be allowed to boil.

CERVELLES DE VEAU AU RÉVEIL-MATIN   FOR 4-6

The anonymous author of *Le Manuel de la friandise* (p. 119) was fond of unusual or mysterious recipe titles. In addition to Omelette charmante, Truite au feu d'enfer and Cuisses de dindon réveillantes, we find these 'alarm-clock calf's brains'. I can only conjecture that mustard was presumed to have awakening properties. However that may be, it is a condiment that, like Parmesan, is ideally suited to the blandness of brains.

2 calf's brains
1 clove garlic
2 tbsp fresh parsley, chopped
2 Welsh or spring onions, sliced
3 cloves
large pinch salt
freshly ground pepper
500 ml (17 fl oz) dry white wine
120 g (4 oz) unsalted butter

4 tbsp juice from a roast *or*
    15 g ($^{1}/_{2}$ oz) meat glaze
    dissolved in 3 tbsp hot water
4 tbsp strong Dijon mustard
150 g ($5^{1}/_{2}$ oz) freshly grated
    Parmesan
100 g ($3^{1}/_{2}$ oz) breadcrumbs
100 ml ($3^{1}/_{2}$ fl oz) veal stock

Soak the brains in cold water for 2 hours. Put 500 ml (17 fl oz) of water in a saucepan with the garlic, parsley, onions, cloves, salt and a little pepper, bring to the boil and simmer for 15 minutes. Add the wine and simmer for a further 15 minutes. Allow to cool. Put the brains in this court-bouillon and bring back to the boil. As soon as it boils, gently lift out the brains with a perforated spoon. Carefully remove the thin membrane covering them, then put them back in the court-bouillon and simmer for 20 minutes. Remove the brains and allow to cool a little. Cut each brain into six equal slices.

On the top of the stove, melt 60 g (2 oz) of butter in a shallow baking or gratin dish large enough to take all the brain slices in one layer. Stir in the meat juice or dissolved meat glaze and 1 tablespoon of mustard. Cook for

1 minute, stirring. Put in the brain slices and, turning them delicately, make sure they are coated by the sauce on all sides. Sprinkle with a little salt and pepper. Strew the cheese and breadcrumbs, mixed together, in quite a thick layer over them. Put into a hot oven (220°C/425°F/Gas mark 7) for 10 minutes or until a crust forms.

While the brains are in the oven, make the sauce. Heat the stock and the rest of the mustard over a high heat in a small saucepan. When the liquid boils, whisk in the remaining butter, chilled and divided into three pieces. Continue whisking over a high heat until the sauce comes to the boil again and transfer immediately to a hot sauce-boat. It should be possible, if your ingredients are prepared in advance, to time things so that the sauce is made just as the calf's brains are ready to come out of the oven.

You can drink a light red wine – a Loire, say – with brains, but in my view they go better with either a dry fruity white or, more adventurously, a lightish sweet one such as a good Monbazillac.

OREILLES DE PORC AU FROMAGE   FOR 4

This unexpected combination is a speciality of the Auvergne. Most Auvergnat farmers, even if they raise battery pigs for the butchery trade, still keep one or two large specimens for domestic consumption. The pigs are cosseted with kitchen scraps, Jerusalem artichokes, skimmed milk, apples and so on, and in some cases are allowed to roam the woods in search of chestnuts and acorns. No wonder they taste good.

Each year the farmer calls in the slaughterer, and the pigs, after what must be considered a happy life compared with the lot suffered by many of their kind, are turned into sausages, ham, *boudin*, pâté and, nowadays, chunks of frozen chops and roasting joints. The Auvergnats, who enjoy the same reputation for thrift as the Scots, abhor waste, so every edible part of the animal is used, including the trotters, tail, snout, lights, spleen – and ears.

4 pig's ears

green leaves of 1 leek

4 parsley sprigs *or* 8 parsley stalks

1 sprig thyme

1 bay leaf

1 large onion

2 cloves

5 peppercorns

2 cloves garlic

500 ml (17 fl oz) Mornay sauce IV
(p. 359) made with young Cantal
instead of Gruyère and Parmesan

Put the pig's ears in plenty of well-salted cold water in a large saucepan and bring to the boil. After 1-2 minutes of vigorous boiling, move the pan partly off the heat and skim. Wash the leek leaves and use the largest of them as an envelope to enclose the parsley, thyme and bay leaf. Secure with string. Put the envelope, the other leek leaves, the onion studded with cloves, the peppercorns and the garlic into the pan with the ears. Lower the heat, cover and simmer for 1¹/₂-2 hours, skimming from time to time.

Remove the ears and set aside 100 ml (3¹/₂ fl oz) of the cooking liquid for the Mornay sauce. Make the Mornay sauce. Butter a gratin dish. Cut the ears into thin strips, arrange in the dish and cover with Mornay sauce. Bake in a fairly hot oven (200°C/400°F/Gas mark 6) for 15 minutes or until the surface begins to turn golden brown.

LANGUE DE BOEUF AU PARMESAN   FOR 4

There are people who have an aversion to ox-tongue – perhaps because, unlike other kinds of offal, tongues can be seen at work in the fields, curling round clumps of grass and guiding them to the animal's teeth. Anyone wishing to conquer their aversion should start by trying this classic of nineteenth-century French *cuisine bourgeoise*, in which the tongue is masked, if not completely disguised, by Parmesan.

1 ox-tongue of about 1 kg (2¹/₄ lb)

2 onions, sliced

2 tomatoes, peeled, halved and
seeded

1 tbsp fresh parsley, finely chopped

1 tbsp fresh chives, finely chopped

large pinch salt

freshly ground pepper

300 ml (10¹/₂ fl oz) dry white wine

140 g (5 oz) freshly grated Parmesan

Bring plenty of water to the boil and blanch the whole tongue in it for 20 minutes. Remove and leave to cool. Skin and put in a large casserole. Add the onions, tomatoes, parsley, chives, salt, plenty of pepper, wine and an equal quantity of water. Cover and simmer for about 2 hours. Towards the end of the cooking period, there should be not much more than a large glassful of liquid left. If there is more, reduce uncovered over a high heat. Remove the tongue and leave to cool.

Purée the vegetables and cooking liquid. Cut the tongue into very thin slices. Arrange the slices overlapping each other in a buttered gratin dish, inserting between each layer about a third of the sauce and cheese. Sprinkle the remaining sauce and cheese over the top. Bake in a fairly hot oven (190°C/375°F/Gas mark 5) for about 20 minutes or until the surface begins to turn golden brown.

This treatment works equally well with lamb's tongues, but they take much less time to cook.

LAPIN AU BROCCIO   FOR 4
Two typically Corsican ingredients, Broccio and pennyroyal (p. 124), go into this simple, summery and aromatic dish.

150 ml (5 fl oz) virgin olive oil
2 tbsp fresh pennyroyal (or mint), finely chopped
2 cloves garlic, crushed
large pinch salt

freshly ground pepper
250 g (9 oz) Broccio or other fresh ewe's-milk cheese
1 small rabbit

Oil a baking dish with 2 tablespoons of olive oil. Mix together the mint, garlic, salt, plenty of pepper, cheese and the rest of the olive oil. Taste and add more salt if necessary. Coat the rabbit all over with this mixture and place on its side in the baking dish. Put in a hot oven (220°C/425°F/Gas mark 7) for 20 minutes. Remove, baste with sauce and return, on its other side, to a moderate oven (180°C/350°F/Gas mark 4) for about 40 minutes or until cooked.

ESCARGOTS AU ROQUEFORT   FOR 4

In the Sixties my greedier friends and I became addicted to a restaurant called Le Galant Verre (a pun on Le Vert-Galant, Henri IV's nickname), in the Rue de Verneuil in Paris. Its hyperactive owner-chef, Guy Girard, had an irrepressible inventive streak: at each visit he would emerge from the kitchens and enthusiastically explain some new dish or dishes on his menu. We were almost never disappointed by his latest *trouvaille*. Girard – who succeeded in bouncing back into business after suffering a serious illness and, later, a bad accident at a wholesale food market – was very different from certain *nouvelle cuisine* stars who give their imagination too free a rein and end up by allowing it to run away with them. His inspiration was firmly anchored in the French culinary traditions of which he had an encyclopaedic knowledge.

Girard believed that snails deserve a better fate than always being swamped in garlic butter, which, however delicious it may be intrinsically, tends to overshadow the snails' own discreet flavour. On one memorable occasion, after Girard's father in Gascony had sent up a consignment of 2,000 *petits gris* (a small, very tasty variety of snail) that he had caught himself, a new dish appeared on the menu: Petits gris à l'échalote. I and a friend ordered them. We were served no less than sixty of the creatures, which had been cooked in a court-bouillon and were simply served cold with a shallot-flavoured vinaigrette dressing on the side. We had no difficulty in dispatching the lot, as they were surprisingly unrich with their light dressing.

This recipe of Girard's for snails with Roquefort, while containing garlic and butter, combines many other judiciously selected flavours as well.

300 g (10¹/₂ oz) unsalted butter,
  softened
100 g (3¹/₂ oz) Roquefort
8 tbsp fresh parsley, finely chopped
4 tbsp fine white breadcrumbs
3 cloves garlic, finely chopped

2 shallots, finely chopped
100 g (3¹/₂ oz) ground almonds
pinch dill seeds or aniseed
freshly ground pepper
48 snails

Blend together all the ingredients except the snails. Put the snails in their shells or in a special earthenware snail dish (with cavities like a solitaire board) and stuff with the butter and cheese mixture. Bake in a hot oven (220°C/425°F/Gas mark 7) for 8-10 minutes or until they just begin to bubble. Do not overcook, otherwise the butter will burn.

Do not omit the bread, said Girard: its purpose is to help prevent the butter and cheese mixture from separating.

Girard, no chauvinist, said that the Roquefort in this recipe may be successfully replaced by the same quantity of Stilton.

CHAPTER THIRTEEN

Cheese and Vegetables

Vegetables, with a few exceptions (cabbage, French beans and carrots, perhaps), have a particularly close affinity with cheese. Although they are often combined in a gratin there are many other ingenious ways of using them together.

A cheese and vegetable main course is particularly useful if you have to cater for a group of people that includes one or more vegetarians. The vegetarians will not feel that attention has been drawn to their vegetarianism, while non-vegetarians are less likely, after, say, a tasty, crusty and rich gratin, to feel they have been cheated of their meat or fish. You can even, if you wish, go to the trouble of procuring cheese made with vegetarian rennet so as not to offend strict vegetarians. Coping with vegans is an altogether more complicated problem that is not within the province of this book.

GRATINS

Because virtually any vegetable can be used in a gratin, this chapter begins by explaining three basic gratin methods. The fourth (where milk is the cooking medium) applies only to Gratin 'dauphinois' (scalloped potatoes with cheese) and its relatives; the method is given under each of those recipes. Quantities of ingredients are given under individual recipes.

Your gratin dish, whatever its size, should be no deeper than about 6 cm (2½ in) and made of Pyrex or, better, earthenware. As regards the practice of dotting the surface of the gratin with butter, see my remarks on p. 29.

Gratin method I

In this method the vegetables and cheese, arranged in layers, are cooked in the gratin dish in a liquid medium (stock, water, wine or a combination of them) and given a cheese crust.

Take a gratin dish into which your ingredients will fit easily without coming too close to the top (some vegetables swell during the early stages of cooking). Place in it the sliced raw vegetables in a series of layers, sprinkled with salt – the amount will depend on the nature of the cooking liquid – and pepper, and interspersed with grated cheese (use half the total amount of cheese at this point; the rest is used for the topping). Add the hot liquid. Cover with aluminium foil, put in a moderate oven (180°C/350°F/Gas mark 4) and cook for the indicated time. When the vegetables are very nearly cooked (by which time they should have absorbed almost all their cooking liquid), remove the foil, sprinkle the surface evenly with the rest of the cheese and return to a hot oven (220°C/425°F/Gas mark 7) or put under a grill until golden brown. The final browning should be relatively brief.

Gratin method II

Here the vegetables are pre-cooked, then mixed with a Mornay sauce, sprinkled with a little cheese and browned on top.

Take a gratin dish of suitable size (the ingredients may fill it more completely than in the preceding method, as they will not swell during their final heating and browning). Place in it the cooked vegetables (sliced or diced) in a series of layers if necessary, interspersed with sauce. Sprinkle the surface evenly with cheese and bake in a fairly hot oven (200°C/400°F/Gas mark 6) until golden brown.

Gratin method III

This time the pre-cooked vegetables are given a 'dry' treatment – a method particularly favoured by the Italians. It has the merit of not masking or interfering with the flavour of the vegetables too much.

Take a gratin dish of suitable size (the ingredients should not be too crowded or too neatly slotted in, so that as much as possible of their surface can brown nicely). Place in it the cooked vegetables (sliced or diced) in a series of layers if necessary, interspersed with sprinklings of grated cheese. Sprinkle the surface evenly with more cheese and bake in a fairly hot oven (200°C/400°F/Gas mark 6) until golden brown. As the gratin is dry, care must be taken not to allow it to burn.

GRATIN 'DAUPHINOIS'   FOR 4

I have put 'dauphinois' in inverted commas as a sop to the purists: the 'correct' version of this classic dish should contain lashings of cream but no cheese. But most people, most restaurant menus, most chefs and many cookbooks assume that gratin dauphinois has cheese in it. And if the version with milk and cheese is not called dauphinois, what should it be called? Some say gratin savoyard. But a 'correct' gratin savoyard, although containing cheese, cooks in stock, not milk. And do the Savoyards *never* leave out the cheese, or the Dauphinois *never* include it?

Instead of running round in circles, let me simply point out that although the 'correct', i.e. cheeseless, gratin dauphinois does not fall within the scope of this book, you can make it quite easily by following this recipe and replacing the cheese with another 150 ml (3½ fl oz) of double cream.

1 kg (2¹/₄ lb) good waxy potatoes,
  peeled
600 ml (21 fl oz) milk
200 ml (7 fl oz) double cream
pinch freshly grated nutmeg

1 large clove garlic, very finely
  chopped
salt
freshly ground pepper
250 g (9 oz) freshly grated Gruyère

Slice the potatoes very thinly. Do not rinse, as the starch in their juice will help prevent the milk and cream from curdling. Bring the milk to simmering point in a large saucepan, add the potatoes and poach gently for 10-15 minutes (the potatoes should be almost cooked). Strain the milk into another pan, add the cream and nutmeg to it, and mix.

Butter a gratin dish generously and strew the garlic over the bottom. Put about a third of the potatoes in a layer with the slices overlapping each other. Sprinkle salt, pepper and about a quarter of the cheese over them. Repeat the layering operation twice more, but, before adding the final generous topping of cheese, pour the milk and cream over the potatoes. By the time the topping has been added, the gratin dish should be no more than three-quarters full, otherwise it may boil over in the oven. Bake in a fairly hot oven (200°C/400°F/Gas mark 6) for 15-20 minutes or until golden brown.

The quantity of garlic can be doubled to excellent effect. Some versions of this dish omit garlic altogether – a terrible mistake in my view.

If you are uncertain about when dinner will be served, prepare the dish up to the point where everything is assembled in the gratin dish. You can then put it in the oven at the last moment, though you should give it 20-30 minutes as the ingredients will have to heat up again. This is a better method than making the whole dish in advance, then re-heating it: the contents tend to dry out and the cheese crust gets leathery.

If you like a strong potato flavour, you can simply wash and slice the potatoes without peeling them. But in that case you must use one of the thin-skinned pink varieties.

Although the correct cheese to be used in gratin dauphinois is Comté or Gruyère, it can also be successfully made with Beaufort (a richer flavour), Emmental (milder) or any good English hard cheese such as Cheddar, Cheshire, or Double Gloucester. For a variant with a completely different flavour, see the next recipe.

GRATIN DE POMMES DE TERRE AU REBLOCHON FOR 4

A genuine farmhouse Reblochon has a wonderfully delicate taste and a pervasive, lingering sweet smell. It melts well and makes an interesting variant for such dishes as raclette or cheese on toast. It lends this gratin a characteristic gamey flavour.

1 kg (2¼ lb) good waxy potatoes, peeled
600 ml (21 fl oz) milk
200 ml (7 fl oz) double cream
300 g (10½ oz) Reblochon, trimmed of its rind and cut into little pieces
pinch freshly grated nutmeg
1 large clove garlic, very finely chopped
salt
freshly ground pepper

Slice the potatoes very thinly. Do not rinse, as the starch in their juice will help prevent the milk and cream from curdling. Bring the milk to simmering point, add the potatoes and poach gently for 10-15 minutes (the potatoes should be almost cooked). Strain the milk into another pan, add the cream, cheese and nutmeg to it, and place over a low heat, stirring frequently, until the cheese has completely melted.

Butter a gratin dish generously and strew the garlic over the bottom. Put about a third of the potatoes in a layer with the slices overlapping each other. Sprinkle with salt and pepper. Repeat this operation twice more, then pour the hot cheese mixture over the whole thing, tilting the gratin dish this way and that, so the liquid reaches into every crevice. The gratin dish should not be more than three-quarters full, otherwise it may boil over in the oven. Bake in a fairly hot oven (200°C/400°F/Gas mark 6) for 15-20 minutes or until golden brown.

GRATIN SAVOYARD   FOR 4

50 g (2 oz) unsalted butter
1 large clove garlic, very finely
  chopped
pinch freshly grated nutmeg
450 ml (16 fl oz) hot beef stock

1 kg (2¹/₄ lb) good waxy potatoes,
  peeled
salt
freshly ground pepper
250 g (9 oz) freshly grated Gruyère

Butter a gratin dish generously and strew with garlic. Mix
the nutmeg into the beef stock. Proceed according to
Gratin method I (p. 264).

GRATIN AUVERGNAT   FOR 4

Much of the lower Auvergne and the Limousin is carpeted
with sweet chestnut forest. There is even an area that
straddles the border between the Cantal and Aveyron
departments that is called the Châtaigneraie (the chestnut
grove). Although dwindling in number, the trees have
managed to hold their own in areas where the terrain is
too steep to be cleared and used for farming.

In the Limousin farmers and *charcutiers* make a succulent kind of *boudin* (black pudding) containing bits of
chestnut. In the Châtaigneraie, where chestnuts were a
staple part of the diet until recently, this filling gratin is
made.

500 g (1 lb 2 oz) potatoes
175-250 ml (6-9 fl oz) milk
500 g (1 lb 2 oz) fresh, frozen *or*
  unsweetened canned chestnuts,
  drained, *or* 250 g (9 oz) dried
  chestnuts, soaked for 24 hours and
  boiled until soft

30 g (1 oz) unsalted butter
salt
freshly ground pepper
100 g (3¹/₂ oz) grated *or* very thinly
  sliced young Cantal

Clean, boil, peel and mash the potatoes with about 100 ml
(3¹/₂ fl oz) of hot milk until a smooth purée is obtained.
Depending on the variety and age of the potatoes you may
have to add a little more milk. If you have fresh chestnuts,
make a circular incision round each of them with a sharp

knife, boil for 5 minutes, remove from the water and peel. Return the chestnuts to the water and continue boiling until they are soft. Mash the chestnuts (whether fresh, canned or dried) with about 75 ml (2¹/₂ fl oz) of milk until they have the same consistency as the potatoes. Beat the two purées together with the butter, salt and plenty of pepper.

Butter a gratin dish and fill with the mixture. Sprinkle with the grated cheese or, if the Cantal is too soft to grate, cover the filling completely with thin slices of cheese. Put in a fairly hot oven (200°C/400°F/Gas mark 6) for about 15 minutes or until golden brown.

FARÇON   FOR 4

Farçon (from *farcir*, 'to stuff') can mean very different things in different parts of France. In the Aveyron a *farçon* is a kind of flat sausage-meat preparation, while in Montélimar, according to Curnonsky, it denotes 'a large, melon-shaped saveloy'.

The *farçon* that concerns us here is a mashed potato and cheese gratin from the Bresse and Savoie region of France. The distinctive ingredient is chervil, a herb that has unjustly fallen out of favour (in nineteenth-century French recipes it is as commonly called for as parsley). Its fresh, faintly aniseed flavour brightens up what might otherwise be a rather boring dish.

750 g (1³/₄ lb) potatoes	freshly ground pepper
150 ml (5 fl oz) milk	pinch freshly grated nutmeg
60 g (2 oz) unsalted butter, diced	1 tsp sugar
3 eggs	2 tbsp fresh chervil, finely chopped
110 g (4 oz) freshly grated Emmental	salt

Wash and boil the potatoes. Peel them while still hot and mash in a mixing bowl with hot milk. When smooth, gradually beat in the butter with a wooden spoon, then the eggs one by one. Add half the cheese, plenty of pepper, the nutmeg, sugar, chervil and salt to taste, and blend thoroughly. Turn out into a buttered gratin dish. Smooth the surface and sprinkle with the rest of the cheese. Bake in a fairly hot oven (200°C/400°F/Gas mark 6) for 20 minutes or until golden brown.

BAKED POTATOES WITH A CHEESE FILLING   FOR 4

Baked potatoes are as versatile as they are bland: they can be stuffed with virtually any combination of ingredients because the taste of potato is so accommodating to other, more assertive flavours.

4 large unblemished potatoes
1 tbsp olive oil
salt

150 g (5^1/$_2$ oz) of any of the following:
butter and freshly grated Parmesan or
    Gruyère in equal quantities
Herb cheese (p. 53), or
    Watercress and curd cheese sauce
    (p. 360)

Scrub the potatoes thoroughly but do not peel. Rub with olive oil and a little salt. Make a small hole in each of them with a skewer. Bake in a fairly hot oven (200°C/400°F/Gas mark 6) for 45 minutes or longer, turning them over at least once. They are done when they are soft to the touch.

Remove the potatoes. When they are cool enough to handle (but still hot), cut them in half and carefully scoop out the pulp without breaking the skins. In a mixing bowl, blend the cooked potato and the filling. Fill the halved potato shells with this mixture, making a smooth mound. If the filling contains green herbs, simply re-heat the potato halves in a moderate oven (180°C/350°F/Gas mark 4) for 15 minutes. If the filling consists of butter and Parmesan or Gruyère, put them in a hot oven (220°C/425°F/Gas mark 7) for 10 minutes or until slightly browned.

PALETS ALLEMANDS   FOR 4

This recipe comes from the 19 July 1908 issue of a fascinating cookery magazine, *La Cuisine des familles*, a 'weekly collection of up-to-date, very clearly explained and easily executed recipes'. The same issue, in addition to its interesting recipes, carries an editorial on the respective merits of five varieties of rhubarb, advice on how to treat your servants ('Be generous but not prodigal'), an article on preserves, and a sprinkling of advertisements (with engravings) for art nouveau jewellery, combs and ladies' belts (braid, silk or leather).

Perhaps the most surprising feature of the magazine was its regular column entitled '*Cuisine cosmopolite*', which carried recipes from all over the world. Such open-mindedness was not all that common at a time when French or French-inspired *haute cuisine* reigned supreme in the culinary cosmos, and when books devoted to 'foreign' recipes were virtually unknown.

1 kg (2¼ lb) floury potatoes	freshly ground pepper
60 g (2 oz) freshly grated Parmesan	pinch freshly grated nutmeg
60 g (2 oz) freshly grated Gruyère	2 whole eggs
60 g (2 oz) unsalted butter, diced	1 egg yolk
and chilled	slightly stale breadcrumbs
salt	oil for frying

Scrub the potatoes but do not peel. Make a small hole in each of them with a skewer. Bake in a fairly hot oven (200°C/400°F/Gas mark 6) for 45 minutes or longer, turning them over at least once. They are done when they are soft to the touch.

Remove the potatoes. When they are cool enough to handle (but still hot), cut them in half, scoop out the pulp, mash quickly and put into a heavy saucepan over the lowest heat possible (just enough to keep it warm). Immediately add the finely grated cheeses and blend well.

Beat in the butter gradually. Add salt to taste, plenty of

pepper and the nutmeg. Remove from heat. Beat one whole egg and the egg yolk together, and blend with the potato mixture until a smooth purée is obtained. Chill for an hour.

Beat the other egg. Divide the potato mixture into pieces the size of a large egg, flatten slightly and form into cakes. Dip these in beaten egg, then in breadcrumbs. Heat the oil in a frying pan to a depth of about 1/2 cm (1/4 in). Fry the cakes on both sides over a brisk heat until golden.

POTATO CHEESE PUFFS   FOR 4
An excellent recipe from that sensible cookbook, and best-seller of the Thirties and Forties, *The Main Cookery Book*, published by the manufacturers of Main gas cookers.

1 kg (2¼ lb) floury potatoes
85 g (3 oz) unsalted butter, diced and chilled
3 eggs, separated
pinch cayenne

200 g (7 oz) freshly grated strong Cheddar
salt
freshly ground pepper
a little milk

Scrub the potatoes but do not peel. Make a small hole in each of them with a skewer. Bake in a fairly hot oven (200°C/400°F/Gas mark 6) for 45 minutes or longer, turning them over at least once. They are done when they are soft to the touch.

Remove the potatoes. When they are cool enough to handle (but still hot), cut them in half, scoop out the pulp, mash quickly, beat in the chilled butter gradually and 3 egg yolks. Blend until smooth. Add the cayenne, the finely grated cheese, salt to taste and plenty of pepper. Whisk the egg whites with a small pinch of salt until very stiff. Carefully fold into the mixture. Place the mixture in rough heaps on a well-oiled baking tray. Brush lightly with milk and put in a very hot oven (230°C/450°F/Gas mark 8) for 15-20 minutes or until brown.

These potato puffs – they do puff up slightly during cooking – go extremely well with roast meat.

ALIGOT   FOR 4

Encountering the Auvergnat dish *aligot* for the first time is a startling experience. A wooden spoon is plunged into what looks like a bowl of mashed potatoes and is raised ceilingwards trailing a mass of rubbery threads that remain attached to the bowl. This unique consistency is given by the cheese that goes into *aligot* – Tomme fraîche de Cantal (which is sometimes incorrectly called Aligot, after the dish). A moist, mild cheese reminiscent in texture of mozzarella, Tomme fraîche is an unsalted, unmatured version of Cantal with its own unassertive but very distinct creamy flavour; it is consumed in large quantities in the Auvergne and the Rouergue.

There is some mystery surrounding the etymology of the word *aligot*. Some claim that it derives from *ail* (garlic); but in several areas *aligot* is made without garlic (there even exists a sweet version flambéd with rum!). Others see a connection with the Latin *aliquid* (something). The most likely origin is, however, the Old French *harigoter* (to tear or cut in pieces), which also gives us *haricot de mouton* (mutton stew). Interestingly, the latest thinking on the etymology of the word *haricot* (haricot bean) is that it comes not from an Aztec word but from *haricot* meaning ragout or stew – a case of a dish giving its own name to one of its ingredients, just as *pistou* (p. 363), in the Nice area, has come to mean basil – and *aligot* sometimes refers to the cheese used in it.

700 g (1¹/₂ lb) floury potatoes	freshly ground pepper
100-150 ml (3¹/₂-5 fl oz) milk	400 g (14 oz) Tomme fraîche de
30 g (1 oz) unsalted butter	Cantal, cut into very thin slices
3 large cloves garlic, very finely chopped	salt

Wash and boil the potatoes. Peel while still hot and mash

in a heavy saucepan with the heated milk, butter, garlic and pepper until a smooth consistency is obtained. Place over a very low heat and stir in the cheese. Beat vigorously with a wooden spoon until the mixture becomes elastic, add plenty of salt to taste (the cheese is unsalted) and continue beating. As the mixture heats up, it becomes slightly softer; if it remains too stiff, add a little more hot milk. As soon as it makes long bubblegum-like strands when lifted with the spoon, serve. Guests must be ready and waiting: there is nothing more sullen than an *aligot* that has cooled off.

Amazingly, in view of the amount of garlic it requires, *aligot* does not have a great deal of character when eaten on its own. It goes well with a very salty or piquant main dish such as *saucisses fraîches* (meaty Auvergnat sausages similar to *saucisses de Toulouse*), fried liver deglazed with a dash of vinegar, or crisp-fried bacon.

There are many variants of *aligot*, in addition to the sweet one already mentioned. It can have chopped parsley in it, lard instead of butter, or, in its more sophisticated 'restaurant' version, much more Tomme fraîche and butter as well as generous amounts of double cream. Already a somewhat indigestible concoction, *aligot* is not, in my opinion, improved by the extra butter, cream and cheese, although these may give it greater elegance. It is basically a humble peasant dish, the kind of thing that cowherds used to survive on for weeks on end when they took their herds up to the high mountain pastures for the summer, living and making Cantal cheese in their *burons* (tiny, almost windowless stone huts).

In the Auvergne *aligot* is often made in large quantities for special events like weddings. On such occasions it is, strangely enough, the Auvergnats rather than Auvergnates who are in charge of making it. In those old-fashioned mountain communities the older generation of men would normally rather be seen dead than do any of their wives' allotted tasks (washing, shopping, cooking, cleaning). Indeed, until recently, it was customary at mealtimes for the women to stand and serve their husbands and sons first, before dining themselves. The reason *aligot* is an exception to this male-chauvinist tradition is simply – as you will discover when you make it – that it requires a good deal of muscle power, and that stirring a big cauldron of the stuff has more in common with ploughing a field than with cooking.

GALETTES DE POMMES DE TERRE AU LAGUIOLE FOR 4
This recipe, given to me by Michel Bras (p. 228), is yet another way of turning mashed potato with cheese into something exciting. The result is very different from preceding dishes, thanks to the carefully worked out proportions of ingredients and the superb quality of Laguiole cheese.

Laguiole is named after the small town of Laguiole, in the Aubrac, which is its centre of production. Although similar to Cantal, it enjoys a separate appellation. Its closest relative is the superior form of Cantal, Salers, which is made solely from the milk of Salers cows, a hardy and agile red-brown breed with long, gracefully pointed horns. The milk that goes into the making of Laguiole is from the equally hardy, similarly horned but more placid Aubrac cows. Both breeds produce relatively little milk, but it is of unmatched quality. Arguably, they might have been allowed to die out, like so many other high-quality livestock breeds, if the faceless uniformitarian bureaucrats of the EU had not been thwarted by the stubbornness of the local cheese-making community – and by a problem of their own making, the milk glut, which removed the temptation for farmers to go for higher-yielding breeds of cow.

340 g (12 oz) potatoes	2 tbsp flour
2 tbsp double cream	2 eggs
pinch salt	140 g (5 oz) freshly grated Laguiole
freshly ground pepper	60 g (2 oz) clarified butter

Wash, peel and steam the potatoes. Drain well, mash and add the cream, salt and plenty of pepper. Leave to cool. Add the flour and the eggs one after the other. Mix well but not too vigorously with a spatula. When smooth, mix in the cheese. Leave to rest for an hour.

Heat the clarified butter in a non-stick frying pan until very hot. Put spoonfuls of the potato and cheese mixture into the pan, flattening them a little. Brown on both sides but do not leave too long in the pan, otherwise the cheese will melt and ooze out.

Bras uses these galettes as a garnish for a dish of his own invention, roast lamb with a mace-flavoured *jus*.

TRUFFADE

This dish, like *aligot* (p. 273), used to be made by Auvergnat cowherds in their *burons* during the summer months. Its ingredients are very similar to those of *aligot*, yet, thanks to the versatility of potatoes, the result is not at all the same in either of the two versions given here.

The word *truffade* immediately brings truffles to mind. There is in fact a connection even though the mushroom is not and never has been used in the dish. When the potato came from South America to the Auvergne, the locals, who at that time spoke only Occitan (or *langue d'oc*), nicknamed it *trufa* (truffle), no doubt because of its shape and earthy origin. A potato dish was consequently called *trufada*, and later given the French form *truffade* (just as the Provençal *boui-abaisso* was turned into *bouillabaisse*).

Truffade I   FOR 4
This recipe was given to me by Yvonne Puech, of the Hôtel Beauséjour in Calvinet (Cantal), whose establishment sported the Michelin's 'red R' (good value for money) for a good twenty years. An experienced cook with a thorough knowledge of local culinary traditions, she handed over to her son, Louis Bernard (p. 253) in 1982. Her late husband, Marcel, made excellent raw hams and

dry sausages, whose reputation travelled as far as Paris.

800 g (1³/₄ lb) potatoes, peeled	salt
60 g (2 oz) fat from raw ham (failing that, use green bacon fat)	200 g (7 oz) Tomme fraîche de Cantal, cut into thin slices

Wash, peel and slice the potatoes thinly. Melt the fat in a large non-stick sauté pan, add the potatoes, mix well so that they are well coated with fat, cover and cook over an extremely low heat for at least 30 minutes. When the potatoes are soft, add salt to taste (the amount will depend on the nature of the fat used). Lay the cheese slices over the potatoes and cover. When the cheese has completely melted, stir it thoroughly into the potatoes and serve immediately.

Truffade made this way goes well with a plain roast of pork, veal or beef.

Truffade II   FOR 4

This is my own version of *truffade*. Because it contains Cantal as well as Tomme fraîche it has more character and is really at its best as a main course. The quantities are therefore larger than for the first version. You can increase them even further if you wish. I have made this dish many times, sometimes using gross quantities so as to be sure of eliciting grunts of satisfaction from particularly gluttonous guests. But, however monstrously large the *truffade*, it has always been finished. This is less a tribute to my cooking than a result of the ability of certain dishes to increase the appetite of the eater as he or she eats. In my experience *truffade* is the dish that comes top on the moreishness scale.

1 kg (2¹/₄ lb) potatoes
30 g (1 oz) unsalted butter
3 tbsp frying oil
large pinch salt
freshly ground pepper
150 g (5¹/₂ oz) Tomme fraîche de
  Cantal, cut into thin slices

150 g (5¹/₂ oz) young Cantal, cut into
  thin slices
2 tbsp parsley, chopped
3 large cloves garlic, finely chopped

Peel the potatoes and cut into *very* small dice. (Young potatoes, which are nicer with the skins left on, should be rinsed in running water after being diced and dried well before you fry them.) Heat the butter and oil in a large non-stick sauté pan, put in the potatoes and cook over a medium heat for about 15 minutes, turning them over frequently with a wooden spatula.

When the potatoes are nearly cooked and slightly browned, add the salt and plenty of pepper. Lay the slices of cheese on top, cover, turn down the heat to low and cook for about 5 minutes, shaking the pan from time to time to make sure the melting cheese is not sticking to the bottom.

When the cheese has completely melted and is bubbling merrily, strew the surface evenly with the parsley and garlic, mixed together. Turn up the heat to medium. Shake the pan from time to time but do not stir its contents. Prise the edge of the truffade away from the side of the pan: if it is golden brown, it means that the bottom is well-browned and the dish is ready. Slide the truffade on to a warmed serving dish or, better, turn it out on to the dish so that it can sport its appetizing crust. Serve immediately.

The reason for putting the parsley and garlic on top, *after* the cheese has melted, is to prevent any bits of garlic coming into contact with the hot pan, burning and giving the dish a bitter taste.

Be sure to use young Cantal, which has a thin rind and smells creamy, and not a mature Cantal with a tang to it, which is not good for cooking.

PAN HAGGERTY   FOR 4

This dish, which has a number of features in common with *truffade* (see preceding recipe), comes from Northumberland, whose rugged landscape is not unlike parts of the Auvergne.

600 g (1 lb 5 oz) potatoes	150 g (5¹/₂ oz) freshly grated Cheddar
300 g (10¹/₂ oz) onions	salt
60 g (2 oz) beef dripping or lard	freshly ground pepper

Peel and slice the potatoes and onions finely. Heat the fat in a large non-stick sauté pan. Put in layers of potatoes, onions and cheese, seasoning each layer with salt and pepper, and finishing with potatoes. Cover and cook very gently, shaking the pan from time to time, until the vegetables are cooked through (make sure the onions are soft and translucent). You can serve it at this point or brown the top lightly by putting the pan under the grill.

POTATO AND CEPE GRATIN   FOR 4

Until recently, most Britons, for some reason, seemed to have a mental block against eating wild mushrooms (apart from field- and horse-, and fairy ring mushrooms). Every year billions of so-called toadstools went to waste. This was a great shame, since it meant that fresh specimens of what is perhaps the very finest of all mushrooms, *Boletus edulis*, or cepe,* eaten by only a very few, enlightened British gourmets. Fortunately, attitudes have since changed, and our woods and fields are now regularly combed by enthusiastic mushroom hunters.

---

* In English mushroom and cookery books *Boletus edulis* is referred to variously as flap mushroom, penny bun, bolete, boletus, cep, *cèpe* and cepe. The first two terms are unlikely to be understood by most people; bolete and boletus are confusing, as there are dozens of boletus species, including the poisonous *Boletus satanas*; the French word for this mushroom, *cèpe*, was borrowed by the English in the mid-nineteenth century to fill a useful gap, and slightly Anglicized to cepe. I have preferred this last term.

In my part of the world (the Auvergne), when the cepes decide to come up – any time between July and November – there is a frantic scramble to pick them. The woods come alive with the rustle of dead leaves and the crack of broken twigs as armies of pickers go about their business. For some of them it is just that: they arrive in vans and fill them with cepes, which they sell in big cities like Toulouse for twice the price of fillet steak. But the locals prefer to keep them for themselves and their relatives, usually eating them sautéd, with a *persillade* (chopped garlic and parsley), and bottling or freezing any surplus for consumption later.

Cepes have a very delicate but pervasive flavour, which enables a little of them to go a long way. In France, when not enough of them have been found for them to be eaten as a vegetable, they might go into a stew, a pie (p. 198) or a gratin like this one.

300 g (10½ oz) fresh cepes, *or* 30 g (1 oz) dried cepes	1 large clove garlic, very finely chopped
800 g (1¾ lb) good waxy potatoes, peeled	salt
1 tbsp parsley, chopped	freshly ground pepper
500 ml (17 fl oz) milk *or* beef stock	pinch freshly grated nutmeg
	250 g (9 oz) freshly grated Gruyère

Carefully wipe all earth or grit off the cepes with moistened paper towels and slice them thinly. If possible, do not put them in water, as they absorb it like a sponge. If using dried cepes, soak them in the milk or stock to be used for the gratin for 1 hour beforehand. Slice the potatoes very thinly.

Butter a gratin dish generously and strew the bottom with garlic. Fill and cook according to Gratin method I (p. 264).

Cepes can vary enormously in weight, depending on whether it has been raining or not. If they are very heavy and waterlogged, reduce the amount of cooking liquid.

Cepes with one or two worm-holes in them can be used

as long as the mushroom's aroma remains sweet and clean. If the tubes (the spongy part underneath the caps) are too mushy and discoloured, prise them off and discard them.

CEPE AND LETTUCE GRATIN FOR 4

It so happens that cepes tend to grow at a time of year when gardeners may find themselves with a glut of lettuces. This dish combines both ingredients felicitously.

400 g (14 oz) fresh cepes *or* 40 g
  (1½ oz) dried cepes, cut up into
  very small pieces
6 tbsp milk (if using dried cepes)
4 medium-sized lettuces
90 g (3 oz) unsalted butter
250 ml (9 fl oz) double cream

2 cloves garlic, finely chopped
1 tbsp parsley, finely chopped
pinch freshly grated nutmeg
1 tsp walnut oil
freshly ground pepper
80 g (3 oz) freshly grated Parmesan
salt

If using dried cepes, soak them in the milk for 1 hour beforehand. Wash the lettuces well, discarding any discoloured leaves, and blanch for 3 minutes in plenty of boiling salted water. Drain, press out as much moisture as possible, chop coarsely, put in a heavy saucepan with 60 g (2 oz) of butter and stew gently, stirring occasionally, until soft. Drain off the cooking liquid, pressing the lettuce down to extract as much as possible, into another saucepan. Reduce it to about 1 tablespoonful and return to the lettuce.

Chop the fresh cepes finely and cook them in a non-stick frying pan with 30 g (1 oz) of butter until they have given up all their moisture and are just beginning to brown. If using dried cepes, poach them gently for 15 minutes in the milk in which they have been soaking. Add the cepes, cream, garlic, parsley, nutmeg, walnut oil, plenty of pepper and 60 g (2 oz) of the Parmesan to the cooked lettuce. Mix thoroughly, add salt to taste, and turn into a buttered gratin dish. Sprinkle the remaining Parmesan over the top, and put in a moderate oven (180°C/350°F/Gas mark 4) for about 20 minutes or until lightly browned.

STUFFED CEPES   FOR 4

Cepes come in widely varying shapes: some have a tiny cap – almost no cap at all – and a huge swollen stem; others have a normal, slightly bulbous stem and a broad, spreading cap. This recipe looks neater if you have cepes of the latter type.

4 cepes measuring 8-10 cm (3-4 in) across	1 tbsp parsley, finely chopped
	12 walnut halves
60 g (2 oz) unsalted butter	60 g (2 oz) freshly grated Parmesan
1 tsp walnut oil	freshly ground pepper
2 cloves garlic, finely chopped	salt

Cut the stems of the cepes delicately from the caps, making a slight hollow if the underside of the cap is flat, not concave. Place the caps on a lightly oiled baking tray with the undersides, lightly scored, facing upwards. Put in a cool oven (150°C/300°F/Gas mark 2) for 15-25 minutes to get rid of some of their moisture (the time will depend on the condition of the cepes).

Meanwhile, chop the stems very finely and sauté them gently in the butter and walnut oil. When they begin to turn russet brown, stir in the garlic and cook for 2 minutes. Transfer this mixture to a mixing bowl. Add the parsley, the walnuts crushed to about the size of peppercorns, the cheese and plenty of pepper. Mix thoroughly and add salt to taste (the filling should be quite salty, as the caps have not been salted).

Remove the caps from the oven and turn it up to 190°C/375°F/Gas mark 5. Pile the mixture neatly on to the caps, making it as compact as possible. Bake in the oven for 10 minutes.

The intentionally rather dry stuffing of this dish contrasts nicely with the juicy cepe caps. The final spell in the oven is designed simply to heat the cepes through, not to brown them (their taste is ruined if they are over-browned).

If the stems are very large in relation to the caps and thus produce an excess of filling, simply spread the filling around, as well as on top of, the caps.

CROQUETTES OF FAIRY RING MUSHROOMS   FOR 4

The fairy ring mushroom, *Marasmius oreades*, is an underrated mushroom even in France, where gastronomes do not commonly overlook goodies that grow in the wild. Its chief characteristic – a slight smell of bitter almonds – which distinguishes it from a number of similar-looking inedible species, is transformed into a pleasantly nutty flavour by cooking.

250 g (9 oz) fairy ring mushrooms
60 g (2 oz) unsalted butter
1 large shallot, finely chopped
170 ml (6¹/₂ fl oz) béchamel sauce II (p. 357)
freshly ground pepper

60 g (2 oz) freshly grated Parmesan
60 g (2 oz) freshly grated Gruyère
2 eggs
salt
slightly stale breadcrumbs
oil for frying

Wash the mushrooms carefully, discarding the stringier stems. Melt the butter in a frying pan, put in the mushrooms and shallot, and sauté gently for 20 minutes. Make or re-heat the béchamel sauce. Put it with the mushrooms, shallots, plenty of pepper, the cheeses and 1 egg into a mixing bowl. Blend well and add salt to taste. Beat the remaining egg. Form the cheese and mushroom mixture into croquettes, dip in beaten egg, cover with breadcrumbs and fry on both sides in hot oil until crisp.

STUFFED PARASOL MUSHROOMS   FOR 4

The taste of the mushroom *Lepiota procera*, which metamorphoses from a drumstick shape in its youth to an elegant parasol with a smart muff-like ring round the stem, is subtle but evanescent. It therefore combines well with cream and with a mild creamy-tasting cheese like mozzarella.

2 shallots, finely chopped
40 g (1¹/₂ oz) unsalted butter
6-8 parasol mushrooms, including at least 4 that have developed into a parasol
salt

100 ml (3¹/₂ fl oz) double cream
1 tbsp fresh tarragon, finely chopped
100 g (3¹/₂ oz) mozzarella, diced
1 egg, beaten
freshly ground pepper

Cook the shallots gently in the butter for 5 minutes in a frying pan. Choose 4 fully extended mushrooms, discard their stems and place the caps, wiped clean and gills side up, on a buttered oven dish. Sprinkle with a little salt. Chop the remaining mushrooms and any of their stems that are not too woody, and add them to the shallots. Cook over a medium heat until the mushrooms begin to change colour (like cepes, they go russet-brown).

In a heavy saucepan, heat the cream with the tarragon. When it is hot, add the mozzarella and stir until melted. Allow to cool slightly, then beat in the egg and add the chopped mushrooms and shallots, salt to taste and plenty of pepper. Mix well. Arrange equal portions of this mixture neatly on the mushroom caps and bake in a moderate oven (180°C/350°F/Gas mark 4) for 20-25 minutes or until lightly crisped on top.

In hot weather parasol mushrooms tend to dry out and their gills to discolour. Such specimens should be avoided.

FEUILLETÉS DE MORILLES   FOR 4

Fresh morels are the second most expensive mushrooms after truffles. Fortunately they dry well and are available in that form at an affordable price. They also have a powerful flavour and do not need to be used in large quantities. Like parasol mushrooms, they have a particular affinity with cream, as in that classic of Norman cooking *Poularde aux morilles*, and with mild cheese.

The problem with most mushroom species is that they are wilful and refuse to grow when and where people would like them to. After two centuries of efforts, man has succeeded in growing only a few mushrooms commercially – cultivated mushrooms, truffles, shitake and oyster mushrooms, for example. So it was a rare event when a couple of American researchers announced in 1982 that they had succeeded in growing morels in the laboratory. They patented their method and naturally expected some financial return for their discovery (though I would have thought that the pleasure of creeping into the lab one morning to find that at last the earth had stirred was reward enough). The sophisticated technique used in growing morels in the lab failed, however, to yield economically practical results. But the price of morels has come down as a result of increased imports from Eastern Europe.

200 g (7 oz) fresh morels *or*
   50 g (2 oz) dried morels
60 g (2 oz) unsalted butter
1 shallot, very finely chopped
3 tbsp Marsala
300 ml (10 fl oz) double cream
80 g (3 oz) mozzarella, diced

30 g (1 oz) freshly grated Parmesan
50 g (2 oz) ham, diced
salt
freshly ground pepper
250 g (9 oz) chilled puff pastry (p. 368)
1 egg, beaten

Wash the morels carefully to get all the grit out of their cavities, and slice them finely. Heat the butter in a non-stick frying pan and gently sauté the morels and shallot for 10 minutes. Pour in the Marsala and, after another minute's cooking, the cream. When the liquid has reduced by about half, add the cheeses, ham, salt to taste and pepper. Stir over a low heat until a smooth consistency is obtained. Keep this mixture warm.

On a lightly floured surface, roll out the pastry to a rectangle 16 x 32 cm (6 x 12 in) and about 5 mm (just under 1/4 in) thick. With a sharp knife, cut it into four rectangles measuring 8 x 16 cm (3 x 6 in). Place these, floured side up, on an oiled baking sheet and brush their tops lightly with beaten egg (do not allow any egg to dribble down the cut edges). Bake them in a hot oven (220°C/425°F/Gas mark 7) for about 15 minutes. Remove and, as quickly as possible, slice each feuilleté delicately in half horizontally. Put the bottom halves on hot individual plates, spoon equal amounts of hot filling over them, cover with the other half of pastry, pour any remaining sauce over the top and serve immediately.

TRUFFES AU PARMESAN   FOR 4
Paul Reboux (p. 44), writing in the Twenties, suggests that
this sumptuous dish should form part of the menu for a
stag party (of the pre-marital kind). In French such an
event is called *un enterrement de vie de garçon* (the funeral
of a bachelor's life). Reboux considers truffles to be the
ideal vegetable course for such a dinner, for black is the
colour of mourning. Truffles with Parmesan are so
delicious, he says, that the bridegroom-to-be's male friends
will still be fondly remembering them the day he divorces.

Even in the Twenties, when truffles were more plentiful
and less expensive than they are now, this dish was
regarded as extravagant; it may seem even more so now.
But, in view of the prices we are prepared to pay for often
mediocre restaurant meals, it is a pity to deny oneself an
occasional indulgence in that most extraordinary of mushrooms. As French gourmets say jokingly: *la faim justifie les
moyens* (hunger justifies expense) – a pun on *la fin justifie
les moyens* (the end justifies the means).

1 clove garlic	freshly ground pepper
50 g (2 oz) unsalted butter	3 tbsp finest Madeira
200 g (7 oz) black truffles	250 ml (9 fl oz) Mornay sauce V
(fresh if possible)	(p. 359)
pinch salt	

Rub a smallish gratin dish with the garlic and some butter.
Place the dish over the lowest heat possible, either on a
heat diffuser over the smallest gas ring or on an electric
plaque at its lowest setting. Slice the truffles fairly thinly
and put into the dish with the rest of the butter. Sprinkle
with salt and plenty of pepper, add the Madeira and cover
the dish as tightly as possible (if it has no lid, place a sheet
of aluminium foil over the top and tie it round with
string). Leave for 15 minutes, shaking the dish from time
to time. There should be no sound of cooking within: this
operation is designed simply to warm the truffles through
and bring out their flavour.

Make or re-heat the Mornay sauce. Remove all the truffle slices from the dish except those covering the bottom. Spoon a little hot Mornay sauce over the truffles in the dish, add a layer of truffles, and repeat the operation as many times as necessary, finishing with a coating of sauce. Bake in a fairly hot oven (200°C/400°F/Gas mark 6) for about 15 minutes or until the surface begins to brown.

This dish naturally prefers the solitary glory of being served as a separate course – on its own or with some thin slices of hot toast or croûtons fried in butter – to playing second fiddle to a main course.

CAULIFLOWER CHEESE   FOR 4

Like many classic British specialities – Yorkshire pudding, mint sauce, suet pudding and sausage rolls are others that come to mind – cauliflower cheese can range in quality from the sublime to the nauseating. Everyone is familiar with the mushy texture and, above all, the lingering cabbagy smell of a badly made, overcooked cauliflower cheese.

Its smell, so similar to that of school cabbage, is analysed scientifically by Harold McGee in his fascinating book *On Food and Cooking:* during cooking

> the mustard oils and cysteine derivatives [in members of the cabbage group] break down to form various odoriferous compounds, including hydrogen sulphide (typical of rotten eggs), ammonia, mercaptans, and methyl sulphide; eventually these may react with each other to form especially powerful trisulphides. The longer the vegetable is cooked, the more of these molecules are produced.

In other words, don't over-cook members of the cabbage family, especially not cauliflower, whose texture as well as taste is thus ruined.

1 medium-sized cauliflower

500 ml (17 fl oz) Mornay sauce III
  (p. 359)

1 clove garlic, finely chopped (optional)

50 g (2 oz) freshly grated Gruyère *or*
  Parmesan, *or* 25 g (1 oz) of each

Break the cauliflower, trimmed of its leaves, into individual flowerets. Wash and plunge them into enough boiling salted water to immerse them easily, and cook uncovered over a medium heat for about 10 minutes. The cauliflower is ready when the stem can be pierced easily with a sharp knife. Remove the flowerets with a perforated spoon, drain in a colander and keep warm.

Alternatively, you can steam the flowerets by placing them in the upper compartment of a steamer with the stems pointing down over about 1 litre (35 fl oz) of boiling water. They will take about 15 minutes to cook. Whether using the boiling or steaming method, reserve 125 ml (4½ fl oz) of the liquid for the Mornay sauce.

Make the Mornay sauce. Butter a gratin dish and strew with garlic if desired (I think it improves the dish). Following Gratin method II (p. 264), fill and bake the dish, breaking up any larger flowerets if necessary, and putting a little extra salt on each layer of flowerets if they have been steamed.

BRUSSELS SPROUTS WITH PARMESAN   FOR 4

700 g (1½ lb) Brussels sprouts

60 g (2 oz) unsalted butter

freshly ground pepper

140 g (5 oz) freshly grated Parmesan

Trim and wash the Brussels sprouts. Boil them uncovered in plenty of salted water for about 10 minutes (they should remain slightly crunchy). Drain.

Heat the butter in a sauté pan, add the Brussels sprouts, sprinkle with plenty of pepper and toss so that the sprouts are thoroughly coated with butter. Butter a gratin dish. Following Gratin method III (p. 265), fill and bake the dish.

BROCCOLI WITH PARMESAN FOR 4

700 g (1¹/₂ lb) broccoli (purple *or*, freshly ground pepper
  better, Calabrese) 140 g (5 oz) freshly grated Parmesan
60 g (2 oz) unsalted butter

Trim and wash the broccoli, peeling any tough bits of stem. Tie into bundles and stand upright in a metal basket (if they fit neatly into the basket it may not be necessary to tie them). Plunge the basket into plenty of boiling salted water, which should cover the stems but not the flowering heads. Sprinkle some salt over the heads and cover (if the heads come above the rim of the saucepan, cover with aluminium foil). Cook for 8-10 minutes or until the stems are tender but still firm. Drain.

Heat the butter in a sauté pan, add the drained broccoli, sprinkle with plenty of pepper and toss so that it is thoroughly coated with butter. Butter a gratin dish. Following Gratin method III (p. 265), fill and bake the dish.

PARSNIPS WITH PARMESAN FOR 4

Parmesan may not seem an obvious partner for that very sweet vegetable, parsnip. But Parmesan is sweet as well as salt and pungent, which is probably why the two flavours interlock successfully in this mellow gratin.

700g (1¹/₂ lb) medium-sized parsnips, freshly ground pepper
  peeled 1 small clove garlic, finely chopped
100 g (3¹/₂ oz) unsalted butter 110 g (4 oz) freshly grated Parmesan
large pinch salt

Slice the parsnips lengthwise and discard their cores if woody. Cut into slender rectangular chunks. Heat the butter in a sauté pan, add the parsnips and enough water to half-cover them, and sprinkle with salt. Cover and cook very gently, turning them over from time to time, until tender. Sprinkle with plenty of pepper.

By the time the parsnips are tender nearly all the liquid

should have been boiled away and the butter absorbed by the vegetables. If there is too much liquid, remove the parsnips and boil it down so that only 2-3 tablespoons remain. Pour the liquid over the bottom of a gratin dish. Sprinkle with garlic. Following Gratin method III (p. 265), fill and bake the dish.

Three other sweetish vegetables – turnip, celeriac and the underrated swede – also respond well to this treatment.

COURGETTES WITH MOZZARELLA   FOR 4

In this very simple dish the elusive flavour of scarcely cooked baby courgettes, modulated only by raw olive oil, mild mozzarella and tiny quantities of herb, comes through loud and strong.

250 g (9 oz) mozzarella
300 g (10^1/$_2$ oz) baby courgettes
2 tsp fresh winter savory, finely chopped

freshly ground pepper
2 tbsp virgin olive oil

Cut the mozzarella into 6-mm (¼-in) slices. Slice the courgettes to the same thickness and blanch them uncovered in heavily salted boiling water for 3 minutes. Drain immediately and lay out on a towel, making sure all the slices lie flat. When cool, arrange them in one layer in a very large gratin dish or baking tray. Sprinkle with winter savory, pepper and olive oil. Cover each courgette slice with a slightly smaller slice of mozzarella. Put under a fierce grill only just long enough for the mozzarella to melt and brown a little. Serve immediately.

This dish can be served on its own as a very light entrée or as an accompaniment for grilled meat or fish. It works only if the courgettes are really small – no longer than 15 cm (6 in).

If you cannot get hold of fresh winter savory, use half quantities of dried, or else the same amount of fresh thyme or wild thyme.

COURGETTE CASSEROLE   FOR 4

Another recipe from Carla Phillips (p. 54). It wears its richness lightly and makes an excellent main course for lunch or supper.

600 g (1¹/₄ lb) young courgettes	2 tbsp lemon juice
275 ml (10 fl oz) double cream	2 tbsp chives, finely chopped
60 g (2 oz) unsalted butter	4 eggs, lightly beaten
175 g (6 oz) freshly grated Cheddar	salt
large pinch paprika	slightly stale breadcrumbs

Cut the courgettes, unpeeled, into small chunks, and blanch uncovered in boiling salted water for 2 minutes. Drain immediately and set aside.

Put the cream, butter, 110 g (4 oz) of cheese, the paprika and lemon juice in a heavy saucepan and place over a gentle heat, stirring all the time, until the cheese has just melted. Remove from the heat and stir in the chives and eggs. Mix well and add salt to taste. Add the courgettes, mix and turn into a buttered gratin dish. Top with breadcrumbs and the rest of the cheese, and bake in a moderate oven (180°C/350°F/Gas mark 4) for 20 minutes or until the surface is golden brown.

STUFFED COURGETTES   FOR 4

This recipe is suitable for courgettes that are *slightly* larger than baby size, say about 20 cm (8 in) long. The dish gets its distinctive flavour from five characterful ingredients lurking in the stuffing – pine-nuts, basil, garlic, Parmesan and olive oil – which are precisely those of pesto (p. 362).

2 medium-sized *or* 4 baby courgettes	2 tbsp fresh basil, finely chopped
3 tbsp virgin olive oil	80 g (3 oz) freshly grated Parmesan
1 onion, finely chopped	2 eggs, beaten
60 g (2 oz) pine-nuts	freshly ground pepper
60 g (2 oz) rice	salt
2 cloves garlic	

Put the washed courgettes, whole, in boiling salted water and blanch for 15 minutes. Heat 2 tablespoons of olive oil in a frying pan and cook the onion gently and without browning until translucent and soft. Put the pine-nuts into a shallow baking tin or tart mould and bake in a moderate oven until they turn the colour of roasted peanuts. Cook the rice in plenty of boiling salted water until tender, and drain.

Cut the courgettes in half lengthwise and scoop out the flesh of each half with a small spoon, taking care not to pierce the skin. Chop finely or blend the courgette flesh and garlic. Put into a mixing bowl along with the onions and their cooking oil. Add the rice, pine-nuts, basil, cheese, eggs, the rest of the olive oil and plenty of pepper. Mix thoroughly and add salt to taste.

Fill the courgette shells with the mixture and arrange in an oiled gratin dish into which they fit as neatly and as horizontally as possible. Bake in a moderate oven (180°C/350°F/Gas mark 4) for about 25 minutes.

Double the quantities when serving this dish as a main course.

PARMIGIANA DI MELANZANE   FOR 4

This gratin of aubergines does indeed contain Parmesan, but some *parmigiana* recipes with other vegetables do not. One can only suppose that the term means 'Parma-style' or 'as made in Parma' (some recipes for this dish call themselves *melanzane alla parmigiana*). Curiously, it is a speciality not of the Parma region at all, but of southern Italy.

1 kg (2¹/₄ lb) good firm aubergines	80 g (3 oz) freshly grated Parmesan
salt	300 ml (10 fl oz) tomato sauce (p. 364)
flour	2 tbsp fresh basil, chopped
virgin olive oil	freshly ground pepper
250 g (9 oz) mozzarella, thinly sliced	breadcrumbs

Slice the aubergines, put into a colander, sprinkle with

plenty of salt and leave for 1 hour under a plate with a heavy weight on top. Rinse, drain and dry with paper towels. Dust the aubergine slices with flour on one side only and, putting a shallow layer of olive oil in a large frying pan, fry them gently in batches on their floured sides until almost completely cooked (this will take about 10 minutes per batch). Add extra olive oil as necessary. Remove each batch as it is ready and drain on paper towels.

Put a layer of aubergine slices, fried side down, in a shallow gratin dish or baking tin. Cover with a few mozzarella slices and some Parmesan, hot tomato sauce, basil and pepper. Repeat the operation until the aubergine slices are used up, and finish with a sprinkling of Parmesan and breadcrumbs. Bake in a hot oven (220°C/425°F/Gas mark 7) for 10-15 minutes or until the surface begins to brown.

Aubergines have the ability to absorb enormous quantities of oil. This is why I have followed Jane Grigson's clever idea of initially frying the slices on one side only.

The flavour of fresh basil is affected and, to my mind, impaired by cooking. This way of making the *parmigiana*, with the aubergine pre-cooked, means that the final spell in the oven, while producing a nice crisp topping, does no more than warm up the contents of the gratin – and thus leaves the flavour of the basil intact. If you want to leave out the basil (or if no fresh basil is available; don't use the dried tea-like product), only half cook the aubergine slices in the frying pan and bake the assembled gratin in a moderate oven (170°C/325°F/Gas mark 3) for about 1 hour. This produces a greater intermingling of flavours.

In Calabria they add little bits of hard-boiled egg and salami to the gratin – a good idea if you are intending to serve it as a main course.

AUBERGINE AND CURD CHEESE PURÉE   FOR 4

This refreshingly garlicky, summery hors d'oeuvre is a variant of the Middle Eastern 'poor man's caviar' (purée of aubergines, olive oil and garlic).

2 aubergines	3 cloves garlic, finely chopped
1 tbsp virgin olive oil	salt
250 g (9 oz) fairly liquid curd cheese	freshly ground pepper
juice of 1/2 lemon	

Bake the aubergines whole in a very hot oven (230°C/450°F/Gas mark 8) until the skin goes black and the flesh is soft. Peel or rub off all the skin under running water, then squeeze out as much of the aubergines' bitter liquid as possible. Put the aubergines in a mixing bowl with the olive oil, cheese, lemon juice and garlic. Mash thoroughly or, better, blend to a purée. Add salt and pepper to taste. Serve slightly chilled.

This dish is also good made with yoghurt instead of curd cheese.

JERUSALEM ARTICHOKE GRATIN   FOR 4

Noting a heap of healthy-looking, freshly-dug Jerusalem artichokes in a farmyard near my home in the Auvergne, I enquired of the farmer if I could possibly purchase some. He seemed a little bemused but agreed. When I told him I wanted only a couple of kilos, a look of blank, uncomprehending amazement came over his face as he realized that the artichokes were going to be consumed by me and not by the pigs he imagined I kept. He gave them to me but refused to be paid for such a footling quantity of 'worthless' vegetables.

Most members of the younger generation in France have never eaten the vegetable, while – and because – their elders on the whole abhor it. This has nothing to do with its extraordinary ability to produce flatulence, a property that would hardly deter the French anyway. Pre-war and nineteenth-century cookbooks are in any case full of recipes for *topinambours*. (The French word, by the way, comes from a Brazilian people, the Tupinamba; the English is a deformation of *girasole*, the Italian word for sunflower, to which family the Jerusalem artichoke belongs.)

No, this curious blind spot has to do with historical circumstances. During the Second World War most potatoes were commandeered by the Germans or the Vichy government, and the population, especially the rural population, had to fall back on the potato's only rival as a heavy-cropping vegetable. So the occupied French were reduced to eating them virtually every day. But, as Jane Grigson points out in her *Vegetable Book*, 'Jerusalem artichokes have such a special flavour that they never could have become a kind of neutral basic food like . . . potatoes. They are for eating now and then, not every day.' Just so. The French have been put off ever since.

One of the more positive contributions of *nouvelle cuisine* has been the rehabilitation of neglected vegetables, and, with the advent of a new generation of Yuppie restaurant-goers in France who did not suffer the privations of wartime, *topinambours* have begun to make a timid comeback on French menus.

Parmesan goes well with Jerusalem artichokes for the same reason that it does with parsnips: it provides a complementary sweetness.

1.25 kg (2¾ lb) unblemished	salt
Jerusalem artichokes	freshly ground pepper
60 g (2 oz) unsalted butter	140 g (5 oz) freshly grated Parmesan

Wash, peel and halve the artichokes, cutting off any hard protuberances. As you prepare them, transfer them to a bowl of acidulated water. Boil in salted water or, better, steam until tender but not mushy. Drain and cut into smallish pieces. Heat the butter in a sauté pan and toss the artichokes in it for 5 minutes without browning them. Add a little salt (more if you have steamed them) and plenty of pepper. Following Gratin method III (p. 265), fill and bake the gratin.

CHARDOONS À LA FROMAGE   FOR 4

As far as vegetables are concerned, I am a dyed-in-the-wool reactionary, i.e. desiring a return to a former state, for it would mean that a far wider range of vegetables would be on the market than are today. Take the cardoon, a delicious leaf-stalk vegetable whose taste is reminiscent of its relative, the globe artichoke. Widely available in Britain in the eighteenth and nineteenth centuries, cardoons are now virtually unobtainable. In France, too, they are becoming hard to find north of Lyon. As Jane Grigson says in her *Vegetable Book*, 'they follow the anchovy belt of the Mediterranean'. Cardoons are relatively easy to grow. But the seeds have unfortunately disappeared from the main British nurserymen's catalogues; they are widely available on the Continent, however, so why not buy a packet next time you cross the Channel – or get friends to bring one back?

In this recipe, taken from an unpublished English cookery manuscript of 1838, cardoons are given their alternative spelling, chardoons. The solecistic 'à la fromage' – the French would say *au fromage* – was common in British cookery books of the period.

1.5 kg (3¹/₄ lb) cardoons, trimmed of their leaves	juice of ¹/₂ orange
500 ml (17 fl oz) red wine	freshly ground pepper
salt	100 g (3¹/₂ oz) freshly grated
30 g (1 oz) *beurre manié* (p. 364)	Parmesan *or* Cheshire

Wash the cardoon stalks, cut into sections and blanch in boiling acidulated and salted water for about 15 minutes. Drain and remove all string and hard skin. Cut into very small pieces and simmer in the wine for about 20 minutes or until tender but not mushy. Add salt to taste. Remove the cardoons with a perforated spoon and set aside.

Divide the *beurre manié* into little knobs. Bring the cooking liquid to just below boiling point, turn the heat down as low as possible and gradually stir in the knobs of *beurre manié*. Do not allow the sauce to boil. When it has reached a creamy consistency, remove from the heat and stir in the orange juice.

Arrange the cardoon pieces in a gratin dish, pour the sauce over them and sprinkle with grated cheese. Bake in a fairly hot oven (190°C/375°F/Gas mark 5) for about 20 minutes or until the surface is golden brown. Serve immediately.

You can also make a gratin of cardoons by continuing to cook them in water, after stringing them, until tender, and then assembling a gratin according to Method II or Method III (pp. 264-5).

GLOBE ARTICHOKE GRATIN   FOR 4

Globe artichokes are companionable vegetables: they get on well with prawns, lobster, mussels, anchovies, chicken livers, foie gras, beef marrow, brains, mushrooms, spinach, broad beans, eggs and cheese, among other things. This dish combines three of those accompaniments.

4 medium-sized *or* 3 large artichokes	2 hard-boiled eggs, shelled
250 ml (9 fl oz) Mornay sauce III (p. 359)	1 small clove garlic, finely chopped
30 g (1 oz) unsalted butter	large pinch salt
4 large whole chicken livers	freshly ground pepper

Wash and boil the artichokes in plenty of boiling salted water. After 30 minutes, pull gently at one of the small outside leaves near the base of the artichoke: if it comes away easily the artichokes are done. Drain facing down in a colander, keeping 6 tablespoons of the cooking liquid for the Mornay sauce. Make the Mornay sauce and keep warm.

When the artichokes are cool enough to handle, pull off the leaves, scraping the edible pulp off each leaf with a spoon (this is a lengthy operation, and an extra pair or two of hands will come in very useful). Pull out the fibrous chokes and cut the artichoke bottoms into 1-cm (½-in) dice. Heat the butter in a small frying pan and gently sauté the chicken livers for about 5 minutes, turning them over once. They should be only *just* cooked, with a hint of pinkness in the middle.

Chop the livers and the hard-boiled eggs coarsely and put them into a mixing bowl with the artichoke pieces and garlic. Add salt, plenty of pepper and the hot Mornay sauce. Mix well but delicately, and turn into a buttered gratin dish. Bake in a fairly hot oven (190°C/375°F/Gas mark 5) for about 20 minutes or until the surface begins to turn golden brown.

CARCIOFI CON MOZZARELLA   FOR 4

4 medium-sized *or* 8 small artichokes	2 tsp fresh *or* dried winter savory, finely chopped
juice of 1 lemon	
150 g (5½ oz) mozzarella, chopped	4 tbsp virgin olive oil
30 g (1 oz) freshly grated Parmesan	salt
50 g (2 oz) breadcrumbs	freshly ground pepper
1 egg, beaten	4 anchovies
1 small clove garlic, finely chopped	

Crack off the stems of the artichokes as close as possible to their base. Cut off the remaining ragged bits so the artichokes can sit upright. Pull off the toughest outer leaves and with a sharp knife slice across the top about half way down. Pull out the central leaves and scrape the choke off the bottom with a teaspoon. As each artichoke cup is prepared, transfer it to a pan of water mixed with lemon juice.

Into a mixing bowl, put the cheeses, breadcrumbs, egg, garlic, winter savory, 2 tablespoons of olive oil, a little salt and plenty of pepper. Mix well. Desalt the anchovies in warm water and dab dry with a paper towel. Drain the artichoke cups and fill with equal amounts of the stuffing. Place the anchovies (or half-anchovies if you are using small artichokes) on top. Arrange the artichokes in a large gratin dish or baking tray. Pour in the rest of the olive oil and enough hot water to make a depth of about 1 cm (1/2 in).

Bake the artichokes in a moderate oven (180°C/ 350°F/Gas mark 4) until cooked through. The time taken for this may vary from 1 to 2 hours, depending on the size and freshness of the artichokes. Test for tenderness with a sharp knife. If the water looks as if it will evaporate before they are cooked, add a little more.

Artichoke bottoms cooked in this way are also very good cold.

FONDS D'ARTICHAUTS SOUFFLÉS   FOR 4

Another elegant entrée from Edouard Nignon's *Eloges de la cuisine française* (p. 114).

8 large or 12 medium-sized artichoke bottoms	salt
	4 egg yolks
juice of 1 lemon	140 g (5 oz) freshly grated Parmesan
120 ml (4 fl oz) well-reduced veal stock *or* 3 tbsp meat glaze dissolved in 6 tbsp hot water	30 g (1 oz) freshly grated Gruyère
	pinch sugar
120 ml (4 fl oz) double cream	freshly ground white pepper
100 g (3½ oz) unsalted butter	3 egg whites

Crack off the stems of the artichokes as close as possible to their base. Cut off the remaining ragged bits so the artichokes can sit upright. Pull off the toughest outer leaves and with a sharp knife slice across the top about three-quarters of the way down. Pull out the central leaves and scrape the choke off the bottom with a teaspoon. As each artichoke bottom is prepared, transfer it to a pan of water mixed with lemon juice.

Put the veal stock or meat glaze and the cream into a very large sauté pan, or two smaller ones. Place over a gentle heat. Drain the artichoke bottoms and put into the pan, cover tightly and simmer over the lowest heat possible, basting from time to time, until their flesh is tender but not mushy. Transfer to a buttered shallow ovenproof dish. Reduce the artichokes' cooking liquid, if necessary, until you have a thin sauce-like consistency, check its saltiness, pour into a sauceboat, and keep hot.

In a large heavy saucepan, melt the butter over a low heat. Beat the egg yolks in a bowl. When the butter has completely melted but *before* it begins to sizzle, remove the pan from the heat and pour in the egg yolks slowly, beating all the time with a wooden spoon. Return to a very low heat and continue beating for about 30 seconds or until the mixture begins to thicken very slightly. Be careful not to allow the egg yolks to curdle. Add the cheeses, a tiny pinch of sugar and a little pepper. Continue stirring until the cheese has melted. Remove from the heat.

Whisk the egg whites with a tiny pinch of salt until very stiff. Take a large spoonful of the whites and stir quickly into the cheese mixture to slacken it, then fold in the rest delicately but thoroughly. Using either a spoon or a forcing bag with a plain nozzle, quickly place little mounds of the mixture on each artichoke bottom and bake immediately in a hot oven (220°C/425°F/Gas mark 7) for about 8-10 minutes. *Do not open the oven door for at least 7 minutes.* Serve immediately with the hot sauce, which, says Nignon, should be 'creamy and the colour of white coffee'.

CHEESE IN VINE LEAVES   FOR 4
A recipe collected by Jane Grigson from the cave village of Trôo, in the Bas-Vendômois region of western France, and published in the *Observer Magazine*.

This recipe can be used for any old end of cheese – it was a way of using up the last dried pieces – and in winter pickled vine leaves make a good substitute for fresh. Buy them in vacuum packs or from the brine tub. Canned leaves are too tender. The fresh, slightly lemony taste of the vine leaves has a revivifying effect on the cheese. In the old days the packages went into the oven when the bread came out, to cook in the dying heat and then to be eaten with the still warm bread.

12 vine leaves, fresh *or* pickled	12 slices bread, fresh *or* crisped for
12 2-cm (³/4-in) cubes cheese	5 minutes in the oven

If using fresh vine leaves, just wash them and wrap them round the pieces of cheese. Place the little packages seam side down, close together in an oven-proof dish. Put them in an oven pre-heated to 230°C/450°F/Gas mark 8 for about 15 minutes or until the leaves darken and catch slightly, and the whole thing feels soft when you press it. Remove the packages from the oven and serve on the slices of bread.

For pickled leaves, pour boiling water over them, separate them carefully with a wooden spoon, and leave them for 20-30 minutes. Drain and cover generously with cold water. Now taste a corner – if the leaves are not too sharply salty, they can now be used. If they are still very strong, repeat the boiling water. Wrap them around the cheese and complete as above.

GLAMORGAN SAUSAGES   FOR 4

This is Jane Grigson's version of a well-known recipe, published in her *English Food*.

140 g (5 oz) freshly grated Caerphilly	1 tbsp fresh parsley, chopped
or Lancashire	1 tsp mustard powder
120 g (4 oz) fresh white breadcrumbs	Salt
2 tbsp spring onion, *or* leek,	Freshly ground pepper
finely chopped	1 egg white
3 egg yolks	extra breadcrumbs
¹/2 tsp thyme	lard for frying

Mix the cheese, breadcrumbs and spring onion or leek. Whisk the yolks, herbs, mustard and seasoning together – use about 1 teaspoon of salt and plenty of pepper – and add to the breadcrumbs and cheese to make a coherent mixture. If the breadcrumbs or cheese were on the dry side, you may need another yolk or a little water before everything hangs together as it should. Divide into twelve and roll each piece into a small sausage about 5 cm (2 in) long. Dip them in egg white, roll in the extra breadcrumbs and fry until golden brown in lard.

PAIN DE POIREAUX   FOR 4

In the heyday of the wireless in France the air was abuzz with recipes. Dr Edouard de Pomiane's authoritative voice was beamed out to millions in the Thirties and Forties (p. 241). But even as early as 1929, not long after the invention of the *sans-fil* (literally 'without-wire') – a neologism that was ousted by *radio* much more quickly than its English equivalent – the publishing house of Flammarion and the French equivalent of Fortnum & Mason, Corcellet, organized a radio recipe competition. Their aim was to unearth little-known regional dishes. Through broadcasting, they were able to 'reach the tiniest hamlets, where the Paris newspapers are scarcely read' and obtain enough material for a book.

The result, *Les Belles Recettes des provinces françaises* by Les Sans-Filistes Gastronomes, contains over 500 regional recipes contributed by the winners of the competition as well as by runners-up. Many of them are excellent, though they tend to be *cuisine bourgeoise* rather than farmhouse fare. The judges of the competition, by the way, included such celebrated gastronomes and cooks as Dr Alfred Gottschalk, Prosper Montagné, Philéas Gilbert and Auguste Escoffier.

This recipe, a very simple kind of leek and cheese pudding, was contributed to the book by a Madame Humbert.

8 medium-sized leeks
4 eggs
large pinch salt
freshly ground pepper
pinch freshly grated nutmeg

50 g (2 oz) stale white bread
3 tbsp milk
90 g (3 oz) freshly grated Gruyère
30 g (1 oz) unsalted butter

Cut off the leek roots and trim the green leaves to within about 3 cm (1 in) of the white stem. Wash and cut into sections. Put the section that came from the green end in some water and peel off its outer layers to remove any lingering grit. Put all the leek pieces in plenty of boiling salted water and cook uncovered for 15 minutes. Drain and chop not too finely.

Beat the eggs in a mixing bowl and add the salt, pepper, nutmeg, bread soaked in the milk, cheese and leeks. Mix thoroughly. Turn the mixture out into a buttered mould, with vertical sides if possible. Make sure it settles properly by tapping the mould on the table. Bake in a fairly hot oven (190°C/375°F/Gas mark 5) for 25-30 minutes. The *pain* is done when an inserted knife comes out clean. Remove from the oven and leave for 5 minutes. Run a knife round the inside of the mould and unmould on to a hot serving plate. If you have used a mould with vertical sides, serve the *pain* with its golden top upmost.

Madame Humbert adds: 'The juice from a veal roast should be served with this *pain*. Slices of roast veal may also be arranged round the *pain*. On days of abstinence this dish should be served without meat juice.'

TWICE-BAKED LEEK, CHEESE
AND TOMATO TIMBALES   FOR 4

A deliciously light yet filling dish devised by Carla Phillips (p. 54).

1 large *or* 2 small leeks	large pinch sugar
40 g (1^1/$_2$ oz) unsalted butter	120 g (4 oz) fresh goat cheese
120 ml (4 fl oz) double cream	2 eggs
salt	large pinch fresh *or* dried oregano,
freshly ground pepper	finely chopped
575 g (1^1/$_4$ lb) fresh tomatoes, peeled,	large pinch fresh parsley, finely
seeded and chopped *or* 400 g	chopped
(14 oz) tinned tomatoes, seeded	30 g (1 oz) freshly grated Gruyère
and chopped	30 g (1 oz) freshly grated Parmesan

Cut the roots and most of the green leaves off the leek(s). Wash, chop finely and put briefly under running water to remove any lingering grit. Sauté gently in butter until soft and very slightly browned. Remove from the heat and set aside.

Put the goat cheese, eggs and 2 tablespoons of cream into a mixing bowl and beat well. Add the leeks, a little salt and plenty of pepper, and mix thoroughly. Lightly oil four smallish ovenproof dishes or ramekins and spoon the mixture into them (they should be about two-thirds full). Place them in a deep baking tray or roasting pan and pour in enough boiling water to come at least halfway up their sides. Bake in a cool oven (150°C/300°F/Gas mark 2) for 15-20 minutes or until a sharp knife inserted in the centre comes out cleanly. Remove from the oven and leave to cool.

Put the tomatoes into a casserole over a high heat and cook for about 15 minutes, stirring from time to time. Add the sugar, oregano, parsley and the rest of the cream. Reduce for another 5 minutes or until a sauce-like consistency is obtained. Add plenty of pepper and salt to taste.

Lightly oil an ovenproof serving dish. Turn the timbales out into it, cover with tomato sauce and sprinkle with the grated cheeses. Bake in a fairly hot oven (190°C/375°C/ Gas mark 5) for about 15 minutes or until the cheese topping has melted and browned.

PATRANQUE   FOR 4-6

This Auvergnat concoction of bread and melted cheese is the ancestor of Aligot (p. 273) and Truffade (p. 276), both of which came into being when the potato was finally accepted for human consumption in the French provinces in the late eighteenth century. Nowadays *patranque* is rarely encountered in homes or restaurants in the Auvergne – which is a pity, as it has plenty of individuality if made with the local bread, which uses 50 per cent rye flour and 50 per cent wheat flour.

600 g (1¼ lb) rye bread	4 cloves garlic, finely chopped
50 g (2 oz) unsalted butter	salt
400 g (14 oz) Tomme fraîche de Cantal, sliced thinly	freshly ground pepper

Slice the bread and soak it in a little water in a large flat dish. There must be enough water to soften it completely, including its crust. Squeeze out any excess water. Heat the butter over a low heat in a large non-stick frying pan, add the bread and stir until it has broken down into a kind of panada. Add the cheese and garlic. When the cheese begins to melt, beat vigorously until the mixture becomes elastic and smooth. Add salt to taste and plenty of pepper.

The *patranque* may be served at this point or left to cook until it acquires a crisp, golden crust underneath. If you choose the latter method, keep the heat low so as not to burn the garlic.

There exists a similar but more liquid dish, halfway between *patranque* and Soupe au fromage, which goes by the evocative name of *cantemerlou* ('sing-blackbird' in Occitan), allegedly because the bubbles of steam escaping the melted cheese make a sound like that of the blackbird.

RISOTTO ALLA MILANESE   FOR 4

This rich, filling classic hardly needs any introduction. When properly made, it offers a marvellously aromatic combination of four flavours: rice (you need the best quality), Parmesan, saffron and chicken stock. In Milan it is the mandatory accompaniment to *osso buco*.

1 g (15 grains) best-quality powdered saffron *or* 4 saffron filaments, pounded

1-1.25 litres (35-44 fl oz) chicken stock

120 g (4 oz) unsalted butter

25 g (1 oz) beef marrow

1 small onion, very finely chopped

300 g (10¹/₂ oz) short-grained rice (Arborio *or* Vialone), briefly washed in running water

salt

freshly ground pepper

80 g (3 oz) freshly grated Parmesan

Put the saffron to soak in 4 tablespoons of hot stock. Heat 40 g (1¹/₂ oz) of butter and the beef marrow in a large non-stick sauté pan and gently sweat the onion until translucent but not browned. Add the rice and stir for 1-2 minutes so all the grains are well coated with the fat. Sprinkle with a little salt. Now add about a tumblerful of hot stock and continue stirring. As the rice absorbs it, add more hot stock. By the time the rice is done (it should remain slightly firm), there should be no more liquid in the pan, just a small amount of creamy sauce.

Gently stir in the saffron and its liquid, plenty of pepper, the cheese and the remaining butter. Turn off the heat and leave the sauté pan where it is for a minute or so to give time for the cheese to melt. Transfer to a hot serving dish and serve immediately. More grated Parmesan should be available on the side.

In another version a glass of white wine is poured over the onions and reduced by half before the rice is added.

KASHA WITH PARMESAN   FOR 4

From *The Russian Cook Book* (1924) by Princess Alexandre Gagarine, this recipe for buckwheat kasha (whole, husked buckwheat grains) is a very White Russian version of a staple peasant dish (I doubt whether Parmesan has ever been available on the steppes of either pre- or post-revolutionary Russia). The distinctive flavour of buckwheat goes well with cheese.

250 g (9 oz) husked buckwheat grain   70 g (2½ oz) freshly grated Parmesan
200 g (7 oz) unsalted butter   salt

Wash the buckwheat, removing any husks, or unhusked grains. Roast in a frying pan without any fat, stirring and shaking all the time, until it begins to pop. Transfer to an ovenproof dish large enough to allow plenty of space for the kasha to swell. Add about 500 ml (17 fl oz) of boiling salted water, stir well, cover and cook in a moderate oven (180°C/350°F/Gas mark 4) with the dish standing in a deep baking tray or roasting pan full of water, for about 45 minutes or until the grains are soft.

Butter a charlotte mould and melt the remaining butter. Remove the kasha from the oven, fluff it with a fork and spoon a layer of it into the mould. Sprinkle with some cheese, melted butter and a very little salt. Repeat the operation until all the kasha is used up, finishing with an extra big sprinkling of cheese and 1 tablespoon of melted butter. Bake in a fairly hot oven (190°C/375°F/Gas mark 5) for about 20 minutes or until the surface begins to turn golden brown.

CHAPTER FOURTEEN

Salads

Cheese often finds its way into salads, especially on vegetarian menus and in buffet, wine-bar and party food. And very nice it can be, too. Unfortunately, however, it is often combined unthinkingly with all manner of unsuitable ingredients; often the cheese used is third-rate, sometimes even processed cheese; often, too, excess liquid from ill-drained canned sweet corn or ill-dried salad vegetables swamps the cheese and turns it soggy.

Texture and flavour are crucial when using cheese in salads. As far as the first quality is concerned, the most successful combinations call for either a relatively hard cheese that keeps its shape and firmness, such as Gruyère, or else a crumbly one that disintegrates without turning to a mush, such as feta or Roquefort. The other vital quality of a cheese that blends well with a salad is an assertive flavour, which is the case with the three cheeses just mentioned (proper Swiss Gruyère has quite a strong taste). The two other requisites for success are the amount of cheese used (a little in a salad goes a long way) and the amount of vinegar or lemon juice that goes into the dressing (not too much).

HORIATIKI FOR 4

This classic Greek salad has a curiously evocative quality. I just happened to be thinking how powerfully it could, especially when washed down by retsina, call up memories of my only visit to Greece – blindingly whitewashed houses, a panpipe player heard but not seen in the countryside near Olympia, a sprig of basil handed to me by an archimandrite at a religious festival on the slopes of Mount Olympus – when I turned to a couple of books that also have the recipe in order to compare ingredients. To my great surprise, I found one author (Claudia Roden, in *A New Book of Middle Eastern Food*) writing: 'This salad brings back for me the garland of islands floating in the deep blue sea, the plaintive sound of the bouzouki and the sugar-cake houses.' And the other (T. A. Layton in *Cheese and Cheese Cookery*): 'To me this immediately conjures up memories of delicious meals eaten under clear Greek skies, often served at the water's edge with yachts and small boats riding lazily at anchor nearby.' What is the mystery ingredient in Horiatiki that produces this quasi-Proustian experience? Probably, as Layton surmises, feta, which, when made with ewe's or goat's milk as it should be, has a surprising depth of flavour. Or could it be the retsina?

The recipe below was given to me years ago by a Greek exile and excellent cook. It was a dish she made regularly – perhaps because it reminded her of the country she had left behind.

freshly ground pepper	1/2 cucumber, unpeeled and sliced
4 tbsp best Greek olive oil	2 large sweet tomatoes, thickly sliced
1 tbsp lemon juice	1 green pepper, cored, seeded and
1 tbsp fresh parsley, chopped	cut into rings
1 tbsp dried rigani (Greek wild	120 g (4 oz) feta, crumbled
marjoram) *or* oregano	12 good Greek black olives
1 sweet onion, sliced	

Put the pepper, oil, lemon juice, parsley and rigani into a salad bowl and mix well. Just before serving, add the other ingredients and toss thoroughly.

The whole point of this salad is its rusticity, so don't peel or seed the cucumber and the tomatoes (try to get hold of huge, misshapen tomatoes with deep grooves in their skins – they have the best flavour), don't slice or chop anything too finely, and don't stone the olives. Salt is unnecessary, as the feta and olives are very salty.

CEPE SALAD   FOR 4

Cepes are among the most aromatic of mushrooms apart from truffles. Left on the kitchen table for an hour or two, they soon make the whole room fragrant with their sweet, complex mushroomy smell. When they are cooked, their aroma dims very slightly: when eaten raw, it remains intact. If you are lucky enough to find or buy young cepes in prime condition (they should be unbruised, dry, heavy and almost as hard as a root vegetable), try this salad. It calls for only a small amount of cepes.

100 ml (3½ fl oz) single cream
8 walnut halves, fresh if possible (p. 30), coarsely chopped
1 tsp Dijon mustard
2 tsp lemon juice
pinch salt

freshly ground pepper
1 tbsp fresh chives, finely chopped
140 g (5 oz) young, very firm cepes
200 g (7 oz) curly endive (only the yellow-white inner leaves if possible)
80 g (3 oz) Gruyère

Put the cream, walnuts, mustard, lemon juice, salt, pepper and chives in a salad bowl and mix well. Wipe the cepes clean with a damp paper towel (on no account immerse in water), having trimmed the earthy bit off the stems. Cut into slices about 3 mm (⅛ in) thick, then cut again into tagliatelle-wide strips. Wash the endive (if using only the inner leaves, this may not be necessary) and dry very thoroughly. Cut the cheese into strips of about the same dimensions as the mushroom. Just before serving, add the salad ingredients to the bowl and toss gently but thoroughly. In hot weather – or if your kitchen is very hot – refrigerate the cheese strips until just before serving.

BATAVIAN ENDIVE AND GRUYÈRE SALAD   FOR 4

2 tsp sherry vinegar *or* good wine vinegar	1 shallot, finely chopped
3 tbsp good salad oil	pinch salt
1 tbsp walnut oil	freshly ground pepper
1 tbsp fresh winter savory, finely chopped, *or* 1 tsp dried winter savory, crumbled *or* pulverized	Batavian endive (1 small specimen, *or* inside leaves of 1 larger one)
	120 g (4 oz) Gruyère, cut into small dice

Put the vinegar, oils, winter savory, shallot, salt and pepper into a salad bowl and mix well. Wash the endive and dry very thoroughly. Add the endive and cheese to the salad bowl just before serving and toss thoroughly. In hot weather – or if your kitchen is very hot – refrigerate the diced cheese until just before serving.

MIXED SALAD WITH ROQUEFORT   FOR 6-8

'Mixed' often means 'muddled' when used in conjunction with salad. Still, I prefer the adjective 'mixed' to the rather pretentious 'composed'. Of course, one of the joys of the salad medium is that it can be used as a vehicle for a miscellany of different ingredients. But what is often overlooked is that the relative proportion of each ingredient is as important as the overall choice of ingredients.

4 tbsp good salad oil	2 tbsp fresh chervil, finely chopped
1 tbsp sherry vinegar *or* good wine vinegar	1/4 celeriac
freshly ground pepper	1 small crisp apple
2 shallots, finely chopped	1/2 small beetroot
12 walnut halves, fresh if possible (p. 30), coarsely chopped	1 curly endive
	60 g (2 oz) Roquefort, crumbled

Put the oil, vinegar, plenty of pepper (but not salt, as the Roquefort will provide enough), shallots, walnuts and chervil into a salad bowl and mix well. Peel the celeriac and cut into julienne strips; peel and core the apple and cut into tiny dice; as they are ready, toss these two ingredients in the dressing to prevent discoloration. Cut the beetroot into tiny dice. Wash the endive and dry very thoroughly (if it is very large, use only the yellow-white inside leaves). Just before serving, add the beetroot, endive and Roquefort to the salad bowl and toss thoroughly.

The celeriac and apple are better prepared not too long in advance. If you expect a long wait before serving the salad, cut them up and add at the last moment – it is only a matter of 5 minutes' work.

If you grow, or can lay your hands on, Hamburg parsley (root parsley), you could replace the celeriac with an equivalent amount of that wonderful vegetable.

CAESAR SALAD   FOR 4-6

This famous American salad, named not after the Roman emperor but a restaurateur in Tiajuana, Caesar Cardini, exists in many 'authentic' versions. Most of them, in my view, call for too much lemon juice and not enough anchovies (or no anchovies at all). Here is a formula that, I think, gets the balance right and does not claim to be authentic.

175 g (6 oz) good white bread, cubed	1 tbsp lemon juice
8 tbsp virgin olive oil	freshly ground pepper
2 cloves garlic, finely chopped	salt
1 Cos lettuce	1 egg
4 anchovies	40 g (1 1/2 oz) freshly grated Parmesan

Fry the bread in half the oil until golden brown and crisp. Add the garlic to the frying pan 2 minutes before the bread is ready. Keep warm. Wash the lettuce and dry very thoroughly. Desalt the anchovies in warm water, dab dry with paper towels and chop coarsely. Put the lemon juice, plenty of pepper and the anchovies into a salad bowl and mix well. Check seasoning and add salt to taste.

Put the egg, brought to room temperature, into plenty of boiling water and cook for 1 minute from the point when the boiling resumes. Cut the lettuce leaves into strips crosswise. As soon as the egg is cool enough to handle, break it into the salad dressing and blend quickly. Add the lettuce and the contents of the frying pan, sprinkle with cheese, and toss thoroughly until all the leaves are well coated with dressing and semi-raw egg. Serve immediately.

Much fatuous ritual surrounds the making and eating of Caesar salad in the United States. To be really chic you must arrive at the table with a trayful of accessories and assemble the salad in front of your guests (with all the risks that such an operation entails). People are expected to use their fingers to eat the lettuce leaves (which are left whole in that version) – this of course provides an excuse to get out the silver finger-bowls – and a knife and fork for the rest.

Some authorities say that the lettuce should be chilled and the salad eaten on chilled plates. Perhaps that was necessary in the broiling Mexican restaurant where the salad originated. I have preferred the French method of tipping hot ingredients into the salad at the last moment.

CHAPTER FIFTEEN

The Cheeseboard

This is a book not about individual cheeses, but about their use in cooking. So I do not intend to go into a lengthy discussion of the pros and cons of this or that method of composing a cheeseboard. It seems to me that this is an area where there can be few hard and fast rules.

For example, you can aim for the greatest possible variety, running the whole gamut from, say, a mild *fromage blanc* to a pungent Boulette d'Avesnes. Or you can opt for variations on a theme, grouping together several similar cheeses in order better to savour their differences: Camembert, Coulommiers, Brie de Meaux, Brie de Melun and Fougeru, for example; or Beaufort, Gruyère, Emmental, Appenzell and Comté; or Bleu d'Auvergne, Stilton, Blue Cheshire and Blue Wensleydale; or a range of goat or ewe's milk cheeses – the possibilities are endless.

My own preference is for a smallish selection, for example four or five cheeses that set each other off well and are all in the absolute peak of condition.

But when the cheese course comes, there are various ways in which you can usefully bring other ingredients into play. Here are some suggestions (others will be found in the chapter on Cold Entrées):

CHEESE WITH CHUTNEY

A combination that can work very well. The chutney should be fairly hot and spicy, and the cheese bland (a mild Cheddar, young Cantal, Emmental or unmatured Gouda, for example); the assertive personality of a strong Cheddar, Double Gloucester or Gruyère does not, to my mind, need the additional zip of the chutney. Indeed, chutney is a good way of knocking some life into rindless, cling-filmed supermarket block Cheddar if ever it should find its way into your house as a result of *force majeure*.

EWE'S-MILK CHEESE WITH QUINCE PASTE

A felicitous combination, much favoured by the Spanish and Portuguese – and consequently the Latin Americans. For the authentic interaction of flavours, try to obtain Spanish Manchego or Portuguese Rabaçal. Failing that, a good Brebis des Pyrénées will do.

STILTON WITH PORT

Blue cheese goes very well with sweet wines. In Bordeaux since at least the turn of the century Sauternes has been traditionally drunk with Roquefort, despite the latter's high salinity. Similarly, port is drunk with Stilton in Britain – and a very good combination they make. The problem is that some people insist on a ritual marriage between the wine and the cheese *in situ*: they cut the Stilton in half, wrap it in a napkin, scoop out some of the cheese and pour in a glass or two of port. People then help themselves – on the whole messily. By the next day the cheese will have turned an unprepossessing shade of grey-green-purple and any residual port will have oxidized nastily. Surely a mouthful of unadulterated Stilton followed by a sip of clean port that still has its bouquet is far preferable?

MUNSTER WITH CARAWAY

Caraway seeds are good for the digestion and prevent flatulence. But the fact that Munster, one of the smelliest of all cheeses, is usually eaten in its region of origin, Alsace, and in Alsatian restaurants with a scattering of caraway seeds probably has less to do with any supposed indigestibility of the cheese than with the osmosis of German culture – caraway is ubiquitous in German cooking, where it finds its way into anything from bread and cakes to sauerkraut and meat dishes.

However that may be, unless you are allergic to the taste – and many people are – caraway does provide Munster with an interesting complementary pungency. The organoleptic experience can be rendered more complex if the cheese and caraway are accompanied by some cool, spicy Gewürztraminer (though purists claim that caraway interferes with the taste of the wine).

Some Munster is marketed with the caraway already in it. It is better to procure your own seeds and roast them lightly before use. Their flavour will be enhanced and you can indulge in the inexplicably satisfying activity of mopping them up with forkfuls of soft, accommodating Munster.

HANDKÄSE MIT MUSIK

Handkäse (so called because it used to be moulded into shape by hand) is a German cheese with an unattractive, wrinkled grey-brown rind and the kind of gustatory attributes that prompt writers on cheese to take refuge in euphemism: 'an acquired taste', 'not to the taste of some', with an 'arresting' smell and '*very* pronounced aroma'. All of which is true, except that the taste of Handkäse, like that of Munster, is not nearly as strong as its smell. In the Frankfurt am Main area, Handkäse (or Handkäs, as it is spelt in the local dialect) is often served 'mit Musik' (sliced sweet onions, often with a vinaigrette dressing) and good coarse bread. It is usually washed down with the local rough dry cider, Apfelwein (or Ebbelwoi). The sharpness of the onion and cider acts as a perfect foil to the flavour of the cheese.

PEARS WITH PECORINO

In the Abruzzi, the wild mountainous region of central Italy where much pecorino is made, people like to eat chunks of their salty, pungent cheese with pears.

Pears and cheese – any cheese – are a classic combination (pp. 318 and 342). There is a medieval French proverb that goes:

Oncque Dieu ne fist tel mariage
Comme de poires et de fromage.
(Never did God make a marriage
Like that of pears and cheese.)

Often, too, they were eaten one after the other in the Middle Ages. As Claude Duneton reminds us in his fascinating anthology of popular French expressions, *La Puce à l'Oreille*, vegetables were notable for their absence at medieval tables. Fruit often followed the meat course, acting like a salad and refreshing the palate for the cheese that followed (the British have maintained this order of courses, whereas the French now eat their cheese *before* their pudding). Hence the French expression *entre la poire et le fromage*, which has now come to mean 'the moment in the meal when one feels satisfied and the conversation gets more relaxed'. In business people's parlance it denotes the critical point during an expense-account lunch at which you clinch a deal because your guest's defences are down.

CHAPTER SIXTEEN

Sweet Dishes

POIRES SAVARIN   FOR 4

While the Italians like to nibble a little pecorino with their pears (p. 316), the French prefer to combine the fruit with a different, equally salty cheese: Roquefort. Here is a recipe for pears and Roquefort from Curnonsky's *Lettres de Noblesse* (p. 102).

80 g (3 oz) Roquefort	4 large lettuce leaves
125 g (4¹/₂ oz) chilled well-drained curd cheese	2 very large juicy ripe pears, chilled
freshly ground pepper	1 tbsp lemon juice
	1 tsp paprika

Mash or blend the cheeses with a little pepper until smooth. Wash the lettuce leaves and dry very thoroughly. Peel, halve and core the chilled pears and brush them immediately all over with lemon juice. Spoon the cheese mixture on to the halves so as to form a dome. Place them on lettuce leaves on individual small plates. Sprinkle with paprika and serve immediately.

This dish can be served as an hors d'oeuvre or as a salad course. In the latter case, you will need to make it in advance – and this poses the problem of pear discoloration. Proceed as follows: make the cheese mixture and refrigerate; prepare the pears as described above; after brushing them thoroughly with lemon juice, put the two halves of each fruit back together, wrap tightly in a wet tea towel (or several wet paper towels) and chill; assemble at the last moment.

GORGONZOLA WITH HONEY AND CREAM   FOR 4

Among the less outlandish combinations to which the Romans were partial was cheese with honey. In this modern reinterpretation, which is surprisingly good, the cheese used is not-too mature Gorgonzola: it has just the right delicate, unassertive flavour for the dish.

250 g (9 oz) not-too-mature   4 tsp liquid honey
  Gorgonzola
8 tbsp crème fraîche *or* very thick
  double cream

Put equal portions of the cheese on four small plates, spoon the cream over it, and decorate with a dribble of honey.

The dish can be served with bread or digestive biscuits.

CRÉMETS D'ANGERS   FOR 4

No sweet cheese dish has a simpler gustatory appeal than these delicious little confections of curd cheese, cream, egg white and sugar. The borderline between recipes for *crémets d'Angers* (which sometimes call for just cream instead of curd cheese and cream) and those for *coeurs à la crème* is blurred – which is why I give no separate recipe for the latter. Their ready-made, mass-marketed descendant is the Fontainebleau.

200 g (7 oz) well-drained curd cheese   2 egg whites
80 g (3 oz) double cream   vanilla sugar

Put the curd cheese and cream into a mixing bowl and blend. Whisk the egg whites with a tiny pinch of salt until very stiff and fold into the mixture delicately but thoroughly, adding sugar to taste while doing so. Spoon into small moulds with draining holes lined with a double thickness of fine muslin (special heart-shaped moulds for crémets can be found in good kitchen equipment shops) and leave to drain in a cool place – if possible not the refrigerator – overnight. Unmould on to chilled plates and serve.

In the Angers region crémets are usually served on their own, sometimes with a little extra cream poured over them. But they are also especially good served with a sharp, sweet fruit such as raspberries, strawberries or, better, wild strawberries. These can be arranged in a circle around the crémets.

CURD CHEESE WITH BILBERRIES AND WALNUTS   FOR 4

Uncooked curd cheese can, as we have seen, be accompanied by a multitude of savoury flavours (see Chapter Three); but it is equally versatile in its sweet uses. Here is a nice autumnal combination that turns the mixture a handsome purple.

300 g (10^1/$_2$ oz) curd cheese	12 walnut halves, fresh if possible
200 g (7 oz) fresh bilberries or	(p. 30)
100 g (3^1/$_2$ oz) bilberry preserve	1 tbsp framboise spirit
sugar	

Beat the cheese vigorously with the bilberries or bilberry preserve. Add sugar to taste (you probably will not need to if using bilberry preserve). Pound the walnuts to a coarse paste and stir into the mixture along with the framboise. Chill for at least 2 hours, beat again energetically and serve with wafer biscuits.

You can use the rarer and more exclusive myrtille (bilberry spirit) instead of framboise if you wish to impress, but the resulting flavour has less resonance.

The recipe can be varied by using mascarpone, ricotta, fresh unsalted ewe's-milk or goat cheese, and even yoghurt, instead of curd cheese. Other variations are possible if you use alternative flavourings to the ones above. Here are just a few suggestions using the same quantity of cheese; in all cases, the mixture should be chilled for at least 2 hours:

30 g (1 oz) candied citron peel, very finely chopped, 50 g (2 oz) lightly roasted pine-nuts, and sugar to taste;

2 tbsp coffee, ground as finely as possible (as for Turkish coffee), 2 tbsp rum, and sugar to taste;

zest of 1 lemon (without any bitter white pith), finely grated, $1/4$ tsp ground coriander, $1/2$ tsp powdered cinnamon, and sugar to taste;

200 g (7 oz) blackberries *or* 100 g ($3^1/2$ oz) each blackberries and raspberries, 1 tbsp cassis liqueur, 1 tsp good Italian amaro (e.g. Radis), and sugar to taste;

2 tbsp good chunky marmalade, chopped, 2 tbsp single malt whisky, 2 tsp lemon juice, and sugar to taste (this is the Scottish Caledonian cream).

FROMAGE BLANC À L'ARMAGNAC   FOR 4

A very simple recipe given to me by that talented cook Marie-Claude Gracia, whose idyllic hotel-restaurant, A la Belle Gasconne – a converted thirteenth-century water-mill – used to straddle the sleepy waters of the river Gélise in the little village of Poudenas, in Gascony.

500 g (1 lb 2 oz) well-drained curd cheese	75 g ($2^1/2$ oz) caster sugar 100 ml (4 fl oz) armagnac

Mix the cheese and sugar thoroughly in a serving bowl. Beat in the armagnac very gradually. Chill slightly. Beat again briefly before serving.

If the mixture ends up too thick and pasty (this will depend on the consistency of the curd cheese), beat in a little cream.

JUNKET   FOR 4-6

Junket . . . is another [like fruit creams and syllabubs]
of the dishes fast becoming obsolete. In the west of
England, especially, this preparation of milk is still
locally popular, but elsewhere there are numbers of
cooks who have no idea how to make it, although the
process is such a simple one that no child who has
been shown the way should fail.

Thus M. M. Mallock in *A Younger Son's Cookery Book*
(1896). The author's explanation of the book's curious
title (it was changed in the second edition to *The
Economics of Modern Cookery*, with the American
market in mind) is of some sociological interest:

First and foremost, then, a class is here addressed,
more numerous in this than in any other country,
which consists of persons belonging to the upper
ranks of society, who have been habituated during
their early lives to the best cooking which time and
money can procure; but who, when they come to
settle in homes of their own, find themselves forced to
live on incomes diminutive compared to those of their
parents or elder brothers, and to content themselves
with, it may be, three or four servants, instead of
twenty or thirty.

Surprisingly – or perhaps not so surprisingly, since the
book is chiefly addressed to the 'younger son's' house-
keeper or cook – the book is a fund of straightforward,
clearly expressed common sense about cookery.

Junket, which is basically just undrained curd cheese
with a sweet flavouring, has been an archetypal English
dish since at least the mid-fifteenth century. The word
comes from the Norman French *jonquette*, the rush basket
in which curd cheese used to be strained. Subsequently
French cooks tended, on the whole, to strain their curd
cheese before using it. But something similar to junket did
also exist in France in the eighteenth century (p. 324).

The older inhabitants of my Auvergne village still love eating junket more or less straight from the cow with sugar and cream – though this practice is becoming increasingly problematic since, because of EU measures to cut back milk production, the number of dairy cows in neighbouring farms has plummeted recently from sixty to four.

Junket, as Mallock suggests, may well have been becoming obsolete in the stately homes of England by the turn of the last century, but it continued to enjoy a long and degenerate career in school canteens and other refectories with a captive clientele. Hence many people's aversion to it.

Yet when properly made – with rich unpasteurized milk or half milk and half cream, with an interesting flavouring and with just the right amount of rennet (too much makes it taste salty) – junket can be a delightful summery dish. Here is the standard recipe, as given by Mallock.

570 ml (20 fl oz) creamy milk *or* the same volume of single cream and milk in equal quantities	1 tbsp caster sugar 2 tbsp rum or cognac 1 tsp rennet

Heat the milk slowly until it reaches blood temperature (about 37°C/98°F) – use a thermometer to be on the safe side). Dissolve the sugar completely in the rum or cognac in a largish bowl. Pour in the milk. Add the rennet (make sure you add *exactly* 1 teaspoon and no more) and stir gently. Leave undisturbed in an ambient temperature of about 20°C (68°F) until set. Transfer to a cool place (if possible not the refrigerator) for 1-2 hours before serving – there is nothing worse than tepid junket.

Mallock concludes:

> According to the more old-fashioned Devonshire practice, junket is made by preference in a china bowl, and is usually covered thickly with scalded [Devonshire] cream and sprinkled with cinnamon or

nutmeg. In the absence of scalded cream to cover it, a spoonful or two of raw cream poured over the top when set is an improvement. When well made, junket should cut into smooth shiny slices like jelly.

FROMAGE À LA DUCHESSE   FOR 4-6

This recipe comes, slightly adapted, from François Massialot's important book *Nouvelle Instruction pour les confitures, les liqueurs, et les fruits* (1692), which is a fund of fascinating recipes. The dish is just a more sophisticated version of junket (see preceding recipe).

400 ml (14 fl oz) double cream	zest of 1 lime, finely grated
250 ml (9 fl oz) milk	3 tbsp best chunky marmalade
segments of ¹/₂ orange	1 tsp rennet
2 dried apricots	caster sugar

Put 250 ml (9 fl oz) of cream and the milk in a saucepan and mix well. Remove all skin from the orange segments so you have nothing but glistening flesh. Pound or blend the orange, apricots, lime zest and marmalade until a fine, smooth consistency is obtained. Put this mixture through a sieve into the saucepan containing the cream and milk (it need not be sieved if you have used a blender). Heat slowly to about blood temperature (37°C/98°F) – use a thermometer to be on the safe side. Remove from the heat and stir in the rennet gently (make sure you add *exactly* 1 teaspoon and no more).

Immediately pour into very slightly warmed individual glasses and leave undisturbed in an ambient temperature of about 20°C (68°F) until set. Transfer to a cool place (if possible not the refrigerator) for 1-2 hours and serve with the rest of the cream and a little sugar.

CHEESECAKES

The modern cheesecake has a long ancestry. Tarts that are cheesecakes in all but name go back to Anglo-Norman times (see Tarte de Bry, p. 326) and Taillevent. The first recorded use of the word cheesecake as such dates from the mid-fifteenth century, and the first published recipe, as far as I know, from 1669 (in *The Closet of the Eminently Learned Sir Kenelme Digbie, Knight, Opened*). Pepys was an enthusiastic consumer of cheesecakes (as he was of much else). English cheesecakes were often served, like their French counterparts, in the form of individual tartlets rather than one large tart. They remained popular in Britain over the next century or two, garnering an ever-wider range of ingredients, sometimes even to the exclusion of curds altogether (lemon cheesecake eventually resulted in the cheeseless lemon curd).

Cheesecake was exported from Britain to the United States, where it was destined to become the president of American puddings. This is hardly surprising. Cheesecake in some form or other was – and is – an integral part of the cooking of virtually every European country (though at some point, curiously, the tradition died out in France). When Europe's various nationalities converged on the United States, it was only normal that one of their cultural common denominators should become a kind of national fetish.

Every modern American has his or her own favourite recipe for, or supplier of, cheesecake. Several books have been published that are devoted exclusively to the art of cheesecake-making. The basic cheesecake-making techniques are few and rather simple; the art resides in the choice of ingredients. One of the great merits of the cheesecake is that it allows considerable scope for individual experiment.

This is why I have included here only a handful of recipes for cheesecake, which have been selected with the following criteria in mind: historical interest, individuality and, of course, tastiness. I have omitted several well-known recipes for cheesecake-like concoctions on the grounds that they resemble too closely other recipes included here. So no complaints, please, if you do not find the Russian *vatrushka* and *zapekanka*, the Hungarian *túrós lepény* and *rétes*, the German *Käsekuchen*, the

English Yorkshire curd tart, the *quesadillas* of the Canary Islands, the Spanish *pastel de queso*, or the Italian *budino di ricotta* and *pastiera napoletana*.

TARTE DE BRY   FOR 4-6

An Anglo-Norman ginger- and saffron-flavoured cheese tart – or early form of cheesecake. Its name suggests that the cheese of the Brie region had already gained a high reputation even in England in the Middle Ages. But it should be remembered that the kind of Brie called for in this tart almost certainly bore little relation to its modern counterpart, for when the name Brie features in later recipes (right up to the eighteenth century), it is clear that what is referred to is a kind of rich curd cheese. So the specific appellation 'Bry' probably denotes a general type of cheese, rather as Petit Suisse does today.

300 g (10^1/$_2$ oz) chilled sweet short pastry (p. 368)	^{1}/$_4$ tsp powdered saffron
	large pinch powdered ginger
400 g (14 oz) well-drained curd cheese	small pinch salt
6 egg yolks, beaten	170 g (6 oz) caster sugar

On a lightly floured surface, roll out the pastry 3 mm (^{1}/$_8$ in) thick. Use it to line a 25-28-cm (10-11-in) flan tin, with a removable base if possible, and bake blind in a fairly hot oven (200°C/400°F/ Gas mark 6) for 15 minutes.

Put the rest of the ingredients into a mixing bowl and blend thoroughly. Turn the mixture into the pastry-lined flan tin and bake in a fairly hot oven (190°C/375°F/Gas mark 5) for about 45 minutes, or until the mixture has set and its surface has begun to brown. If it seems to be browning too soon, protect by laying a sheet of aluminium foil on top. Remove from the oven, leave to firm up for 5 minutes and serve hot or warm.

CHESE CAKES   MAKES ABOUT 15 TARTS

This recipe, which is fairly typical of those of its period, comes from an unpublished eighteenth-century cookery manuscript. I have halved the quantities and slightly altered the proportion of pastry to filling. The 'coffins' in the recipe are blind-baked tartlet shells.

375 g (13 oz) chilled short pastry with egg (p. 366)	pinch mace
	pinch cinnamon
500 g (1 lb 2 oz) well-drained curd cheese	3 tbsp rosewater
	3 tbsp sweet sherry
60 g (2 oz) slivered almonds	4 tbsp double cream
3 lady's finger *or cuiller* biscuits	115 g (4 oz) currants
2 egg yolks	115 g (4 oz) caster sugar
pinch freshly grated nutmeg	

On a lightly floured surface, roll out the pastry 3 mm (1/8 in) thick. Cut fifteen 10-cm (4-in) rounds. Fit each round into a lightly oiled 7-cm (3-in) tartlet tin, crimping the surplus pastry on the edge to form a border. Bake blind in a fairly hot oven (200°C/400°F/Gas mark 6) for 10 minutes.

Put all the ingredients into a mixing bowl and beat thoroughly. Leave for at least 2 hours in a cool place (this will soften the currants and enable the flavours to intermingle). Beat the mixture again and spoon into the tartlet shells. Bake in a fairly hot oven (190°C/375°F/Gas mark 5) for about 15 minutes, or until puffed up and golden brown. Remove from the oven, leave to firm up for a minute or two, then transfer to hot individual plates and serve immediately.

Rose petals or rosewater were a frequent ingredient of cheesecakes in earlier centuries. If rosewater reminds you too strongly of cheap scent, you may wish to reduce the generous quantity indicated in this recipe.

MAIDS OF HONOUR   MAKES ABOUT 12 TARTS

It is claimed that the maids of honour of Queen Elizabeth I, who had a palace at Richmond, gave their name to these very lemony miniature cheesecakes. Until fairly recently, they could be bought at a pastry shop called The Maid of Honour in Hill Street, Richmond.

400 g (14 oz) chilled sweet short
  pastry (p. 368)
225 g (8 oz) well-drained curd cheese
175 g (6 oz) unsalted butter, softened
4 egg yolks
120 g (4 oz) caster sugar
1 small floury cooked potato, mashed

60 g (2 oz) freshly ground almonds
2 drops bitter almond essence
zest of 3 lemons (without any bitter
  white pith), finely grated
juice of 1 lemon
$1/2$ freshly grated nutmeg

On a lightly floured surface, roll out the pastry 3 mm ($1/8$ in) thick. Cut twelve 10-cm (4-in) rounds. Press into lightly oiled tartlet tins about 7 cm (3 in) in diameter. Prick with a fork and bake blind in a fairly hot oven (200°C/400°F/Gas mark 6) for 10 minutes.

Blend the cheese and butter in a mixing bowl. Put the egg yolks and sugar into another bowl and beat vigorously until pale yellow. Add the potato, ground almonds, bitter almond essence, lemon zest, lemon juice and nutmeg, and blend thoroughly. Stir in the cheese mixture and beat until smooth. Spoon the filling into the pastry-lined tins and bake in a fairly hot oven (190°C/375°F/Gas mark 5) for 20 minutes. Serve either warm or cold.

CURD FLORENTINE   FOR 6-8
This deliciously almondy recipe comes from *Cookery, Pastry, Confectionary, Pickling and Preserving*, by Mrs Fraser, 'teacher of these arts in Edinburgh'. Edinburgh at the beginning of the nineteenth century was a hive of culinary activity and curiosity.

250 g (9 oz) spinach	110 g (4 oz) unsalted butter, softened
300 g (10¹/₂ oz) blanched almonds	140 g (5 oz) caster sugar
600 g (1 lb 5 oz) well-drained curd cheese	350 g (12¹/₂ oz) chilled flaky pastry (p. 367)
150 g (5¹/₂ oz) currants	

Wash the spinach thoroughly and blanch, uncovered, in plenty of boiling water for 10 minutes. Drain, squeeze as dry as possible and chop finely. Put the almonds in a tart tin and bake in a cool oven until the colour of roast peanuts. Pulverize. Put the cheese, almonds, currants, chopped spinach, butter and sugar into a mixing bowl and blend well.

On a lightly floured surface, roll out the pastry 3 mm (¹/₈ in) thick. Use just over three-quarters of it to line a 25-28-cm (10-11-in) flan tin, with a removable base if possible. Turn the filling into the pastry-lined tin. Lay strips of pastry across the top in criss-cross fashion. Bake in a fairly hot oven (200°C/400°F/Gas mark 6) for about 30 minutes or until the pastry has cooked through, covering the surface with aluminium foil to prevent burning, if necessary. Serve warm or cold.

CHEESECAKE, A VERY OLD RECEIPT   FOR 8
A sumptuous early American recipe that does not exactly stint on ingredients. It comes from *Famous Old Receipts* (1906), 'used a hundred years and more in the kitchens of the North and the South, contributed by descendants'. The recipe was 'used by Mrs George D. Weatherill with success, contributed by Mrs Morris Hacker'.

250 g (9 oz) chilled sweet short
  pastry (p. 368)
115 g (4 oz) unsalted butter, softened
115 g (4 oz) sugar
115 ml (4 fl oz) good sweet white
  wine
115 ml (4 fl oz) cognac
4 eggs, separated
250 g (9 oz) well-drained curd cheese

200 ml (7 fl oz) double cream
225 g (8 oz) cake crumbs
  ('Any good cake: the richer the
  better your pie will be')
1 whole small nutmeg,
  freshly grated
pinch cinnamon
zest of $1/2$ lemon (without any
  bitter white pith), finely grated

Lightly oil the sides of a 23-cm (9-in) springform pan, separated from its base. On a lightly floured surface roll out the dough 4 mm ($1/6$ in) thick to form a disc and place on the lightly oiled base of the springform pan. Trim off the excess pastry. Prick with a fork, cover with aluminium foil and an empty tart tin, and bake blind in a fairly hot oven (200°C/400°F/Gas mark 6) for about 20 minutes or until light brown. When cool, clamp the sides of the springform pan on to the base.

Cream the butter and sugar, and add the wine, cognac and egg yolks. Mix the cheese and cream together thoroughly and add to the mixture. Stir in the cake crumbs, nutmeg, cinnamon and lemon zest. Whisk the egg whites with a tiny pinch of salt until very stiff. Take a large spoonful of whites and stir into the mixture, then fold in the rest delicately but thoroughly.

Turn the mixture into the springform pan and bake in a moderate oven (170°C/325°F/Gas mark 3) for about 1 hour or until a sharp knife, when inserted, comes out clean. Turn off the oven and leave the cheesecake to cool in the oven for about 1 hour. Loosen the filling from the sides of the pan with a palette knife, but do not unclamp. Leave in a cool place, preferably not the refrigerator, for at least 12 hours. Gingerly remove the sides of the pan and serve. If you have been forced by climatic conditions to refrigerate the cheesecake, leave it at room temperature for 1 hour after unclamping.

PASKHA FOR 12

Paskha, which means 'Easter' in Russian, is also the name of a special Russian Easter dish that influenced the American cheesecake. Sadly, in the traditional version of *paskha*, where the cheese mixture is put into a special and often very decorative pyramid-shaped mould with holes, a little of the delicious flavouring is allowed to drain away. In the formula given here, which is halfway between a traditional *paskha* and a cheesecake, the precious liquid is cleverly trapped by the surrounding sponge cake.

The recipe comes from Jacques Médecin's *La Cuisine du Comté de Nice*. I did not include it in my English translation of that book (*Cuisine Niçoise*) because it is not an indigenous Niçois recipe: it was brought there by the White Russian aristocracy (or rather by their cooks) when they went into golden exile on the Côte d'Azur after the Revolution.

1.5 kg (3¹/₂ lb) well-drained curd cheese	50 g (2 oz) candied orange peel
450 g (1 lb) unsalted butter	30 g (1 oz) candied lemon peel *or* grapefruit peel
450 g (1 lb) vanilla sugar	250 ml (9 fl oz) double cream
9 whole eggs	4 egg yolks
250 g (9 oz) sifted plain flour	100 g (3¹/₂ oz) blanched almonds, finely chopped
30 g (1 oz) candied cherries	

Line a colander with a double thickness of wet muslin, put in the cheese, fold over the muslin, place a plate and a heavy weight on top, and leave to firm up for 3 hours.

Melt 200 g (7 oz) of butter so it is just liquid but not hot. Keep warm. Put 250 g (9 oz) of sugar and 9 eggs into a mixing bowl placed on top of a saucepan of simmering water. Whisk vigorously until the mixture becomes frothy and increases in bulk. Remove the bowl from the top of the saucepan and continue beating for a while. Little by little, fold in the flour gently but thoroughly. Stir the melted butter into the mixture.

Turn into a shallow, lightly oiled and floured large

baking tray (the mixture should be about 2 cm (3/4 in) deep), and bake in a moderate oven (180°C/350°F/Gas mark 4) for about 45 minutes or until well risen and golden brown. Remove from the oven and leave for 5 minutes. Unmould the cake and cool on a rack.

Cut all the candied fruit into 6-mm (1/4-in) pieces. Remove the cheese from the muslin and push through a fine sieve into a mixing bowl. Melt 250 g (9 oz) of butter and beat into the cheese until thoroughly blended. Pour the cream into a heavy saucepan over a moderate heat. As soon as a ring of bubbles forms round the edge, turn the heat down as low as possible. Beat 200 g (7 oz) of sugar into 4 egg yolks in another mixing bowl until pale yellow, add the hot cream gradually, beating all the time, then pour the whole mixture back into the saucepan.

Place the pan in a larger saucepan half full of boiling water. Immediately turn the heat down to very low and stir the mixture constantly with a wooden spoon until it acquires the consistency of a thick egg custard. This will take 15-20 minutes. Remove from the double boiler, stir in the candied fruit and leave until completely cooled.

Line a large charlotte, cake or *paskha* mould (or even a large flower pot lined with aluminium foil) with about three-quarters of the sponge cake. Stir the cold custard and chopped almonds into the cheese mixture gently but thoroughly, and turn into the mould. Cover with the remaining sponge cake, place a fairly heavy round flat object on top, and leave for at least 12 hours in the refrigerator. Remove and unmould 1 hour before serving.

CHEESECAKE   FOR 4-6

This is cheesecake in its simplest, Central European form.

40 g (1¹/₂ oz) unsalted butter
140 g (5 oz) digestive biscuits *or*
  graham crackers, crushed
680 g (1¹/₂ lb) well-drained curd
  cheese
200 g (7 oz) caster sugar
4 eggs

zest of 1 lemon (without any bitter
  white pith), finely grated
2 tsp lemon juice
3 drops vanilla essence
50 g (2 oz) sultanas
250 ml (9 fl oz) soured cream

Melt the butter, stir in the biscuits and mix well. Press into the bottom of an assembled springform pan. Put the cheese, 175 g (6 oz) of sugar, eggs, lemon zest, lemon juice, vanilla essence and sultanas into a mixing bowl and blend well. Turn the mixture into the flan tin and bake in a fairly hot oven (190°C/375°F/Gas mark 5) for 30 minutes. Mix the soured cream with the rest of the sugar. Without turning off the oven, remove the cheesecake, pour the soured cream over the top and bake for a further 7 minutes. Remove and allow to cool. Refrigerate for at least 12 hours. Remove from the refrigerator and unmould 1 hour before serving.

This cheesecake can be decorated with fresh or candied fruit if desired. The very precise cooking times are essential for the success of the dish. Do not be alarmed by its apparent liquidity after baking. It sets well after its spell in the refrigerator.

VIENNA CURD CAKE   FOR 4-6

This cheesecake, another simple expression of the cheese-cake genre, does not need to be baked and is therefore a useful standby if there is no oven available.

4 tsp gelatine
40 g (1¹/₂ oz) unsalted butter
140 g (5 oz) digestive biscuits *or*
  graham crackers, crushed
130 g (4¹/₂ oz) caster sugar

340 g (12 oz) well-drained curd
  cheese
3 drops vanilla essence
210 ml (7¹/₂ fl oz) double cream
3 egg whites

Put the gelatine to soak in a small bowl with 2 tablespoons of water. Melt the butter with 30 g (1 oz) of sugar. Stir in the biscuit crumbs and mix well. Press half this mixture on to the base of an 18-20-cm (7-8-in) springform pan. Refrigerate. Put the rest of the sugar and the curd cheese into a mixing bowl and beat vigorously.

Place the bowl containing the gelatine on top of a small saucepan of simmering water and stir until dissolved. Beat the dissolved gelatine and vanilla essence into the curd cheese and sugar mixture. Oil the sides of the springform pan very lightly. Remove the base from the refrigerator and clamp the sides on to it. Whip the cream lighty. Whisk the egg whites with a tiny pinch of salt until very stiff. Fold the cream and egg whites into the mixture. Turn into the springform pan, smooth with a palette knife and crumble the rest of the biscuit crumb mixture evenly over the surface. Refrigerate for at least 12 hours.

One hour before serving, remove from the refrigerator, loosen the filling from the sides of the pan with a palette knife and unclamp.

LIME, CHOCOLATE AND MINT CHEESECAKE   FOR 4-6

Like Vienna curd cake (see preceding recipe), this refreshing, summery cheesecake does not require baking.

20 g (3/4 oz) gelatine
70 g (2 1/2 oz) unsalted butter, softened
175 g (6 oz) digestive biscuits or graham crackers, crushed
3 limes
280 g (10 oz) bitter chocolate

4 tbsp crème de menthe
2 sprigs fresh mint, with at least 20 leaves in all
500 g (1 lb 2 oz) well-drained curd cheese
60 g (2 oz) caster sugar
500 ml (17 fl oz) double cream

Put the gelatine to soak in a small bowl with 4 tablespoons of water. Assemble a 23-cm (9-in) springform pan and oil very lightly. Combine the butter and biscuits in a bowl with the fingers or a fork. Press evenly on to the base of the pan and refrigerate.

With the finest holes of your grater, grate the zest of the limes, making sure not to include any bitter white pith. Squeeze their juice into a small saucepan, place over a gentle heat, add 250 g (9 oz) of chocolate, broken into small pieces, and stir constantly until it has completely melted. Away from the heat, add the crème de menthe and 12 mint leaves, very finely chopped. Put the remaining mint sprig(s) in a glass of water to keep fresh.

Put the cheese and sugar into a mixing bowl and blend well. Stir in the melted chocolate. Place the bowl containing the gelatine on top of a small saucepan of simmering water and stir until dissolved. Allow to cool slightly, then beat well into the mixture. Whip 300 ml ($10^{1}/_{2}$ fl oz) of cream until stiff, and fold into the mixture delicately but thoroughly. Turn into the springform pan and refrigerate for at least 12 hours.

For the final assembly, loosen the filling from the sides of the pan with a palette knife and unclamp. Run the knife carefully between the cheesecake and the base, and slide on to a serving dish. Scrape the rest of the chocolate with a vegetable peeler to obtain little scrolls. Whip the rest of the cream until stiff and put into a forcing bag with a serrated nozzle. Decorate the top of the cheesecake with the whipped cream, the chocolate scrolls and the remaining mint leaves.

The basic formula of this cheesecake (curd cheese, cream and gelatine) can be adapted to almost any other flavour or accompaniment of your choice.

FIADONE   FOR 4
A simple, quickly made Corsican pudding made with fresh ewe's milk cheese.

500 g (1 lb 2 oz) Broccio *or* Brousse   zest of 1 lemon (without any bitter
100 g (3¹/₂ oz) caster sugar   white pith), finely grated
4 eggs

Put the ingredients into a mixing bowl and blend thoroughly. Turn the mixture into a buttered cake or charlotte mould, which it should only three-quarters fill, and bake in a fairly hot oven (190°C/375°F/Gas mark 5) for about 45 minutes or until a knife, when inserted, comes out clean. Remove from the oven and leave to stand for 15 minutes, then unmould on to a serving dish. Serve cold.

MELOPITTA   FOR 6
A Greek version of cheesecake flavoured with honey and cinnamon.

300 g (10¹/₂ oz) chilled sweet short   140 ml (5 fl oz) honey
  pastry (p. 368)   4 eggs
500 g (1 lb 2 oz) well-drained curd   2 tsp cinnamon
  cheese

On a lightly floured surface, roll out the pastry 3 mm (¹/₈ in) thick. Use it to line a 25-28-cm (10-11-in) flan tin, with a removable base if possible. Prick with a fork and bake blind in a fairly hot oven (200°F/400°F/Gas mark 6) for 15 minutes.

Put the cheese into a mixing bowl and stir in the honey and eggs. Beat until well blended. Turn into the pastry-lined tin, making sure the surface is even. Bake in a fairly hot oven (190°C/375°F/Gas mark 5) for 30-40 minutes or until golden brown. Remove from the oven, sprinkle the surface evenly and thickly with cinnamon and leave to firm up for 5 minutes, then transfer to a serving dish. The tart may be served warm or cold.

TOURTEAU FROMAGÉ   FOR 6
This speciality of the Poitou region in France exists in
several versions. Commercially sold *tourteaux* have a
rather unpleasant (to my mind) blackened crust. The
recipe given here is basically just a straightforward
cheesecake made with fresh unsalted goat cheese.

300 g (10¹/₂ oz) chilled short pastry	5 eggs, separated
(p. 366)	80 g (3 oz) potato starch
300 g (10¹/₂ oz) fresh unsalted	2 tbsp cognac
goat cheese	salt
100 g (3¹/₂ oz) caster sugar	

On a lightly floured surface, roll out the pastry 3 mm
(¹/₈ in) thick. Use it to line a 25-28-cm (10-11-in) flan tin,
with a removable bottom if possible. Prick with a fork and
bake blind in a fairly hot oven (200°C/400°F/Gas mark 6)
for 15 minutes.
  Put the cheese, sugar, egg yolks, potato starch and
cognac into a mixing bowl, and beat until well blended.
Whisk the egg whites with a small pinch of salt until very
stiff. Take a large spoonful of whites and stir quickly into
the cheese mixture, then fold in the rest delicately but
thoroughly. Turn into the pastry-lined tin, making sure the
surface is even, and bake in a fairly hot oven (190°C/
375°F/Gas mark 5) for 30-40 minutes or until the top is
well browned. Remove from the oven and leave for 5
minutes to firm up, then transfer to a serving dish. The
tourteau may be served warm or cold.

APPLE AND QUINCE PIE WITH CHEESE PASTRY   FOR 4
Apples, like pears, have a great affinity with cheese, hence
no doubt the saying: 'An apple without cheese is like a kiss
without a squeeze.' In this pie the apple and cheese combination is given an additional, almost gamey nuance by
quince.

450 g (1 lb) sweet eating apples
225 g (8 oz) cooking apples
1 quince (*or* 3 tbsp quince jelly)
80 g (3 oz) unsalted butter
50 g (2 oz) caster sugar
zest of $^1/_2$ lemon (without any bitter

white pith), finely grated
225 g (8 oz) chilled cheese pastry
(p. 369)
1 egg, beaten
150 ml (5 fl oz) double cream

Peel, core and slice finely the apples and quince. Melt the butter in a sauté pan, add the sugar, lemon zest, apples and quince (or quince jelly if no fresh quince is available), and cook over a medium heat for 5 minutes, stirring and tossing all the time so all the fruit is well coated with butter. If no liquid is given off, moisten with a few table-spoons of water. Transfer to an oval or round pie dish with a capacity of about 1.4 litres (50 fl oz).

On a lightly floured surface, roll out the pastry to a shape larger than the pie dish 6 mm (¼ in) thick. Cut strips from the edge of the pastry, press down on to the rim of the dish and brush with beaten egg. Roll the remaining pastry on to the rolling pin and unfurl over the top of the filling to form a lid. Press down to seal and knock up the edges. Make a central hole and ensure it stays open by inserting a small roll of card or aluminium foil folded double. Brush the surface well with beaten egg.

Bake in a fairly hot oven (200°C/400°F/Gas mark 6) for 20 minutes, then reduce the heat to moderate (180°C/350°F/Gas mark 4) and bake for another 20-25 minutes or until the pastry is golden brown. Bring the cream to almost boiling point in a small saucepan. Remove the pie from the oven and pour the cream through a funnel into the hole in the middle of the pastry lid. Serve immediately.

Depending on the sweetness of the eating and cooking apples used (Cox's Orange Pippins and Bramley's, respectively, are the best, but other varieties will do) and on whether you use fresh quince or quince jelly, you may wish to use either more or less sugar than the amount suggested.

SFOGLIATELLE   FOR 4

A Neapolitan speciality.

400 g (14 oz) ricotta	30 g (1 oz) sultanas soaked in
100 g (3¹/₂ oz) caster sugar	2 tbsp rum
15 g (¹/₂ oz) plain flour	450 g (1 lb) chilled flaky pastry
3 egg yolks	(p. 367)
30 g (1 oz) candied orange peel	1 egg, beaten
30 g (1 oz) pine-nuts	30 g (1 oz) icing sugar

Put the cheese, caster sugar, flour, egg yolks, candied orange peel, pine-nuts and sultanas into a mixing bowl and blend thoroughly.

On a lightly floured surface, roll out the pastry 2 mm (¹/₁₂ in) thick and cut into rectangles measuring about 10 x 13 cm (4 x 5 in). Place a small mound of the filling on one end of each rectangle. Brush the edges of the pastry with a mixture of beaten egg and a little water, fold the uncovered end over the filling, press down to seal well, and crimp with a fork. This quantity should make about 16 *sfogliatelle*.

Place on a lightly oiled baking sheet (or sheets) and bake in a fairly hot oven (190°C/375°F/Gas mark 5) for 25-30 minutes or until golden brown. Just before they are ready to be removed from the oven, sprinkle the *sfogliatelle* with icing sugar and glaze for a minute or two more. *Sfogliatelle* are normally eaten cold, but they are also very good warm.

CHEESE STRUDEL   FOR 4-6

60 g (2 oz) sultanas	80 g (3 oz) caster sugar
3 tbsp apricot brandy	1 tbsp cinnamon
225 g (8 oz) ready-made strudel *or*	250 g (9 oz) well-drained curd cheese
filo pastry	4 eggs, separated
60 g (2 oz) unsalted butter, melted	120 ml (4 fl oz) soured cream
60 g (2 oz) fresh white breadcrumbs	

Put the sultanas to soak in the apricot brandy for at least

2 hours beforehand. Lay out the strudel or filo pastry with the sheets overlapping each other, and brush with melted butter. Sprinkle with the breadcrumbs, half the sugar mixed with the cinnamon, and the soaked sultanas. Beat the cheese and egg yolks until well blended, and stir in the rest of the sugar and the soured cream. Whisk the egg whites with a small pinch of salt until very stiff. Fold into the cheese mixture delicately but thoroughly.

Spread the mixture on the strudel pastry, roll up carefully and not too tightly, cut into suitable lengths, and bake on a lightly oiled baking sheet in a fairly hot oven (200°C/400°F/Gas mark 6) for 15 minutes, then lower the heat to moderate (180°C/350°F/Gas mark 4) and bake for a further 30 minutes or until crisp. Serve hot or cold.

If you are feeling festive, you can douse the hot strudel with heated apricot brandy, sprinkle it quickly with a little icing sugar through a fine strainer and immediately flambé the lot.

CRÊPES À LA FLORENTINE   FOR 4

The recipe for these delicate pancakes comes from Pierre de Lune's *Le Cuisinier* (1656). There is nothing particularly Florentine about the crêpes: seventeenth-century chefs were fond of giving their recipes superfluous geographical tags.

6 egg yolks	pinch nutmeg
120 ml (4 fl oz) milk	2 tbsp orange-blossom water
140 g (5 oz) fairly liquid curd cheese	80 g (3 oz) icing sugar
140 g (5 oz) sifted plain flour	
50 g (2 oz) candied lemon peel, very finely chopped	

Put the egg yolks, milk, cheese, flour and lemon peel into a blender and blend for 1 minute. Pour into a bowl, cover and leave in a cool place for 2 hours. Make the pancakes in the usual way (p. 175). Roll them up and arrange in a shallow baking tray, sprinkle with nutmeg, orange-blossom water and plenty of icing sugar, and glaze under a moderate grill.

CURD PANCAKES   FOR 4

In this Central European recipe the curd cheese goes not into the batter as in the preceding recipe, but into the filling of the pancakes.

140 ml (5 fl oz) milk	150 g (5½ oz) sifted plain flour
3 eggs	2 tbsp oil
small pinch salt	zest of ½ lemon (without any bitter
oil *or* clarified butter for frying	white pith), finely grated
140 g (5 oz) well-drained curd cheese	40 g (1½ oz) caster sugar
1 egg, separated	175 ml (6 fl oz) soured cream

Put the milk, an equal amount of water, 3 eggs, salt, flour and oil into a blender and blend for 1 minute. Pour into a bowl, cover and leave in a cool place for 2 hours. Cook 8 pancakes in the usual way (p. 175).

Mix together the cheese, egg yolk, lemon zest and sugar. Whisk the egg white with a tiny pinch of salt until very stiff and fold gently but thoroughly into the mixture. Spread this filling on the pancakes, roll them up and arrange in a shallow baking dish. Smother with sour cream and place in a hot oven (220°C/425°F/Gas mark 7) for 5 minutes or until well heated through. Serve with more sugar if desired.

PEAR PANCAKES   FOR 4

Pears have an exceptional affinity with ewe's-milk cheese, whether mature, such as Roquefort and pecorino (pp. 317 and 318), or fresh and mild, such as Broccio or Brousse, as in these pancakes.

4 eggs, separated	2 pears (of an aromatic variety),
small pinch salt	peeled, cored and diced
200 ml (7 fl oz) milk	juice of $1/2$ lemon
250 g (9 oz) Brousse *or* Broccio	freshly ground pepper
250 g (9 oz) sifted plain flour	caster sugar

Put the egg yolks, salt, milk, cheese and flour into a blender and blend for 1 minute. Pour into a bowl, cover and leave in a cool place for 2 hours. Add the pears, lemon juice and plenty of pepper, and blend until smooth. Whisk the egg whites with a tiny pinch of salt until stiff, and fold gently but thoroughly into the mixture. Make the pancakes in the usual way (p. 175) and sprinkle with sugar to taste.

Pepper may seem the odd man out in this recipe, but it goes as well with pears as it does with strawberries or melon. In France the syrup of preserved pears sometimes contains whole black peppercorns.

MACCHERONI CON LA RICOTTA   FOR 4

A curious semi-sweet macaroni dish from the region of Bari in south-east Italy.

170 g (6 oz) ricotta	1 tbsp caster sugar
1 tsp cinnamon	340 g (12 oz) macaroni *or* rigatoni

Put the cheese, cinnamon and sugar into a large serving bowl, blend well and warm over a saucepan of just simmering water. Cook the pasta in plenty of boiling, slightly salted water until *al dente* (pp. 150-1), drain, turn into the bowl containing the cheese, mix well and serve immediately.

HUNGARIAN SWEET NOODLES FOR 4

The Hungarians, like the Italians, occasionally eat pasta with a sweet accompaniment, as in this rich and aromatic dish of baked noodles.

1 orange	60 g (2 oz) caster sugar
60 g (2 oz) sultanas	200 g (7 oz) well-drained curd cheese
250 g (9 oz) fresh flat noodles	100 ml (3¹/₂ fl oz) soured cream
(of the tagliatelle type)	2 tbsp poppy seeds
80 g (3 oz) unsalted butter, melted	

Grate half the zest of an orange finely, without including any bitter white pith. Squeeze the juice of the orange and put the sultanas to soak in it (this should be done 1-2 hours ahead of time if possible). Cook the pasta in plenty of boiling slightly salted water until *al dente* (pp. 150-1). Put the melted butter, sugar, cheese, soured cream, orange zest, sultanas and any orange juice not absorbed by the sultanas into a mixing bowl. Combine thoroughly. Add the pasta and mix. Turn into a buttered gratin dish, sprinkle with poppy seeds and bake in a moderate oven (180°C/350°F/Gas mark 4) for about 30 minutes.

SWEET PIEROGI WITH CHEESE FOR 6

A sweet version of Polish pierogi (p. 168).

175 g (6 oz) buckwheat flour	30 g (1 oz) currants
225 g (8 oz) plain wheat flour	1 egg, beaten with a few drops
small pinch salt	of water
250 g (9 oz) well-drained curd cheese	50 g (2 oz) unsalted butter
1 egg yolk	250 g (9 oz) soured cream
80 g (3 oz) caster sugar	
30 g (1 oz) candied orange peel,	
finely chopped	

Put the sifted buckwheat flour into a mixing bowl and very gradually add about 100 ml (4 fl oz) of boiling water, kneading all the time. Add the wheat flour and salt, and continue to knead until a smooth dough is obtained. Roll out or put through a pasta-making machine: the sheet of dough should be slightly thicker than that of Italian pasta.

Beat the cheese thoroughly with the egg yolk, sugar, orange peel and currants. Using this mixture and the sheet of dough, make, cook and drain the *pierogi* according to the same procedure as for ravioli (pp. 164-5). Lay them in a heated deep serving dish and pour melted butter over them. Serve with soured cream on the side.

GNOCCHI DOLCI   FOR 4

340 ml (12 fl oz) milk	2 egg yolks
90 g (3 oz) unsalted butter	1 tbsp cinnamon
salt	60 g (2 oz) caster sugar
170 g (6 oz) semolina	200 g (7 oz) fresh ewe's-milk cheese

Bring the milk to the boil in a saucepan with 30 g (1 oz) of butter and a very little salt. Pour in the semolina gradually, stirring all the time. Continue cooking and stirring over a medium heat until the mixture takes on the consistency of thick porridge and begins to come away from the sides of the pan. Remove from the heat, allow to cool slightly and stir in the egg yolks one after the other. Blend well, turn out on to a slightly moistened marble slab or smooth worktop, spread out with a palette knife to an even thickness of about 1 cm (1/2 in). Dip the knife in hot water from time to time so the mixture does not stick to it. Leave to cool. Cut circular shapes out of the semolina layer with a glass or pastry cutter and arrange them, overlapping each other, in a lightly buttered gratin dish.

Dissolve the cinnamon and sugar in 60 g (2 oz) of melted butter, add the cheese, mix well and pour over the gnocchi. Bake in a hot oven (220°C/425°F/Gas mark 7) for 10 minutes or until just beginning to sizzle and serve immediately.

CURD CHEESE DUMPLINGS   FOR 4

Throughout Central Europe there are countless versions of sweet dumplings made with curd or cream cheese – most of them, it has to be said, rather humdrum. Here is a recipe with plenty of character.

40 g (1¹/₂ oz) unsalted butter, softened	1 tsp baking powder
40 g (1¹/₂ oz) caster sugar	90 g (3 oz) fine semolina
2 eggs, beaten	25 g (1 oz) fine slightly stale breadcrumbs
225 g (8 oz) well-drained curd cheese	small pinch salt
zest of ¹/₂ lemon (without any bitter white pith), finely grated	40 g (1¹/₂ oz) raisins
	40 g (1¹/₂ oz) slivered almonds, roasted

Cream the butter and sugar thoroughly in a mixing bowl. Beat in the eggs, cheese and lemon zest. In another bowl, mix the rest of the ingredients. Stir into the cheese mixture and combine well. Form the resulting dough into small dumplings and poach in a large quantity of simmering, slightly salted water for about 15 minutes. These dumplings may be served with double cream or, better, soured cream.

CASSATA ALLA SICILIANA   FOR 8-10

A chocolate-coated *semi-freddo* that contains a succulent double-sandwich of *pan di Spagna* (a kind of sponge cake), ricotta and candied fruit. Originally a rustic Sicilian speciality, it has since travelled the world – and even been transmogrified into a variety of commercial ice cream.

150 g (5¹/₂ oz) vanilla sugar	140 g (5 oz) caster sugar
zest of ¹/₂ lemon (without any bitter white pith), finely grated	50 g (2 oz) candied citron peel, chopped
4 eggs	50 g (2 oz) candied cherries, halved
pinch salt	30 g (1 oz) angelica, finely chopped
80 g (3 oz) sifted plain flour	250 g (9 oz) bitter chocolate
40 g (1¹/₂ oz) potato starch	4 tbsp maraschino
225 g (8 oz) unsalted butter	100 ml (3¹/₂ fl oz) very strong coffee
1 kg (2¹/₄ lb) ricotta	

Put the vanilla sugar, lemon zest, eggs and salt into a mixing bowl placed on top of a saucepan of simmering water. Whisk until the mixture becomes frothy and increases in bulk. Remove the bowl from the top of the saucepan and continue beating for a while. Mix the flour and potato starch together, sprinkle a little on to the egg and sugar mixture, and fold in delicately. Repeat the process until the two mixtures are completely blended. Melt 25 g (1 oz) of butter, allow to cool slightly so that it is warm but not congealed, and stir gently into the mixture. Turn into a buttered and floured loaf tin about 25 cm (10 in) long and bake in a moderate oven (180°C/350°F/Gas mark 4) for about 45 minutes or until well risen and golden brown. Remove from the oven and leave for 5 minutes. Unmould the cake and cool on a rack.

While the cake is baking, prepare the filling. Put the sieved cheese, caster sugar, citron peel, cherries, angelica and 50 g (2 oz) of finely grated chocolate into a mixing bowl, and beat well. When the cooked cake has cooled, cut it lengthwise into four slices of equal thickness. Pour the maraschino and an equal quantity of water into a shallow rectangular or oval dish and stir. Dip both sides of one slice of cake briefly in this mixture and place on a rectangular or oval serving dish. Spread neatly with a third of the filling. Repeat this operation twice more, finishing with a slice of cake (having made sure you have soaked up all the maraschino-and-water mixture).

Break the rest of the chocolate into little pieces and put into a small heavy saucepan with the coffee. Heat gently, stirring all the time, until the chocolate has completely melted. Cut the remainder of the butter into small dice and, away from the heat, stir into the melted chocolate until thoroughly blended. When the mixture has cooled to the consistency of thick custard, spread it all over the cake with a palette knife. Refrigerate for 2 hours, by which time the chocolate coating will have hardened. Completely envelop the dish with cling-film so the cassata is tightly sealed, and refrigerate again for at least 24 hours (or longer if possible) before serving.

CHAPTER SEVENTEEN

Appetizers and Biscuits

GOUGÈRE — FOR 4

A Burgundian dish that the Burgundians claim is the ideal accompaniment to good Burgundy. They are right: the flavour of Gruyère-flavoured choux pastry is muted enough not to interfere with the subtleties of a great wine.

90 g (3 oz) unsalted butter, diced
large pinch salt
175 g (6 oz) sifted plain flour
5 eggs

pinch freshly grated nutmeg
freshly ground pepper
125 g (4½ oz) Gruyère, cut into tiny dice

Put the butter, salt and 275 ml (10 fl oz) of water into a heavy saucepan and heat slowly. Make sure the butter has completely dissolved by the time the water comes to the boil. When it boils, remove from the heat, pour in the flour in one go and beat vigorously with a wooden spoon. Return to the heat and continue beating until the mixture comes away from the sides of the pan. Remove the pan from the heat and stir in the eggs one after the other, making sure each one has been thoroughly blended before putting in the next. Add plenty of pepper and 100 g (3½ oz) of diced cheese, and stir well.

Place spoonfuls of this mixture, touching each other, in

a neat circle on a lightly oiled baking sheet, smoothing the surface with a palette knife dipped in water so you have a perfect quoit shape. Dot the surface of the quoit with the remaining diced cheese and bake in a moderate oven (190°C/375°F/Gas mark 5) for 35-45 minutes. *On no account open the oven door for at least 20 minutes after putting in the* gougère. It is cooked when it feels firm and crisp to the touch on top and at the sides. Transfer to a rack, pierce with a pointed knife at several points and leave for about 10 minutes, with the oven off and the door ajar, before serving.

RAMEQUINS   FOR 4

The English word 'ramekin' (also spelt ramakin, ramkin or ramaquin) and the French *ramequin* have been used over the centuries to describe almost anything from Welsh rabbit or a melted cheese sandwich to a cheese-flavoured egg custard, tartlet, soufflé, pudding or puff. It later came to be applied also, by metonymy, to the receptacle in which some types of ramekin were cooked. The word derives from *rammeken*, the diminutive of *ram*, the Flemish word for cream (cf. the German *Rahm*). So a ramekin is a 'little cream', just as a manikin, also of Flemish origin, is a 'little man'.

The following recipe comes from *Le Cuisinier impérial* (1806), by A. Viard, an important French cook of the early nineteenth century. In the course of subsequent and ever enlarged editions, his book changed its title to *Le Cuisinier royal* after the Restoration of 1814, and again to *Le Cuisinier national* after the Revolution of 1848.

90 g (3 oz) unsalted butter
large pinch salt
175 g (6 oz) sifted plain flour
6 eggs

freshly ground pepper
150 g (5¹/₂ oz) freshly grated Gruyère
60 g (2 oz) freshly grated Parmesan

Put the butter, salt and 340 ml (12 fl oz) of water in a heavy saucepan and heat slowly. Make sure the butter has completely dissolved by the time the water comes to the boil. When it boils, remove from the heat, pour in the flour in one go and beat vigorously with a wooden spoon. Return to the heat and continue beating until the mixture comes away from the sides of the pan. Remove the pan from the heat and stir in the eggs one after the other, making sure each one has been thoroughly blended before putting in the next. Add plenty of pepper and the cheeses, and stir well.

Using a tablespoon or a forcing bag with a plain nozzle, place neat little circular mounds of the mixture on two oiled baking sheets, leaving plenty of space between each *ramequin* (they swell considerably during cooking). Bake both sheets at a time in a hot oven (220°C/425°F/Gas mark 7) for 20-25 minutes. The *ramequins* are done when they feel firm and crisp to the touch. Transfer to a rack, prick with a pointed knife and leave for about 5 minutes, with the oven off and the door ajar, before serving.

A version of *ramequins* using less cheese can be made by preparing the mixture according to the same proportions as for *gougère* (see preceding recipe), then placing individual mounds of it on baking sheets as above, instead of forming a ring. The result should not properly be called *gougères*, as some British menus and cookery articles imply, since the word *gougère* has no plural form.

GÂTEAU DE FROMAGE DE BRIE   FOR 6
A rich kind of cheese cake, as opposed to cheesecake, from the 25 November 1906 issue of the magazine *La Cuisine des familles* (p. 271).

125 g (4¹/₂ oz) ripe Brie	250 g (9 oz) unsalted butter, melted
pinch salt	3 eggs, separated
500 g (1 lb 2 oz) sifted plain flour	1 egg yolk

Trim the cheese of any hard or brown bits of rind. Mash it well with 1-2 tablespoons of hot water until a smooth paste is obtained. Put the salt (allowing for the fact that the cheese is salted) and the flour into a mixing bowl. Make a well and put in the mashed cheese. Blend well, then gradually add the butter, only just melted, mixing all the time. Beat in 3 egg yolks, one after the other. Whisk 3 egg whites with a tiny pinch of salt until stiff and fold in. Knead the dough vigorously, form into a ball, wrap in aluminium foil and leave to rest in a cool place for 1 hour.

Roll out the pastry 2-3 cm (1 in) thick and press into a lightly oiled circular flan tin. Brush with a mixture of egg yolk and a little water. Bake in a fairly hot oven (200°C/400°F/Gas mark 6) for about 30 minutes or until the surface is golden brown.

KÄSEBROD   1 LOAF

A cheese bread of Central European origin, delicious toasted.

14 g (¹/₂ oz) yeast	1 egg, beaten
100 ml (3¹/₂ fl oz) milk	110 g (4 oz) freshly grated Cheddar *or*
1 tbsp sugar	Gruyère
1 tsp salt	250 g (9 oz) sifted plain flour

Dissolve the yeast in 3 tablespoons of warm water. Heat the milk, add the sugar and salt, and stir until dissolved. Allow to cool a little, then put into a mixing bowl with the yeast, egg, cheese and some of the flour. Beat until smooth, then add the remaining flour. Knead and punch the dough with greased hands until you have a smooth mass. Put the dough in a greased mixing bowl, cover with a damp tea towel and leave in a warm place, not in direct heat, and away from draughts for about 2 hours or until the dough's volume has doubled.

Knead and punch the dough again, shape so the folds are underneath and put into a warmed, lightly oiled baking tin. Cover and leave in a warm place until the dough has risen to the top of the tin. Bake in a hot oven (220°C/425°F/Gas mark 7) for 20 minutes, then reduce the heat to fairly hot (190°C/375°F/Gas mark 5) for about another 25 minutes or until the top is crusty and golden brown. Take the tin from the oven and wait 5 minutes before removing the loaf. The bread should sound hollow when tapped on the bottom.

GALETTES BRIARDES   FOR 4
Aromatic, crusty Brie-flavoured biscuits.

200 g (7 oz) ripe Brie	pinch freshly ground white pepper
70 g (2¹/₂ oz) unsalted butter, diced	pinch freshly grated nutmeg
2 egg yolks	250 g (9 oz) sifted plain flour
pinch salt	1 tbsp milk

Trim the cheese of any hard or brown bits of rind. Mash it in a mixing bowl, add the butter, egg yolks, salt, pepper and nutmeg, and blend. Gradually add the flour and knead everything together until a rather stiff, smooth dough is obtained. If necessary add a few drops of cold water. Wrap in aluminium foil and chill for 1 hour.

On a lightly floured surface, roll out about 6 mm (¹/₄ in) thick. Cut serrated rounds of about 7 cm (3 in) in diameter. Arrange on lightly oiled baking sheets, score lightly in a criss-cross pattern with a fork, brush with milk and bake in a fairly hot oven (190°C/375°F/Gas mark 5) for about 15-20 minutes or until golden brown. Cool on a rack.

CHEESE BISCUITS
Not Bath Olivers or Thin Captains, of course, but biscuits with cheese *in* them. They range from very rich biscuits that are almost like a savoury shortbread to light, wafery concoctions. I shall give only a brief selection here, for, delicious though they can be, they are hardly the most compulsive department of cheese cookery.

Rich Cheese Biscuits

MAKES 16-20 SMALL BISCUITS

90 g (3 oz) sifted plain flour
90 g (3 oz) unsalted butter, softened
90 g (3 oz) freshly grated Cheddar,

Cheshire *or* Gruyère *or* half of any
of them mixed with the same
quantity of freshly grated Parmesan

Blend the flour, butter and cheese, adding a little cold water if necessary in order to obtain a manageable paste. On a lightly floured surface, roll out 6 mm (1/4 in) thick. Cut rounds of about 7 cm (3 in) in diameter and prick well with a fork. Arrange on lightly oiled baking sheets and bake in a hot oven (220°C/425°F/ Gas mark 7) for 10-15 minutes or until golden brown. Cool on a rack.

Plain Cheese Biscuits

MAKES 16-20 SMALL BISCUITS

120 g (4 oz) sifted plain flour
60 g (2 oz) unsalted butter, softened
60 g (2 oz) freshly grated Cheddar
pinch salt

freshly ground pepper
pinch cayenne
1 egg yolk

Blend the flour, butter, cheese, salt, pepper and cayenne. Add the egg yolk and a little water, and mix until you have a rather stiff paste. Knead lightly. On a lightly floured surface, roll out 6 mm (1/4 in) thick. Cut into rounds of about 7 cm (3 in) in diameter and prick well with a fork. Arrange on lightly oiled baking sheets and bake in a hot oven (220°C/425°F/Gas mark 7) for 9-12 minutes or until golden brown. Cool on a rack.

Light Cheese Biscuits

MAKES 16-20 SMALL BISCUITS

These biscuits, called *petites galettes au parmesan* by the author of this recipe, Edouard Nignon (p. 114), are so light they almost float away.

250 g (9 oz) puff pastry
90 g (3 oz) freshly grated Parmesan

1 egg yolk

Make the puff pastry as described on p. 368, sprinkling

each of the 6 layers or turns with 15 g ($^1/_2$ oz) of cheese. Wrap in aluminium foil or cling-film and chill for 1 hour. On a lightly floured surface, roll out 1 cm ($^1/_2$ in) thick and quickly cut serrated rounds of about 7 cm (3 in) in diameter. Place these face down and not too close together on a slightly moistened baking sheet, prick their surface with the prongs of a fork, brush with egg yolk (do not allow any yolk to dribble down the cut edge) and bake in a very hot oven (230°C/450°F/Gas mark 8) for about 15 minutes or until well puffed up and golden brown on top. Cool on a rack.

Nignon adds: 'Served hot, [the *galettes*] are a perfect accompaniment for 5 o'clock tea.' Anglomania in Nignon's day made English-style tea all the rage in France and a verb meaning 'to have tea' was coined: *five-o'clocker*. Nowadays we should probably prefer to eat these biscuits a little later in the day, with pre-dinner drinks.

Puff pastry is time-consuming, if deeply fulfilling, to make. You can cheat by buying the same amount of frozen flaky pastry, giving it a couple more turns, each interspersed with 30 g (1 oz) sprinklings of Parmesan, and proceeding as above.

THICK PARMESAN BISCUITS MAKES 16-20 SMALL BISCUITS
Excellent scone-shaped little biscuits from *The Cookery Book of Lady Clark of Tillypronie* (p. 138).

150 g (5$^1/_2$ oz) plain flour
pinch salt
80 g (3 oz) unsalted butter, chilled and diced

80 g (3 oz) freshly grated Parmesan
1-2 egg yolks
pinch cayenne

Mix the flour and salt together in a mixing bowl. Add the butter. Holding a pair of table knives scissors-fashion, with their blades touching and your hands crossed over, pull them apart repeatedly so that the butter is cut into the flour. (Rub in the butter if you prefer.) Continue until the mixture has the consistency of fresh breadcrumbs. Add the cheese, egg yolk and cayenne and work into a dough, adding a little water if necessary.

On a lightly floured surface, roll out 1 cm ($\frac{1}{2}$ in) thick. Cut into rounds about 2.5cm (1 in) in diameter. Arrange on a lightly oiled baking sheet and bake in a moderate oven (170°C/325°F/Gas mark 3) for about 20 minutes. Serve hot.

Lady Clark of Tillypronie adds: 'These biscuits will keep in a tin, but when wanted they must be made hot.'

CHEESE STRAWS

In most restaurants cheese straws are made by cutting the trimmings left over from puff or flaky pastry into sticks, sprinkling them with grated cheese and baking them. Here are two other methods.

Method I

If you want to make really superlative cheese straws, intersperse layers of puff pastry with Parmesan, exactly as in the recipe for light cheese biscuits (p. 352). Then roll out the dough 6 mm ($\frac{1}{4}$ in) thick, cut with a sharp knife into sticks about 1 x 5 cm ($\frac{1}{2}$ x 2 in), place them face down on a slightly moistened baking sheet, brush their tops with egg yolk (being careful not to allow any egg yolk to dribble down the cut edge) and bake in a very hot oven (230°C/450°F/Gas mark 8) for about 12 minutes or until well puffed and golden brown on top. Cool on a rack. You can, if you like, twist the straws once before baking.

Method II

If you cannot spare the 3 or 4 hours necessary to make puff pastry or do not have any of the frozen product, here is a simpler, less ethereal but also less rich version of cheese straws.

200 g (7 oz) sifted plain flour
pinch salt
100 g (3¹/₂ oz) unsalted butter,
   chilled and diced
150 g (5¹/₂ oz) freshly grated Cheddar,

Cheshire *or* Gruyère *or* half of any of
them mixed with an equal quantity
of Parmesan
1 egg, beaten
pinch cayenne

Mix the flour and salt in a mixing bowl. Add the butter. Holding a pair of table knives scissors-fashion, with their blades touching and your hands crossed over, pull them apart repeatedly so that the butter is cut into the flour. Continue until the mixture has the consistency of fresh breadcrumbs. (Rub in the butter if you prefer.) Add the cheese, egg and cayenne. Blend until a smooth, firm dough is obtained. Cover with aluminium foil and chill for 1 hour.

On a lightly floured surface, roll out 6 mm (¹/₄ in) thick. With a sharp knife, quickly cut into strips measuring about 1 x 5 cm (¹/₂ x 2 in). Arrange on lightly oiled baking sheets and bake in a fairly hot oven (190°C/375°F/Gas mark 5) for 10-15 minutes or until golden brown. Cool on a rack.

If you like, you can twist the straws before baking.

These cheese straws may be given all sorts of extra flavourings before baking: they can be strewn with pine-nuts, flaked almonds or crushed fresh peanuts, sprinkled with aromatic seeds (cumin, caraway, poppy or sesame) or spread with anchovy paste.

Other tasty versions can be made by using, instead of one of the cheeses indicated above, an equal quantity of:

   smoked cheese (as in Hungary),
or Camembert *or* Brie (trimmed of hard or brown rind),
or a good blue cheese such as Stilton, Bleu d'Auvergne, Fourme
   d'Ambert or Roquefort (if using Roquefort, do not put any salt in the dough).

CHAPTER EIGHTEEN

Sauces, Pastry and Home-made Cheese

BÉCHAMEL SAUCE

Here are two versions of béchamel sauce, the first a coating sauce, the second a thick panada.

Béchamel I   TO MAKE ABOUT 400 ML (14 FL OZ) OF SAUCE

25 g (1 oz) unsalted butter   pinch freshly ground white pepper
325 ml (11 fl oz) milk   pinch freshly grated nutmeg
25 g (1 oz) plain flour   salt
90 ml (3 fl oz) double cream

Melt the butter gently in a heavy saucepan. Heat the milk in another pan. Blend the flour with the butter and cook slowly, stirring all the time with a wooden spoon, for 2-3 minutes without browning. When the milk almost reaches boiling point, pour it over the butter and flour mixture, away from the heat, and stir until absolutely smooth. Return the pan to the heat, bring to a gentle boil and cook gently for about 1 minute, stirring. Pour in the cream gradually and stir until smooth. Add the pepper, nutmeg and salt to taste.

Béchamel II   TO MAKE ABOUT 400 ML (14 FL OZ) OF SAUCE

40 g (1¹/₂ oz) unsalted butter	pinch freshly grated white pepper
40 g (1¹/₂ oz) plain flour	pinch freshly grated nutmeg
370 ml (13 fl oz) milk	salt

Proceed as for Béchamel I, but without adding any cream. The sauce will be very thick.

MORNAY SAUCE

Oddly enough, this versatile and classic cheese sauce, which has a peculiar affinity with fish, is a relative new-comer to the culinary scene. Joseph Favre, in his monumental *Dictionnaire universel de cuisine et d'hygiène alimentaire* (1883-7), says that it was invented in the mid-nineteenth century by one Joseph Voiron, chef at the celebrated Restaurant Durand on the Place de la Madeleine in Paris, apparently as a tribute to another chef, named Mornay. Voiron may have been the first to serve it under that name. But Mornay sauce already had a virtual existence in a number of earlier dishes, such as the Maccaroni à la Reine (p. 159), where a béchamel sauce is combined with grated cheese.

Mornay sauce has got rather a bad name because its masking properties are often used by unscrupulous chefs and restaurateurs as a way of fobbing off less-than-fresh fish on unsuspecting customers. Parisian restaurant-goers, who are aware of such practices, tend to be wary of, say, Turbot sauce Mornay when it appears on Monday's menu (there is no fish market on Monday) and especially if it is strongly recommended by the waiter.

But a carefully made Mornay sauce can make a perfect marriage when accompanying the right kind of food. It has plenty of character and therefore lends interest to otherwise rather low-key ingredients (pasta, eggs, etc.) or to the less subtle-tasting species of fish (whiting, coley, pollock, 'rock salmon'). But it tends to crowd out the delicate flavours of, say, sole, red mullet or salmon, or indeed freshwater fish in general.

I have given five versions of Mornay sauce, to be used

in different dishes. Whichever one is called for, it is a good idea to remember that when in doubt keep the consistency on the thin side. There is nothing worse than an over-thick, porridgy Mornay sauce.

ALL QUANTITIES WILL MAKE FRACTIONALLY MORE THAN 400 ML (14 FL OZ) OF SAUCE

Mornay sauce I: Basic

25 g (1 oz) unsalted butter
325 ml (11 fl oz) milk
25 g (1 oz) plain flour
100 ml (3$^{1}/_{2}$ fl oz) double cream
25 g (1 oz) freshly grated Gruyère

25 g (1 oz) freshly grated Parmesan
pinch freshly ground white pepper
pinch freshly grated nutmeg
salt

Melt the butter gently in a heavy saucepan. Heat the milk in another pan. Blend the flour with the butter and cook slowly, stirring all the time with a wooden spoon, for 2-3 minutes without browning. When the milk almost reaches boiling point, pour it over the butter and flour mixture, away from the heat, and whisk until absolutely smooth. Return the pan to the heat, bring to a gentle boil and cook gently for about 1 minute, stirring. Add the cream gradually. Bring back to boiling point. Remove from the heat and stir in the finely grated cheese until it has melted completely. Add the pepper, nutmeg and salt to taste.

Mornay sauce II: For fish dishes

25 g (1 oz) unsalted butter
250 ml (9 fl oz) milk
25 g (1 oz) plain flour
80 ml (3 fl oz) fish *fumet,* made with bones and trimmings, *or* fish's cooking liquid

100 ml (3$^{1}/_{2}$ fl oz) double cream
25 g (1 oz) freshly grated Gruyère
25 g (1 oz) freshly grated Parmesan
pinch freshly ground white pepper
pinch freshly grated nutmeg
salt

Proceed as for I, adding the fish stock to the milk at the start of the recipe.

Mornay sauce III: For vegetable dishes

25 g (1 oz) unsalted butter
250 ml (9 fl oz) milk
25 g (1 oz) plain flour
80 ml (3 fl oz) vegetables' cooking
  liquid
100 ml (3^1/$_2$ fl oz) double cream

25 g (1 oz) freshly grated Gruyère
25 g (1 oz) freshly grated Parmesan
pinch freshly ground white pepper
pinch freshly grated nutmeg
salt

Proceed as for I, adding the vegetables' cooking liquid to the milk at the start of the recipe.

Mornay sauce IV: For meat dishes

25 g (1 oz) unsalted butter
250 ml (9 fl oz) milk
25 g (1 oz) plain flour
80 g (3 fl oz) meat's cooking liquid *or*
  strong meat stock
100 ml (3^1/$_2$ fl oz) double cream

25 g (1 oz) freshly grated Gruyère
25 g (1 oz) freshly grated Parmesan
pinch freshly ground white pepper
pinch freshly grated nutmeg
salt

Proceed as for I, adding the meat's cooking liquid or stock to the milk at the start of the recipe.

Mornay sauce V: Rich

20 g (^{3}/$_4$ oz) butter
300 ml (10^1/$_2$ fl oz) milk
20 g (^{3}/$_4$ oz) plain flour
2 egg yolks
100 ml (3^1/$_2$ fl oz) double cream

25 g (1 oz) freshly grated Gruyère
25 g (1 oz) freshly grated Parmesan
pinch freshly ground white pepper
pinch freshly grated nutmeg
salt

Melt the butter gently in a heavy saucepan. Heat the milk in another pan. Blend the flour with the butter and cook slowly, stirring all the time, for 2-3 minutes without browning. When the milk almost reaches boiling point, pour it over the butter and flour mixture, away from the heat, and whisk until absolutely smooth. Return the pan to the heat, bring to a gentle boil, and cook gently for about 1 minute, stirring. Remove from the heat.

Blend the egg yolks and cream in a mixing bowl. Add to this mixture about half the hot sauce, very gradually at first, beating all the time. Pour this mixture back into the saucepan and continue beating until smooth. Put back on a gentle heat and stir for about a minute. Remove from the heat and stir in the finely grated cheeses until they have completely melted. Add the pepper, nutmeg and salt to taste.

Re-heating Mornay sauce
Use a double boiler for this. Re-heat very gently, stirring from time to time. Do not allow the sauce to get hotter than the temperature of a hot bath.

WATERCRESS AND CURD CHEESE SAUCE　　　　FOR 4
Watercress is an unfairly treated vegetable. In steak houses and their like, where its role is usually one of mere decoration, it adds a touch of greenery and, to judge from the way it has usually been washed, is not expected actually to be *eaten*. Yet watercress soup is one of the greatest of all soups. And in a sauce such as this, where it is used almost as a flavouring herb, watercress shows itself capable of a surprising depth of flavour.

about 140 g (5 oz) watercress, trimmed of its tougher stalks
1 tbsp fresh tarragon, chopped
1 small shallot

200 g (7 oz) fromage blanc *or* fairly liquid curd cheese
1 tbsp orange juice
Salt

Wash the watercress well, blanch in boiling water for 2 minutes, drain, refresh under a cold tap and dry well. Put it into a blender with the tarragon, shallot and cheese. Blend until smooth. Mix in the orange juice and salt to taste. Chill briefly before serving.

This sauce goes best with cold steamed or poached fish, but is also good with hot fish or hard-boiled eggs. Do not make the sauce too long in advance, as the bright green of the watercress may turn dirty yellow-green.

RAITA   FOR 4

Cooling and aromatic raita (yoghurt relish), even when itself fiery (as in this version), is a marvellous foil to the hot spices of Indian cuisine.

400 ml (14 fl oz) plain yoghurt	salt
large pinch cayenne	freshly ground pepper
1 spring onion, finely chopped	
1 tbsp fresh coriander leaves, finely chopped	

Beat the yoghurt until smooth, then add the cayenne (don't be timid), onion, coriander, and salt and pepper to taste. Mix thoroughly. Serve chilled.

CURD CHEESE MAYONNAISE   FOR 4

A sauce from Central Europe.

100 g (3½ oz) well-drained curd cheese	2 tsp lemon juice
	pinch salt
2 egg yolks	pinch caster sugar
2 tsp Dijon mustard	pinch freshly ground pepper
175 ml (6 fl oz) good salad oil	4 tbsp fresh dill, finely chopped

Beat the cheese, egg yolks and mustard together in a small mixing bowl. Add the oil drop by drop at first stirring all the time, as if making a classic mayonnaise. When firm, add the lemon juice, salt, sugar, pepper and dill and stir gently but thoroughly.

This sauce is excellent with cold fish or hard-boiled eggs, or as a dressing for salads (use half the above quantities for 1 good-sized lettuce). The fresh dill can be replaced with crushed dill seeds or caraway seeds, or omitted altogether – but then the sauce will lose much of its character.

ROQUEFORT SALAD DRESSING
FOR ONE GOOD-SIZED LETTUCE, OR EQUIVALENT

Nearly all Roquefort dressings in my experience have one, if not all, of the following flaws: too much Roquefort, too much salt, too much vinegar. Roquefort has such a powerful flavour that very little goes a long way in a salad. Salt and vinegar are very much a matter of personal taste, habit and upbringing. As a general rule, though, in moderation both ingredients enhance flavour, but in excess assassinate it.

40 g (1¹/₂ oz) Roquefort

1 tbsp sherry vinegar *or* good wine vinegar

3 tbsp good salad oil and 2 tbsp walnut oil *or* 5 tbsp good salad oil

1 clove garlic, finely chopped

freshly ground pepper

Mash the cheese in the vinegar. When soft, add the oil and beat until a smooth consistency is obtained. Add the garlic and plenty of pepper.

Salt is quite unnecessary, as the Roquefort is very salty.

PESTO   TO MAKE ABOUT 250 G (9 OZ) OF PESTO

The ingredients of this sublime sauce – basil, garlic, olive oil, pine-nuts and Parmesan or pecorino – uniquely combine a series of contrasting tastes: spicy, sharp, smooth, mellow and pungent respectively.

The places where pesto is eaten in the largest quantities are the Genoa area and the Comté de Nice (where it is known as *pistou*, and where the pine-nuts are usually omitted). Historically, Genoa has always had strong ties with Nice, and it is generally believed that pesto originated in Genoa and travelled westwards – though some Niçois claim that the migration of the sauce was in the other direction. Today there can be no doubt which of the two cities takes its pesto more seriously: Genoa is surrounded by vast basil plantations.

Pesto, which literally means 'pounded' (cf. the English 'pestle'), has the consistency of a paste rather than a sauce. In Italy it accompanies minestrone, gnocchi and various kinds of pasta, usually being added at the last moment, since basil loses much of its flavour if it cooks. In Nice, it is best known as the dominant ingredient of a minestrone-like soup, *soupe au pistou*, which is often abbreviated simply to *pistou* (by extension, *pistou* is sometimes even used to mean basil). In the mountains behind Nice *pistou* sauce is frequently eaten with mutton.

60 g (2 oz) pine-nuts	6 cloves garlic
60 g (2 oz) fresh basil leaves (a large handful), gently washed and dried	60 g (2 oz) freshly grated Parmesan *or* pecorino (*or* half of each)
pinch salt	4-6 tbsp virgin olive oil

Bake the pine-nuts in a baking tin or tart mould in a moderate oven until they turn the colour of roast peanuts (this is a better method than browning them in a frying pan, which almost inevitably burns them on one side). Take out and leave to cool.

Put all the ingredients into a blender, and blend until smooth. Check seasoning.

You can, if you prefer, aim for etymological authenticity and use a pestle to pound the ingredients in a mortar. But with these quantities it will prove a very strenuous operation. It is worth making more pesto than you need at a given time, as any that is left over can be frozen or packed into small jars, covered with a film of oil and kept in the refrigerator for several weeks.

Basil turns blackish-green when cut or crushed. The Italians therefore sometimes add some spinach or lettuce leaves to the pesto to keep it bright green.

The pesto that is commercially available in jars (sometimes containing no garlic!) makes a poor substitute, as the basil has been subjected to the sterilizing process and tastes of tea leaves. Fortunately, more and more delicatessens now sell fresh pesto made with fresh (or, in winter, frozen) basil.

TOMATO SAUCE

TO MAKE ABOUT 400 ML (14 FL OZ) OF SAUCE

1 tbsp virgin olive oil	$1/2$ tsp fresh or dried thyme
1 onion, finely chopped	$1/4$ bay leaf
2 small cloves garlic, chopped	large pinch salt
1 kg ($2^1/4$ lb) ripe tomatoes, peeled and chopped	freshly ground pepper
1 tbsp fresh parsley, finely chopped	sugar
	2 tsp fresh basil, finely chopped

Heat the oil in a large heavy enamel saucepan and sweat the onion and half the garlic until translucent but not brown. Add the tomatoes, parsley, thyme and bay leaf, and simmer uncovered for about 30 minutes until reduced to a pulp. Away from the heat, season with salt, pepper and sugar to taste, and stir in the basil and the rest of the garlic.

Tomato sauce must have the right balance of acidity and sweetness. The amount of sugar you add will depend on the ripeness and sweetness of the tomatoes used. If all you can obtain are unsweet, tasteless, juiceless greenhouse tomatoes, you are better off using Italian canned tomatoes.

If a raw garlic flavour is out of key with the dish in which the tomato sauce is being used, you can omit the second clove.

If you want the sauce to have a sleeker appearance, seed the tomatoes before chopping them.

This sauce can be kept in the refrigerator for a few days – or frozen.

BEURRE MANIÉ

A useful last-minute sauce thickener, which consists simply of equal quantities of butter and flour mashed together. Bring your sauce to the boil and, away from the heat, whisk a few tiny knobs of this mixture into it. Return to a low heat and simmer until the required consistency is obtained. Do not allow to boil.

DUXELLES   TO MAKE ABOUT 225 G (8 OZ) OF DUXELLES

Here is Edouard Nignon's version of this classic mushroom flavouring.

30 g (1 oz) unsalted butter	5 tbsp dry white wine
2 tbsp virgin olive oil	5 tbsp well-reduced veal stock
4 shallots, finely chopped	salt
250 g (9 oz) mushrooms, finely chopped	freshly ground pepper

Heat the butter and oil in a heavy frying pan and sweat the shallots until translucent. Squeeze as much moisture as possible out of the chopped mushrooms, then add them to the pan. Cook gently until the mixture is completely dry. Add the wine and stock, and simmer for 15 minutes or until the liquid has reduced by half. Add salt and pepper to taste.

You can use 60 g (2 oz) of butter instead of a mixture of butter and olive oil. Ordinary cultivated mushrooms are generally used for duxelles; but a better result will be obtained with wild mushrooms (e.g. very small field mushrooms, young parasol mushrooms, or, better, fairy ring mushrooms, young horse mushrooms or cepes).

The finest duxelles of all is of course made with black truffles (use fresh ones if possible), in which case Nignon suggests that the white wine be replaced by an equivalent quantity of Madeira.

Duxelles, in a well-sealed container, can be kept for 1-2 weeks in the refrigerator.

PASTRY

Nowadays, most ready-made frozen pastry is of excellent quality. It is a convenient and time-saving standby, but cannot compare with a successful home-made product. Here are a few basic pastry dough formulae called for by recipes in this book. You can rub in the butter if you prefer it to the knife method indicated.

ALL QUANTITIES ARE FOR ABOUT 450 G (1 LB) OF PASTRY

Short pastry

250 g (9 oz) sifted plain flour	125 g (4^1/$_2$ oz) unsalted butter, diced
6 g (^{1}/$_4$ oz) salt	and chilled
^{1}/$_4$ tsp icing sugar	5 tbsp iced water

Mix the flour, salt and sugar in a mixing bowl. Add the butter. Holding a pair of table knives scissors-fashion, with their blades touching and your hands crossed over, pull them apart repeatedly so that the butter is cut into the flour. Continue until the mixture has the consistency of fresh breadcrumbs. Gradually sprinkle the iced water over the mixture, quickly stirring all the time with a fork until the dough forms into a compact and unsticky mass (you may need slightly less or more water than the amount indicated). Shape the dough into a ball.

If you have a blender that makes pastry, simply put all the ingredients into it and blend for about 30 seconds or until the mixture forms into a ball.

Wrap the dough in aluminium foil or cling-film, and refrigerate for at least 30 minutes, and overnight if possible, before use.

Short pastry with egg

250 g (9 oz) sifted plain flour	1 tbsp iced water
6 g (^{1}/$_4$ oz) salt	1 egg, well beaten and refrigerated
^{1}/$_4$ tsp icing sugar	
125 g (4^1/$_2$ oz) unsalted butter, diced	
and chilled	

Mix the flour, salt and sugar in a mixing bowl. Add the butter. Holding a pair of table knives scissors-fashion, with their blades touching and your hands crossed over, pull them apart repeatedly so that the butter is cut into the flour. Continue until the mixture has the consistency of fresh breadcrumbs. Mix the iced water with the beaten egg and gradually pour over the mixture, quickly stirring all the time with a fork until the dough forms into a compact and unsticky mass (you may need to add a little more iced water). Shape the dough into a ball.

If you have a blender that makes pastry, simply put the flour, salt, sugar and butter into it and blend for about 15 seconds. Add the egg and water, and blend for a further 15 seconds or until the mixture forms into a ball.

Wrap the dough in aluminium foil or cling-film, and refrigerate for at least 30 minutes, and overnight, if possible, before use.

Flaky pastry

180 g (6¹/₂ oz) sifted plain flour	180 g (6¹/₂ oz) unsalted butter, chilled
5 g (¹/₆ oz) salt	6 tbsp iced water

Mix the flour and the salt in a mixing bowl. Add 40 g (1¹/₂ oz) of butter diced. Holding a pair of table knives scissors-fashion, with their blades touching and your hands crossed over, pull them apart repeatedly so that the butter is cut into the flour. Continue until the mixture has the consistency of fresh breadcrumbs. Gradually sprinkle the iced water over the mixture, quickly stirring all the time, until you can press the dough into a compact and unsticky mass (do not worry if the surface is not smooth).

If you have a blender that makes pastry, simply put the flour, salt, water and 40 g (1¹/₂ oz) of butter into it and blend for about 25 seconds or until the mixture forms into a ball.

Flatten the dough slightly, slash in one or two places, wrap in aluminium foil or cling-film, and refrigerate for at least 1 hour. Chill the rest of the butter.

Beat the butter with a rolling pin to soften it slightly and form into a square of about 12 cm (5 in). On a lightly floured surface (which, like the rolling pin, will require light re-flouring during operations), roll out the dough to a square of about 20 cm (8 in). Place the butter diagonally on the dough and fold the corners of dough over the butter envelope-fashion. With a series of short gentle movements, roll the envelope away from you, stopping the rolling pin just before it reaches the edge, to form a rectangle twice as long as it is wide. Fold the farthest third back towards you, then fold the nearest third over it. Rotate the dough 45°. Gently roll out into a rectangle and fold over as before. Wrap in cling-film and refrigerate for any period of time from 30 minutes to 12 hours.

Remove the dough from the cling-film and, if it is hard, tap it all over with a rolling pin to soften slightly. Repeat the previously described rolling out and folding operations twice more, and refrigerate again for at least 30 minutes before use. After rolling out to the required thickness, use a very sharp knife to cut the shape(s) you need (a blunt blade will crush the butter-and-flour layers together).

Puff pastry

180 g (6¹/₂ oz) sifted plain flour   6 tbsp iced water
5 g (¹/₆ oz) salt   180 g (6¹/₂ oz) unsalted butter, chilled

Proceed exactly as for flaky pastry, but, after the final refrigeration, repeat the rolling out and folding operation a fifth and sixth time, refrigerating again for at least 30 minutes between each operation and before use.

Sweet short pastry

225 g (8 oz) sifted plain flour   1 tbsp iced water
pinch salt   1 egg, well beaten
60 g (2 oz) caster sugar
115 g (4 oz) unsalted butter, diced
   and chilled

Mix the flour, salt and sugar in a mixing bowl. Add the butter. Holding a pair of table knives scissors-fashion, with their blades touching and your hands crossed over, pull them apart repeatedly so that the butter is cut into the flour. Continue until the mixture has the consistency of fresh breadcrumbs. Mix the iced water with the beaten egg and gradually pour over the mixture, quickly stirring all the time with a fork until the dough forms into a compact and unsticky mass (you may need to add a little more iced water). Shape the dough into a ball.

If you have a blender that makes pastry, simply put the flour, salt, sugar and butter into it and blend for about 15 seconds. Add the egg and water, and blend for a further 15 seconds or until the mixture forms into a ball.

Wrap the dough in aluminium foil or cling-film, and refrigerate for at least 30 minutes, and overnight if possible, before use.

Cheese pastry

200 g (7 oz) sifted plain flour	90 g (3 oz) freshly grated strong
1/4 tsp icing sugar	Cheddar, Gruyère *or* Parmesan
100 g (3 1/2 oz) unsalted butter, diced and chilled	5 tbsp iced water

Proceed exactly as for Short pastry (p. 366), omitting the salt, and stirring in the finely grated cheese before adding the iced water.

BAKING BLIND

Partly or fully baked pastry shells are an essential feature of cheese cookery: many tart fillings take less time to cook than raw pastry, so the pastry needs to be given a head start.

Here is the procedure:

Oil very lightly all surfaces that will be in contact with the pastry (inside of tart/flan tin or mould, flan ring, flan ring base, baking sheet, etc.).

Roll out the chilled dough to the required dimensions. Roll on to the rolling pin and unroll over the tin or mould, or, in the case of a flan ring, line the ring and base (or baking sheet), sealing the join well. Prick the pastry all over with a fork.

Gently press a single piece of aluminium foil into and against the whole surface of the pastry shell. Weigh it down with dry beans or rice (kept permanently for that purpose in a roasting bag if you like).

Bake as directed by the recipe. The usual baking time for a partly cooked shell is 10-15 minutes in a fairly hot oven (200°C/ 400°F/Gas mark 6), and for a fully cooked shell about half as long again. Remove the pastry shell from its mould 1-2 minutes after baking and cool on a rack.

In the case of tartlet shells, instead of using aluminium foil and beans to weigh down the pastry, place the pastry-lined tins one on top of the other, finishing with an empty tin. Start by baking in a fairly hot oven (200°C/400°F/Gas mark 6) for 5 minutes for a partly cooked shell or 10 minutes for a fully cooked shell, then unstack the tins and complete baking for a further 5 minutes.

CURD CHEESE

For a discussion of curd cheese, see p. 16.

TO MAKE ABOUT 1 KG (2¼ LB) WELL-DRAINED CURD CHEESE

4.5 litres (160 fl oz) whole milk   2 tbsp live (cultured) buttermilk

Fill a large saucepan or casserole half-full with water. Heat until the water reaches blood temperature (about 37°C/98°F), then remove from heat. Pour the milk into a slightly smaller enamel or stainless steel saucepan and place it over the other pan as for a double-boiler. When the milk reaches a temperature of 27°C (81°F), add the buttermilk and stir thoroughly. Leave the mixture at about 20°C (68°F) for 18-24 hours or until it sets to curds and whey. You can tell when it is ready as follows: place the back of your hand on the surface; if it picks up milk and/or fragments of curd, the coagulating process has not been completed; if it is simply moistened with whey, you can proceed to the next stage.

Place a sterilized piece of muslin, folded double, in a large colander. Spoon the curds gently into the muslin.

Leave to drain for a few hours in a cool place. Scrape the curds down towards the centre of the muslin, tie it up into a bundle and suspend over a bowl or sink. Leave for about 10 hours. Untie the bag, peel off the muslin and turn the curd cheese out into a bowl. It is now ready to use. If fairly liquid curd cheese is called for, leave the bundle suspended for only 5 hours.

LABNA   TO MAKE ABOUT 500 G (1 LB 2 OZ) LABNA
Labna (or lebanie) is a Middle-Eastern yoghurt cheese with quite a sharp flavour. When unsalted, it can be eaten with honey and cinnamon. More often it is salted, then accompanied by olives and pitta bread or by raw vegetables. It goes into pies (p. 197) and can be preserved in oil (p. 51).

1 litre (35 fl oz) cow's- *or*   1 tsp salt (optional)
  goat's-milk yoghurt

Place several layers of damp muslin over a large colander and pour in the yoghurt. Leave for several hours or overnight in a cool place, then tie the cloth up into a bundle and suspend over a bowl or sink for a day or so to extract more whey and make the labna firmer. The best results are obtained with thick home-made yoghurt.

Selected Bibliography

Acton, E., *Modern Cookery for Private Families*, London, 1845.

Allhusen, D., *A Medley of Recipes*, London, 1936.

Arm, A., *Meatless Menus for Lunch, Dinner and Supper*, London, 1917.

Ayrton, E., *The Cookery of England*, London, 1974.

Beck, S., Bertholle, L. and Child, J., *Mastering the Art of French Cooking, 2 vols.*, London, 1966 and 1978.

Beeton, Mrs, *Dictionary of Every Day Cookery*, London, 1865.

Bonnefons, N. de, *Les Délices de la campagne*, Paris, 1654.

Boorde, A., *A Compendyous Regyment, or a Dyetary of Helth*, London, 1542.

Clark, Lady, *The Cookery Book of Lady Clark of Tillypronie*, London, 1909.

The Closet of the Eminently Learned Sir Kenelme Digbie, Knight, Opened, London, 1669.

Croze, A. de, *Les Plats régionaux de France*, Paris, 1928.

Le Cuisinier gascon, Amsterdam, 1740.

La Cuisinière genevoise, 4th edn., Geneva, 1817.

Curnonsky, *Lettres de noblesse*, Paris, 1935.

David, E., *An Omelette and a Glass of Wine*, London, 1986.

   English Bread and Yeast Cookery, London, 1979.

   French Provincial Cooking, London, 1964.

   Summer Cooking, London, 1969.

Dods, M., *The Cook and Housewife's Manual*,

Edinburgh, 1826.

Dolby, R., *The Cook's Dictionary*, London, 1830.

Dudley, Georgiana Countess of, *The Dudley Book of Cookery and Household Recipes*, London, 1909.

Edinburgh College of Domestic Science, *The Edinburgh Book of Plain Cookery Recipes*, Edinburgh, 1932.

Favre, J., *Dictionnaire universel de cuisine et d'hygiène alimentaire*, 4 vols., Paris, 1883-1887.

Fishman, E., *The Staffordshire Oatcake Recipe Book*, Stoke-on-Trent, 1984.

Fraser, Mrs, *Cookery, Pastry, Confectionary, Pickling and Preserving*, Edinburgh, 1800.

Gagarine, Princess Alexandre, *The Russian Cook Book*, London, 1924.

Glasse, H., *The Art of Cookery Made Plain and Easy*, London, 1747.

Gompertz, M., *The Main Cookery Book*, London, 1946.

Le Grand Cuisinier de toute cuisine, Paris, 1540.

Grigson, J., *English Food*, London, 1977.
   Good Things, London, 1973.
   Vegetable Book, London, 1980.

Haeberlin, P. and J.-P., *Les Recettes de l'Auberge de l'Ill*, Paris, 1982.

Hudson, Mrs, and Donat, Mrs, *The New Practice of Cookery, Pastry, Baking and Preserving*, Edinburgh, 1804.

Jaffrey, M., *Madhur Jaffrey's Indian Cookery*, London, 1982.

Kenney Herbert, A., *Fifty Lunches*, London, 1902.

La Varenne, F. P. de, *Le Cuisinier françois*, Paris, 1651.

Layton, T. A., *Cheese and Cheese Cookery*, London, 1971.

Leyel, C. F., *Savoury Cold Meals*, London, 1927.

Lune, P. de, *Le Cuisinier*, Paris, 1656.

McGee, H., *On Food and Cooking*, London, 1986.

Mallock, M. M., *A Younger Son's Cookery Book*, London, 1896.

Le Manuel de la friandise, ou les talents de ma cuisinière Isabeau mis en lumière, Paris, 1796.

Marin, F., *Les Dons de Comus ou les délices de la table*, Paris, 1739.

Marshall, A. B., *Larger Cookery Book of Extra Recipes*, London, 1899.

Massialot, F., *Nouvelle Instruction pour les confitures, les liqueurs, et les fruits*, Paris, 1692.

Médecin, J., *La Cuisine du Comté de Nice*, Paris, 1972. *Cuisine Niçoise*, London, 1983.

Le Ménagier de Paris, ed. J. Pichon, 2 vols., Paris, 1846.

Menon, *Les Soupers de la cour*, 4 vols., Paris, 1755.

Midgley, W., *Cookery for Men Only*, London, 1948.

Miller, E. S., *In the Kitchen*, Boston, Mass., 1875.

My Receipt Book: A Treasury of Six Hundred Receipts in Cooking and Preserving, London, 1861.

Nignon, E., *Eloges de la cuisine française*, Paris, 1933.

Parry, E. H., *Cookery and Other Recipes*, Allahabad, 1910.

Pomiane, E. de, *Radio-Cuisine*, Paris, 1936.

Ponsonby, R., *Lady Sysonby's Cook Book*, London, 1935.

Rance, P., *The Great British Cheese Book*, London, 1982.

Reboux, P., *Plats nouveaux! 300 recettes inédites ou singulières*, Paris, 1927.

Les Recettes des 'Belles Perdrix', ed. G. Réval and M. Croci, Paris, 1930.

Roden, C., *A Book of Middle Eastern Food*, London, 1970.

A New Book of Middle Eastern Food, London, 1985.

Les Sans-Filistes Gastronomes, *Les Belles Recettes des provinces françaises*, Paris, 1929.

Scotson-Clark, G. F., *Eating without Fears*, London, 1925.

Senn, C. H., *Savoury Breakfast, Dinner and Supper Dishes*, London, 1904.

Smith, J. H., and Halsey, S., *Famous Old Receipts*, Philadelphia, Pa., 1906.

Stobbs, W., *Guide to Cheeses of France*, London, 1984.

Tuite, E., *Lemco Dishes for All Seasons*, London, 1905.

Vergé, R., *Les Fêtes de mon moulin*, Paris, 1986.

Viard, A., *Le Cuisinier impérial*, Paris, 1806.

Wilson, C. A., *Food and Drink in Britain*, London, 1976.

Index